PETRARCH'S *FRAGMENTA*

The Narrative and Theological Unity of *Rerum vulgarium fragmenta*

THOMAS E. PETERSON

Petrarch's *Fragmenta*

The Narrative and Theological Unity of *Rerum vulgarium fragmenta*

UNIVERSITY OF TORONTO PRESS
Toronto Buffalo London

Toronto Buffalo London
www.utppublishing.com

ISBN 978-1-4875-0002-3

Toronto Italian Studies

Library and Archives Canada Cataloguing in Publication

Peterson, Thomas E. (Thomas Erling), author
Petrarch's fragmenta : the narrative and theological unity of Rerum vulgarium fragmenta / Thomas E. Peterson.

(Toronto Italian studies)
Includes bibliographical references and index.
ISBN 978-1-4875-0002-3 (cloth)

1. Petrarca, Francesco, 1304–1374. Rime. I. Title. II. Series: Toronto Italian studies

PQ4479.P48 2016 851′.1 C2016-900175-X

University of Toronto Press acknowledges the financial assistance to its publishing program of the Canada Council for the Arts and the Ontario Arts Council, an agency of the Government of Ontario.

Funded by the Government of Canada
Financé par le gouvernement du Canada

[Nolo ducem me prohibēre] ubi velim pedem ponere et preterire aliqua et inaccessa tentare; et breviorum sive ita fert animus, planiorem callem sequi et properare et properare et subsistere et divertere liceat et reverti.

I do not want a guide to forbid me to step where I wish, to go beyond him in some things, to attempt the inaccessible, to follow a shorter or, if I wish, an easier path, and to hasten or stop or even to part ways and to return.

Rerum familiarium libri, xxii, 2[1]

Contents

Preface

One of the motivations for writing this book was to examine the link between moral change and formal change in a series of semi-autonomous texts in sequence. The goal was to uncover in the microtexts of *Rerum vulgarium fragmenta* (*Fragments of Vernacular Matters*) the details of the inner life of the Petrarchan subject and to connect those details to the properly poetic organization of the whole. In the lively field of Petrarch studies, much attention has been paid recently to questions of narrative. As Rossana Bettarini writes in the introduction to her 2005 edition, *Canzoniere. Rerum vulgarium fragmenta*:

> Anche nel *Canzoniere*, il grande Libro che per la prima volta nella letteratura romanza raccoglie le «rime sparse» del 'genere' lirico in un disegno retrospettivamente unitario sotto il segno dell'Eros-frustrazione, la materia non è tutta Amore, mescolandosi nell'eventuale 'racconto' vari e diversi amori, come l'amicizia, la passione civile, il gusto per l'invettiva [...,] l'*amor Sapientiae* [...].

> Also in the *Canzoniere*, the great Book that for the first time in romance literature collects the "scattered rhymes" of the lyric "genre" into a retrospectively unitary design under the sign of Eros-frustration, the subject matter is not just Love, as various and diverse loves, such as friendship, civic passion, the taste for invective, [...], the love of Wisdom, are mixed into the eventual "story."[1]

The thematic complexity alluded to by Bettarini is matched by a formal (phonetic, metrical, syntactic) complexity that is equally daunting. These combined orders comprise a narrative and theological unity that makes the *Fragmenta* a seminal text at the origins of humanism and the development of the modern conscience. Petrarch's theology is Augustinian, though – as suggested by the book's epigraph – he was ever willing to follow his own path, even when it meant diverging from a revered model.

By writing poems in the vernacular Petrarch was attempting something he didn't accomplish in any other work: to tell the interior story of the soul in its confrontation with desire, followed by the sublimation of desire and the undertaking of a journey towards God. It was natural for him to exploit the medieval tendency towards narrative, and narrative's capacity to communicate truths that other discursive forms could not. This was exemplified for him by the classical literary tradition and especially the Bible – itself a book of fragments – and other sacred texts of the Judaeo-Christian tradition.

Readers of the *opera omnia* discover a rich mosaic of texts in diverse genres that repeatedly return to the core themes of the *Fragmenta*. For that reason I have paid special attention to those scholars (mostly writing in Italian) who corroborate "il carattere unitario dell'opera del Petrarca" (the unitary character of Petrarch's work).[2] There is a unity of the work as a whole that is manifest in its component parts, starting with the *Fragmenta*.

Petrarch's use of Italian is characterized by a generality and lexical selectivity that made it a model for future poets. It is a language of artifice and stylistic brilliance that adheres to certain conventions of the courtly love tradition even as it radically alters that tradition. With his new poetic system Petrarch wove a universal story of desire and enamourment, self-examination and friendship, of great philosophic and religious value.

This is first a poetry of the voice, spoken and sung, only later transcribed for posterity. It is critical, therefore, to consider the orality and musicality of the Petrarchan poem as an intrinsic part of the reading, since it is only through an accurate sounding of the verse that one can grasp the "divine inbreathing" the author intended.[3] By according a thematic role to the voice, one is better able to penetrate the hermeneutic density, the figurative and figural imagery, and the dramatic loci and personae of the *Fragmenta*, and to perceive it as a single text comprising 366 parts, each contributing to the narrative and theological unity of the whole.

Acknowledgments

An earlier version of chapter 3, section 1, titled "Petrarch's *Canzone-frottola*: A Parable of Return" appeared in *Symposium* 57, 1 (2003): 13–23; an earlier version of chapter 2, section 2, titled "The Fabulous Petrarch: *La raccolta del 1342* as Source of the Fabulous in *Rerum vulgarium fragmenta*," appeared in *Annali d'Italianistica* 22 (2004): 61–84.

This project benefited from a grant from the American Council of Learned Societies and the Center for Contemplative Mind in Society in 2000, and from a Willson Center Research Fellowship at the University of Georgia, in 2007–8. Publication assistance was provided at the University of Georgia by the Department of Romance Languages, the Franklin College of Arts and Sciences, and the Willson Center for Humanities and Arts. The project was also supported by the President's Venture Fund through the generous gifts of the University of Georgia's Partners and other donors.

I am grateful to my professors at Brown University for their guidance in Petrarchan and other medieval matters: Anthony Oldcorn, Franco Fido, Remo Ceserani, and Maria Corti. I would also like to thank Giuseppe Mazzotta for organizing and directing the 1989 Yale Petrarch Institute, where I was privileged to meet and study with an extraordinary cohort of scholars too numerous to mention by name.

I would like to remember the late Ron Schoeffel of the University of Toronto Press, a beacon in our field, who shepherded this book through its early stages. I am very grateful to Ron's colleagues at the Press – Suzanne Rancourt, Anne Laughlin, and Margaret Allen – for their kind and professional dedication and commitment to this project.

PETRARCH'S *FRAGMENTA*

The Narrative and Theological Unity of *Rerum vulgarium fragmenta*

Introduction

1. Petrarch Today: A Focus on Narrativity

In Petrarch's composition of *Rerum vulgarium fragmenta* (*Fragments of Vernacular Matters*) over more than four decades, the conscious manipulation of narrative time is critical.[1] The story that is told and the account of the telling are constantly interwoven and complicated by their relationship to the author's life. In recognition of the intrinsic complexity of the work's narrative and compositional scheme, recent commentators have voiced scepticism about long-accepted interpretations of the work.[2] As Marco Santagata writes, "Delle strutture simboliche, dei sovrasensi, della complessa trama di richiami di cui il libro è gravato, né i contemporanei, né i posteri si sono accorti. Insomma, buona parte della storia raccontata in questo libro non ha mai circolato sulle bocche degli ammiratori o tra le carte degli studiosi" (Neither Petrarch's contemporaries nor posterity realized the extent to which the book is laden with symbolic structures, second meanings, a complex weave of references. In short, a good part of the story told in this book has never circulated on the lips of its admirers or in the pages of scholars).[3]

Not only is this story not that of a melancholy lover perennially divided between earthly desires and spiritual aspirations, but its author is not "il lirico dei particolari, il poeta dal corto respiro" (the lyric poet of details, of shallow inspiration), an elegant formalist whose style is consistent with a self-defeating psychology and tenuous religious faith.[4]

In his 1993 study, *I frammenti dell'anima. Storia e racconto nel Canzoniere di Petrarca*, Santagata discusses the actual parallels between the author's life and his fiction. He clarifies the character of each of the "forms" of the *Fragmenta* along with two definitive redactions, arguing that within this codicological perspective the facts of Petrarch's fictional chronologies remain autobiographically consistent.[5] Beginning with the early, frustrated attempt to write a "romanzo" (romance) and progressing to the realized but layered "racconto" (story) of the *Fragmenta*, one sees the characters of Francesco and Laura take shape. As the "theatres" of Avignon, the Sorgue Valley, and Italy acquire specificity, reversals of fortune heighten the tension between the apparent stylistic ease of the poems and the moral difficulty of the progression.

Writing in 1898, Henri Cochin was one of the first moderns to assess the narration (or *histoire*) of the collection as a factor of its internal ordering and chronology; he compared Petrarch's narrative to Dante's: "J'en arrive à croire que, semblable à plusieurs de ses prédécesseurs, il conçut l'histoire de ses amours comme un roman moral analogue au moins dans son intention générale, au roman où Dante avait enveloppé, déguisé et symbolisé des histoires d'amour" (I have come to believe that, similar to many of his predecessors, he conceived the story of his loves as a moral romance analogous, at least in its general intention, to the romance in which Dante had enveloped, disguised, and symbolized stories of love).[6] While somewhat approximate, Cochin's idea of a moral romance composed of retrospective segments granted to Petrarch's work a complex, overarching narrativity, in contrast to the oversimplified, romantic readings of the past.

Despite the advances in Petrarch studies marked by E.H. Wilkins's *The Making of the "Canzoniere" and Other Petrarchan Studies* (1951), Gianfranco Contini's "La lingua del Petrarca" (1953), and Contini's edition of the *Canzoniere* (1964), discussions of the Petrarchan narrative were lacking, reflecting the general state of Petrarch studies. As Santagata writes, even in the twentieth century, "gli studi sul Canzoniere hanno [...] sofferto di una sorta di schizofrenia" (studies of the *Canzoniere* have [...] suffered from a sort of schizophrenia).[7] While philologists provided new data concerning Petrarch's writerly practices, they were less concerned about thematics or stylistics. And while commentators addressed literary matters, they failed to incorporate new philological data into their studies and delayed discussing narrative continuity until long after Wilkins's study had suggested the saliency of such an approach. It is only recently that studies of the *Fragmenta* have succeeded in bridging the gap between philology and criticism by considering the work integrally, connecting its formal structure and the stages of its composition to the interrelated questions of narrative and theology.[8]

Like Santagata, Rossana Bettarini has written of the difficulties of connecting the philological labour of the "apparato" (apparatus) to the critical work of the "commento" (commentary), noting that the editor of a critical edition follows strict scientific criteria while commentators are free to select traits of a text that capture their imagination and give weight to their interpretations.[9]

Bettarini makes the point that the "racconto" of the *Fragmenta* includes within it all the types, subject matters, and genres that commentators from the sixteenth century forward have chosen to split apart (as when non-love poems were separated from love poems). In order to rectify this, one must see Petrarch's history as a history of books, of books read and authored, the latter being self-inscribed and documented by the author in a way that was unprecedented. Petrarch's addressees constitute a broad community of readers ranging from the circle of *intenditori* (experts) or *fedeli d'amore* (Love's Faithful) to the generic reader addressed in the opening sonnet.[10] Bettarini stresses the extraordinary historical moment and archival importance of Petrarch's "autografo-idiografo" (autograph-idiograph) (Vat. Lat. 3195), and she notes how the supporting "Codice degli abbozzi" (Draft Codex) (Vat. Lat. 3196) serves as an invaluable working record of Petrarch's decision making in compiling and transcribing Vat. Lat. 3195.

From his late twenties onward Petrarch experimented with vernacular lyrics, re-editing and emending the poems into groupings and sequences. While there is much uncertainty about the dating of poems and the significance of their positioning in the earlier "forms" of the collection, the general chronology is known and provides insight into the poet's intellectual and creative process.[11] In 1349 or early 1350 Petrarch writes in the first letter of *Familiarium rerum libri* (hereafter *Familiari*) of his triple plan, to compile that book, the *Fragmenta*, and the *Epystole metrice* (Latin letters in verse) in parallel. It is clear that he was laying the groundwork for his work's investigation by posterity, and that such investigation would need to be conducted across diverse literary genres and types with an eye to history.[12] A critical date in this process is 1358, the final year of both the narration (*récit*) and of the internal narrative (*histoire*).[13] Not coincidentally it is also the year in which Petrarch completes the Correggio form:

> Petrarca, dunque, pone un termine preciso alla sua storia sentimentale, che non dura per tutta la sua vita, ma che giunge ad esaurimento nel 1358. Questo è anche l'anno in cui termina la redazione del primo *Canzoniere*.

> La coincidenza non mi sembra casuale: la vicenda d'amore termina nel momento in cui la letteratura l'ha tradotta in una storia. [...] Da quel momento in poi, però, le interferenze non saranno più possibili: la letteratura terrà da sola il campo.
>
> Petrarch, thus, places a precise end to his sentimental history, which does not last for his whole life, but which reaches exhaustion in 1358. This is also the year in which he completes the redaction of the first *Canzoniere*. The alignment does not strike me as coincidental: the love scenario ends in the moment in which literature has translated it into a story. [...] From that moment on, however, the interferences will no longer be possible: literature alone will hold the field.[14]

Another critical period in the compilation of Vat. Lat. 3195 begins at the end of 1367 when Giovanni Malpaghini ends his work as a scribe and Petrarch assumes those duties. This begins the final phase of "quel grande gesto di *colligere* gli sparsi frammenti lirici" (that grand gesture of gathering up the scattered lyric fragments), a labour guided by the poet's quest for knowledge and wisdom.[15] The final phase of compiling the poems will extend into 1374, the year of the poet's death.

Certainly the quest for knowledge is to be prioritized in appraising the compilation, editing, and ordering of the *Fragmenta*. This cognitive quest is invariably connected to Petrarch's hermeticism and use of indeterminacy, ambiguity, and evasiveness to refine his poetic message. Such obliquity has often not been considered as a positive factor, losing out to such reductive readings as Pietro Bembo's, which analysed the Petrarchan language in terms of a dichotomous system: "il persistente 'canone' del Bembo, che stende un velo su questa lingua limpida nell'aspetto ma elaborata nella sostanza, piena di parole cangianti dentro una rappresentazione polisemica della realtà, intrisa di zeugmi e scorci sintattici, di mirabili fughe affidate all'aspetto sonoro della rappresentazione verbale" (the persistent "canon" of Bembo, which draws a veil over this language limpid of aspect but elaborate in substance, full of words changing within a polysemic representation of reality, dripping with zeugmas and syntactic foreshortenings, with marvellous flights entrusted to the sonoric aspect of verbal representation).[16] To say with Bettarini that there is nothing unessential about Petrarch's poetic language – "niente aggiunto di descrittivo, veridico, opaco, esistenziale" (nothing added of the descriptive, truthful, opaque, existential) – is to acknowledge its compactness and organicity, its elimination of the arbitrary and its elevation of syntactical and phonetic tropes to a thematic level.[17]

The critical editions by Santagata and Bettarini have marked a sea change in Petrarch studies and made the current project possible. They have added considerably to our understanding of Petrarch's use of literary and sacred sources, the intratextual network of references within the *Fragmenta* and the larger oeuvre, the historical nature of Petrarch's authoring and compiling of the sequence, and the difficulties of reception noted above. They have also provided much support for the view of the *Fragmenta* as a narrative text that possesses its own dynamic unity, a unity that is complex, comprising 366 separate texts written in five different poetic genres.

While lyric poems are usually lacking in narrative development, in a sequence such as Petrarch's, having a persistent temporal progression and development of themes and characters, that is not the case. By the same token, a narrative embedded in a lyric sequence is resistant to the kind of analysis one would apply to a verse epic or romance, as it arises incrementally through the formal patterns of verse and the scattered vignettes and episodes of the microtexts that are gradually accumulated in the macrotext. To capture the complexity of such a narrative one must assess an array of structural and rhythmic elements; beyond the questions of literary personae and relationships, one must address the patterns of verbal and tropic iterativity and references to myths and other narrative motifs, including those arising from the courtly love tradition and sacred texts.

Medieval texts were overwhelmingly narrative in character. "Vita fabula est" was a well-known proverb.[18] Several years ago, when I began to assess the narrativity of the *Fragmenta*, I realized that the classic triad of fable, history, and parable could be used provisionally to assess Petrarch's treatment of narrative subjects in his lyrics. These sub-genres allowed for a differentiation into types based on contrasting diegetic schemes (see figure I.1). While the modes of fable, history, and parable could not be used literally, or to support a closed and essentialist poetics, they could be applied conditionally.[19] While Petrarch's style deviates greatly from that of a prose writer, his retention of the syntactic norms of prose allows for narrative and thematic unity to persist within the collection. (It is worth bearing in mind, as Giacomo Leopardi writes, that the linguistic tools available to Petrarch and Boccaccio were more similar than one might realize.)[20]

As a man of the Middle Ages he was well aware of Cicero's "tria genera narrationum" or division into three narrative genres:

> l'"historia," che propone le "res gestae" del passato, corrispondente alla "narratio aperta" di Cicerone o "narratio dilucida" della *Rhetorica ad herennium*; la *parabola*, corrispondente all'*argumentum*, che con le sue "res fictai" ma possibili ripete la "narratio probabilis" ciceroniana o "verismilis" della *Rhetorica ad Herennium*; infine la "fabula," che con le sue narrazioni "neque verae, neque verisimiles" corrisponde alla "narratio brevis" della retorica classica.

> the "historia," which proposes the "res gestae" of the past, corresponding to "narratio aperta" of Cicero or "narratio dilucida" of the Rhetorica ad herennium; the parable, corresponding to the argumentum, which, with its things fictional ["res fictai"] but possible, repeats the "narratio probabilis"of Cicero or "verisimilis" of the Rhetorica ad Herennium; finally the "fable" [fabula], with its narrations "neither truthful nor probable," corresponds to the "narratio brevis" of classical rhetoric.[21]

The fictional tale or fable (*fabula*) is defined by Cicero as neither truthful nor probable, and concerns events that have not occurred and are unlikely to occur. A non-linear mode, the fable anticipates the improbable. The history (*historia*) rather provides a linear account of chronological time; it asserts the veracity of a pattern of events and attempts to give an accurate account of how those events occurred or were experienced. The parable (*parabola*) involves a dual plane of signification in which the time of history comes into contact with a more mysterious, allegorical or providential time.[22]

As an unvariable, authorized, and ordered sequence in an unambiguously written form, Petrarch's *Rerum vulgarium fragmenta* stands apart from other medieval sequences.[23] It presents a new humanistic subject whose development over the course of the 366 poems is informed by the author's commitments to history, moral philosophy, and theology. Unlike the anonymous figure of the poet within the medieval canzoniere (songbook), Petrarch's "I" figure is rooted in his actual identity in the world.[24] In addition, as a rigorously ordered sequence, the book asks the reader to traverse its narrative phases and conceive of its story; this is, by any estimation, an arduous task.

In narratological terms, the *Fragmenta* presents an author, a narrator, and a character who are at times identical and at times discrete: the author is the historical person who arrived at the definitive pattern of his book

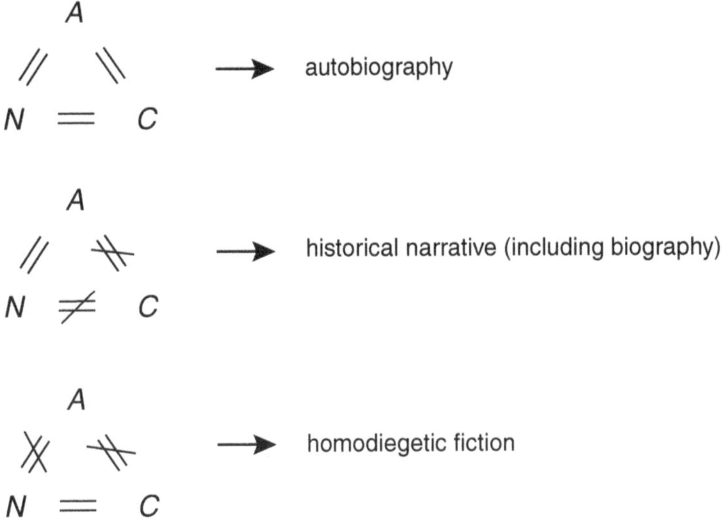

Figure I.1. Narrative schemas applicable to the *Fragmenta*

in the final years of his life; the narrator is the speaking voice within the lyrical-fictive framework of the poems; the character is the personage whose purported experiences are recounted. Gérard Genette has presented the following alignments of these diegetic roles as they give rise to distinct types of narrative:[25]

In the homodiegetic mode the author is distinct from the combined figure of the narrator-character: "In the type of narrative called personal, or first-person (or, in more narratological terms, narrative with a *homodiegetic* narrator), the enunciator of the narrative, herself a character in the story […] is herself fictional."[26] Such a narrative form recommends itself to the purely fictional work, such as the fable, in which the author's voice is absent, there being no superior viewpoint to that of the narrator-character. In line with the definition of fable as a story neither truthful nor probable, Petrarch's early poems combine the familiar and the strange, hope and despair, from within the perspective of a homodiegetic narrator-character. As I argue in chapter 2, the fabulous Petrarch depicts the subject as helpless against the obstacles of sin – *lacci* (snares), *giogo* (yoke) – and *l'amore sensibile* (sensual love). Here one is in the space of "exilio" ("exile"), bewildered by beauty and frozen by the fear of annihilation.[27] The time is one of incessant repetition, defining the psychological suffering of the unregulated soul: "vi discovrirò de' mei martiri / qua' sono stati gli anni, e i giorni et l'ore" ("I'll unfold my sufferings to you– / Woes that have shaped my years, and days, and hours") (12, 10–11).

In the mode of historical narrative, the character is distinct from the author-narrator, as for example in poem 1 (discussed in chapter 1, section 3) where the character is viewed retrospectively as "altr'uom da quel ch'i' sono" ("a different man than now I am") (1, 4).[28] By distancing himself in this way, the author-narrator lifts himself out of the predicaments of fable, reframing the arguments of love and desire in terms of process and history. In historical narrative there are conative markers that assure the reader of the veracity of the account. As I argue in chapters 4 and 5, many of the poems in the second half of Part 1 of the *Fragmenta* lend themselves to an analysis of this type, as they are concerned with actual situations – everyday relations, responses to worldly adversity, and, naturally, the experiences of love and faith. With the narrator now distinct from the character, by virtue of being a writer, the writerly self-awareness obtains a prominent place in the central poems of the collection.

In the mode of autobiography, the figures of author, narrator, and character coincide. Since in Petrarch's case the "I" figure is preoccupied with matters of the spirit, it is not surprising to see him adopt the modes of parable, exemplum, and allegory to convey the higher truths of the religious experience. As I discuss in chapter 6, when Part 1 of the *Fragmenta* concludes with poem 263 and Part 2 begins, one sees the mode of history slowly give way to that of parable; while there is much continuity between Parts 1 and 2, the greater singularity of the "I" figure in Part 2 actually has the paradoxical effect of de-individualizing and universalizing the content. Upon the cataclysm of Laura's death (announced in poem 267), one is cast into grief, words grow less, and poetry is equated with weeping. Though one still has the Petrarchan dualisms – of joy and sorrow, hope and despair – they are mitigated by the logic of limit-expressions, including parables, proverbs, and eschatological sayings.[29] And finally, as I argue in chapter 7, in the last fifty poems the duplicities of Petrarch's poeisis are completely absorbed into the twofold unity of parable, which combines the familiarity of the here and now with the exalted realm of the spirit, the "kingdom of God."

If in recognition of the complexity of the Petrarchan sequence one can exploit the tools of narratology to analyse the diverse phases of the collection, this comes with a caveat: no analytical tool can be applied deterministically if one wishes to penetrate the mystery of the *Fragmenta*. In interrogating the text the reader is to exploit only those tools – lexical, syntactic, phonetic, rhetorical, thematic – that the text puts forth. In appraising the macrotext as a unitary whole, the reader is asked to consider a progression, from the mode of homodiegetic fiction to historical narrative to spiritual autobiography, keeping in mind that the textual itinerary is not without relapses and interruptions, as well as intervals of non-narrative, purely lyrical poems.

2. Humanism and Poetic Theology

The late Middle Ages was a time of great instability in which the idea of catastrophic change was pervasive. With the Hundred Years War (1337–1453) and the Black Death, this idea was more than confirmed. Viewed against the backdrop of crisis and the endemic corruption and decadence of church and empire, the developing relationships among humanists acquired a sense of urgency as a means of shoring up the impoverished moral tenor of the society. A common misconception about humanism is that it was less religious than the scholasticism that preceded it, when in fact it favoured a closer relationship with God.[30] Another is the idea that, by precipitating the Renaissance, humanism demolished the Middle Ages, when in fact it represented the finest medieval scholarship in the classical world.[31] Given that Petrarch is the most prominent early humanist, it is not surprising that these misconceptions were applied to him as well. At times this has meant that Petrarch's humanism and concept of universal harmony were viewed in isolation from his actual experience of history: of dissonance and unruliness, and life in a chaotic and unjust society. Yet, no less than with Dante, Petrarch's experience of disharmony, sorrow, and estrangement – including political conflict – had a decisive impact on his poetry. While he tended to exclude the baser elements of the chronicle and of worldly struggle from the *Fragmenta*, this is a work imbued with historicity, viewed as an essential aspect of human experience.

This viewpoint is supported by Petrarch's prose, where the author is involved in the same process of moral self-examination undertaken in the *Fragmenta*.[32] Thus one confronts the need to read the vernacular poems with an eye trained on the major Latin texts – the *Familiari*, *Rerum senilium libri* (*Letters on Old Age*, hereafter *Senili*), *Secretum*, *De otio religioso* (*On Religious Leisure*), *De vita solitaria* (*The Life of Solitude*), and *De sui ipsius et aliorum ignorantia* (*On His Own Ignorance and That of Many Others*, hereafter *De ignorantia*). Here the author was involved in moral philosophy and the arts of the word as he proposed a new relationship in society between the role of "eloquence" and the "care of souls."[33]

If the reigning scientific and theological culture of the Middle Ages stressed dialectic (or logic) over grammar and rhetoric, Petrarch preferred to see logic as a property of all three arts of the trivium, the highest of which was rhetoric. This view is salient in the *Familiari* and *Senili*, epistolary works in which the author's dialogical engagement with his addressees is fundamental.[34] To endow one's addressee with selfhood was to arrive at a sense of literary intersubjectivity, embedded in the form of speech one adopted. As Eugenio Garin writes of Petrarch's epistolary style, "Speech – *sermo* – is a form of expression which exhibits its own measure as well as that of the soul of which it is an expression. [...] There is an insoluble connection between the interior and the exterior, between mind and speech. There is no point in praising the solitary form of speech, or monologue, which man conducts with himself. If we wish to be human, we must communicate with other men."[35]

Petrarch took as his models for epistolary dialogue Cicero and Seneca, Stoic philosophers whose embrace of virtue he saw as compatible with Christianity. He defends the meeting of ancient knowledge and Christian doctrine, and celebrates Platonic idealism, stating that pagan writers, if read with modesty and a religious heart, cannot harm faith but can actually benefit it: Plato and Cicero, Paul and Augustine are the true philosophers.[36] Moreover, the rebirth of classical letters would lead to a restoration of Italy and the Catholic church.[37]

In Petrarch's adoption of Senecan and Ciceronian ideals, based on the depth of feeling and interiority he found in their writings, one sees an Augustinian model as well, centred on the cultivation of friendship and contemplation, in solitude:

> This retreat in solitude [...] is a spiritual communication. It is not the refusal of the world, but of the falseness of the world, of the sadness of the world, in order to find once more the truth of the world within the truth of God.[38]

The reconciliation of Cicero and Augustine is emblematic of Petrarch's syncretism. His dialectical understanding of existence and experience contrasted with the confession-oriented sermons and tracts of the Dominican mendicants, a major force in the Italian church of the fourteenth century.[39]

The Dominicans had responded to the evident crisis in the religious life by stressing the centrality of the intellect and the *ratio* for the life of the soul, and relegated emotional and temporal considerations to a lower, inferior level, emphasizing the need for order in the spiritual life. This order confirmed the social hierarchy of the church and the superiority of the clerics to the laity. In the systematic order of Thomistic theology, the act or substance of Aristotelian metaphysics preserved its superiority to the contingency or accident. In contrast to this system, Petrarch asserted the importance, for moral philosophy and theology, of the question of time and the exploration of history. A practitioner of inductive thinking, he rejected the authority-based intellectual culture of his day and opted to explore the centrality of the emotions to the life of the soul. This research presupposed the intrinsically moral practice of rhetoric. As a historian he maintained a detached position, yielding neither to the technical approach to history that equated the magnitude of events with the power achieved through struggles of interest, nor to the mystical approach that attributed reality only to the life of the spirit. He was, for all intents and purposes, a historical realist who saw divine law as a vital component of human culture and aimed to integrate his awareness of his times with his understanding of the Bible as a historical document.[40]

Without disputing the major tenets of the *Summa theologica*, Petrarch found that Aquinas's rationalism resulted in a closed system.[41] He shared Aquinas's view that philosophy was the handmaiden of theology, and the classic view that the active life depended on the contemplative life, but he felt that medieval monasticism had shut out the world.[42] He was strongly influenced by the current of medieval spirituality that Gilson labelled "Christian Socratism," this being the pursuit of self-knowledge by contemplating God in one's own soul, trusting that one was made in the image of God.[43] Thus he was unambiguous about poetry's compatibility with theology:

> theologie quidem minime adversa poetica est. Miraris? parum abest quin dicam theologiam poeticam esse de Deo: Cristum modo leonem modo agnum modo vermem dici, quid nisi poeticum est? mille talia in Scripturis Sacris invenies que persequi longum est. Quid vero aliud parabole Salvatoris in Evangelio sonant, nisi sermonem a sensibus alienum sive, ut uno verbo exprimam, alieniloquium, quam allegoriam usitatiori vocabulo nuncupamus? Atqui ex huiusce sermonis genere poetica omnis intexta est. Sed subiectum aliud. Quis negat? illic de Deo deque divinis, hic de diis

> hominibusque tractatur, unde et apud Aristotilem primos theologizantes poetas legimus.
>
> In truth, poetry is not in the least contrary to theology. Does this astonish you? I might also say that theology is the poetry of God. What else is it if not poetry when Christ is called a lion or a lamb or a worm? Indeed, what else do the parables of the Savior in the Gospels echo if not a discourse different from ordinary meaning or, to express it briefly, figurative speech, which we call allegory in ordinary language? Yet poetry is woven from this kind of discourse, but with another subject. Who denies it? That other discourse deals with God and divine things, this one with God and men; whence even Aristotle says that the first theologians were poets.[44]

Poetry, like theology, uses obscure language in order to communicate what "plebeian" language cannot. If this is done "introducendo [...] nelle strutture linguistiche deputate alla trasmissibilità della parola, ciò che alla parola si oppone (appunto come 'indicibile')" (by introducing [...] into the linguistic structures assigned to the transmissibility of the word, what is opposed to the word (precisely as "unsayable")), such a practice still remains committed to communication.[45] The unsayable retains a referent in Petrarch's semiotic system, just as the inexpressible is a condition of the will for which he seeks verbal equivalents.[46] In order to extend theology in the direction of human life and history, he based himself on a few principles: that God is truth and can be known through faith alone; that the cultivation of virtue is essential to prepare one for the love of God; and that the expression of free will is not in conflict with the experience of divine grace.[47]

Petrarch's daily practice of reciting the Holy Offices led him to incorporate sacred and biblical citations, and their particular cadence and rhythm, into the verse.[48] This is apparent when he imitates the archaic forms of oral and written transmission present since proto-Christian times: *logia*, formulae, parables, and stories based on historical accounts. He realized that he would never fully understand God with his reason – and thus that poetry could not be bound by the doctrinal modes of predication or rationalization – but needed to find new and unprecedented verbal forms.[49] It is abundantly clear that Petrarch's practice of a poetic theology deepens over time.[50]

As one considers the narrative features of the *Fragmenta*, the model provided by the *Confessions* is pivotal. The notion of a spiritual autobiography that encompasses a pilgrimage towards God provides Petrarch with a template upon which to chart the events of his spiritual life. The time frame afforded by the Augustinian model tends to integrate the recursive aspect of time, as in the circularity of the diurnal or annual cycle, with the linear or historical aspect of time. These periodicities are absorbed in the finite "hours" and "seasons" of one's life, giving rise to a contemplative time that can be compared to the harmonies of music and the cosmos.[51] Ultimately this sense of a cosmic harmony is audible in the fugue structure of the poems themselves as they weave together felicitous combinations of phonetic and rhythmic elements.

In thematic terms, Petrarch seeks to recuperate the classical past and integrate it with the ethos of Christian humanism, which presupposed a figural and typological reconciliation of the Old and New Testaments, in the manner of Paul and Augustine. Like Augustine, Petrarch identified the faithful with the Holy Spirit, and his notion of life change implicated a turning in time, towards and with God. As with that saint, the experiences of justification and life change were understood by Petrarch as a lengthy process. In the *Fragmenta*, as in the *Confessions*, it is through the narrative discourse that the author evinces his developing relationships with God and the world. The operating premise of either work is that the story being told is based on the truths of one's self-examination and journey. As the reader of either text comes to appreciate, the past is aligned with memory, the present coincides with the understanding, and the future corresponds to the will in such a way that the writing process itself is absorbed into the reality of the *mutatio vitae.*

Another key religious figure is St Francis. It was the spiritualist side of the Franciscan ideal that appealed to Petrarch, born in the Franciscan town of Arezzo and named in honour of the saint. The aspects of Francis's life and works that most impressed him have to do with his pursuit of the solitary life in remote, desert-like locations and his mystical life of prayer. Not coincidentally, Francis is the only modern cited in the *De otio religioso* as an example of one who resisted physical desires and made the body obedient, freeing the soul.[52] Francis is also singled out in *De vita solitaria* as having practised three types of solitude – of place, time, and the mind – that Petrarch emulated:

> Triplex nempe, si rite complector, solitudo est: loci scilicet, de qua maxime michi nunc sermo susceptus est; temporis, qualis est noctium, quando etiam in rostris solitudo silentiumque est: animi, qualis est eorum qui vi profundissime contemplationis abstracti luce media et frequenti foro quid illic geratur nesciunt, qui quotiens et ubicunque voluerint soli sunt.

> Has quidem simul omnes solitudinum species nulli quam Francisco magis frequentatas video.
>
> Solitude is considered threefold, if I grasp the matter rightly: that of place, with which my present discourse is specially taken up; that of time, as in the night, when there is solitude and silence even in public squares; that of the mind, as in persons who, absorbed in deepest contemplation, in broad daylight and in a crowded marketplace, are not aware of what is going on there and are alone whenever and wherever they wish. I know of no one who had recourse to all these kinds of solitude at the same time more commonly than St. Francis.[53]

In the Franciscan view, to worship God is to collaborate in the Resurrection. The more one prays, the more the wonders that are revealed in the creation become an allegory for one's soul-work. The widespread popularity of Franciscanism in the fourteenth century represented a threat to the church, as did the related religious practice involving the worship of the Virgin Mary.[54] At the heart of St Francis's practice was the belief that

> against spiritual pride the soul is defenceless, and of all its forms the subtlest and the meanest is pride of intellect. If "nostra domina paupertas" had a moral enemy, it was not the pride beneath a scarlet robe, but that in a schoolmaster's ferule, and of all the schoolmasters the vainest and most pretentious was the scholastic philosopher.[55]

Knowing at first hand the corruption of the papacy and having little sympathy for the schoolmen, Petrarch adopts the saint's practices of solitude, retreat, itinerant evangelism, and praise of the humblest objects of the Creation, including devotion to the Virgin Mary. While this is most evident in the final poem, *Rvf* 366, "Vergin bella, che di sol vestita" ("O Virgin fair, in sunshine all arrayed"), Petrarch is unequivocal about his lifelong devotion to the Madonna.[56]

3. A History of Return

In his discussion of the history of the "forms" of the *Fragmenta*, Domenico De Robertis asserts that the true character of the Petrarchan subject only emerges from the "intermediate" relations of contiguity and similarity between the texts.[57] Contiguity, based on the syntagmatic axis of language, and similarity, based on the paradigmatic axis, share a complementary relationship. If one considers the entire collection of 366 poems, one's perception of unity will depend on this relationship. Far from imposing a predetermined structure on the sequence, Petrarch devised an open-ended system that progressed because of the gaps and uncertainties in its development.[58] The syntagmatic axis concerns the syntactic relation of contiguity and combination and is commonly named in the discussion of narrative, while the paradigmatic axis involves the relation of selection and equivalency and is commonly invoked in discussions of lyric poetry.[59] Conjunction and metonymy characterize the syntagmatic, while rhythm and repetition are among the primary features of the paradigmatic.[60] Contiguous elements assembled on the syntagmatic axis of a text constitute a world of interdependencies linked by tropes of the unexpected that are an important part of common speech and prose narrative. In poetry, however, the threshold of what is allowed in terms of these tropes is expanded; the lifting of prohibitions allows for an intensification of poetic structure, still disposed along the syntagmatic axis.

Critical reception of Petrarch has favoured a paradigmatic approach, privileging metaphor.[61] As a result, speculation on narrative has devolved into discussions of the romance that normalize the subject, rendering him static. If instead one integrates the two axes and visualizes the poems as progressive links in a chain, as one moves forward in the sequence one can recapitulate the earlier segments and compress them in memory, whether of objective references to the world or subjective views of the self. Memory possesses an almost Proustian dimension and provides the intratextual connections that enable the syntagmatic progression to occur. Herein lies the radical novelty introduced by Petrarch. Moving out of a confessional self-accounting, the Petrarchan subject proposes a new literary type of spiritual autobiography that combines the theological concerns of the *Confessions* and the *Commedia* (and the model of Bonaventure's *Itinerarium mentis in deum*) with the intense pathos and interiority peculiar to the lyric.[62]

The decision of Petrarch's brother Gherardo to enter the monastery in 1343 was the most immediate example to him of religious self-abnegation; yet that kind of monastic decision does not appeal to him.[63] In terms of the moment of decision at the classical trivium – represented by the Pythagorean "Y" – to right for virtue, to left for vice – Gherardo had turned right, Francesco had turned left.[64] Even if one's initial choice is in error, one can return on the left hand stave of the "Y" to the crossroads and select the path of virtue. In essence this is the story of the *Fragmenta*, the story of a man who has returned to the trivium, possessed of the knowledge of error, and then proceeded on his upward journey. This crossroads coincides with the arts of language, insofar as language is the path the poet has chosen to express his desire to be part of a new religious and cultural community. For Petrarch, grammar and dialectic (or logic) do not possess the prominence they had for the scholiasts. Rhetoric assumes the lead, rather, as a companion to moral philosophy and aligned with the heaven of Venus.[65] Since rhetoric is assumed to be ethical, even when the poet sublimates reality by the stylizations of poetry, he is investing in the truthfulness of a historical discourse.

History is a primary means by which Petrarch conceives of himself in the world. While a certain conventional criticism has dwelt overly on the themes of weariness, the pursuit of glory, the fear of death, and self-absorption in nature, these signs of psychological lassitude are corrected by the functionality of the historical within the syntagmatic continuity of Petrarch's text. As Andrea Zanzotto writes (introducing a 1976 edition of the *Fragmenta*), the fixation on these themes has led to the erroneous view of the work as possessing a circular structure and being essentially a psychological romance. Yet if one looks more closely at this "romance," one detects a radical change in the "I" character once he has entered into the historical landscape and allowed poetry to reshape his experience; at that juncture he discovers a continuity in the discontinuities of the past:

> È una vicenda che si svolge come insistita continuità nel discontinuo di una disseminazione di attimi che sembrano nutrirsi dei loro stessi detriti ...
>
> It is a situation that develops as an insistent continuity within the discontinuous, of a dissemination of moments that seem to nurture themselves on their own detritus ...[66]

Zanzotto is referring to Petrarch's decision to gather up the fragments of his past and make them whole. By taking this prospect seriously, he avers, the reader can perceive the dynamic presence of a new historiography in the *Fragmenta*:

> Da quelle zone confinarie in cui si costituisce come evento-limite, la poesia manifesta allora la capacità di mettere in crisi la dinamica degli altri eventi

("questa" realtà storica), rende inaccettabilmente banali tutti gli schemi secondo cui tale dinamica è stata decifrata. Allora: di fronte al groviglio per così dire bestialistico [...] della storia, sta, col no della poesia, una nuova, "oscura" proposta di umano che potrà avere esplicitazione, lasciato da parte il groviglio astrale della poesia stessa, in una eventuale storia "di ritorno," "autre."

From those border zones in which it is constituted as a limit-event, poetry manifests its capacity to place in crisis the dynamics of other events ("this" historical reality) as it renders unacceptably banal all the schemes according to which such a dynamic has been decoded. Then: faced by what might be called the bestial tangle [...] of history, there exists, with the no issued by poetry, a new "obscure" proposal of the human that can be explicated, once the immense tangle of the poetry itself is set aside, in a possible history "of return" or "other" history.[67]

By detaching himself from "le maglie rigidissime dei vettori della violenza che fa la storia" (the rigid weavings of the vectors of violence produced by history), Petrarch created a complex poetic discourse in which human history is legible, not in the outward struggles for power or authority but in the inward struggles of the individual and the collectivity for knowledge, justness, and morality.[68]

The idea of a history of return coincides with the Petrarchan motif of turning back from the road of vice onto the road of virtue. It is this scenario that confirms the moral and theological underpinning of the *Fragmenta* in its bipartite structure. Here, too, one discovers the significance of the "calendrical" structure, according to which the 366 poems constitute a kind of breviary within which the days of the church year align themselves with individual poems: if poem 1 corresponds to Good Friday, 6 April 1327, the day of the first encounter with Laura, then the first poem of Part 2, poem 264, falls on Christmas.[69] Another temporal structure – the fifteen "anniversary" poems by which the narrator establishes the number of years that have passed since 1327 – also aids in ordering the narrative.[70]

The emphasis on time and movement in the poems results in a "complementarity between history and fiction" in which the past, present, and future have discrete yet interpenetrating roles.[71] The itinerary begins in youth, when the horizons of expectation are myriad and cloudy, saturated with emotion and illusion. It moves towards a more conscious steering of the means of discourse by which the subject charts out the course of his future trajectories. And it concludes with the catharsis of loss and consecration and the becoming whole of the subject. Petrarch's return to a path of moral rectitude was repeatedly presented in his oeuvre as a life-long journey towards God. Such a journey coincided providentially with the return of society to an earlier and more primitive period of purity. In conceiving of this radically humanist historiography, Petrarch gave rise to the birth of the modern conscience.

As stated at the beginning of this section, a myth persists that humanists were less religious than their scholastic predecessors. It is important to recognize that Petrarch is unwavering in his faith, from his earliest writings forward. The rigours of self-examination evidenced in the *Fragmenta* and elsewhere ask to be understood in the spirit they are offered, of modesty, sincerity, and vulnerability, and as offering a new affective dimension to medieval theology, to accompany its well-established intellective dimension.[72]

A seminal text in this regard is the *De otio religioso* (*On Religious Leisure*), a sermon-like tract addressed to the Carthusian friars of Montrieux who had recently hosted him. *De otio religioso* is a theological treatise about grace and faith in which Petrarch summarizes the challenges, or "enemies," facing humanity: these are "the enticements of the flesh," "the traps of this world," and the "the guiles of demons."[73] These challenges are confronted in the *Fragmenta*, roughly in this order. In the earliest poems, rife with fabulous imagery, the character's quest is for a sensual-spiritual creature named Laura. The adventures of fable are such that the narrator does not question them but accepts them on face value; he is absorbed, in Bakhtin's expression, in "life's manifold *fabulas*, that complete nothing and leave everything open."[74] Preoccupied with the trial of sexual desire, the narrator-character contends with fear and mystery, a condition he can only understand as something fated. Though there is a spiritual aura to the phantasm as well, he cannot extract himself from the experience.

When the narrator ceases to identify with the character and openly confronts the traps of the world, he rises above them, making clearer distinctions of time and memory. "Outsidedness" (or "transgredience") is not possible in fable, says Bakhtin, since the author does not assume the veracity of the account; rather one is in the mode of "historical inversion" where magical thinking prevails over critical thinking.[75] Conversely, once the historical challenge is met, the author-narrator can recapitulate his character's actions and redimension the question of glory, understood as a product of virtue and not as worldly fame. By turning the methods of historical accounting inward, the subject can document the stages of a turning away from worldliness and towards the wholesome desire for happiness and God.

There gradually intervenes a providential time of the will that suspends the time of the world, whether that is understood as the cyclical temporality of nature or the chronological linearity of history. This is the mode of parable, which exists at the point of contact between daily events and the divine. It has as its primary subject the experience of renunciation and liberation. Generally speaking, the parabolic and Davidic area of the book is found in Part 2 and is characterized by a diminishing concern with linguistic and psychological contradictions and a greater dependency on Holy Scripture. It is here that one perceives a steady movement away from the "time of the world" of Aristotle and towards the "time of the soul," or "of the mind," of Augustine – that is, towards the time of the parable.

For Aristotle, who asserted the "primacy of movement over time," there is a fundamental difficulty and mystery in negotiating "the unstable and ambiguous status of time itself, caught between movement, of which it is an aspect, and the soul which discerns it."[76] As change or movement occurs, a second "aporia" arises: "Does [movement] not appear to be 'something indefinite' with respect to the available meanings of Being and Nonbeing? And is it not in fact undefinable, since it is neither power nor act?"[77] This double aporia devolves onto Aristotle's understanding that "it is indeed the 'now', the instant, that is the end of the before and the beginning of the after"; in contrast, for Augustine "the future and the past exist only relating to a present, that is, to an instant indicated by the utterance designating it."[78] As Ricoeur summarized this distinction, the "great aporia of the problem of time [...] lies entirely within the duality of the instant and the present" and "the narrative operation both confirms this aporia and brings it to the sort of resolution that we term 'poetic.'"[79] By following the Augustinian conception, one arrives at "a hierarchization of the levels of temporalization, which requires distinct denominations: temporality, historicality, and within-time-ness."[80]

In Petrarch, these denominations correspond to the three narrative modalities I have indicated. In the last category ("within-time-ness") one sees the narrative develop into a figural, or typological, dimension rich in subjectivity and pathos. Petrarch shared with Augustine the conviction that only by exposing one's errors could one commence to rectify them. He also articulated the view that one's earthly desires could be refined and sublimated into a desire for God and the divinity that resides in God's creation, in the world of immanence.

With the title *Rerum vulgarium fragmenta*, Petrarch indicates the work's materiality, multiplicity, and linguistic character. As with the titles *Rerum familiarium libri*, *Rerum senilium libri*, and *Rerum memorandarum libri*, the genitive *rerum* indicates that the poems propose to communicate about the *res ipsae* of existence. *Vulgarium* designates the decisive choice of the vernacular language and the insertion of the work into the extant vernacular tradition.[81] With *fragmenta* the poet designates the poems not simply as separate textual entities but as pieces of a whole that will be unified and regathered with a sacred purpose, as in John 6:12–13 (and, with variations, Matthew 14:20, Mark 6:43, and Luke, 9:17): "colligite quae superaverunt fragmenta ne pereant" ("gather up the fragments that remain, lest they be lost").

Petrarch was aware of Augustine's homily on the Feeding of the Five Thousand at the Sea of Galilee, paraphrased as follows: "The fragments left were truths of hidden import, such as they were unable to receive (they took the carnal, left the spiritual)."[82] The significance of the "fragments" is that the meal of the spirit remains one of scarcity and difficulty. Thus the deeper understanding of the parable of the loaves and fishes concerns Christ's compassion.[83] With this gloss, the term *fragmenta* is an apt descriptor for a composite poetic sequence intensely concerned with the problems of piety and compassion and requiring an attentive reader to grasp its deeper significance.

In chapter 1, I lay the theoretical groundwork for the study by examining Petrarch's relation to recent poetic tradition, the nature of his style and linguistic practice, his use of genre, including the "canzoniere" genre that he radically alters, and the concept of unity that one can infer for the book. My reading of *Rvf* 1, "Voi che ascoltate in rime sparse" ("O you that hear in scattered rhymes the sound"), sees it as a poem of deferral in which the "I" figure's early experiences, which led him to be the topic of gossip – "favola fui gran tempo" ("I have long been a fable") (1, 10) – are neutralized by the nascent desire for truth, just as the natural desire for the beloved is channelled and sublimated beyond the will to possess her. I note how the outward impulse to shun the vulgarity of the world coincides with an inner mandate to follow the path of repentance. With this sonnet as a point of departure I assess the extended proem of *Rvf* 1–10, seen as introductory poems that prepare the reader for the work that follows.

Chapter 2 considers how in poems *Rvf* 17–100 one sees a parallel between the fabulous, passionate trials of youth and the mythic absorption in the marvellous, and how, in the initial stage of the character's enamourment with Laura, one finds the characteristic markings, the external signs and effects, of love. In these earliest-written of the poems one sees little of the "I" figure who rues his past and much of the "I" figure who participates in the amorous passion. These poems contain the highest concentration of proper nouns, mythic periphrases, and geminological, astronomical, and geographical references. Here one sees poems of a fabulous nature that typically express a wish, desire, or hope with respect to a future that is vague and uncertain. Some of the commonplaces are taken from myth, starting with Daphne and Apollo but including others such as Diana and Actaeon, Narcissus and Echo, and Perseus and Medusa; others are taken from the Bible and popular religious practice. The imagery of fixation, the stupor of enamourment, and the suffering of loss are integral to this mode in which the narrator-character is debilitated by the weight of sin, as symbolized by the *vincolo* (chain), *laccio* (snare), *giogo* (yoke), *vischio* (bird-lime), or *vomero* (ploughshare). While there are numerous exceptions, the first centenary is dominated by the distorting mirror of a subjective personal mythology. My discussion of the fourteen sonnets of the Raccolta of 1342 draws attention to the fact that Petrarch had begun to assemble his lyrics into a collection. This selection offers an array of interconnections that reveal the author's tendency to build on the internal temporalities of the work. The presumptive opening poem of the Raccolta, poem 34, centres on the myth of Daphne and Apollo, a myth that evolves through the course of the *Fragmenta* from its original status as a fable of metamorphosis into a parable of Christian transformation.[84]

Chapter 3 investigates a turning point at the start of the second centenary, highlighted by the *canzone-frottola* (*Rvf* 105), an enigmatic tour de force that portrays the author's historical and existential sense of being in the world. At this point in the sequence, a symmetry is sought between the forward reachings or protensions of fable and the retentions in memory of history. Here the "giovanile errore" ("youthful error") is increasingly immured in the past. A catalyst in this transition is provided by the poet's further investment in the hermetic, archaic, and antique style of Provence that has often been overlooked by commentators.

As seen in chapter 4, after canzone 119, which recapitulates some of the thematics of the Latin prose dialogue, the *Secretum*, the author narrator views his character with historical detachment; thus he establishes a link between the psychological aspects of the individual drama and the history of Christian piety. In the great sequence of canzoni 125 to 129, the landscape takes on a prominent role, including the Italian political landscape and the solitary landscape of Vaucluse. As the combined persona of the author-narrator emerges with greater clarity, we see his desire to distance himself from worldliness. Within this moral framework, the subject takes a stand against the Avignonese papacy (*Rvf* 136–138), seen to have been responsible for leading the church into a "Babylonian captivity." Also in chapter 4, I examine the use of parallelism and antithesis in the second centenary, arguably the "Petrarchist" span of the collection. Through antithesis one sees the moral character of the subject in his historical confrontation with error. Antithesis is not a trope of self-contradiction or dispersal but rather of developing interiority. This is seen in the *amaro/dolce* opposition through which the poet projects a middle ground and style of semantic neutrality. In delineating a parallel to Petrarch's *Psalmi penitentiales* (Penitential Psalms), I show how the elements of contrition and faith in these poems provide a model for the change in the *Fragmenta* to a more Davidic style and the anticipation of a state of ataraxia or quietude.

In chapter 5, I turn my attention to the final eighty poems of Part 1, a series that includes many late poems added after the Correggio manuscript, in which the author-narrator establishes the groundwork for a penitential engagement of memory and learning. By now the pagan deities are nominalized and Laura is humanized. With the "Petrarchist," heavily troped and conceit-ridden, interval of the second centenary concluded, the poems anticipate the arrival at a contemplative "at-one-ness" with time and a separation from the moral and intellectual errors of the past.

Chapter 6 concerns the first fifty-four poems of Part 2, starting with canzone poem 264 – probably written at the same time as poem 1, in 1347. Here the investigation of the soul becomes overt as its itinerary is delineated unambiguously as a road of repentance. The religious poems intercalated with poems of distress and longing possess the Augustinian imprint of disquietude leading to hope. At the outset of Part 2, the subject cannot conceal his inner condition from those who see him; but his weeping is a liberation from the limits of stoicism. By virtue of this inner change, one has a more tangible portrait of Laura in death than in life. Amore, now a figure of charity, is still capable of disputing with the subject, as the trope of the "giogo antico" ("ancient yoke") (270, 1) acquires a sacred and penitent cast.

Chapter 7 follows the subject through his mourning to its end in consecration. As the signs of *chronos* diminish, there intervenes an atemporal, ascensional experience of time, diversified by the whole range of verb tenses. The "friend" that emerges as the unifying element between Laura and the subject is Christ. Forming a part of the Christian mystery, Laura is spiritually alive and listening, a guide. The subject's love for Laura is undying after her death, this being a sentiment that had not been expressed with such candour in verse previously in the Middle Ages.[85]

The present study is divulgative in nature. More than a new interpretation of the *Fragmenta*, it aims to be an accurate reading, situated in the author's philological reality.[86] The poems' order is respected, so as to best imagine how the text was present in Petrarch's memory.[87] By adopting a fictional voice, Petrarch was able to dramatize the problems of a self that aspired to the exemplarity of classical and Christian ideals. This was undertaken with the characteristic ambiguity of the medieval author who fulfils a double role, as individual and as the bearer of a collective cultural message. Endowed with the gift of self-analysis, Petrarch was able to mix his song and his story, deriving thereby a narrative that emerges from the text not as a compilation of episodes but as an evolving moral discourse. Through the love of knowledge the Petrarchan subject arrives at the love of God, but this depends on his knowledge of the world and his involvement in the selfhood of the Other.

Chapter One

Historical Context and Poetic Form

Eo tamen dulcior fit poesis quo laboriosius quesita veritas magis atque magis inventa dulcesit.

Poetry is all the sweeter since a truth that must be sought out with some care gives all the more delight when it is discovered.

Petrarch, *Collatio laureationis*[1]

1. The Poetry of the Tradition

Starting with the court of Frederick II and the poetics of the Sicilian school, a doctrine of love with its origins in philosophy and medical science was disseminated. The elevation of the imagination by the Sicilian school had its highest manifestation in Giacomo da Lentini, for whom the image of the beloved, painted in the lover's heart, corresponded to the Aristotelian notion of the phantasm, the *quo* of sense cognition. This *fantasma* could preserve the beloved's presence in the heart when she was absent. The imagination could exist independently of any physical object or perception, being, as Aquinas would argue, immaterial. The imagination could assume a transcendent power in the subject as reminiscences served as a bridge to the intellect, which was separate from the domain of the senses. Giacomo's canonical sonnet "Amor è un[o] desio che ven da core" ("Love is a desire which comes from the heart") presents two options to the lover: to yield to the love of the senses or to elevate the woman in the imagination by means of the image. In the final line Giacomo asserts "e questo amore regna fra la gente" ("and this love prevails among the people") (l. 14): the love of the senses leads to madness, as the organism, controlled by its biological impulses, cannot tolerate their denial.[2] In contrast, the love of the imagination elevates the soul, and this is the love carried forward from the Sicilian school to the Tuscan-Bolognese poets Guido Guinizelli, Guido Cavalcanti, Dante, and Cino da Pistoia.

This tradition stemmed in part from the poetry of the troubadours, in which erotic love was mediated by a series of conventional elements: the woman's superiority to the vassal-lover, the secret encoding of the love signal, the centrality of the gaze, the figure of the *lauzengier* or deceiver, the absence of the beloved and the anguish it causes. In the troubadouric poetry of the *amor de lonh*, the poet-lover was distant from the beloved, but the unrequited love was compensated for by the nobility of the emotion and the dignity conferred on the Lady. As the poetics of courtly love was adapted by the Tuscan and Bolognese schools, it gained new complexity as a semiotic system of correspondences, acquiring a philosophical and religious framework. Averroës's commentary on Aristotle's *De anima* had a profound impact as the poets devised a new technical terminology, theorizing the intellectual knowledge of God as being capable of transporting one above the plane of the physical senses, and even above the imagination.

Cavalcanti is the most sophisticated transmitter of the new philosophy, such that his doctrinal canzone "Donna me prega" ("A lady asks me") is an obligatory point of reference. This *summa* relates the love of the woman through the preservation of her noble image in memory, cultivated in the heart and sent upwards to the soul and intellect as a vehicle to the knowledge of the divine. For Cavalcanti the division between the subject (*subiectum*) – the plaintive and wounded lover, whose death is imminent if the Lady does not return to save him – and the object (*obiectum*) – the knowledge of the divinity – is mediated by "spiritelli" ("little spirits"), materialistic agents that work within the hearts of the lover and the beloved in order to favour love's enaction, in line with the movement from potency to act in Aristotelian terms.

Dante splits with Cavalcanti over the pessimistic implications of Averroism, but not nearly as much as Petrarch will do. For Dante, the weightiness of the Cavalcantian doctrine was dealt with in the *Rime petrose*, poems directed to a woman of stone, while the Dante of the *Commedia* rejected the subjective suffering side of the Cavalcantian polarity in favour of a transcendent elevation of the woman to the status of an agent of God, a *beatrice*.[3] While Petrarch's allusions to Dante's poetry are considerable, historically they have been underestimated.

Numerous scholars, and the editions of Santagata and Bettarini especially, have set out to rectify that situation, so as to recognize the parity and commonality between the two poets, each of whom enacted a spiritual journey through love poetry that was elevated and dignified by their understanding of Christian theology. How Petrarch altered the earlier phenomenology of love is a complex matter, typified by modulation and variation of key terms and a radical change in theology.[4] As he retained the pulsations of desire of the courtly love tradition, he encoded that desire in Augustinian terms. While continuing to employ much of the stilnovistic imagery and language, he shifted the emphasis away from the Beloved onto the subjectivity and conscience of the Lover.[5] In this way the Lady herself was humanized.

If there is one poet who serves as a bridge in this regard, it is Cino da Pistoia. The lexical and rhythmic commonalities between the poets derive from their shared ability to mediate the voices of the Provençal poets and the Italians.[6] Petrarch can be said to share a level of affective knowledge with Cino, or what Marti has called his "realismo psicologico" (psychological realism).[7] His attention to Cino's language begins with canzone 23 and is then seen in canzoni 37, 70, 72, and 73; it is most apparent in *Rvf* 90 to 97 and 267 (indebted to the *planh* for Cino's Selvaggia), and in the final series of poems. Cino's ability to absorb within his style the influences of others is a gift inherited by Petrarch, whose borrowings amount to "sottili e dissimulanti modulazioni" (subtle and dissimulating modulations).[8] Petrarch's derivation from Cino occurs, first of all, on the lexical and syntagmatic levels: shared elements include the attributes of the Lady, the suffering of the lover, and the use of common rhyme words. Thematically, the shared idea of mediation concerns the Lady's ability to transmit divine knowledge to the lover in a manner that is more intersubjective and less rigid and doxological than in Dante.[9] Cino's poetic existence is also coloured by his exile, which provides the element of distance from the beloved that is the subject of his most celebrated canzone, "La dolce vista e 'l bel guardo soave" ("The loveliness, the glances soft and clear").

While Cino was part of a group of poets who exchanged sonnets of correspondence based on questions of poetics, Petrarch was more isolated. When he does address another poet directly, as in sonnets 112, 113, and 144 to Sennuccio del Bene, the poems are about enduring the passionate experience of love. The importance of Cino's example is apparent in the sonnet written on his death in 1336, "Piangete, donne, et con voi pianga Amore" (*Rvf* 92) ("O ladies weep, and may Love weep with you"), which is the only obituary poem in Part 1 and is preceded by two other poems, "Erano i capei d'oro a l'aura sparsi" (*Rvf* 90) ("Her golden hair was scattered on the breeze") and "La bella donna che cotanto amavi" (*Rvf* 91) ("That beauteous lady whom you loved so much"), rich in reminiscences of Cino.[10]

As one considers Petrarch's debts to earlier poets one must contrast his cultural situation to theirs. While negotiating the Siculo-Tuscan and Bolognese traditions noted above, he was isolated in Provence and lacked the close social community enjoyed by the earlier *rimatori*.[11] Given this situation, his return to his Italian poetic roots was a rite of passage by which he introduced into the disorderly world of fourteenth century Avignon the discipline, formal clarity, and aristocraticism that belonged to the most compact schools of the thirteenth century.[12]

Petrarch's knowledge of Provençal was unexcelled among Italian poets, and his continuation of the Occitan tradition was unique.[13] If in the Provençal lyric the poet was a liege in the service of a superior Lady, the courtly love could still result in his erotic ecstasy or *joi*. As that tradition was altered by the Italians, *joi* became a philosophical concept. In Petrarch this abstraction does not take place; rather the figures of desire and Eros are reclaimed, internalized, and endowed with an intersubjective character as pertains to a relationship between equals. This leads to a greater sense of ambivalence in the interiority of the characters. Another novelty with respect to earlier canzonieri was the fact that the *Fragmenta* met the requirements of a completed work, existing in an authorized and definitive version.[14] As he altered the language of the Italian lyric, Petrarch refined it to meet the needs of the self, enhancing its capacity for genericness and ambiguity, expanding its ability to dialogue with the worldly and the transcendent.[15]

A critical moment in his emergence as an Italian poet is marked by his coronation as poet laureate in Rome on 8 April 1341.[16] In his *Collatio laureationis* (Coronation Oration, hereafter *Collatio*), Petrarch defined poetry – citing Cicero – as an activity requiring divine inspiration: "Ceterarum rerum studia et ingenio et doctrina et arte constare, poetam natura ipsa valere et mentis viribus excitari et quasi divino quodam spiritu afflari" ("Whereas attainment in other activities depends upon talent, learning, and skill, the poet attains through his very nature, is moved by the energy that is within his mind, and is as it were inspired by a *divine inbreathing*").[17] Petrarch is clear that he would not be content to be merely a poet, as that practice was currently understood, since he shares the goals of the philosopher and historian: "cum offitium poete in eo sit ut ea, que vere gesta sunt, in alia spetie, obliquis figurationibus, cum decore aliquo conversa traducat" ("The office of the poet consists in this, that he should take things that have really come to pass and transform them by means of subtle figures into things of a different sort").[18] The poet can only realize his commitment to the truth by following a divine inspiration: "in arte poetica secus est, in qua nil agitur sine interna quadam et divinitus in animum vatis infusa vi" ("nothing can be accomplished unless a certain inner and divinely given energy is infused in the poet's *spirit*").[19]

As one considers the literal understanding of inspiration, it is useful to recall that, in the medieval world, the heart "sees" and the mind "feels" in terms of simulacra and other images, ordered in a complex system of correspondences: "According to the medieval model, or code, things and events of our real world speak; things and events are words in the book of creation."[20] While modern texts are generally "founded on signification, expression, [and] representation," medieval texts are typically focused "on production and on the self-representation of production."[21] When the modern reader approaches the *Fragmenta*, therefore, it is critical to assess its values of production and process and not assume that the author is primarily involved in self-representation. Another common error is the neopositivist tendency to collapse the reading of the *Fragmenta* into the formalistic tradition of the medieval lyric, which "excludes narrative elements" and is dedicated to "situations rather than actions."[22] While Petrarch continues to rely on these models, emblems, and types, he transforms the lyric by adding to it the dramatic loci and typological imagery that were common to narrative poetry.[23]

In the medieval lyric the type is a "higher function" of language by means of which poets transformed the "informative function" of the vernacular language; as a poetical sign, the type possesses a given structure but is also polyvalent.[24] Types are present in the form of expression (lexical and syntagmatic patterns) and the form of the content (motifs and fictional situations) of poems: "As soon as [the types] were adopted by the tradition, they tended to generate one another and to combine into broad, more or less fixed sets of patterns, forming within the literary language [the] restricted number of systems [...] named 'registers.'"[25] Within the registers (or "styles") certain idealized elements could be seen to recur among a range of poets: "For instance, the allusion to an obstacle in the (affective) way from man to woman [...] *signifies* the erotic impulse in the infinite variety of its actual manifestations."[26] The fact that the registers "allude to and suggest real things and events" is posited at a distance, such that the tendency to "escape from the specific into the general" is aided by the recourse to emblem, a figure of semantic duality that ties a literal meaning to a figurative one.[27]

It is clear that as Petrarch absorbed the Provençal tradition into his poetics, he transformed the "achronic, circular, centripetal" usage of types by those troubadours into a narrative form.[28] Similarly, as regards the Italian poets of the thirteenth century, it is critical to recall the radical innovation of Petrarch with respect to his Italian predecessors and the astonishing modernity of his language.[29] He rejected the position and technical lexicon of earlier poets with respect to the "objectifying analysis of love" and drastically limited the number of distinct lemmas he would include in his book.[30] The author's lexical selectivity is not a matter of preciosity so much as a means of amplification in support of the work's overall unity.[31] The lack of empirical particulars and realistic depictions of natural objects actually serves to intensify the affective dimensions of the text, such that beneath the monotone surface of *soavità* (gentleness) there exists another Petrarch of political denunciation and anchoritic devotion, of interrogation, enigma, and mystery. Here one finds allusions to Petrarch's travels, his epistolary activity, his religious vocation, and his immersion in historical studies. In addition, there is a hermetic and *trobar clus* Petrarch whose use of irony, iconicity, and mnemotechnics gives the work an added element of authenticity.

2. Style, Genre, Structure

Paucitas autem est que precium rebus facit.

It is scarcity that gives value to things.

Fam. xvi, 11[32]

If Petrarch's novelty as a poet and humanist lies in his reticence to accept the great "cathedrals of ideas" of medieval theology, and if this novelty is actualized in the world by a new language of the self, then readers of the poetry are compelled to make an assessment of his style.[33] Style implies point of view and thus a sense of personal unity, diversified by the range and distribution of poetic materials. As the Petrarchan narrator states in poem 1, the poems are written in a "vario stile" ("various style") (1, 5). The principle of *variatio* – of poetic forms and themes – is the arch principle of Petrarch's poetics, as it allows for iteration and modification of key terms over the course of the sequence, along with the preservation of ambiguity and uncertainty, a practice enhanced by the use of hypothetical, optative, and interrogative modes. As seen above, Petrarch was deeply invested in rhetoric; the third art of the trivium was a partner to moral philosophy and was needed to persuade the reader as to the rightness, dignity, and virtue of the events being reported. As a Christian, he understood the role of rhetoric theologically, so that its use in poetry could expose the tensions and disquietude, the joy and the exultation of the soul.[34]

The fact that Petrarch's style later became the model for widespread imitation (with the phenomenon of Petrarchism) has at times obscured one's view of it, almost making it seem a specular or ornamental version of itself. Another error has been the idea that Petrarch's poetry can somehow be reduced to a binary system, such as one proposed by Pietro Bembo, who divided Petrarch's style into the poles of "gravità" ("gravity") and "piacevolezza" ("pleasantness"), "maestà" ("majesty") and "dolcezza" ("sweetness").[35] The danger with such simplistic views is that they ignore the middle ground of signification and marginalize the syntagmatic and narrative elements as primary means of ordering the text.

At the heart of Petrarch's style is the notion of scarcity, a quality that suited his ideal reader as well.[36] By employing a select vocabulary, he was able to expand the range of meaning through a technique of lexical concentration and combination:

> È stupefacente [...] la capacità petrarchesca di ottenere, con un repertorio lessicografico estremamente selezionato e poco icastico, effetti così intensi e sorprendenti; si direbbe che proprio a misura della sua povertà e monotonia, in virtù delle straordinarie capacità combinatorie dell'autore e delle frequenti riprese ritmiche, il linguaggio ne guadagni in condensazione e concentrazione, dilatando in profondità il campo delle possibilità semantiche.

> Petrarch's ability to obtain such intense and surprising effects with an extremely selective and non-vivid lexicographic repertory is astonishing; one would say that exactly in proportion to its poverty and monotony, thanks to the author's extraordinary combinatory abilities, and the frequent rhythmical reprises, the language gains in condensation and concentration, by expanding in depth the field of semantic possibilities.[37]

In his landmark essay "La lingua del Petrarca," Gianfranco Contini demonstrated how linguistic selectivity and monolinguism were factors that contrasted Petrarch with Dante. The plurilingual Dante is characterized by the "sperimentalità incessante" (incessant experimentality) of a poet inclined to self-interruption, allegoresis, and constant movement outward: "l'enciclopedia e dottrinale e stilistica di Dante può trovare un centro solo all'infinito" (the Dantean encyclopedia, both doctrinal and stylistic, can find its centre only at infinity).[38] In contrast, the only "experiment" that Petrarch is said to have made concerns the structure itself of the *Fragmenta* as it is elaborated over time.[39]

The labour of editing and compilation focused on refining the formal perfection of the style and the macrotextual coherence of the whole. We are fortunate to possess Petrarch's considerations about the editing process in his annotations to his manuscripts: "Le postille, frequentissime, sono autoesortazioni ad eliminare dal contesto parole o frasi che possano ingenerare nel lettore equivoci [...], ad evitare ripetizioni e l'eccessiva frequenza di certi nessi fonici o sintattici [...]; oppure ad obbedire a precetti di retorica esterna o scolastica" (The frequent marginalia are self-exhortations to eliminate from the context words or phrases that could lead to misunderstandings in the reader [...], to avoid repetitions and the excessive frequency of certain phonic or syntactic nexus [...]; or to obey the precepts of external or scholastic rhetoric).[40] The work of revision, correction, and expansion proceeded slowly, by "inlay," until the final changes were made in 1374. The editing process was undertaken in conformity with Petrarch's conviction that language (and not just the vernacular) was an imperfect material vehicle in the service of a higher, immaterial truth and unity.

As Contini states, the expressive variety and freedom of Petrarch's text is due to its written and recitative nature. The esteemed philologist provides insights on how stylistic and linguistic data inform the moral, affective, and spiritual planes of Petrarch's text and how lexical and syntactic details coincide with its overall thematic contours. He also notes the presence of an arcane Petrarch, characterized by linguistic violence and polyglottism.[41] By concentrating on the syntagm and poetic passage, as defined by the rhythmic (phonetic, syntactic) tensions within it, Contini underscores the relation between Petrarch's linguistic practice and his life.

Related to Petrarch's use of the Tuscan language is his transformation of the stilnovistic phenomenology of love: "Petrarca si esercita nella fenomenologia amorosa, fa dell'autobiografismo trascendentale, accentuando con rilievo meramente formale i dati biografici sinceri o fittizî" (Petrarch practises the phenomenology of love; he produces a transcendental autobiographism by accentuating the biographical events, whether sincere or fictitious, with a purely formal relief).[42] Coinciding with this modification is the linguistic system Contini attributes to Petrarch's "fiorentinità trascendentale" (transcendental Florentinity), being the result of his long residence outside Italy and idealization of the lyric genre.[43] Petrarch's self-restriction to the lyric results in a "metaphysical heroism" that is humble in nature and prolongs the earlier lyric tradition of Cino, Dante, and others, reinforcing the positive side of their "genius, patience, constancy, and exhaustive abilities."[44] Contini further writes of the dominance of rhythm over semantics in Petrarch's verse, as evidenced in the variety of syntactic, metrical, and phonetic tropes (enjambment, suspension, litotes); his use of the verb, said to be "metaphorical, not yet active in the true sense"; his generic use of the noun as "neuter" rather than "masculine"; and his adjectives, which function as "epithets" rather than "predicates."[45] The reference to the neuter is a glottological distinction, which, in a gendered language like Italian, allows one to distinguish between the generic noun and the particular noun.

In a larger sense, the idea that the Petarchan noun is neuter can be extended to a theory of semantic neutrality that carries over into questions of tone and judgment. To say that the noun is ungendered is to leave it in its ideal or indeterminate form. This idea is epitomized by the phonic-semantic cluster *l'auro / l'aura / Laura / lauro / l'oro / l'alloro* (gold / aura / Laura / laurel / gold / laurel) with its intrinsic polysemy. The theme of the fleetingness of time – as announced in the opening book of the *Familiari* and present throughout the *Fragmenta* – is energized by this sense of semantic neutrality. The neutral is further enabled by the hypothetical character of Petrarch's thought, since by imagining multiple outcomes to the scenarios of existence the poet elevates potentiality (*potenza*), in the widely diffused Aristotelian system, to an equal status with actuality (*atto*).

Summarizing Contini's work, Bettarini makes a crucial point: "le stesse parole singole verbalmente innocenti si caricano d'ogni differenza e movimento" (while verbally innocent, the individual words themselves are charged with every possible difference and movement).[46] Indeed, the Petrarchan style is rich because of the variability of the contexts, whereby a single word may acquire – in the rhythmic context of a poem – a "lexical coloring" and "secondary meaning" that overtake its "principal sign of meaning."[47]

No better example of this latitude can be given than the word "stile" itself, which presupposes the physical act of writing. It is of great consequence – in light of this lexical-stylistic datum – that Petrarch's handwriting is the first handwriting of the great poets that is known to us and that the graphic aspect of his book possesses its own semantic value; the *Fragmenta* "è [...] il primo esempio di *liber* contenente liriche sparse di materia amorosa, sapientemente impostato sotto l'aspetto grafico, considerato anch'esso come messaggio" (is [...] the first example of a book containing separate lyric poems, on an amorous subject, knowingly ordered with a graphic presentation, this also considered to be a message).[48] "Autoscrittura" (self-writing) emerged as an authorial practice in the Middle Ages. As the number of literate people grew in the twelfth century, and as paper became available, the earlier practice of dictating texts to a scribe who recorded them on a waxed tablet was slowly replaced by self-writing. This movement towards the self-drafting of documents that were thus "authorized" was led by archivists, notaries, chroniclers, and chancellors. The historical and philological investigation of the problem was complicated by the subsequent phenomenon of "riscrittura" (rewriting).[49]

While for Dante the process of self-writing and rewriting were of great importance, we possess no autographic evidence. In contrast to Dante, whose sociocultural profile is that of an isolated figure writing in opposition to "la cultura ufficiale in lingua Latina" (the official Latin language culture), Petrarch has a complex strategy aimed at renovating the writerly and book culture of his era: "per lui l'autoscrittura rappresentò lo strumento primario ed essenziale di una complessa strategia scrittoria e libraria, che mirava al rinnovamento radicale sia delle tipologie grafiche in uso al suo tempo, sia della stessa forma-libro" (self-writing represented for him the primary and essential instrument of a complex writerly and book-related strategy which aimed at a radical renewal, both of the graphic typologies in use in his time and of the book-form itself).[50] This strategy takes shape in the *Fragmenta* through the persona of the author-narrator, who self-consciously drafts, orders, and delivers the poems to a reader. The act of self-writing presupposes the intention to transcribe the poems for posterity in a manner befitting their quality as a verbal music.

Recent research into the calligraphic practices of Petrarch (and Malpaghini) suggests that much work remains to be done in connecting those practices to our understanding of the work's unity. Giuseppe Savoca's studies of Vat. Lat. 3195 blend the insights of ecdotics – the practices that govern the preparation of critical editions – and codicology – the study of manuscript books in their material and cultural individuality.[51]

Savoca rejects arguments that Vat. Lat. 3195 is a working copy, arguing on the basis of palaeographic and philological evidence that "il libro del Canzoniere si presenta rigorosamente compiuto e definito, tanto sul piano della scrittura e della lezione dei singoli testi quanto su quello dell'architettura e della organicità narrativa dell'insieme" (the book of the Canzoniere is presented rigorously complete and defined, as much on the plane of the writing and the reading of the individual texts as on that of the architecture and narrative organicity of the whole).[52] In his critical edition Savoca aims to reproduce what Petrarch and his scribe actually wrote in Vat. Lat. 3195, recovering his system of punctuation and capitalization, in contrast to the Contini text, which is based on the Modigliani diplomatic edition of 1904. In this way the text is opened up to greater fluidity, musicality, and possible ambiguity in the reading. It is also Savoca's intent to direct the reader to the orality of Petrarch's text, and the palpability and mutability of his voice.

In syntony with Savoca's research, H. Wayne Storey urges us to take seriously Petrarch's intentions to unify the microtext and the macrotext, citing the strict connection between the visual-graphic unity of Vat. Lat 3195 and its thematic unity.[53] Once again one can speak of the author's self-writing as implemented by his embedding the role of the scribe into the narrative, so that from the start one has a distinction between the character and the narrator. This distinction obliges the reader to treat the "I" character with deference and latitude and inquire into its particular references, its orientations of time and place, and its relationship with Laura.[54]

In recognition of the fact that genre is a major organizing device in the *Fragmenta*, in marking out a moral itinerary and architecture, Storey explicates how Petrarch arrived at a unique means of transcribing each of the five genres in the manuscript.[55]

Each poem's position, dimensions, and proportionality with respect to the whole is essential. A crucial identifier of each of the poems is its genre. There are 317 sonnets, 29 canzoni, 9 sestinas, 7 ballatas, and 4 madrigals. The canzoni account for 7.9 per cent of the poems but fully 37.3 per cent of the lines (if the sestinas are included in the canzoni, the figures are 10.4 per cent and 42.2 per cent). The canzoni tend to stand together in clusters, like pillars that free up the architectural space of the whole for extended sonnet sequences. Not coincidentally, the longest canzone, poem 23, is the first to appear, and the second and third longest, poems 360 and 366, are the last to appear. Moreover the canzoni are evenly distributed. In addition to the sonnet and canzone forms, one sees ballatas, madrigals, and sestinas. The madrigal, a short humble lyric open to diverse formal solutions, provides an outward-looking view of a pastoral scene; appropriately, all four madrigals appear in the first third of the book. The ballatas (poems 11, 14, 55, 59, 63, 149, 324) are divided into an early group of five followed by one occurrence in the second centenary and a final occurrence in the fourth centenary, arriving at the "perfect" number of seven. The seven regular sestinas (poems 22, 30, 66, 80, 142, 214, 237, 332) occur in Part 1, with only the double sestina, poem 332, in Part 2, drawing a parallel to the single ballata of Part 2, poem 324. The differentiation of lyric genres follows the rhetorical practice of the topoi or topics, as each genre occupies a "place" in language and a particular place in memory.[56] While it was common to employ diverse genres to address diverse aspects of life in the medieval literary culture, it was unprecedented to blend within a single work poems of a low register, such as the ballata and the madrigal, with poems of a high and illustrious register.

As I detail over the course of this study, each of the genres has a particular contribution to make to the whole; though seemingly obvious, this critical distinction has not traditionally received the attention it deserves. So, too, certain themes and topics have been overlooked, such as the civic and historical poems. Yet fully 23 per cent of the supposed Correggio form are non-love poems, a fact that points to Petrarch's propensity "to use the poetic text as a means of communication."[57] In short, the order of the canzoniere in Petrarch's hands is not imposed but flows organically from the semantic content and disposition of each poem, and this order is based on meaning.[58]

The most critical division of all is provided by the work's bipartite structure. Scholars concur on the fact that Petrarch arrived at the bipartite plan of his book well in advance of the Correggio "form" (1356–8), probably in 1348 or 1349 in the immediate aftermath of Laura's death. As is known, the Chigi manuscript (1359–63, drafted by Giovanni Boccaccio) is the first actual redaction containing the bipartite division into Part 1 and Part 2.[59] As Martinelli suggests, the bipartite structure is Pauline in character, a "negative parable of sin" that moves from "error" to "grace":

> Le due parti sono strutturate secondo un ritmo binario, discendente e ascendente, come parabola negativa del peccato, in quanto allontanamento da Dio, e come vittoriosa affermazione della luce della grazia; il registro verticale-ascetico del libro tuttavia fa sì che i segni della crisi morale e della ripresa religiosa siano *evidenti ovunque*, per cui il *Canzoniere* si struttura più realisticamente come un'opera *in progress*.

The two parts are structured according to a binary rhythm, descending and ascending, as the negative parable of sin, in as much as a distancing from God, and as the victorious affirmation of the light of grace; nevertheless the vertical-aescetic register of the book causes the signs of moral crisis and religious renewal to be *everywhere apparent*, such that the *Canzoniere* is structured more realistically as a work in progress.[60]

As Martinelli also suggests, Petrarch's use of structure as an ordering principle derived from his awareness of the understanding of "structura" in medieval exegesis:

Il termine e l'immagine di *structura*, in uso a partire soprattutto da S. Gerolamo (*Ep.* 168, 26), occupa un posto fondamentale nell'esegesi biblica medioevale. La Sacra Scrittura è un'organica costruzione, non soltanto una successione di libri, ha cioè una struttura: è *spiritualis fabrica, structura spiritualis, aedificium*. [...] Anche il *Canzoniere* è *spirituale aedificium*, di cui le singole *pièces* non sono che i materiali. [...] L'ordine e la disposizione dei nostri pensieri si fonda soprattutto sulla nozione del *colligere*, che è uno dei primi gradini della scala ascetica. L'ordine dell'edificio umano e di ogni altra opera dev'essere modellato sull'ordine della realtà (*ordo rerum*) e fondato su una scala e graduatora degli esseri. Il fondamento di questo ordine è Dio stesso ...

The term and image of *structure*, in use especially after St Jerome (*Ep.* 168, 26), occupies a fundamental place in medieval biblical exegesis. The Bible is an organic construction, not just a succession of books, that is, it has a structure: it is a *spiritualis fabrica, structura spiritualis, aedificium*. [...] The *Canzoniere* too is a *spirituale aedificium* whose single *pièces* are but the materials. [...] The order and disposition of our thoughts is based especially on the notion of *colligere*, which is one of the first steps of the ascetic ladder. The order of the human edifice and of every other work must be ordered on the order of reality (*ordo rerum*) and based on a ladder and scaled list of beings. The foundation of this order is God himself ...[61]

The model of a biblical architectonics is sufficiently general to accommodate the continuous variations of Petrarch's poetic discourse while constituting "a compact vertical structure ... rising on the foundation of humility."[62] In such a way the moral struggles of the subject can be seen as steps on an ascetic ladder. Within this view, the autonomy of the individual poem is respected. As Martinelli writes, "L'architettura del libro non si sovrappone alle singole *pièces* e non è secondaria ed ulteriore rispetto all'esigenza di una scelta e organizzazione esclusivamente estetica dell'opera, ma si sviluppa direttamente attraverso l'ordine e la successione delle poesie stesse" (The architecture of the book is superimposed on the single *pièces* and is not secondary and ulterior with respect to the need for choice and an exclusively aesthetic organization of the work, but is developed directly through the order and succession of the poems themselves).[63] Martinelli argues for the narrative unity of the *Fragmenta* under the sign of salvation, refuting the claims of those critics, including Natalino Sapegno, who persist in separating the unitary "structure" of the *Fragmenta* from its fragmentary "poetry" (reminiscent of Croce's critical division of the *Divine Comedy* into its "poetry" and "non-poetry").

In assessing the unique structural adaptation of the medieval canzoniere form, Santagata discourages the tendency to treat the *Fragmenta* as a romance-type narrative and places into relief its investment in memory:[64] "Ma questa idea di canzoniere si afferma decisamente solo con i *Fragmenta* e con la scoperta petrarchesca della memoria" (But this idea of a songbook is decisively affirmed only with the *Fragmenta* and with the Petrarchan discovery of memory).[65] It is through memory that Petrarch adapts a "lyric" sequence into an "ordered" sequence.[66]

As Maria Corti has written (citing Santagata), the unity of the *Fragmenta* results from the intersection of two possible sets of organizational criteria. Either "there exists a combination of thematic and/or formal elements that runs through all the texts and produces the unity of the collection" or "there is a progression to the discourse for which each single text can occupy only one place."[67] She concludes that "the *Canzoniere* meets the conditions of both," as elements recurring in the work – the *patterns of equivalence* – alternate with the *patterns of transformation*. By alternating the emphases between these two patterns, Petrarch is able to situate transformative events in a context that is believable and consistent with the overall unity of his text.

3. The Proem of the *Fragmenta* (*Rvf* 1-10)

Poem 1 begins with a direct address to the reader, stating that the "scattered rhymes" presented here concern "another man" from the one who is writing. The earlier man was enmeshed in "error" and reduced to a subject of "gossip," while the man speaking, the narrator, has learned the nature of "vain hopes" and "vain sorrows" for which he still feels deep "shame." In this way the sonnet encapsulates a narrative situation in two moments:

> Voi ch'ascoltate in rime sparse il suono
> di quei sospiri ond'io nudriva 'l core
> in sul mio primo giovenile errore
> quand'era in parte altr'uom da quel ch'i' sono,
> del vario stile in ch'io piango e ragiono
> fra le vane speranze e 'l van dolore,
> ove sia chi per prova intenda amore,
> spero trovar pietà, nonché perdono.
> Ma ben veggio or sí come al popol tutto
> favola fui gran tempo, onde sovente
> di me medesmo meco mi vergogno;
> et del mio vaneggiar vergogna è 'l frutto,
> e 'l pentersi, e 'l conoscer chiaramente
> che quanto piace al mondo è breve sogno. (1, 1–14)

> O you that hear in scattered rhymes the sound
> Of those sighs that I used to feed my heart
> In my first youthful error, when I was
> In part a different man than I now am,
> Whoever knows of love by trial, from him
> If pardon none, compassion then I hope
> To find, for this the various style in which
> I weep, debate these vain hopes, this vain woe.
> Now I see clearly how to everyone
> I long have been a fable, and of that
> Deep in myself I often am ashamed;
> Shame is the fruit of my delirium;
> As is repentance, and the knowledge sure
> That worldly joy is but a passing dream.[68]

The direct engagment of the plural addressee ("Voi") will remain implicit throughout the collection, as will the startling simplicity of the poet's speech and his reliance on the music of the voice – "il suono / dei sospiri" – to communicate his message.[69] The opening line also contains the words "rime sparse" ("scattered rhymes"), in which the image of scattering suggests its opposite, the gathering up of pieces into a whole.

As further iterations of the word *spargere* suggest, the scattering – whether of stars or seeds, fronds or locks of hair, tears or prayers – denotes an underlying unity. What is scattered, like the crumbs of bread by the Sea of Galilee, will be collected. So too the poetic "harvest" will be reaped in accordance with how it is sown.[70] Though phrased in the language of poetry, this is at heart a theological idea.

The separation of historical selves in poem 1, as demarcated by the alternation of past and present tenses, demands consideration from a narrative perspective. The separation is placed in relief by the line "quand'era in parte altr'uom da quel ch'i' sono" ("When I was / In part a different man than I now am") (1, 4), and by the sense of shame visited on the subject looking back to his errant youth. The final two lines – "e 'l pentersi, e 'l conoscer chiaramente / quanto piace al mondo è breve sogno" ("As is repentance, and the knowledge sure / That worldly joy is but a passing dream") (1, 13–14) – confirm the need to repent and to know the illusory nature of worldly pleasure. These lines are powerful yet tentative, an utterance but not yet a positive action. Thus the entire moral problematic of the book is introduced *in medias res* and dialogically, as the reader – but only the reader who understands love! – is asked for compassion.[71]

It is worth noting that the "I" figure in poem 1 will subsequently be imbricated in a diverse array of narrative configurations. As the poem makes clear, the changes and fluctuations in this figure are keyed into his moral development. And while the poem is palinodic, the overturning of the earlier moral position has only occurred "in part," meaning that the subject has only made relative progress; one can say that the narrator has passed beyond the love of the senses of the character, and has arrived at a sublimated love as aided by the imagination, but has not yet reached the goal of a pure love of the intellect. In theological terms, "Voi ch'ascoltate" marks the passage from the love of the creature to the sublimating love of the creation, but it lacks the act of will by which the unified subject will eventually arrive at the pure love of the Creator.

Francisco Rico has aptly described the state of the narrator in poem 1 as stoical with respect to his earlier errors. As Rico has shown, poem 1 has a determinative role in the formation of the bipartite canzoniere; the antithetical structure of the sonnet serves as a projection of the architectural divisions of the entire macrotext. Citing the shared language between *Rvf* 1 and the prologue letters of the *Familiari* and the *Epystole metrice*, Rico places the poem's *terminus ad quem* as 30 November 1349 (though for a consensus of scholars 1347 was the date of composition).[72]

The nine poems that follow poem 1 complete a proem that will be referred to over the course of the work. These sonnets contain a mixture of pastoral, scriptural, and amorous themes and are written under the sign of renunciation, in opposition to the illusions of dreams, "sogno" (1, 14), and the reality of shame, "vergogna" (1, 11). Poems 2, 3, and 4, all sonnets, introduce Laura in a providential light: 2 and 3 deal with the moment of the enamourment with Laura while 4 boldly compares her birth in Avignon to that of St Francis in Assisi. In sonnet 6 one has a portrait of the lover, guilty of lust, and in sonnet 7 a letter elevating the life of the mind and impugning strayed humanity, as embodied by the Avignon papacy. The apparent intent is to establish, here in the proem, the widespread nature of sin in the world and the need of humanity to correct its moral-theological path. The thrust of Petrarch's declamation here – "povera e nuda vai philosophia" – reports on the disregard in which philosophy was held by a world dedicated to lucre:[73]

La gola e 'l sonno et l'otïose piume
ànno del mondo ogni vertú sbandita,
ond'è dal corso suo quasi smarrita
nostra natura vinta dal costume;
[...]
Povera et nuda vai philosophia,
dice la turba al vil guadagno intesa. (7, 1–4, 7–8)

Gorging and sleep and lazy feather-beds
Have banished every virtue from the world,
And thus our nature, almost overcome
By habit, from its course is led astray
[...]
"Naked and poor go forth, Philosophy,"
The rabble cries, intent on paltry gain.

Poems 11 to 100 – all of which were written by 1342 – constitute a macrotextual span in which the experience of love is alternately one of bedazzlement and fatigue, obsessive specularity and "sperar fallace" ("deceptive hope") (32, 4). In general these poems are concerned with the subjection to Laura as Daphne, a fabulous Ovidian projection remote from the sacred role that Laura will later embody.[74] Nevertheless, Daphne (Δάφνη = laurel) also stands for the tree of knowledge, the tree of life, and the cross of the Crucifixion. Since for the Christian there is a fabulous consciousness as well, the soul can be seen pursuing its faith through ritualistic practice, penetrating to the spiritual core of its existence, as in canzone 29 in which the subject pierces through a self-destructive dependency on the amorous phantasm to arrive at the purified state of contemplation; or sonnet 62, "Padre del ciel" ("Father of heaven"), a text grounded in the Crucifixion and the subject's turning to "altra vita" ("another life") (62, 6). Also noteworthy is the establishment of the civic and historical theme in canzone 37, "Sí è debile il filo a cui s'attene" ("So feeble is the thread by which is held"), and canzone 53, "Spirto gentil" ("Noble spirit"). The healthy mixture of tones and subject matters of the first centenary demonstrates Petrarch's intent to treat the topic of sin with candour and to focus on the centrality of the will in the subject's eventual return to the correct path. It was because of Christianity's retention of the elements of the pagan world that it succeeded among the less educated populations. Petrarch does not trivialize this fact but incorporates the memory of classical motifs within the Christian mythology, including the descent to the underworld, the worship of physical representations of the deity, and the cult of relics.

Five of the seven ballatas and three of the four madrigals are found in *Rvf* 11–90, generally treating the themes of hope and sorrow, projection and introspection. Petrarch's ballatas are metrically consistent with those of Dante and the stilnovists; their novelty lies in their monostrophism.[75] Had Petrarch employed multiple strophe ballatas, the iterations of the same rhymes would have disrupted the continuity of the macrotext and lowered the tone to an unacceptably plebeian level.[76] The ballatas typically possess a chiasmic structure, recreating the movement and temporality of a circular dance. This is seen in "Lassare il velo o per sole o per ombra" ("I have not seen you draw aside your veil"), a single stanza of twelve hendecasyllables and two septenaries structured around the theme of the veil. While the veil covers the Lady's face, the lover's desire cannot be hidden, a condition that leads him to the mortification of thought in a manner reminiscent of Cavalcanti:

Lassare il *velo* o per sole *o* per ombra,
donna, non vi vid'io
poi che in me conosceste il gran *desio*
ch'ogni altra voglia d'entr'al cor mi sgombra.
Mentr'io portava i be' pensier' celati,
ch'ànno la mente *desïando* morta,
vidivi di pietate ornare il volto;

ma poi ch'Amor di me vi fece accorta,
fuor i biondi capelli allor *velati,*
et l'amoroso sguardo in sé raccolto.
Quel ch'i' piú *desiava* in voi m'è tolto:
sí mi governa il *velo*
che per mia morte, et al caldo et al gielo,
de' be' vostr'occhi il dolce lume adombra. (11, 1–14)

I have not seen you draw aside your *veil,*
Lady – not for sun or shade –
Since first you recognized the grand *desire*
That drives all other longings from my heart.
While I bore secretly those lovely thoughts
That have decreed [*desired*] the death of sanity,
I saw compassion grace your countenance,
But from the time Love made you notice me,
Your golden hair has been forever *veiled,*
Your amorous glance withdrawn into itself;
What I most *longed for* in you I'm denied;
So that *veil* governs me
Which by my death – in cold as well as heat –
Will darken the sweet light of your fair eyes.

With its terms of desire framed by iterations of the veil (*velo / desio / desiando / velati / desiava / velo*), the symmetrical ballata closes as it begins, repeating the same pairing of light and shadow in lines 1 and 14 (sole [...] ombra / ... lume adombra), with the emphasis being on the shadow, the hidden, the denied, the mysterious. One has in essence a recollection of when the Lady first perceived the subject's desire, a pastoral situation involving a play of spaces in which the subject's failure to capture the Lady's gaze is compensated by the fact that she has taken notice of him and pitied him.

Poem 14, the second ballata, is also made up of twelve hendecasyllables and two septenaries and is the first poem to repeat the motif of weeping ("pianto") from poem 1:

Però, dolenti, anzi che sian venute
l'ore del pianto, che son già vicine,
prendete or a la fine
breve conforto a sí lungo martiro. (14, 11–14)

Therefore, you're filled with grief before the hour
For tears has come – and it is near at hand –
Take now in your extremity
Brief comfort in such lengthy suffering.

The theme of lamentation recurs in sonnet 16, a well-known vignette featuring an old man who has travelled to Rome to see the Veronica shroud (or veil) before he dies, a quest the narrator-character compares to his pursuit of Laura. At the centre of the conceit is the fact that the Veronica was believed to contain the imprint of Christ's face. The lower, or popular, style at work in the sonnet is seen in the style of Cavalcanti, be it in the diminutives of "famigli*uola*" ("little family") and "vecchi*erel*" ("good old man") or the adjective "sbigottita" ("dismayed"). Since the "I" figure's search for a likeness of Laura is compared to the old pilgrim's search for a relic before dying, the question has arisen as to whether Petrarch is comparing Laura to the Christ. In actuality, what is compared are the two quests, both of which are motivated by a natural instinct to move towards the "forma vera":

cosí, lasso, talor vo cerchand'io,
donna, quanto è possibile, in altrui
la disïata vostra forma vera. (16, 12–14)

Just so, worn out, I wander questing too
Seeking in others, if it's possible,
Lady, your true form, yearned-for and desired.

The failure to find in other women the substance of Laura's ideal beauty serves to confirm that beauty, and stands to that degree as an expression of faith in the "true form" of beatitude that exists within her. As Silvia Chessa writes,

[*F*]*orma vera* è l'oggetto filosofico e mistico di un'esperienza ripetutamente e ontologicamente fallimentare; non la forma perfetta o un generico eterno femminile, ma l'eterno di Laura. La sua anima. Petrarca può trovare *in altrui* la *pulchritudo* dell'amata, ma non la sua *forma vera*, proprio come l'altro *discipulus veritatis* vedrà nella veronica l'immagine di Cristo ma non godrà della visione di Dio.

True form is the philosophic and mystical object of a repeatedly and onto logically failed experience; not perfect form or a generic eternal feminine,

> but the eternal of Laura. Her soul. Petrarch can find *in others* the pulchritude of the beloved, but not her *true form,* just as the other truth-seeking pilgrim will see in the Veronica shroud the image of Christ but will not enjoy the vision of God.[77]

While the subject's search is not successful, it can be seen as as spiritually analogous to that of the old pilgrim, and to that extent an attempt at iconolatry, the religious practice of worshipping a representation as the embodiment of the divinity.[78] This seminal poem introduces into the *Fragmenta* the theme of spiritual visualization, which Petrarch – following Augustine and more recent thinkers such as Bonaventure – saw as a model for the transformation of the heart.[79] As Chessa suggests, the locution "forma vera" ("true form") extends beyond the mythic situation of the microtext to the greater sense of the sacred at work in the macrotext. The words "forma vera" are inserted into the syntagmatic continuum as a kind of seed. If the subject is beguiled by love, his desire contains within it the potential for transformation.[80] Just so, the old man's desire to go to Rome to see the image of Christ serves to confirm Petrarch's belief that Rome is the legitimate seat of the papacy to which the church must providentially return in order to manifest its "true form."

Chapter Two

Temporality and Desire (*Rvf* 22–100)

Et quis non viator ex nobis est? brevi omnes adversoque tempore, tanquam hiberno pluviali die, longum ac difficile iter agimus; cuius dyaletica pars esse potest, utique terminus non est.

And who among us is not a pilgrim? We all are on a long and difficult journey in a period of time as brief and difficult as a rainy winter's day. Dialectic can be part of the journey; but it is certainly not its goal.

Fam. i, 7[1]

1. Entering the *Selva* of the First Centenary

To tell a fable requires great cultivation of language but also great simplicity. The fabulist confronts an enigma, as in the "daily bread" of the Gospel, which is ordinary bread to eat but also the "supersubstantial" bread of the sacrament.[2] Within the space of the early poems of the *Fragmenta*, the Petrarchan subject has experiences that are difficult, dominated by beauty and fear, a wondrous imprisonment. This is the space of fable.

Fables rely on magical objects, more powerful than the characters; around these objects a force field exists that determines the narrative links of cause and effect. These events are typically stark, abnormal, inexplicable; they embrace reality by standing apart from it. In such a way, "the unreality of fables becomes truth. No falsehood is possible in myth."[3] This paradoxical assertion by a great contemporary scholar of fables strikes us as a suitable guide to the earliest phase of the "giovanile errore" ("youthful error") when the chimeric figure of Amor arbitrarily wields his power. Petrarch's use of language in this phase dramatizes the affective intensity of a soul in exile, split from the object of desire: one is presented with a static condition that carries with it a sense of moral and psychological entrapment.

Petrarch was inclined to draw his metaphors from the natural world, a practice that allowed him to remain focused on the interiority of the subject in his relations with others. One such system of metaphors was characterized by the wild and sylvan, the site of the dark wood and the relationship with animals. This is the case in the first sestina, "A qualunque animale alberga in terra" ("Among such creatures as dwell on this earth"), which contrasts the distress of the lover, compared to a wild beast at loose in the woods, to the calm harmony of the animal world absorbed in the natural cycle. A dichotomy is developed in alternating stanzas between the human distinction from animals – animals are in repose, man is restless – and the human's subjugation to its animal instincts, as Laura, too, is an "aspra fera" ("harsh creature") (22, 20). In the following lines, stimulated by "lo mio fermo desir" ("my love unchanging") – a homage to Arnaut Daniel, the originator of the sestina – the narrator-character voices the most direct and unambiguous statement of carnal desire in the entire collection:

Con lei foss'io da che si parte il sole,
et non ci vedess'altri che le stelle,
sol una nocte, et mai non fosse l'alba; (22, 31–3)

Oh, might I be with her from set of sun
And let no others see us but the stars –
One night alone: And never come the dawn,

In the poem's coda one has a synthesis of its sylvan argument expressed in the form of an *adynaton*, rooted in the dark wood:

Ma io sarò sotterra in secca selva
e 'l giorno andrà pien di minute stelle
prima ch'a sí dolce alba arrivi il sole. (22, 37–9)

But under earth I'll be in withered woods,
And day will pass by filled with little stars
Before, on that sweet dawn, forth shines the sun.

In contrast to the arduousness of the sestinas of Dante and Arnaut, Petrarch's sestinas stand out for their subtlety and apparent ease.

The six end words (almost always nouns) possess a certain generality, so that associations can accrue to them as the poem unfolds. In the present instance, the end words limn the sylvan setting as a place where the human being experiences the excesses of the four classical passions: fear, sorrow, hope, and joy.

The arch example of the fabulous mode is found in canzone 23, the longest and probably the earliest poem of the collection. Here one finds fragments of myths representing six episodes of metamorphosis of the lover's body, symbolizing his subjection to Laura. There are numerous references to speech along with an overdetermined set of references to the lover's struggle to regain his identity: "Lasso, che son! che fui" ("Woe: What I am: What I was":) (23, 30); "Non son mio, no. S'io moro, il danno è vostro" ("No: I'm not mine; if I die, yours the cost") (23, 100). The dominant tone is one of naive wonder that will eventually be transmuted into something more solid and lasting.[4] Clearly this poem was written before Petrarch's intensive study of Augustine.[5] Conversely, one sees the strong influence of Dante, as in these lines – "m'aperse il petto, e 'l cor prese con mano, / dicendo a me: Di ciò non far parola" ("That girl [...] / Unsealed my breast, seized with her hand my heart, / Instructing me: 'Breathe not a word of this'") (23, 75–6) – which call to mind Dante's dream in the *Vita nuova* in which Beatrice is given his heart to eat. When the lover declares his desire – which Laura has forbidden him to do – she changes him to a stone, after which she attempts to clarify her identity:

> Ella parlava sì turbata in vista,
> che tremar mi fea dentro a quella petra,
> udendo: I' non son forse chi tu credi. (23, 81–3)

> She spoke with such a troubled countenance,
> It made me tremble there within that rock
> To hear: "I am perhaps, not whom you think";

The scene calls to mind Virgil's instructions to Dante-pilgrim when he is mistaken by the simoniac pope Nicholas III for the (still living) Boniface VIII:

> Allor Virgilio disse: "Dilli tosto:
> 'Non son colui, non son colui che credi'" (*Inf.* xix, 61–2)

Then Virgil said: "Tell him immediately:
'I am not he, I am not the one you think I am'"

The lover prays to be un-stoned and returned to his former state; he regains his feet but he is unable to speak, and can only "cry out" by writing:

ond'io gridai con carta et con incostro:
Non son mio, no. S'io moro, il danno è vostro. (23, 99–100)

So I cried out with paper and with ink
"No: I'm not mine; if I die, yours the cost."

The mythic fantasies of canzone 23 are exaggerated forms of human individuality. Among the myths is that of Actaeon, who spies Diana bathing at a pool and is transformed into a stag. In the narrator's insistence that the fabulous account of the metamorphosis is true, he recognizes he is indulging the reader's credulity:

l'acqua nel viso co le man mi sparse.
Vero dirò (forse e' parrà menzogna)
ch'i' sentí' trarmi de la propria imago
et in un cervo solitario et vago
di selva in selva ratto mi trasformo:
et anchor de' miei can' fuggo lo stormo. (23, 155–60)

With her hands splashed the water in my face.
The Truth I'll tell (though it may falsehood seem):
I felt myself drawn forth from my own shape,
And to a stag, alone and wandering
From wood to wood, I swiftly was transformed,
And still I flee the baying of my hounds.

While the sylvan theme – "di selva in selva ratto mi trasformo" ("From wood to wood, I swiftly was transformed") (23, 159) – naturally recalls poem 22, the focus here is on disabling transformation, not the static quality of the tranquil woods. As the first two canzoni in the sequence, poems 22 and 23 work as a dyad, with the latter poem representing the "earlier" sensibility (a familiar pattern in the *Fragmenta*).

In canzoni 27 and 28, written in 1333, Petrarch urges the powerful Romans Orso dell'Anguillara and Giacomo Colonna to support the

Holy Crusade and join forces with Philip VI of Valois. By so doing he hopes to persuade Pope John XXII of the wisdom of returning the papacy to Rome. Orso will host Petrarch during his first trip to Rome in 1337 and will, as a Roman senator, bestow on him the laurel crown during his next trip in 1341. In canzone 27, Rome is figured as a woman, a usage Petrarch will repeat in the civic canzone 53.

The third canzone in a row, *Rvf* 29, "Verdi panni, sanguigni, oscuri o persi" ("Green fabrics, blood-red, dark or violet"), demonstrates Petrarch's relation to the *trobar clus* tradition and is an anomaly at this stage of the collection, as it praises Laura in angelic terms. Its opening lines concern the topos of the body as one's worldly dress, a topic of great importance in the *Fragmenta*. Metrically complex, its use of *coblas unissonas* recalls Arnault Daniel (as does sestina 30, with which it forms a dyad, establishing chiasmic symmetry with the earlier dyad of *Rvf* 22 and 23: sestina / canzone // canzone / sestina). In the opening lines, the phantasm of the beloved, evoked by the sensory images of fabrics and colours, eyes and hair, is mistaken for the woman herself, an illusion that leads the subject to the verge of self-destruction:[6]

[…] et dal camin de libertade
seco mi tira, sí ch'io non sostegno
alcun giogo men grave. (29, 5–7)

It draws me in such fashion from the path
Of liberty that no less heavy yoke
Can I endure to bear.

The extraordinary art of "Verdi panni" is found in the hermetic language that draws the reader inside the subject's thoughts of suicide, to witness how in the moment that he realizes he is being acted on beneficently by the woman herself – rather than the phantasm – he is transported to a state of grace. If in the early portion of the canzone Petrarch refers to a severe Laura (not unlike the woman in Dante's *Rime petrose*), in the penultimate stanza he refers to Laura's birth from a holy womb such as Mary's, making her a Christological figure:

Benigne stelle che compagne fersi
al fortunato fianco
quando 'l bel parto giú nel mondo scórse! (29, 43–5)

O stars benign that were companions of
That blessed womb when its
Fair issue slipped into this world below:

Then in conclusion, the praise of the Lady echoes conventional tropes of praise such as those Dante uses for Beatrice:

quanta vede vertú, quanta beltade,
chi gli occhi mira d'ogni valor segno,
dolce del mio cor chiave?
  Quando il sol gira, Amor piú caro pegno,
donna, di voi non ave. (29, 54–8)

Such virtue, such great beauty as one sees
Who gazes in those eyes – mark of all worth
And sweet key of my heart.
  While the sun wheels, Love will not have a pledge
Lady, more dear than you.

The extraordinary range of the poem, moving from thoughts of suicide (identifying with Dido) to the sacred laud, suggests it was written at a much later date than its position in the sequence would suggest. Arduous but graceful (and having the shortest stanzas of any canzone), the poem seems to offer a synthesis and foreshortened map of the subject's future trajectory, even as it is situated in an "older" position presumably because of its engagement of the Provençal tradition and its close metrical affinity with the sestinas.

To speak of a Petrarchan *trobar clus* is to recognize the author's privileged status as a sustainer of the Provençal tradition. It is to acknowledge the presence of a deep structure beneath the phonetic tissue of signifiers that reflects the psychic dynamism of the subject (as will be seen in my discussions of *Rvf* 105 and 206). The goal of writing in a closed style is not obscurity itself but the search for an equivalent to a psychic state in which physical desire is sublimated into a sacred, purifying desire.[7] (The fact that desire has a key role in forming identity has not escaped psychoanalytic critics.)[8]

Sestina 30, "Giovene donna sotto un verde lauro" ("A youthful lady under a green laurel"), returns to the sylvan landscape of sestina 22, but with a clearer focus on time. The spell of a circular time, typical of the sestina, cannot conceal the passage of the years. As in sestina 22, the end words of sestina 30 are all nouns: *lauro, neve, anni, chiome, occhi, riva.* Because of the *retrogradatio cruciata* rhyme scheme of the sestina, the end word that completes one stanza recurs as the end word of the following stanza, as here with "riva" ("shore"), a key word whose values of liminality and imminence will increase over the course of the sequence:

e 'l suo parlare, e 'l bel viso, et le chiome
mi piacquen sí ch'i' l'ò dinanzi agli occhi,
ed avrò sempre, ov'io sia, in poggio o 'n *riva*.
  Allor saranno i miei pensier a *riva*
che foglia verde non si trovi in lauro; (30, 4–8)

I liked her speech, fair features, and her hair
So much that I keep her before my eyes –
And ever shall, though I'm on my hill or shore.
  And thus my thoughts will stay along the shore,
Where no green leaf is found upon the laurel;

In the following passage one has the first internal dating of the character's *historia*, as seven years have passed since the enamourment. Notable is the syntagm "vivo lauro" ("living laurel"), signifying the wood from which the "idolo" ("idol") is sculpted:

  I' temo di cangiar pria volto et chiome
che con vera *pietà* mi mostri gli occhi
l'idolo mio, scolpito in *vivo lauro*:
ché s'al contar non erro, oggi à sett'anni
che sospirando vo *di riva in riva*
la notte e 'l giorno, al caldo ed a la neve. (30, 25–30)

  I fear the changing of my face and hair
Before, with pity true, she shows her eyes –
My idol, sculpted in the living laurel;
For if my count errs not, it's seven years
Today that I have sighed from shore to shore
By night and day, in heat and in the snow.

Through this ambiguous image of the idol – a bodily form suggestive of a crucifix – the sacred argument is inserted synecdochally into the text. As De Robertis writes, "[Petrarca] accampa quella parola, 'idolo,' come significazione d'un'impassibilità esaltata a confronto della propria trasmutabilità, e che trova la sua raffigurazione nell'immagine del simulacro scolpito" ([Petrarch] asserts that word, "idol," in contrast with his own transmutability, as the signification of an exalted impassivity which finds its representation in the image of a sculpted simulacrum).[9] If the "idol" suggests a certain worship of Laura as deity, the syntagm "vivo lauro" indicates another possibility, in line with the changes in worship undertaken in the New Testament: "il legno è *vivo, lignum vitae,* è *arbor* fatto carne e creatura, contrapposto in veloce sintesi all'inanimata vanità dell'idolo veterotestamentario" (the wood is *alive, living wood,* it is the *tree* made flesh and a creature, counterposed in rapid synthesis to the inanimate vanity of the Old Testament idol).[10] According to this reading, the fear that one will age physically without maturing spiritually serves as a prolepsis for the positive change that will take place as the anniversary poems progress under the sign of "pietà" ("pity"). During that process of soul change the living wood will be manifest by repeated and varied references to the laurel.

In canzone 37, "Sí è debile il filo a cui s'attene" ("So feeble is the thread by which is held"), the image of the absent Laura holds absolute control over the subject. Though he is desperate, simultaneously he is cultivating her image in his heart, allowing the blending of sensual love with a higher love sponsored by the imagination. What distinguishes the portrait of the absent Lady from that in Cino da Pistoia, who is alluded to at several points, is the astonishing physicality of her image, along with the reduction of her figure to a few essential traits, a portrait intensified by the frequency of septenaries and the quick rhythm of the polysyndeton:

Et per pianger anchor con piú diletto,
le man' bianche sottili
et le braccia gentili,
et gli atti suoi soavemente alteri,
e i dolci sdegni alteramente humili,
e 'l bel giovenil petto,
torre d'alto intellecto,
mi celan questi luoghi alpestri et feri; (37, 97–104)

And still to make me weep with more delight,
Those white and slender hands
And noble, tender arms,
And all those looks of hers, so gently proud,

And sweet disdain, so arrogantly meek
Her fair and youthful breast,
A tower of lofty thoughts,
These savage, alpine places hide from me.

In the theme of *not* seeing Laura, with the concealing agent being the remote alpine landscape, one has a clue to the circumstances surrounding the relationship. The limited vocabulary used for describing her does not prevent the communication of desire, nor is desire in contradiction with the higher goals of the relationship signified by "occhi" and "piangere," which anticipate the religious importance weeping will have in later poems.

In sonnet 40, a missive to an unknown addressee from whom the author would like to borrow a key volume (probably of Livy), the writing process is foregrounded and the text metaphorized as a "fabric" in which the author would weave together two otherwise unspecified "truths":

S'Amore o Morte non dà qualche stroppio
a la tela novella ch'ora ordisco
et s'io mi svolvo dal tenace visco,
mentre che l'un coll'altro vero accoppio,
i' farò forse un mio lavor sí doppio
tra lo stil de' moderni e 'l sermon prisco, (40, 1–6)

If Love or Death does not create some flaw
Or rend this fabric new whose warp I lay
If from the limed snare I can free myself,
Till this one with that other truth I wed,
Perhaps so doubly my one work I'll shape
Between the moderns' style and ancient tongue

What strikes one from the textual conceit is the force of the author's involvement and intent to knit together the ancient and modern styles (in Latin and the vernacular).[11] Though his statement of need has not resulted in the arrival of the book requested, there is a positive upshot in this conclusion, which is the idea that without the assistance of others, without a community, the great "work" – including implicitly the *Fragmenta* itself – will not be achieved and is not worth achieving.

A similar logical existential situation is presented by sonnet 51, which posits a negative hypothesis based on the lover's inability to control the force of events in his daily life. The premise is that if Laura had drawn closer to the lover he would have been transformed by her brilliance – as she (as Daphne) was transformed – so as to become one with her. Since that is not possible, he desires to be petrified:

di qual petra piú rigida si 'ntaglia
pensoso ne la vista oggi sarei,
  o di diamante, o d'un bel marmo biancho,
per la paura forse, o d'un dïaspro,
pregiato poi dal vulgo avaro et sciocchо; (51, 7–11)

Then of the hardest stone one carves would I
Be made today, with thoughtful visage grave,
  From diamond, or from marble fine and white,
(With fear perhaps), or jasper, and be prized
Thenceforth by rabble – stupid, greedy folk.

The prospect of petrification is desired and feared by the subject. His desire to become one with the beloved's substance is frustrated but not futile, since the metamorphoses alluded to intimate the potential for theological transformation. To intimate the divine is characteristic of the first centenary, in which the etymons of "selva" – associated with the wild, the inhospitable and stony, the animal – serve to establish the condition of yearning and need that characterizes the Christian pilgrim. It is Petrarch's genius to convey this condition as intrinsic to the immanent condition of humanity itself.[12] On the imagistic level, there is a telluric attraction to the image of stone that bespeaks the subject's stoic defence against passion and is a hidden autograph of earth and rock (*petra*) that contrasts to the *senhal* of light and air (*aura*) of Laura.[13] The sonnet concludes with a second Ovidian allusion, that of Atlas (51, 13–14) turned into a mountain by Medusa, referring back to the initial allusion to Daphne (51, 3) and reinforcing the reciprocity of transformations, as well as the potential of a change of "sign" from negative to positive in one's theological understanding of metamorphosis.

This potentiality is the focus of madrigal 52. As he compares his view of a shepherdess washing her veil to Actaeon's vision of Diana naked at the fountain, the narrator reverses the pagan transformation scene of *Rvf* 23, 148 to 60, along with the focus of the Ovidian text (*Metamorphoses*, III:171–252), which is Diana's anger. Here the centre of attention is the subject, an innocent Actaeon figure who stumbles upon a chaste and fully clothed shepherdess. In such a way the erotic direction of the *pastourelle* is suppressed, and the violent passions of sylvan myth are transformed into the idyllic sentiments of the madrigal, as enabled by the image of the veil, which normally shields the shepherdess's hair from the breeze. As if to confirm Petrarch's theological intentions in this madrigal, the scene occurs at midday, the hour of Paul's conversion:[14]

  Non al suo amante piú Dïana piacque,
quando per tal ventura tutta ignuda
la vide in mezzo de le gelide acque,
  ch'a me la pastorella alpestra et cruda
posta a bagnar un leggiadretto velo,
ch'a l'aura il vago et biondo capel chiuda,
  tal che mi fece, or quand'egli arde 'l cielo,
tutto tremar d'un amoroso gielo. (52, 1–8)

  Diana did not please her lover more
When by like happenstance he looked on her,
Entirely naked 'midst the waters cold,
  Than did the rustic, Alpine shepherdess
Please me – she poised to wash a charming veil
That shields blond, straying hair from gentle breeze –
  So although heaven's burning now, she sets
Me all atremble with an amorous chill.

The "veiled" presence of the *senhal* – "ch'a *l'aura* il vago et biondo capel chiuda" (52, 6) – signalling Laura's absence (as in the other madrigals) is an instance of what are aptly called "the isotopies of Laura."[15] The isotopy is a marked recurrence of semic categories, which can be thematic (or abstract) or figurative; unlike the simple rhetorical figure, the isotopy preserves the semantic link between recurring signifiers and their signifieds. Thus "aura," the breeze that carries the memory and scent of the beloved, retains its denotative meaning even as it connotatively evokes "Laura" (the name only occurs four times, all in Part 2).

This poem is followed by canzone 53, "Spirto gentil" ("Noble spirit"), probably written upon return from Petrarch's first trip to Rome in 1337. The poem is addressed to a Roman senator and voices an appeal for political change. Even as Petrarch decries the squalor and degradation into which Rome has fallen, he deems it to be the just home of the papacy.

che fur già sí devoti, et ora in guerra
quasi spelunca di ladron' son fatti,
tal ch'a' buon' solamente uscio si chiude,
et tra gli altari et tra le statue ignude
ogni impresa crudel par che se tratti.
Deh quanto diversi atti! (53, 49–54)

What formerly were sacred places now
Almost the caves of thieves in war become.
Thus to the good alone the doors are closed;
Among stripped altars, and 'midst statues bare
It seems that ever cruel trade is plied.
Oh, what inhuman acts!

If one examines the poem's recurrent metaphors, one is struck by the force of the cry to extirpate the "male piante" ("noxious weeds") (53, 76) and the apostrophe to the "nova gente" ("newcomers") (53, 80), a reference to *Inferno* xvi, 73: "La gente nuova e i sùbiti guadagni" ("Newcomers to the city and quick gains"). Also reminiscent of an earlier poetic sensibility is the use of the allegorical female figure, first standing for Italy, then her weeping mothers, then Rome, and finally Fortune, who steers the fate of the nation. One can say that the poem represents Petrarch's political position circa 1337, a republican position that will lead eventually to his break with his patrons, the Colonnas. If "Spirto gentil" projects a utopian state of affairs that will not come to pass, it also lays the groundwork for "Italia mia" (*Rvf* 128), a canzone of great civic impetus and actuality.

"Spirto gentil" is followed by the second madrigal, which conveys the hobbling nature of sinfulness and the impotence of evil. As the subject pursues a woman through the woods, he is warned off by a voice "on high" and decides to retreat:

Perch'al viso d'Amor portava insegna
mosse una pellegrina il mio cor vano,
ch'ogni altra mi parea d'onor men degna.
Et lei seguendo su per l'erbe verdi,
udí dir alta voce di lontano:

Ahi, quanti passi per la selva perdi!
  Allor mi strinsi a l'ombra d'un bel faggio,
tutto pensoso; et rimirando intorno,
vidi assai periglioso il mio vïaggio;
  et tornai indietro quasi a mezzo 'l giorno. (54, 1–10)

  Because she bore Love's emblem in her face,
A pilgrim stirred my empty heart, for all
The rest less fit for honor seemed to me.
  Yet as I followed her through fields of green,
I heard a lofty voice speak from afar:
"Ah, in that wood you waste so many steps!"
  At once I pressed myself deep in the shade
Of a fine beech; all pensive, gazing round,
I knew my journey very perilous;
  And it was almost noon when I turned back.

The act of retreat, an essential moment in the history of return, is introduced in a fantastic setting, but its message is clear: it is in disquietude that one finds the configurations of faith. For Nicolae Iliescu this madrigal reflects Petrarch's focus on Augustine, perhaps the identity of the "lofty voice" ("alta voce") that gives him counsel in times of crisis. While sharing the sacred interpretation of the poem, Martinelli argues that the lofty voice is God, and that the root text is – as it is for Augustine in *Confessions* viii – Acts 22:6–7, which recounts the conversion of Paul at midday on the road to Damascus. The madrigal would thus refer to the pilgrim's retreat from sinfulness, the act of return that gives closure to the poem and serves as a signpost of moral and psychic development.

This madrigal is followed by a ballata, then by two sequences of three sonnets and one ballata each, thus an alternation of the musical forms of the madrigal and ballata amidst neighbouring sonnets. As Capovilla has written, the four madrigals "[sono] destinati ad assolvere a precise funzioni di raccordo entro la struttura logica del Canzoniere" (are destined to accomplish precise functions of linkage within the logical structure of the Canzoniere).[16] The same could be stated for the ballata, like the madrigal a form in the low register that appears primarily in the first centenary; in either case, Petrarch's use of the forms is never popular or plebeian. Ballata 55 is a case in point, an intricate and late composition whose insertion at this early point reinforces the historicity of the entanglements of Eros present in the subject:[17]

Amor, avegna mi sia tardi accorto,
vòl che tra duo contrari mi distempre;
et tende lacci in sí diverse tempre,
che quand'ò piú speranza che 'l cor n'esca,
allor piú nel bel viso mi rinvesca. (55, 13–17)

Love – it happens I realized it too late –
wants me to waste away between two contraries;
and lays traps in such varying manners, that
when I am most hopeful my heart shall escape,
he entraps me even more in the beautiful face.

The implacable face of the Lady yields only bitter suffering. It is an emblem of contradiction of the sort found in Cavalcanti's opposition of the spirit-intellect to the body. Yet there is a mitigating factor seen in the insert "avegna mi sia tardi accorto" (55, 13), a retrospective statement that confirms that the immobility of the wounded lover will eventually pass into consciousness and be corrected.

Emilio Bigi identifies such parenthetical inserts as typical and unique to Petrarch's literary persona: "elementi di ripiegamento elegiaco-meditativo e insieme di variato equilibrio ritmico" (elements of elegiac-meditative internalization and at the same time of varied rhythmic equilibrium).[18] He divides the inserts into "intimate interrogations," "doubtful suspensions," "ecstatic or elegiac exclamations," and "melancholy sententious declarations," stating that their musical effect is to provide pauses that round out the syntactic and metrical units. While Petrarch did not use the diacritical mark of the parenthesis, he employed the parenthetical mode on a number of levels, from the microtext, where frequent digressions are made, to the macrotext, where an entire poem can stand apart from those around it. These insertions integrate diverse thematics into the whole and broaden the conative relationship between the author and reader.[19] In some cases the parenthetical inserts are a means to confirm that what one is reading is true: "(or chi fia che mi 'l creda?)" ("(now who is there to credit me?)") (129, 40). The liminality of the inserts allows the author to include heterogeneous forms of discourse, including the invocation of God, while maintaining stylistic equilibrium.[20]

Ballatas 55, 59, and 63 stand together as a group, each depicting a conventionalized setting in which the Lady's eyes make the lover a prisoner of love. The ballata, like the madrigal, captures love at its inception in the freshness of youth. Ballata 59 introduces the continuing theme of a good death with the *sententia* "ben morendo honor s'acquista" ("by dying well one honor gains") (59, 15). In ballata 63 the Lady's eyes are considered by the lover as a guide to his identity, with strong stilnovistic associations: through her greeting the Lady has given birth to the man's soul, freeing him to "sail" where the wind will take him: "presto di navigare a ciascun vento" ("Eager to sail with any wind") (63, 13). It is notable that ballatas 59 and 63 frame three sonnets (60–2) that constitute the first sacred thrust of the collection.

If the "dark wood" of the first centenary is a labyrinthine space of passions and snares, yokes and chains, these traps are slowly revealed to the narrator to have been self-devised. Thus a poem like "Padre del cielo" (*Rvf* 62), discussed below, occupies a critical place within the macrotext, reminding us that the sylvan imagery of the early poems provides the antefact to a more universal understanding of the *selva* as a symbol of the transitoriness of life, which inheres to subsequent poems, and, as Petrarch describes in one of his *Letters of Old Age* (*Sen*. iv, 5):

> Silva vero vita hec, umbris atque erroribus piena perplexisque tramitibus atque incertis et feris habitata, hoc est difficultatibus et periculis multis atque occultis, infructuosa et inhospita, et herbarum virore et cantu avium et aquarum murmure, idest brevi et caduca specie et inani ac fallaci dulcedine rerum pretereuntium atque labentium …

> The wood is this life, full of shadows and pitfalls, confusing and unsure byways, inhabited by wild beasts, that is, beset with many hidden trials and perils. Sterile and inhospitable, at times it confronts and soothes the ears and eyes of the inhabitants with the lush greenery, the songs of birds, and the murmuring of waters, that is, the short-lived and frail image, the empty and deceptive sweetness of things that pass on and slip away.[21]

2. The Dimension of Fable in the "Raccolta of 1342"

In January 1337, tiring of life in Avignon, Petrarch travelled to Rome for the first time; the journey had a lasting impact on his sense of vocation as a poet and a historian. Returning to Provence, he moved to a remote location in the Vaucluse. That summer his son Giovanni was born and he turned thirty-three. In the fall of that year he spent three nights at the Cavern of Sainte-Beaume where, according to legend, Mary Magdalen (to whom he dedicates a Latin poem) spent thirty years of penitence. These facts suggest a turning towards solitude as a means to escape the deceit and illusion witnessed at the papal court. One can speculate that the experience of travelling to Italy and then settling in the Vaucluse contributed to Petrarch's desire to give a macrotextual order to his vernacular lyrics. While the first ordered form of a canzoniere containing the division of the poems into Parts 1 and 2, with Part 2 beginning with canzone 264, "I' vo pensando, et nel penser m'assale" ("I wander thinking, and within my thoughts"), was probably compiled in 1347, there were earlier attempts at compiling a lyric sequence, starting with the "Raccolta of 1342," a series of fourteen sonnets ultimately situated between poems 34 and 60 of the *Fragmenta*.[22]

In his essay "Petrarch's First Collection of His *Rime*" (1932), E.H. Wilkins argues that four sheets of Vat. Lat. 3196 constitute Petrarch's first attempt at compiling a collection of his lyric poems.[23] Of the twenty-three sonnets by Petrarch on the sheets, five were later rejected; those that were included in the final collection are poems 34, 35, 36, 41, 42, 43, 44, 45, 46, 49, 58, 60, 64, 69, 77, 78, and 179. Wilkins's theory of an early *Liederbuch* has not met with universal acceptance, but there is consensus that Petrarch was thinking about a book of his vernacular lyrics in the late 1330s and early 1340s.[24] Santagata's position is that the pages referred to by Wilkins – dated between 1336 and 1338 – did not meet the standard of proof for a separate collection, but that there is evidence in the same service collection, where Petrarch makes annotations in 1342, that he has initiated a finished copy. What Santagata calls "La raccolta del 1342" includes these poems – 34, 35, 36, 41, 42, 43, 44, 45, 46, 49, 58, 60, 64, 69 – each of which is cancelled and marked as having been transcribed ("transcriptus") in the service collection, where the page in question

> presenta, nella sua metà superiore, un solo testo, il son. 34, preceduto dalla postilla: "iniziata la trascrizione da questo punto, il 21 agosto del 1342, all'ora sesta." Manca l'espressione "in ordine" che sarà tipica delle postille riferite alla formazione della Correggio, ma non vi sono dubbi che la nota segnala l'inizio di una trascrizione in bella copia, cioè di una raccolta. [...] Oltre che cancellati, i testi sono accompagnati, *senza eccezione* dalla nota

"trascritto" ("transcriptus") o per esteso, o in forma abbreviata. Ecco tutto ciò che sappiamo di quella che, allo stato attuale, possiamo considerare la prima raccolta poetica petrarchesca.

presents, in its upper half, a single text, sonnet 35, preceded by the note: "transcription begun at this point, 21 August 1342, at the sixth hour." The expression "in order" that will be typical of the notes referred to in the formation of the Correggio is missing, but there are no doubts that the note marks the beginning of a transcription in a finished copy, that is of a collection. [...] As well as being stricken out, the texts are accompanied, *without exception* by the note "transcribed" ("transcriptus") either in toto or in abbreviated form. That is all we know about that which, at the current time, we can consider to be the first poetic collection by Petrarch.[25]

It is not known if the collection was circulated or contained other poems that were lost. Since the poems were annotated and cancelled in the manner indicated, a study of their common intratextual and stylistic features would seem to be merited. Since Petrarch "intendeva evidentemente costruire una vera e propria raccolta, dall'ordine autonomo, con forti allusioni classiche e collegamenti tematici e poetico-retorici interni" (clearly intended to construct a genuine collection, of an autonomous order, with strong classical allusions and internal thematic and poetical-rhetorical connections), it seems appropriate to study the poems in the order they possess in the *Fragmenta*, where they come after poem 23, "Nel dolce tempo della prima etade" ("In the sweet season of my early youth"), and before poem 70, the canzone of citations that cites that *capoverso* in its final line.[26] The codicological evidence suggests that these sonnets were grouped together in 1342 and constitute a collection in process. There are numerous contiguities between the texts, overlapping lexis, figures, themes, and shared syntagmatic strings, such that some of the sonnets fall into pairs or trios and gain meaning when read together. In addition, the idea of fourteen poems of fourteen lines each suggests a "squaring" of the sonnet; a scheme that might have appealed to Petrarch's numerological sensibility.[27]

The poems of the group are dominated by a historical-mythological and Daphnean thematics.[28] These elements are engaged in a way that is typical of fable; thus one sees emerge the dominant theme of the severe limitations of the human when faced by the powers of nature. Poem 34, "Apollo, s'ancor vive il bel desio" ("Apollo, if that fair desire still lives"), centres on the myth of Daphne and Apollo. The invocation to Apollo is set in a single period introduced by two "if" clauses, followed by the request that the god bless Laura with his healing powers. Apollo is asked to recall his desire for Daphne before her change into the laurel, and to protect that sacred tree; he is asked to clear the morning air and recognize this new Apollo – the Petrarchan subject – and this new Daphne (Laura) sitting in the glen.[29] Another world beckons, yet the terms of concealment and entrapment ("oblio," "invescato," "impressïon," "vita acerba") make the prospect of "meraviglia" uncertain. The verb tenses are those of the mythic past and the present of its figural re-enactment, with the final tercet projecting a future tense in which one hears an echo of the invocation to Apollo in *Paradiso* i, 13 to 16. Yet in the static frontality of the representation one has an only dubious sense of repose:

sí vedrem poi per meraviglia inseme
seder la donna nostra sopra l'erba,
et far de le sue braccia a se stessa ombra. (34, 12–14)

Thus you and I will see a wondrous sight:
Our lady sitting down upon the grass
And making, with her arms, shade for herself.

Though, as Kenelm Foster writes, it is a "happy poem [...] pictorially," the scene that one confronts is fundamentally ironic. The bower of bliss – so flatly painted – is illusory.[30] What is intriguing about this paradigmatic poem is the religious significance that lies *in potentia*, a feature that Marjorie O'Rourke Boyle glosses as follows: "In the inaugural apostrophe to Apollo, the poet allied himself with that god by whose inspiration 'we shall then see together a marvel.' [...] The laurel was most nobly [...] a 'holy' tree."[31] As if to acknowledge the connection between the illusory beauty of the bower and the religious significance that the poem seems to forecast, De Robertis writes of the relationship between poem 34 and poem 188, "Almo sol, quella fronde ch'io sola amo" ("O vital Sun, the only tree I love"), in which one finds a suggestion of Apollo the healer who states in *Metamorphoses* I, 517 to 518: "per me, quod eritque fuitque / estque, patet" ("I am the revealer / of present, past and future").

Standing in contrast to poem 34, which turns around the subjectivity and beauty of Laura-Daphne, poem 35, "Solo et pensoso i piú deserti campi" ("Alone in thought with lagging paces slow"), is centred on the lover and the theme of solitude. Written entirely in the present tense, this celebrated dialogue with Amor seems to ask: of what value is man? what are his natural limitations? of what importance is the experience of solitude?[32] The response is that if man is not to be an animal or a liar, he must come to terms with his mortality in a way that generates an ethics and recognizes divine providence. Wilkins, who identifies an elegy of Propertius as a probable source, remarks that in comparison to that poet's "implicit […] avoidance of mankind," and in response to the woman's cruel non-response to his "undistinguished love," Petrarch's avoidance is more "explicit," his "love is calmer and more profound, mature and meditative."[33] The wanderer rightly fears he will not be understood; thus the instinct to flight is supported by reason. "Humano" and "natural" are negative terms that exemplify the want, the lack, the unreliability of the human and the natural. Only in the deserted landscape can one measure the slowness of one's steps, the weight of one's thoughts. This is a wild terrain that Giorgio Orelli compares to the "selva oscura" of early *Inferno,* citing the lines "Ma pur sí aspre vie né sí selvagge" ("Yet no path can I trace so savage, wild") (35, 12) and "esta selva selvaggia e aspra e forte" ("that savage forest, dense and difficult") (*Inf.* i, 5).[34] By the same token, the theme of solitary wandering suggests the poet's espousal of the tenets of eremitic Franciscanism, making the place of solitude a place of potential penitence.

> sí ch'io mi credo omai che monti et piagge
> et fiumi et selve sappian di che tempre
> sia la mia vita, ch'è celata altrui. (35, 9–11)

> Thus, now I think that even hills and shores,
> Rivers and forests know the quality
> My life must have, though masked from human kind.

The measuring of one's steps stands in contrast to the sense of victimization and helplessness one sees in poem 36, "S'io credesse per morte essere scarco" ("If I believed through death I'd gain release"), in which the narrator states that suicide is not a way out of the predicament of love's entrapment. By treating the topic of self-destruction, he presents the problem of a man existing outside the natural harmony observed in the animal world, a man denatured by love. Phrased in the form of a hypothesis, the sonnet possesses a static sense of enclosure reflecting the extreme limits of life, of being imprisoned by the force one expected to be freed by. By raising the topic of suicide, a mortal sin,

Petrarch engages the power of the will and articulates the futility of self-destruction, foreseeing a more serene condition than previously. As in poem 34, the tenses of poem 36 are the past absolute and the future; looking to the past, the fable remains proleptic, anticipatory of the world ahead.[35] It is this linking of the perspectives of non-knowing and seeming that characterizes the purely hypothetical situations of the counterfactual. Poems 34 and 36 are of this hypothetical mode, as are poems 43, 45, and 64.

Poems 35 and 36 provide an example of a Petrarchan technique of having two contiguous poems interlock, with the first poem looking forward to a higher moral reality and stability while the second poem looks back to a negative *status quo ante*. In this way the pair serves in a cautionary way to signal a thematic transition in the macrotext. In the moral-spiritual itinerary of the *Fragmenta*, the delineation of a contemplative place of solitude is a necessary escape from the spiritual death and baseness of sin. And that potentiality is already inscribed in some of the earliest poems.

If the wounds to the lover Apollo in poem 36 are caused by Love's arrows, in poem 41 the arrows are Jove's thunderbolts: the laurel tree is immune from lightning, but when it is absent the thunder will rage. This is the conceit adopted to express the inner turbulence of the subject when Laura is absent from Avignon.

> Quando dal proprio sito si rimove
> l'arbor ch'amò già Phebo in corpo humano,
> sospira et suda a l'opera Vulcano,
> per rinfrescar l'aspre saette a Giove (41, 1–4)

> When from its rightful place that tree is gone
> Which in a human form once Phoebus loved,
> Then Vulcan at his labor sweats and sighs,
> Replenishing the cruel bolts of Jove;

There are eleven proper nouns in this sonnet, denoting a kind of cosmic participation in the meteorological turbulence. Laura-Daphne, "l'arbor ch'amò già Phebo in corpo humano" (41, 2), is simultaneously the tree that was human and the woman who has travelled away from home. Her absence serves proleptically to suggest in the final line the ultimate departure that will coincide with her death, "il bel viso dagli angeli aspectato" ("that fair face / Awaited by the angels") (41, 14).

Poem 41 cannot be grasped without its pair sonnet, poem 42, "Ma poi che 'l dolce riso humile et piano" ("But once the modest, sweet and humble smile"), which flows directly from its conclusion (as reinforced by the rhyme *viso / riso*).[36] Now that the rare beauty of Laura-Daphne has reappeared, Jove's "sister" (Juno, the atmosphere) grows calm again: "sua sorella par che si rinove" ("And bit by bit Jove's sister reawakes") (42, 7).[37] In the symmetry and reversal is the advent of something new, though this cosmic serenity lies completely beyond the control of the subject. The two poems share the same rhymes but in inverted positions that reflect a thematic reversal.[38] A formal element worth noting here is the presence of the absolute superlative – "l'antiquissimo fabbro ciciliano" ("the most venerable Sicilian smith") (42, 4) – which projects one backward, syllable by syllable, into the mythic time of Vulcan, whose forge was in Mount Etna.[39]

Poem 43 repeats the rhyme scheme of 41, concluding the second trio of like sonnets. Here there is only one proper noun, Latona, the female deity, Apollo's mother. The subject focuses on Apollo the man – "mostrossi a noi qual huom per doglia insano" ("He seemed to us like one insane with grief") (43, 7) – who searches for Daphne in vain from his celestial firmament. In the course of expressing pity for Laura, who after an absence of nine days has returned weeping and pale, the narrator-character introduces the topic of poetry, stating his intention to praise her, if he should live, in more than a thousand pages:

> Et cosí tristo standosi in disparte,
> tornar non vide il viso, che laudato
> sarà s'io vivo in piú di mille carte;
> et pietà lui medesmo avea cangiato,
> sí che' begli occhi lagrimavan parte:
> però l'aere ritenne il primo stato. (43, 9–14)

> Thus gloomy, standing far away, he failed
> To see that face return that, if I live,
> In pages by the thousand shall be praised.
> And pity so had changed her countenance
> That meanwhile those fair eyes were shedding tears;
> And thus the air retained its former state.

Here in the last of three sonnets in which the mutable identities of Laura, Daphne, and the laurel are matched by those of Phoebus, Apollo, and the sun, the groundwork is being laid for a more pious use of the laud form. Though the subject remains bedazzled by Laura's person, when her beauty is compared to that of a divinity one has a foreshadowing of future poems in which her attributes will commonly be those of the Madonna.[40]

Poem 44, "Que' che 'n Tesaglia ebbe le man' sì pronte" ("That man who with such eagerness prepared"), concludes the first half of the Raccolta, meshing within a swift sequence of proper nouns the figures of Julius Caesar, David and Goliath, Saul, and Amore.

> e 'l pastor ch'a Golia ruppe la fronte,
> pianse la ribellante sua famiglia,
> et sopra 'l buon Saúl cangiò le ciglia,
> ond'assai può dolersi il fiero monte. (44, 5–8)[41]

> The shepherd who Goliath's forehead smote
> Wept for the rebel in his family,
> And knit his brows above the worthy Saul –
> For this the savage mount can much lament;

In contrast to the pity of David for King Saul, Laura utterly lacks compassion, causing the subject to write "mi vedete straziare a *mille* morti" ("You see me tortured with a *thousand* deaths") (44, 12). In the echo of the subject's stated intent to praise Laura "in piú di *mille* carte" ("in pages by the *thousand*") in poem 43, one has an example of the interlocking patterns that Petrarch uses to link contiguous poems.

Poems 45 and 46, concerning the allegory of the mirror, are interlocking in the manner of poems 35 and 36. The mirror is named as "adversario" of the lover in 45, but its Medusa-like fixity threatens Laura as well: she, not he, is the Narcissus figure imprisoned in the gaze. The subject states: If I were nailed to the wall to receive your gaze, you wouldn't need a mirror to be so proud. The focus on the destructive levelling that occurs when the lover is reduced to an object recalls Cavalcanti. But there is an important distinction: Petrarch's self-denigration concerns a necessary humbling that is potentially uplifting. There are Christic resonances in the unworthiness of the lover to be in Laura's company (the reference being to Matthew 8:8):[42]

> misero exilio, avegna ch'i' non fôra
> d'abitar degno ove voi sola siete.
> Ma s'io v'era con saldi chiovi fisso,

non devea specchio farvi per mio danno,
a voi stessa piacendo, aspra et superba. (45, 7–11)

A wretched exile, since I was unfit
To sojourn where you now abide alone.
  But if there I were fixed with massive nails,
You'd need no glass to make you haughty, stern
To my undoing while you please yourself.

To be in love with one's own image, as Laura is, leads only to melancholy. But the obsessive self-reflection of Narcissus also has a positive side as it signifies a first access to the self, to consciousness, and thus to the subjectivity of the Other.[43] Thus when the initial allusion to a Christic subtext is followed with line 9, "Ma s'io v'era con saldi chiovi fisso," the subject can be seen to place himself hypothetically in the position of Christ. The dual functionality of a signifier like "chiovi" (45, 9) is seen as an example of what Stefano Agosti, in a study of Petrarch's uses of metaphor, calls the "poly-isotopic structures of enunciations."[44] Within such plural structures, the grammatical level of an enunciation, which is grounded in the poem's syntax, coexists with its semantic value, which is not. Thus in the context of *Rvf* 45, on the grammatical level, the "chiovi" refer to the nails from which a mirror hangs, while semantically the "chiovi" suggest the nails that pierced Christ's flesh.

Poem 46, a pair sonnet with 45, brings this issue to a head. By relativizing his suffering, the "I" figure introduces a mise-en-scène in which Laura's splendid attributes – "L'oro et le perle e i fior' vermigli e i bianchi" ("The gold, the pearls, the crimson blooms and white") (46, 1) – are threatened with destruction by time and vanity. Thus the subject's tribulation and sorrow are channelled again through Laura's eyes, seen as lethal mirrors turned on themselves:

  Però i dí miei fien lagrimosi et manchi,
ché gran duol rade volte aven che 'nvecchi:
ma piú ne colpo i micidiali specchi,
che 'n vagheggiar voi stessa avete stanchi. (46, 5–8)

  And thus my days are full of tears and few;
For seldom does so great a grief grow old.
Yet I blame homicidal mirrors more,
For with fond gazing you exhaust yourself.

The powerful syntagm "i micidiali specchi" echoes Dante's "li occhi micidiali" (applied to Beatrice in the *Rime*), but in contrast to that usage Petrarch has put a didactic frame around the image in order to reinforce his position that the threat of the mirror is shared by both parties.[45] This frame is seen in the tercets where the locus for the death of Narcissus is the "aquam abyssi" of Isaiah 51:10, and the figure of Amore is silenced. The final line, "onde 'l principio de mia morte nacque" ("From them was born the first cause of my death") (46, 14), with the paronomasia "morte nacque," recalls the conclusion of the previous sonnet, where the end envisaged was the death of Narcissus-Laura.[46]

Poem 49, written during the stay in Rome, is an allegory in which the poet personifies his tongue, his tears, and his sighs. One recalls a similar use of personification by Cavalcanti in "Noi siàn le triste penne isbigotite, / le cesoiuzze e 'l coltellin dolente" ("We are the stunned and mourning quill, / the doleful knife and tiny shears"), a sonnet in which the poet gives life to his writing tools.[47] Yet here the objects that stand synecdochically for the writer's craft are the breath and body of the poet: the animate made inanimate made animate again in a cycle that suggests a fabulous "pathos of the detail."[48] The tongue stands for speech and for its opposite, and, with reference to the previous two poems, the figure of Echo and the presence of tears.

Poem 58, "La guancia che fu già piangendo stancha" ("Ah, rest that cheek, already worn with tears"), written upon the move to Vaucluse in mid-1337, is a sonnet sent to a friend, sent along with three gifts – a pillow, a prayer book, and a drinking cup – that will aid the friend in resisting the same enemies that beset the writer. The poem itself – personified here in the final tercet – is the fourth gift, and conveys the high value of friendship. Following Augustine's thought, friendship is a gift from God through the Holy Spirit.

Me riponete ove 'l piacer si serba,
tal ch'i' non tema del nocchier di Stige,
se la preghiera mia non è superba. (58, 12–14)

Tuck me away, where pleasure is saved up
So I won't dread the boatman of the Styx –
If this request of mine is not too proud.

Poem 60, "L'arbor gentil che forte amai molt'anni" ("That noble tree, which I so dearly loved"), historicizes the love for Laura. If, as Petrarch states in the *Collatio*, the laurel remains evergreen, protected from lightning, here the narrator asks that Jove strike it, that the sun – Apollo – inflame it, and that its leaves be left to dry up and die:

> Che porà dir chi per amor sospira,
> s'altra speranza le mie rime nove
> gli avessir data, et per costei la perde?
> Né poeta ne colga mai, né Giove
> la privilegi, et al Sol venga in ira,
> tal che si secchi ogni sua foglia verde. (60, 9–14)

> What can one utter – one who sighs for love –
> If, when my early rhymes had given him
> Another hope, through her he loses it?
> "Then let no poet ever pluck its fruit,
> Nor Jove grant privilege; and may it feel
> The Sun's full wrath, so each green leaf may sear."

The Petrarchan language dramatizes the affective intensity of a peregrine soul split from the object of his desire and thus in "exile." Yet here, too, in lines 10 and 11, one sees the shade of an evangelical prophecy, as in Matthew 10:39: "He who has found his life will lose it, and he who has lost his life for My sake will find it" (and, similarly, in Mark 8:35, Luke 17:13, and John 12:25).[49] Logically, in the medieval reading of "L'arbor gentil," the "spietato legno" (60, 6) ("wood ... obdurate") of the laurel represents the wood of the cross, expressing *in potentia* what the conclusion of poem 62, "Padre del ciel," expresses *in substantia*:

> *Miserere* del mio non degno affanno;
> reduci i pensier' vaghi a miglior luogo;
> ramenta lor come oggi fusti in croce. (62, 12–14)

> *Miserere*; pity my worthless woe;
> My straying thoughts, lead to a better place;
> Remind them: this day You were on the cross.

This is the third anniversary poem and is dated eleven years after the enamourment, on Good Friday of 1338; thus it is a sonnet of devotion memorializing the Crucifixion. As suggested by the proximity to "L'arbor gentil," for Petrarch the tree symbol – the laurel, the tree of life, the tree of knowledge – ultimately has one final significance and one true antecedent. The verbal crux of line 14, "oggi fusti," in which the verb in the absolute past occurred "today," conveys the eternity of Christ's sacrifice on the cross: the eternal present of the past.

Poem 64, "Se voi poteste per turbati segni," proposes an impossible hypothesis to Laura: If you could but leave my heart, then I would be deserving of your scorn; but since it is your destiny to reside there, that is not possible, so you should take care not to scorn me:

> ma poi vostro destino a voi pur vieta
> l'esser altrove, provedete almeno
> di non star sempre in odïosa parte. (64, 12–14)[50]

> But since your destiny forbids that you
> Live elsewhere, at the least take measures lest
> In loathsome regions you forever stay.

In sonnet 68 the subject projects a battle between two voices of his conscience, the one returning to see Laura and the other embarking directly on the heavenly road – "qual vincerà, non so; ma 'nfino ad ora / combattuto ànno, et non pur una volta" ("which will win I do not know; but until now / they have battled, and not just once") (68, 13–14). Then in sonnet 69 a third voice emerges, that of the placid and road-weary man of peace, whose symbolic journey continues on foot; thus the narrator-character reconciles himself to the inevitable, that "natural advice" or prudence is of little use against love: "Ben sapeva io che natural consiglio, / Amor, contra di te già mai non valse" ("I surely knew that natural advice / Was never any use against you, Love") (69, 1–2). By so doing, he anticipates a middle road, between the extreme poles of a dichotomous vision. In comparison to the infernal waters of poem 46, "sopra l'acque / d'abisso," one confronts the actual waters of a sea journey, "l'acque salse, / tra la riva toscana et l'Elba et Giglio" ("the briny sea, / Off Giglio, Elba, and the Tuscan shore") (69, 7–8), during which, in colloquy with Amor, the subject accepts his destiny, which is not to struggle against love but to seek to ennoble it, an act of the will that will see Amor transformed in later poems.

> quando ecco i tuoi ministri, i' non so donde
> per darmi a diveder ch'al suo destino
> mal chi contrasta, et mal chi si nasconde. (69, 12–14)

Here came your ministers, I knew not whence,
To show me he fares ill who strives against
His fate, and ill fares he who hides from it.

In the Raccolta of 1342 one finds a repertory of objects, myths, and *topoi* that will be extended in later poems. Considered as a first collection, the fourteen sonnets embody the stylistic origins of the *Fragmenta*. Here one confronts the self-portrait of a sinner who nevertheless possesses an awareness of sin's powerlessness over the redeemed soul. Episodes of despair are followed by moments of self-recognition and the lesson of historical experience to stop idealizing the past. This is suggested in poem 43, in which the sorrowful subject vows to praise Laura "in più di mille carte" ("In pages by the thousand") (43, 11), and in the passages that acknowledge Laura's subjectivity and vulnerability. The relation between weeping and praise emerges as an aspect of Petrarch's text that will connect to his itinerant evangelism and anchoritic practice. Therein lies the idea of a "cure" analogous to the one the subject recommends to a friend, a healing infusion of bitter grasses, "dolce a la fine, et nel principio acerba" ("Sweet at the end, though bitter at the start") (58, 11).

3. Further Consequences of Fable

Perché la vita è breve (71, 1)

Because life is so brief

Canzone 70, "Lasso me, ch'i' non so in qual parte pieghi la speme" ("Alas, I do not know where to direct my hope"), signals the end of the inital phase of the *Fragmenta*, in which the Ovidian figuration of Daphne and Apollo was dominant. That construction is now replaced by a theological understanding of the myth. The "not knowing where to turn" of the canzone's incipit is a narrative premise that allows the poet, in the course of writing the poem, to articulate his position with respect to Arnaut Daniel, Guido Cavalcanti, Dante, and Cino da Pistoia – whom he cites in the final lines of stanzas 1 to 4, before ending the poem by citing the first line of canzone 23: "Nel dolce tempo de la prima etade" ("In the sweet season of my early youth") (70, 50).[51] While paying homage to the earlier poets, Petrarch detaches himself from their doctrines of love and idealizations of the Lady.[52] But he also draws a distance between his current perspective and his earlier work. Insofar as the question of artistic filiation is one of maieutics – the drawing out of a didactic content from a perceived lineage – Petrarch's references to the earlier poets carry a doctrinal importance.

In citing Dante's canzone "Cosí nel mio parlar voglio esser aspro" ("I want to be as harsh in my speech") (70, 30), Petrarch selects a poem from the *Rime petrose* in which Dante sought to counter the coldness and severity of the Lady by speaking harshly. Dante's poem had marked a historical breakthrough by enacting, in Santagata's words, "la rottura della distinzione medievale degli stili e [la] conseguente mescidazione linguistica" (the breaking of the medieval distinction of styles and the resultant linguistic intermixing).[53] Before citing this *capoverso*, Petrarch espouses a poetics of harshness of his own, alluding to those many poems of the first centenary (in particular the poems of the Raccolta of 1342) in which the hardness of Laura leads the poet to a style of asperity.

> onde, come nel cor m'induro e n'aspro,
> *cosí nel mio parlar voglio esser aspro.* (70, 29–30)[54]

> As I grow hard and bitter in my heart,
> "So in my speech I want to be severe."

In citing Cino's canzone, "La dolce vista e 'l bel guardo soave" ("Her features sweet and her fair, gentle glance") (70, 40), Petrarch interiorizes the problem of sin as a problem of the will:

> Se mortal velo il mio veder appanna,
> che colpa è de le stelle,
> o de le cose belle?
> Meco si sta chi dí et notte m'affanna,
> poi che del suo piacer mi fe' gir grave
> *la dolce vista e 'l bel guardo soave.* (70, 35–40)

> And if a mortal veil obscures my sight,
> What fault's that of the stars?
> What fault of lovely things?
> One stays with me who grieves me day and night
> Since by her charm I was afflicted with
> "Her features sweet and her fair, gentle glance."

The visual limitations of the body – "mortal velo" (70, 35) – cannot be attributed to celestial influences (as they are in Cavalcanti's cited canzone) but are the subject's own responsibility.[55] As stated in the concluding stanza, the susceptibility to sinful desire and the failure to fully absorb the goodness and beauty of the creation cannot be blamed on the Other or on the spell cast by her beauty. Thus one reaches a provisional equilibrium, an epoché of desire mediated by a fuller understanding of the past:

Tutte le cose, di che 'l mondo è adorno
uscïr buone de man del mastro eterno;
ma me, che cosí adentro non discerno,
abbaglia il bel che mi si mostra intorno;
et s'al vero splendor già mai ritorno,
l'occhio non po' star fermo,
cosí l'à fatto infermo
pur la sua propria colpa, et non quel giorno
ch'i' volsi inver' l'angelica beltade
nel dolce tempo de la prima etade. (70, 41–50)

All things with which the world's graced, issue forth
In goodness from the eternal Shaper's hand;
But I, since inner things I don't discern
Am dazzled by the beauty all around,
And if to splendor real I don't return
My eye cannot stay true,
So feeble it has grown
Through its own guilt, and not because that day
I turned to face angelic loveliness,
"In the sweet season of my early youth."

Poem 70 is followed by three canzoni on the eyes of Laura, which (uniquely) share the same versification. As with other poems set in the Vaucluse, in canzoni 71 to 73 Laura has a beatifying presence. In the second of these the image of sweetness "descending" into the "heart" recalls Cino's lines "La grazia sua a chi la può mirare / discende nel coraggio / e non vi lassa alcun difetto stare" (Her grace descends to the heart / of one who can gaze on her / and allows no defect to remain there):[56]

Vaghe faville, angeliche, beatrici
de la mia vita, ove 'l piacer s'accende

che dolcemente mi consuma et strugge:
come sparisce et fugge
ogni altro lume dove 'l vostro splende,
cosí de lo mio core,
quando tanta dolcezza in lui discende,
ogni altra cosa, ogni penser va fore,
et solo ivi con voi rimanse Amore. (72, 37–45)

Bright sparks angelic, how
You bless my life, where pleasure kindles that
Both swallows me and melts me quite away.
As every other light
Entirely fades and flees when yours shines clear,
So when such sweetness great
Flows down into my heart, all else from him
Departs, and every care of mine makes way,
And there alone with you Love still remains.

The image of the eyes as flames tracing pathways to the heart was present in the pre-stilnovistic and stilnovistic traditions where it was responded to either by slavish devotion and suffering (as in the Cavalcantian mode of bewilderment and paralysis) or by transcendence. The latter option could be undertaken in a secular manner – by allegorizing the light into *sophia* or knowledge – or religiously, or in a combination of the two (as in Cino). But Petrarch is moving beyond the abstract, stilnovistic solutions by including the woman's eyes in an actual temporal process. Thus in the above lines, the love of the senses is ephemeral and dissolves into the past, leaving only the phantasm as the retention in memory of the Lady's spirit. While borrowing the convention of the debilitating power of the eyes from the earlier poets, Petrarch replaced the technical idea of the phantasm – as created by the lover's *pneuma* or spirit – with one based on a theology of the will. If for Cino the love of the intellect is "in totale antagonismo" (in total antagonism) with the love of the senses and the imagination, for Petrarch the senses and the image reinforce the sacred presence of the woman in memory.[57]

Poem 73 completes the *cantilena oculorum* and continues its focus on the power of song to assuage the pain of the lover. In stanzas 1, 2, and 3 the dominant verb is *dire* (lines 2, 10, 27, 31), as the subject announces that, as a result of his condition, singing or saying no longer works as it once did to lessen pain. In stanzas 4, 5, and 6 the Lady's eyes are compared to the stars guiding a navigator over the nighttime sea. If Laura's eyes have always been present when the lover has gone towards the good, and if the peace they bring is like heaven itself, their excessive light has tied his tongue and left him weak and pale. Therefore one has a two-part experience: the recognition of an illuminated presence capable of steering one along the path to beatitude, and the inability to pursue that path. In stanza 5, the recognition that singing no longer lessens the pain as it once did takes the form of the inexpressibility topos, for which one will never be able to recount ("narrar") the experience. As the poem concludes, the *status quo ante* of the lover's entrapment has been overturned, as the scribe, with pen in hand, reaffirms the salutary effect of his continuing interior dialogue:

> Canzone, i' sento già stancar la penna
> del lungo et dolce ragionar co·llei,
> ma non di parlar meco i pensier' mei. (73, 91–3)

> Song, I feel my pen already weary
> of this discourse, so long and sweet, with her,
> But my thoughts don't grow tired of talk with me.

It is clear from the cycle of canzoni 70 to 73 that love poems can cross the boundary into maieutics, particularly in extended sequences. In fact, the statement of awareness that one is *not* discerning, that one has *not* returned to the "vero splendor" ("splendor real") (70, 45), sets the stage for what is to follow. To expand on an argument set forth by Luisa Del Giudice, I would suggest that poems 63 to 79, all love poems, together with the religious and confessional poems 80 and 81, concern the subject's personal history, while those that follow – up to poem 105 – are mostly occasional poems concerned with the demonstration of artistry and poetic skill, as befitting a poet-laureate.[58] The first section contains the trio known as the canzoni of the eyes and several poems containing the motif of fatigue (74, 75, 76, and 81), a condition that has replaced despair as the dominant mood in the fiction. Thus in poem 76 the subject is seen oscillating – as in a fable – between the "prison" of his love for Laura, which he ironically refers to as his "freedom," and the awareness that this prison-freedom (of concupiscient desire) is exhausting his soul, a fact whose veracity or unbelievability he frames parenthetically for the reader:

> et or con gran fatica
> (chi 'l crederà perché giurando i' 'l dica?)
> in libertà ritorno sospirando (76, 6–8)

> and now, with effort great
> (Who'll credit it unless I give my oath?)
> I return sighing to my freedom.

Sonnets 77 and 78 concern a portrait of Laura painted by Petrarch's Sienese contemporary Simone Martini.[59] In the first of these, the poet uses hyperbole to extol the genius of Simone, who in his portrait of Laura must have been divinely inspired. It is hypothesized that the sculptor Polyclitus could not have equalled Simone's efforts had he laboured for a thousand years. Nevertheless, the resultant painting *cannot* be equated with the divine image of Laura. Petrarch is introducing a theory of the image that contrasts with that of Giacomo da Lentini, for whom a picture of the beloved could be painted in the heart, transcending the material plane. Petrarch's emphasis is on the limits of representation and ultimately on the inability to grasp the divine "opra" which remains occluded by the "velo" of the body:[60]

> L'opra fu ben di quelle che nel cielo
> si ponno imaginar, non qui tra noi,
> ove le membra fanno a l'alma velo. (77, 9–11)

> This work, assuredly, was one of those
> Conceivable in Heaven, but not here
> Among us, where the body veils the soul.

Poem 78 continues the discussion, again with a hyperbolic hypothesis involving a sculptor, this time Pygmalion. It suggests that if Simone had used words rather than paint, the poet would have been spared his labours and anguish in attempting to depict Laura.

> Quando giunse a Simon l'alto concetto
> ch'a mio nome gli pose in man lo stile,

s'avesse dato a l'opera gentile
colla figura voce ed intellecto,
  di sospir' molti mi sgombrava il petto,
che ciò ch'altri à piú caro, a me fan vile:
però che 'n vista ella si mostra humile
promettendomi pace ne l'aspetto. (78, 1–8)

  Simone, when he found that high conceit,
Took pencil in his hand on my behalf;
But had he given to that noble work,
Along with shape, both voice and intellect,
  My breast would be relieved of many sighs
That make whatever others hold most dear
Seem base to me; for in her picture she
Seems meek, and her face promises me peace.

Poem 78 continues to praise Simone's artistry, in parallel with the extraordinary virtue of Laura; but it states in greater detail that art is unable to capture the ineffable and the divine. If an ideal of mimetic accuracy is present in poem 77, here that ideal is abandoned in favour of a symbolic understanding of the art work as an ethical guide to the viewer, not to the object of his desire but to the divine idea that she embodies. (Inevitably one recalls poem 16, "Movesi il vecchierel canuto et biancho" ("The good old man, gray-haired and pale, stirs forth"), in which the lover unsuccessfully pursued the "forma vera" of Laura in the images of other women; but here the ambivalence of that early lyric is not in evidence.)[61] The sonnets to Simone ground artistic representation in the immanent, so that it is sufficient for the divinely inspired Christian artist to aspire (in contrast to the aims of Polyclitus and Pygmalion) simply to create an idea of the divine vision.

Sestina 80 reintroduces the navigation metaphor, a complex trope having classical and vernacular precedents, and an apt tool for marking beginnings and endings. One recalls Dante's image of "la navicella del mio ingegno" ("my talent's little vessel") (*Purg.* i, 2), where the ship is an image of the poem and the poet's skill, and – by way of the Petrarchan sestina's seven uses of "porto" – the closing pages of Dante's *Convivio*, where the image of the port represents the solace arrived at at the end of a well-lived life.[62] Here, too, the navigational theme concerns the allegory of safe return over dangerous waters. If the poem's point of departure is the oppressive circularity of time, its point of arrival is the prospect of safe harbour in the welcoming arms of the "Signore" ("Lord"):

> Chi è fermato di menar sua vita
> su per l'onde fallaci et per li scogli
> scevro da morte con un picciol legno,
> non pò molto lontan esser dal fine:
> però sarebbe da ritirarsi in porto
> mentre al governo anchor crede la vela.
> [...]
> S'io esca vivo de' dubbiosi scogli,
> et arrive il mio exilio ad un bel fine,
> ch'i' sarei vago di voltar la vela,
> et l'anchore gittar in qualche porto!
> Se non ch'i' ardo come acceso legno,
> sí m'è duro a lassar l'usata vita.
> Signor de la mia fine et de la vita,
> prima ch'i' fiacchi il legno tra gli scogli
> drizza a buon porto l'affannata vela. (80, 1–6, 31–9)

> Whoever has resolved to lead his life
> Upon deceitful waves, among the shoals,
> From death divided just by a small craft,
> Cannot be very distant from his end.
> And thus he should withdraw into a port
> While to the rudder still responds the sail.
> [...]
> If, living, I escape those doubtful shoals,
> And if my exile comes to a fair end,
> How happy I should be to furl the sail
> And then let down my anchor in some port!
> Unless I burn as does a flaming craft,
> I find it hard to leave my wonted life.
> Lord of my end and also of my life,
> Before I wreck my craft among the shoals
> Direct to a good port my troubled sail.

While the navigation metaphor implicates the amorous subtext, as suggested by the flames of desire, there is no ambiguity about the addressee, "Signore" ("Lord").[63] Moreover the sestina fits into this transitional maieutic section of the sequence, advancing its implicit narrative.

In the following sonnet, written on the death of Giacomo Colonna in September 1341, the religious theme merges with that of friendship. The "journey" presented is a kind of parable, enabled by "a great friend":

> Io son sí stanco sotto 'l fascio antico
> de le mie colpe et de l'usanza ria
> ch'i' temo forte di mancar tra via,
> et di cader in man del mio nemico.
> Ben venne a dilivrarmi un grande amico
> per somma et ineffabil cortesia; (81, 1–6)

> I am so tired beneath the ancient load
> of my guilt and my evil ways
> that I fear terribly I shall fall
> on the road into my enemy's hands.
> Once a great friend came to deliver me
> With highest courtesy, ineffable,

As I suggested above, poems 81 to 104 are mostly occasional poems that draw into focus the poet's craft; additionally, in poems 83 to 97 one has a high concentration of archery imagery (*arco, saette, strali, colpo*), suggesting a juxtaposition between the observer of Love's actions (the narrator) and the recipient of his arrows (the character). In addition, in poems 88, 91, 92, 98, 99, 103, 104, 108, 112, and 113 one sees the tangible rise of the topic of friendship, a fact that allows the internal monologue to expand into dialogue with one's neighbour. The language of friendship is endowed with a specific morality compatible with the pursuit of "libertà" (as above in poems 29 and 76), not the ironic freedom from love's prison but the freedom promised by civil society and the freedom of spiritual liberation (as in poems 89, 96, and 97). It is suitable, therefore, that the diction of poems 83 to 89 features a degree of linguistic violence, *hapaxes,* and rare words and rhymes, a change glossed by Contini as follows:

> È questa un'esperienza antica, condizioni e premesse del vero Petrarca, benché non essa il Petrarca proverbiale; un'esperienza antica che suppone un concentramento d'energia nei punti salienti (in rima), e al massimo una distribuzione a ritroso, non un equilibrio.

(This is an ancient experience, the conditions and premises of the true Petrarch, though it not be the proverbial Petrarch; an ancient experience that supposes a concentration of energy in the salient points (in rhyme), and at the most a distribution backwards, not an equilibrium.)[64]

The "ancient" or archaic register is seen below in the *hapax* "larve," referring to the amorous phantasm; behind this word deriving from *larua* (a mask or skeleton-like ghost, but also a skin or hide) is the hidden *senhal* of *Laura*:

Diceami il cor che per sé non saprebbe
viver un giorno; et poi tra via m'apparve
quel traditore in sí mentite *larve*
che piú saggio di me inganato avrebbe. (89, 5–8)

My heart told me that, by itself, it could
Not live a day; and then along the way
I saw that traitor in such false disguise
That wiser men than I would have been tricked.

Poem 91 continues in the worldly mode and concerns the death of a woman loved by Gherardo, a dire event that the poet responds to by advising his brother to "ricovrare ambo le chiavi / del tuo cor" ("take back both the keys / Of your own heart") (91, 5–6), reminding him of the ubiquity of death:

Poi che se' sgombro de la maggior salma,
l'altre puoi giuso agevolmente porre,
sallendo quasi un pellegrino scarco.
Ben vedi omai sí come a morte corre
ogni cosa creata, et quanto all'alma
bisogna ir lieve al periglioso varco. (91, 9–14)

Once you're unburdened of your heaviest weight
The rest with more ease you will put aside,
And like a pilgrim now unladen, climb.
Now you can see how each created thing
Runs on toward death, and see how light the soul
Must travel to that pass so dangerous.

One is presented here in the space of the transitory with a maxim concerning the inevitability of death: "a morte corre / ogni cosa creata" (91, 12–13). Such maxims are common in the earlier poems and serve to link them to larger themes in the macrotext; other examples include "ché perfetti giudicii son sí rari" ("For someone's crime, another takes the blame") (84, 13); and "Ma sofferenza è nel dolor conforto" ("Endurance, though, brings comfort in […] woe") (139, 12).

In his early career, Petrarch dedicated himself to the verbal arts of the trivium. As a humanist, he no longer conceived of the liberal arts as an immutable hierarchy but saw them in practical terms as finite tools to be used for virtuous ends:

> Adde quod nec grammatica nec septem ulla liberalium digna est in qua nobile senescat ingenium. Egregium viatorem nec viarum asperitas terret nec mulcet amenitas et montem hispidum transit et prata virentia; totus in finem prominet.

> Neither grammar nor any of the seven liberal arts deserves the entire lifetime of a noble talent, for they are transitory, not ends in themselves. The roughness of the road does not frighten the seasoned traveller nor does the pleasantness attract him; in crossing rugged mountains and green meadow he is completely engrossed in arriving at his journey's end.[65]

As a proponent of a new theory of knowledge, Petrarch derived his view of the arts of language empirically and was guided – as stated in the Introduction – by moral philosophy and inductive thinking. To the Aristotelian dialectic of potentiality and actuality he adds the mediating element of experience and the natural process of becoming.[66] Thus, guided by his perceptions and his conscience, he will continue to develop in the poems of the second centenary an alternative landscape to the threatening and fabulous world of the *selva*.

Chapter Three

The Language of Tears (*Rvf* 92–122)

1. A Parable of Return

The language of tears seen in poem 92, "Piangete, donne, et con voi pianga Amore" ("O ladies weep, and may Love weep with you"), mourning the death of Cino da Pistoia, establishes the act of weeping not simply as a natural part of grief but as a means of prostrating oneself before God together with the community.[1] To weep openly is to break stoic apathy. In fact, the prominence of tears in Petrarch's poetry is not unrelated to his practice of the Holy Offices and recitation of scripture (especially the Psalms): weeping is an ingredient of his prayers that finds its way into the poems: "Ora il lavoro centonario del poeta si concentra con un'insistenza singolare sull'elemento acqueo. Prevalenza di lacrime che definiscono la poesia di Davide, nonché con quelle bibliche, sparse nei *Rerum vulgarium fragmenta* 'mille a mille' [...]" (Now the poet's citational patchwork is concentrated with a singular insistence on the aqueous element. The prevalence of tears that define the poetry of David, and those of the Bible, shed "by the thousands" in the *Rerum vulgarium fragmenta*) [...].[2] It is clear not only that "difendendo la nobiltà teologica della poesia, egli intendeva parlare della propria" (by defending the theological nobility of poetry, he meant to speak of his own poetry) but that the biblical prophets were a primary model in that regard.[3]

Poem 93 continues the lachrymose thematic as it provides a paraphrase of an address made by Amor on various occasions. The sonnet can be organized into three parts: Amor's command to the subject to write down in "golden letters" his past experience as a lover; the subject's departure from Amor, when he set out on "altro lavoro" ("another work") (93, 7); and the recapturing of the subject by Amor, who warns him that the same suffering he once experienced will return again. In the conclusion, Amor exposes his own subjectivity, suggesting that sad days lie ahead for the subject: "forse non avrai sempre il viso asciutto: / ch'i' mi pasco di lagrime, et tu 'l sai" ("Perhaps your face won't be forever dry – / I feed myself on tears as you well know") (93, 13–14). There are two fundamental aspects to this sonnet: first, it presents a marked diegetic split between the character and the author-narrator, the victim of Amor and the writer; second, by its reference to "another work," it provides a limit-expression applicable to the subject's past but also his future.[4] Looking backwards, this other work (possibly the *Africa*) drew the poet away from his love poems, but the potential remains in the remark by Amor that the "other work" still continues within the lyric sequence. Perhaps the finest example of a contrasting style is given by canzone 105, which continues in the archaic and ambiguous register of canzone 29, one that will later recur in canzoni 135 and 206. What these and similar poems share is a reliance on encrypted poetic language that has roots in the Provençal tradition, notably in the poetry of the *trobar clus*.

After receiving the *laurea*, in Rome in 1341, Petrarch had an extended stay in Parma, where his friend Azzo da Correggio had come into power. Parma would come to represent the Italian alternative to Provence in these years when the poet's alienation from the Avignon court grew more bitter. At the same time he is broadening and diversifying the subject matter of his vernacular lyrics. Representative of this profoundly communicative and ecumenical work, poems 101, 102, 103, 104, and 108 are among the fifty-six "non-love" poems in the *Fragmenta*; the first two are deemed confessional poems while the latter three are concerned with friendship.[5] These provide a frame for *Rvf* 105, surely the most anomalous poem in the collection.[6] Sonnet 101 – marking the year 1341 – acknowledges that love has made one a prisoner but that one is not deceived:

So come i dí, come i momenti et l'ore,
ne portan gli anni; et non ricevo inganno,
ma forza assai maggior che d'arti maghe (101, 9–11)

I know how the moments, days and hours bear off
Our years, and I'm not fooled; but I endure
A power stronger far than magic arts.

Then, in poem 104, addressed to Pandolfo Malatesta, the narrator compares the worldly fame he seeks as a writer to the *res gestae* of four celebrated Roman generals:

'l nostro studio è quello
che fa per fama gli uomini immortali. (104, 13–14)

our pursuit is one
That makes men grow immortal through renown.

The final line calls to mind Dante's homage to Brunetto Latini, "m'insegnavate come l'uom s'etterna" (*Inf.* xv, 85), who taught him to gain the "eternal" through the "study" of letters, not least because Brunetto's teachings, which combined the love of God and of one's neighbour with a civic awareness and ethical involvement in politics, were adopted by Petrarch.[7] It is clear with this sonnet, addressed by name to a contemporary active in the civic life, that Petrarch is inserting a historically based self-consciousness into the sequence. It is precisely here that he places the canzone-frottola, the maximum expression of a more archaic, antique style, that will resurface in canzoni 145 and 206 and elsewhere.[8]

Poem 105 introduces the popular poetic form of the *frottola* into the *Fragmenta*, along with hermetic elements of the *trobar clus*.[9] When Petrarch reshapes this loose and extravagant genre of obscure proverbs of the oral minstrel culture into the lofty and demanding canzone form, what results is a tour de force of ambiguity, emotion, and wit.[10] The poem is unique in many respects, possessing the largest quantity of internal rhymes in the whole collection, the only use of masculine rhyme, the only *rima tronca*, the only instance of a double *sirma*, and, on a thematic level, a formidable obstacle to its own exegesis.[11] As Nicola Zingarelli writes: "Bisogna liberare la fama del Petrarca dalla taccia di un'arte leggiera, e tutta esteriore, e incurante del sentimento e della coscienza, in occasione di questa canzone, che appunto fa pensare ai temi tradizionali della poesia anteriore" (One must free Petrarch's fame from the reproach of a light, completely exterior art neglectful of feeling and conscience, in the case of this canzone, which leads one to think, precisely, of the traditional themes of the poetry which preceded him).[12] Petrarch has taken from the Provençals the *descort*, which has as its content the separation from love and from the woman, and the enigmatic *devinalh* form. These forms, like the *frottola*, are appropriate to the declared intention to never sing again as one once did.

The incipit, "Mai non vo' piú cantar com'io soleva" ("I never want to sing as I once did"), is canonical and connects with the openings of canzoni of renunciation of one's habit of singing by Arnaut Daniel ("D'autra guiz' e d'autra razo / m'aven a chantar que no sol" [In another way, on another subject, / from what I'm used to, I'd better sing]), Guittone d'Arezzo ("Ora parrà s'eo saverò cantare / e s'eo varrò quanto valer già soglio" [We will soon find out if I can sing / and if I command the respect I once did]), and Dante ("Le dolci rime d'amor ch'i solia / ... / convien ch'io lasci" [The sweet rhymes of love I used to sing / ... / I now must leave]). For students of the Italian lyric, the reminders are particularly evocative, formally and artistically but also in terms of a Christian situation of moral decision of life change.

In the poem's opening sections this life change is simply desired or willed, but by poem's end it will be understood in terms of a *mutatio anime*. Though the poem's subject is love, it polemicizes against the courtly love of the troubadors and grouses against Laura herself. It advocates for a turning back to a humbler, more devotional life but does so with great obscurity of form and content, and with the disarming simplicity of its many paratactic declarations derived from popular oral discourse. These are proverbs, adages, and aphorisms that both stand alone and constitute a sequence; in this latter way they tell a story, or, as I suggest, a parable of return (where "return" is understood in the renunciatory way discussed above).

The commentary on the canzone is divided between those who find no coherent sense in it and those who do. Pietro Bembo essentially rejected the poem; though he recognized its formal superiority to another *frottola* attributed to Petrarch, he denied that it had any sense or logical consequentiality.[13] Leopardi in his commentary skipped over the poem, stating it had to be Petrarch's intention that it not be understood.[14] Among those who find sense in the poem, some focus on biographical motives, speculating that it might have been an attack against some specific clerics; but as Zingarelli writes of such motives, "a ricordarli darebbero più disgusto che diletto" (to recall them would bring more disgust than delight).[15] Giosuè Carducci rejected the explanations based on political-polemical motives, saying that Petrarch had written the canzone "per dolersi ora di aver servito a corte indarno, ora d'aver amato Laura senza profitto alcuno, ora contr'a'costumi di corte" (to complain first about having served at court in vain, then for having loved Laura without success, then again against the customs at court); and that finally one must see in it a love poem addressed to Laura "che non più gli impedisce la via del cielo" (who no longer blocks him from the way of heaven).[16] For Arnaldo Foresti the poem is a decisive and unique rebuttal of the unresponsive Laura. I agree with Foresti's focus on the "I" character's "indifference" towards the love object, and I see it as the necessary starting point for the subject's further development, as permitted by the *frottola*. Through his momentary dismissal of Laura (l. 80: "disdetto"), he establishes himself as one capable of acting and not simply reacting. The active rejection of this medieval version of *la belle dame sans merci* is another aspect of the poem's uniqueness. Antonio Daniele has provided the most eloquent defence of the poem's multi-levelled coherence. Demonstrating its similarity to the Provençal "*comjat:* the canzone of farewell with which the lover departs from the beloved," Daniele relates this to the historic demands of the *frottola* and canzone forms, "dando vita ad un ibridismo semantico-formale (senso scollato e struttura ferrea) e ad un'operazione sincretica originale, quella della *canzone frottolata*" (thus giving life to a semantic-formal hybridism (unrestrained meaning and rigid structure) and to an original syncretic operation, that of the *canzone frottolata*).[17] While individual lines cause critics to pause, the narrative shape of the poem is coherent. As Daniele states, "il quadro di riferimento [è] quello di una tenzone interiore tra doloroso rifiuto d'amore, riprovazione della propria debolezza sentimentale e desiderio di ristoro religioso" (the frame of reference is that of an internal dispute between the painful rejection of love, the self-reproach of one's sentimental weakness and the desire for religious relief).[18]

Poem 105 possesses considerable sense, continuity, and equilibrium for the reader who is able to negotiate its engagement of paradox and polysemy. The *new* mode of singing will be defined above all by the intention to turn back from a former mode in which one was the victim of a worldly love, as one reads in the final lines of the first strophe:

Chi smarrita à la strada, torni indietro;
chi non à albergo, posisi in sul verde;
chi non à l'auro, o 'l perde,
spenga la sete sua con un bel vetro. (105, 12–15)

Who's lost upon the road may turn around;
Who has no home may rest upon the grass;
Who's lost his gold or who
Has none, may slake thirst from a lovely glass.

The obscure lines project a Petrarchan sublime, an archaic sense of the limits of representation; the sublime is a counter-principle to the "beautiful," which, together with fear, permeated the first centenary of poems.[19] Daniele traces a host of prior poems in the collection (poems 54, 62, 68, 74, 80, 81, 88, 96–8, 99, 101) that anticipate the decisive turn of poem 105, towards God and away from the physical person of Laura. To speak of the sublime in this sense is to speak of recognition, of religious wonder and satisfaction at the limits of knowledge. In fact, the openings of the poem's first four stanzas repeat the theme of a positive understanding garnered by a turning away:

Mai non vo' piú cantar com'io soleva,
ch'altri no m'intendeva, ond'ebbi scorno;
et puossi in bel soggiorno esser molesto. (105, 1–3)

I never want to sing as once I did,
For since she did not heed me, I was scorned;
On pleasant sojourns one can come to grief.

§

I'die' in guarda a san Pietro; or non piú, no:
intendami chi pò, ch'i' m'intend'io.
Grave soma è un mal fio a mantenerlo:
quando posso mi spetro, et sol mi sto. (105, 16–19)

Saint Peter I put trust in; no more, now;
(Judge this who can; I understand myself).
Ill tribute is so burdensome to bear;
I pull free – as I can – stand by myself.

§

Proverbio "ama chi t'ama" è fatto antico.
I' so ben quel ch'io dico. Or lass'andare,
ché conven ch'altri impare a le sue spese. (105, 31–3)

That proverb: "Love who loves you" – ancient truth!
I know well what I say. Now let it go,
For everyone must learn at his own cost.

§

Forse ch'ogni uom che legge non s'intende;
et la rete tal tende che non piglia;
et chi troppo assotiglia si scavezza. (105, 46–8)

Perhaps not all who read will understand,
Who sets the net may not bring in the catch;
Who sharpens wits too fine will break his neck.

All four openings allude to past errors, using aphorisms to project a knowledge that might obviate the sorrows of the past. Their seeming discontinuities are a product of the sheer accumulation of sayings or examples, each expressing the desire to break with former rationales, which only led to unhappiness. On the basis of these four openings, we might say that rationality itself – of the scholastic sort that pervaded "Saint Peter" (the church) and grew so subtle it undermined the integrity of the thinker – is at the centre of the poet's concern.

The second half of the poem reflects a more optimistic tone in which the common, or popular, sense of the proverbial voice translates into a detachment from amorous desire itself. To appreciate the moral-philosophical scope of the canzone, one must examine its numerous references to the artistic and cognitive process. The use of so much secondhand material (the proverbs belong to the dimension of folklore) is itself a comment on the importance of the oral code and culture vis-à-vis the written (or chirographic) code.[20] Proverbs and riddles possess their own truths, independent of text-formed thought. The proverb is a trope of modesty and humility: it advises against the quest of too-lofty goals or grandiose expectations. The lexis of poem 105 is also unusual; the several *hapax legomena* ("scavezza," "assottiglia," "disdetto") add colour without lowering the tone. Here again, the canzone represents a limit and not a deviation; it is strange and ambiguous but intimately tied to the usages, forms, and motives of the other poems, and to that single "fixed rule" of the *Fragmenta*, that of pleasing variability.

In the absence of any continuous landscape, one must contend with a new kind of referentiality; the external landscape is not truly absent, but it is in competition with the intensely rhymed and otherwise sound-figured verbal texture, as well as with the existential present of the "I" figure, suspended between his disappointing memories and his hopeful projections for the future. The plenitude of this moment forces Petrarch to step down from the exclusivity of authorship, to not embellish the situation or discourse "as he once did"; it causes him to abandon the *many* hopes of amorous obsession in order to trust in the *one* hope that is God. God is figured on the poetic-rhetorical plane by the coincidence of opposites (or resolution of paradoxes), the transmutation of thought, and, finally, by and in the re-formed, sublimated person of Laura. Modifying the *descort* form, whose theme is disagreement with the Lady, Petrarch slowly returns to an affirmation of devotional love or *pietà*. In this sense he exploits the genre without being limited to it. Fubini writes, "Ha assoggettato il libero giro della *frottola* alle leggi della canzone, costringendo quel componimento popolaresco entro le linee aristocratiche della sua arte e ottenendone suggestivi effetti di sentenze e d'immagini" (He subjected the free course of the *frottola* to the laws of the canzone, constraining that popular composition within the aristocratic boundaries of his art and obtaining from it suggestive effects of maxims and images).[21] Petrarch takes the essence from the proverbs, employing them in an experiential, intuitive, and affective way rather than as logical abstractions or syllogisms. A sign of this aristocratic bent is the arduous metrics of the poem, which with *rimalmezzo*, features 138 rhymes in 90 lines. This metric rigour is foreign to both the *descort* and the *frottola giullaresca*.

Having introduced the poem, I would like to summarize the six stanzas and follow up with a series of stylistic considerations. The initial attack reveals an "I" figure (as in Dante's canzone "Così nel mio parlar voglio esser aspro" ["I want to be as harsh in my speech"]) who declares himself compelled to seek a more arduous artistic path. My end could come at anytime, he says, so I must remain vigilant. I am aging; I am resolving to change my way of singing and writing. The change is comparable to a journey where one turns back, having lost his way. This turning back means being content with more modest means and a franker, wiser view of love, love that "rules its empire without a sword." He suggests that Laura has temporarily lost her disdainful dignity by growing proud – "et in donna amorosa anchor m'aggrada / che 'n vista vada altera e disdegnosa, / non superba et ritrosa" ("And in a loving lady still I'm pleased / When hauteur and disdain show in her face, / Not pride and bashfulness") (105, 8–10), this latter being an echo of Dante's Sordello, "O anima lombarda, / come ti stavi altèra e disdegnosa!" ("Oh Lombard soul, what pride / and what disdain were in your stance!") (*Purg*. vi, 61–2). Now a chain of proverbial sayings (or *paroemia*) beginning with the pronoun "chi" lists commonplaces about rejected lovers. Let those who do not find love be satisfied with a secure shelter and the comfort of "un bel vetro" ("a cool drink"), though it not be from a cup of "auro" (gold, glory, Laura).[22] Such allusions are attempts to communicate by images the complex reasons that steer the affective life towards the spiritual life.

Stanza 2 relates the renunciation to St Peter, that is, the institution of the papacy and curia and Petrarch's employ therein, which grew steadily less satisfactory (as discussed in the final section of this chapter). He stands alone, knowing he is obscure: "Intendami chi pò, ch'i' m'intend'io" ("(Judge this who can; I can understand myself)") (l. 17). In the declaration "Quanto posso mi spetro e sol mi sto" ("I pull free – as I can – stand by myself") (l. 19), there is also a punning on the poet's name, and thus a detachment from the sameness of one's anagraphic identity, as well as from the stoniness that results from impure emotions and attachments. My journey, he says, must now be a calm one, for venturing out to sea is a risk I cannot afford: "Non è gioco uno scoglio, in mezzo l'onde" ("A shoal amidst the waves is not a jest") (l. 23). Now the proverbial "rispondi a chi ti chiama" (answer those who call) is essentially reversed in the line, "Alcun è che risponde a chi nol chiama" ("A few will answer when nobody calls") (l. 27), as if to say that I erred in this way; I answered when I was not called. I was like Phaeton or a bird trapped by birdlime; thus a series of examples of the madness brought on by love conclude the stanza.

In stanza 3, which opens "Proverbio, ama chi t'ama, è fatto antico" ("The proverb 'Love him who loves you' is an ancient fact") (l. 31), the "I" figure expresses his desire to have a practical attitude towards life's difficulties: I will dedicate myself to God. I have been too vulnerable to appearances, he says, especially external beauty. I now know that it is wise to undertake modest projects that are realizable and to appreciate the presence of goodness everywhere; man is free insofar as he realizes that "per ogni paese è bona stanza" ("in every country there are pleasant dwellings") (l. 37); man is a pilgrim by nature. As such, I dedicate myself to Christ, the good shepherd.

Quel poco che m'avanza,
Fia chi no 'l schifi, s'i' 'l vo' dare a lui.
I' mi fido in Colui che 'l mondo regge.
Et che' seguaci Suoi nel boscho alberga,
che con pietosa verga
mi meni a passo omai tra le Sue gregge. (105, 40–5)

What little I have left
He won't shun If I wish to yield it up.
I trust myself to Him who rules the world
And cares for his disciples in the woods,
For with His loving crook
He guides my steps at last among His flock.

The rhymes with "gregge" and the homophones of "legge" are strongly consonantic and rare in the *Fragmenta*, putting into relief the vocalic rhymes that denote with pronouns ("altrui," "lui," "Colui") and a key verb ("fui") the limits of possible worldly experience. The series of relative clauses ("che," "che," "che") continue the periphrasis of God ("lui," "Colui") and echo the iterative form of the preceding stanzas. The affirmation of faith suggests a resolution to the canzone. But were it to conclude here it would do so prematurely. The *frottola* would remain disordered, and the renunciation of Laura of the *descort* form would prevail.

In stanza 4 we read that mental and verbal subtlety, like opulent beauty, are fatal. Rather a concealed beauty – in the woman and in the poetry – is more gentle. To unlock this secret there is a symbolic "key" that opens the heart and releases the burden of anguish. The obscurity of these lines is tied to the amorous situation, as both are transmuted into spiritual values. The paradoxes are not the usual antitheses found in Petrarch (in which the opposite terms of a binomial soften and mitigate one another); instead the sweetness of this sorrow is transcendent, free from the fragility of time. The following lines build up to an exclamation and a slew of alliterations:

Benedetta la chiave   che s'avvolse
Al cor, e sciolse   l'alma, e scossa l'àve
Di catena sí grave,
E 'nfiniti sospir del mio sen tolse!
Là dove piú mi dolse,   altri si dole,
et dolendo adolcisse il mio dolore:
Ond'io ringratio Amore
che piú nol sento, et è non men che suole. (105, 53–60)

Ah, blessed be the key that turned within
My heart, unbound my soul and freed it from
Such heavy chains, and that
Unshackled from my breast signs infinite!

> There where I sorrowed most, another mourns,
> And by that mourning makes my sorrow sweet.
> So I thank Love that I
> Feel it no more; yet it's not any less.

Laura is the other here, "altri," as in the cited "ch'altri no m'intendeva" ("she did not heed me") (l. 2), and possesses her own subjectivity: she feels a pain equal to that of the "I" figure. For both, we might say, love's sorrow is leading them beyond themselves to an unsuspected harmony. To know the self as other, and the other as oneself, is to conceive of the self no longer in terms of a sameness of identity over time but rather as a soul, a living creature of God. This in turn is a very Franciscan concept, suggesting a marriage to poverty, simplicity, and a healthy primitiveness. He who is too concerned about rational justifications for his actions will get lost. The "I" figure was a lost sheep who has now been found and returned to Christ's flock. The necessary descent of "molte miglia" ("many miles") (l. 50) is to be read in this light as a figure of repentance and humility. Only thus can the purifying force of Love lead to a qualitative change in one's life.

The opening of stanza 5, "In silentio parole accorte e sagge" ("And in the silence, words adroit and sage") (l. 61), concerns the importance of listening to and in the silence for the living Word of God. Having declared above "I' mi fido in Colui che 'l mondo regge" ("I trust myself to Him who rules the world") (l. 42), he now acknowledges the contemplative practice of prayer and receptivity to the living word. A complex sentence follows whose several subjects – including Love and Jealousy, and all having to do with aspects of the love object – are ruled by one predicate, "m'ànno il cor tolto" ("have seized my heart") (l. 69). The direct object, the suffering heart, stands for a destructive passion. Once that heart is removed, in its place the spiritual heart emerges in the subject to be guided on a flat and level road, not a steep incline, with Laura as the prudent guide. It is this heart's role to listen: faith depends on the listening of the heart to the Word of God. The stanza ends with the plea that this goodness not abandon the "I," that he might keep the knowledge of the other in himself, this sacred transcendence, for all his days. The use of anaphora (ten of the final thirty lines begin with "E") helps simplify the syntax and concentrate the attention on the intense rhymings, quickening the pace of a poem that has now abandoned the use of proverbs which crowded the first four stanzas ("frotta" means crowd). Laura is now a figure ever more revered, but not to be followed save in their common hope in God, and towards death, "il fin degli affanni" ("the end of all my pains") (l. 72).

Stanza 6 opens with a retrospective view, and a vow to live in the present. The bird figure of stanza two (Phaeton falling, the bird snared in the birdlime) is now comfortably nesting.The "I" figure senses a liberation based on the awareness of past wrongs. He regales and trusts in what he hears in the present, as in the line "perché molto mi fido in quel ch'i odo" (l. 77), again recalling the cited lines "I'mi fido in Colui" (l. 42) and "In silentio parole" (l. 61).

De' passati miei danni piango e rido,
Perché molto mi fido in quel ch'i' odo;
Del presente mi godo, e meglio aspetto. (105, 76–8)

For my past injuries I weep and laugh,
Because I trust so much in what I hear.
The present pleases me; the best I wait.

One thinks of the tradition of *lectio divina*, a religious practice that traditionally includes four stages of involvement with the word and with silence: reading, ruminating, praying, and communion with God or contemplation. The "I" has come to the point of thanking Laura for having resisted his entreaties. These lines give the sense of the faith that allows man to cry or laugh at his own fortune. The "I" is now joined to the substantial facts of his existence; no longer weakened by delusion, he contemplates an earlier version of himself:

E 'n bel ramo m'annido, et in tal modo
ch'i' ne ringratio et lodo il gran disdetto
che l' indurato affecto alfine à vinto,
et ne l'alma depinto "I' sare' udito,
et mostratone a dito," et ànne extinto
(tanto inanzi son pinto,
ch'i' 'l pur dirò) "Non fostú tant'ardito": (105, 80–6)

And on a fair branch I so build my nest
I'm grateful, and I praise that great denial
Which overcame engrafted love at last,
And painted in my soul: "I would be known
And pointed at for that"; next was crossed out
(I'll even say it, since
I'm deeply moved) "You were not very bold":[23]

Here there emerges, I would argue, the first instance of Laura as divine guide, and a first use of the low or popular register in a Davidic or psalm-like manner reminiscent of the *Psalmi penitentiales*. It is by means of this soteriological register that Petrarch is able to advance the sequence as a story that travels beyond contradiction, pain, and sorrow to salvation. It is interesting to note that Boyle concludes her book on Petrarch with a series of citations from the *frottola*, indicating its importance in the author's developing theology and his arrival in his poems at a "spirituality of the secular."[24] Boyle writes that Petrarch is speaking in parables, as did Christ: "Like all valid prophetic verse, it engages men in the act of interpretation, as in Petrarch's enduring challenge of Delphic wisdom: Understand me who can, for I can understand myself."[25] It is apparent that Petrarch's use of the Bible is not utilitarian but emulates the Bible's integration of obscure symbolic messages into the language of narrative. As Ricoeur writes, "The biblical form of imagination is indivisibly a narrative and a symbolic form of imagination."[26]

When viewed in the context of the entire sequence, the *frottola* and the poems around it occupy a transitional position, moving beyond those poems in which the "I" figure was complacent about his amorous sufferings, his virtuosity, and his pursuit of glory.[27] In its conclusion, the *frottola* reflects the tendency of the collection as a whole to chart out a return to God.[28] The *frottola* is perhaps the clearest example by Petrarch of the knowing use of *obscuritas* to engage the sort of sacred truths one finds in the Psalms and the Gospels. The poet concerns himself not with a single duration or location but with several loci unified under the sign of *paroemia* – the string of proverbs that speak to one's concrete experience without recourse to abstractions or syllogisms.

It is only in the final two stanzas that these proverbs are absent, allowing the poem to return to centre and attain closure in a kind of religious and mystical reawakening. The lack of an envoi, whose normal function is to frame the canzone and dispatch it to the world, is significant. An envoi would require a shift in voice and level in a canzone that is already multi-voiced and multi-levelled. Daniele sees the lack of an envoi as an affirmation of Petrarch's initial declaration to change his register and thus not to adopt the courtly convention of the envoi. One can consider the eight-line madrigal inserted immediately afterwards as a kind of *pendant* or substitute envoi.

The word "Nova" that opens madrigal 106, meaning "new," "marvellous," "wondrous," but also "youthful," could refer to the poem itself.[29] By interrupting the semantic continuum of an "I" figure subjugated to

Laura – who is not present in the madrigals – and by reversing the traditional male dominance (and carnality) of the *pastourelle* form, "Nova angeletta" demarcates a new metatextual space in the sequence "in su la fresca riva" ("on the cool shore") (106, 2): [30]

> Nova angeletta sovra l'ale accorta
> scese dal cielo in su la fresca riva,
> là 'nd'io passava sol per mio destino.
> Poi che senza compagna et senza scorta
> mi vide, un laccio che di seta ordiva
> tese fra l'erba ond'è verde il camino.
> Allor fui preso, et non mi spiacque poi,
> sì dolce lume uscia degli occhi suoi! (106, 1–8)

> A wondrous angel came down from the sky
> on nimble wings to that cool river where
> it was my destiny to walk alone.
> Without a friend or guide I wandered by,
> and, seeing this, she laid a silken snare
> amid the grass that made the pathway green.
> Then was I caught, and after had no care,
> her eyes were shining with a light so fair.

Because of the connotative and allusive character of this third madrigal, one is inclined to consider it as a paragram, or text in support of a secondary level of communication in the *Fragmenta*.[31] Within the logic of the paragram, the "fresca riva," here the site of a miraculous encounter between the subject and an angelic female figure, also refers, by way of its semantic variability, to the "fresca riva" of sonnet 148, where the cool riverbanks are those of the Sorgue.[32] Since poem 106 serves as a *pendant* to the coda-less *frottola*, it is worth adding that the "laccio" ("snare") the woman uses on the man has roots in Psalms 34:7, 139:6, and 141:4, sharing that semantic field with the *frottola*.[33] The lightness and brevity of the madrigal constitutes an interval in the horizontal progression of the sequence and a decisive moment for reflection.

2. Nature, Landscape, Solitude

As we have seen, in 1337 a new life begins for Petrarch. Though he will remain in the service of the Colonna family for another ten years, he has moved to the Vaucluse fifteen miles from Avignon, to the source of the Sorgue River. Midway through that decade comes the critical year 1342, decisive in the author's compilation of his text but also a key date in the poem's internal history. Assigned to this year are sonnets 107 to 118, all set either in Avignon, dominated by the presence of Laura, or in the Vaucluse, the place of solitude.[34]

Sonnet 107, an anniversary poem, articulates two voices within the fiction: that of the "I" figure of fifteen years earlier, of the "primo giovenile errore" ("first youthful error") (1, 3), and that of the narrator who remembers and still suffers from that condition. Despite the narrator's continued subjugation by love, the once dualistic image of the laurel has achieved singularity and possesses the power to unify the scattered images of Laura in the lover's memory:

> Fuggir vorrei; ma gli amorosi rai,
> che dí et notte ne la mente stanno,
> risplendon sí, ch'al quintodecimo anno
> m'abbaglian piú che 'l primo giorno assai;
> et l'imagine lor son sí cosparte
> [...]
> Solo d'un lauro tal selva verdeggia
> che 'l mio adversario con mirabil arte
> vago fra i rami ovunque vuol m'adduce. (107, 5–9, 12–14)

> I'd like to flee; yet still the amorous rays
> That, day and night, stay in my memory
> Blaze so that in this fifteenth year much more
> They dazzle me than that first day they did.
> Their images are scattered so about
> [...]
> From just one laurel, such a forest thrives
> That with amazing art my foe leads me
> Astray amidst the branches, where he will.

As the mnestic quality of the laurel acquires prominence, in line with the mythic and moral powers enunciated in the *Collatio*, that tree cannot be construed as an object of secular wonder or worldly fame; rather it is capable of engendering an entire forest in the service of Amor.[35]

In a psychoanalytic reading of sonnet 109, Stefano Agosti demonstrates how the phantasm of the love object occupies the psychic space of the subject, whether it is the remote stars ("faville") of her eyes or the nearness of her breath ("L'aura soave"). The "structural opposition" of near and far reveals a "proxemic relation" between the subject and the Other, a "deep structure" that is the key to the poem's interpretation.[36] In the following lines, Laura's presence during the day is remembered at night, bestowing on the sleepless subject a kind of sacred calm:

Ivi m'acqueto; et son condotto a tale,
ch'a nona, a vespro, a l'alba et a le squille
le trovo nel pensier tanto tranquille
che di null'altro mi rimembra o cale. (109, 5–8)

There I grow quiet, am so guided that –
At nones and vespers, dawn and angelus –
In thoughts of them I find such peacefulness,
There's nothing else I care for or recall.

Like the other poems fictively set in 1342, this poem conveys the role of the amorous phantasm in the growth in consciousness, as Laura's presence is recalled in inverse temporal order following the hours of the church day. This proleptic pattern, moving from restlessness to calm, suggests the larger pattern of moral transformation that will be enacted in later poems.

As Petrarch's work for the Avignon court grew more sporadic, he set his sights on the Vaucluse. Sonnets 108 to 112 are set in Avignon, and in 113 one has the departure for this rustic location, which is the setting for poems 114, 116, and 117.[37] While Petrarch met Laura in Avignon – "Aventuroso piú d'altro terreno" ("Land, more than any other fortunate") (108, 1) – the prevalent image of the city is of bitterness – "l'empia Babilonia, ond'è fuggita / ogni vergogna" ("From impious Babylon, whence every sense / Of shame has fled, and every good's withdrawn") (114, 1–2). Leaving Avignon meant leaving Laura behind, as dramatized in poem 116 by the contrast between verbs in the past absolute tense and those in the present; here one has the first "naming" of the Vaucluse, "una valle chiusa" ("a closed valley"), whence the subject contemplates Laura:

lassai quel ch'i' piú bramo; et ò sí avezza
la mente a *contemplar* sola costei,
ch'altro non vede, et ciò che non è lei
già per antica usanza odia et disprezza.

In una *valle chiusa* d'ogni 'ntorno,
ch'è refrigerio de' *sospir'* miei lassi,
giunsi sol com Amor, pensoso et tardo.
Ivi non donne, ma fontane et *sassi*,
et l'imagine trovo di quel giorno
che 'l pensier mio figura, ovunque io sguardo. (116, 5–14)

I left what most I yearn for, and have schooled
My mind to *contemplate* her only, so
It sees no other, and what is not she,
Indeed by custom old it loathes and scorns.
Into a *valley closed* on every side
Where there is solace for my weary *sighs*,
Pensive and slow I went alone with Love.
No ladies there, but rather founts and *stones*
I find, and find in every place I look
The likeness of that day which shapes my thoughts.

The verb "contemplar" is a *hapax* and connotes, etymologically, the gaze to the sky and thus an association of Laura with this landscape. The sonnet shares four key terms (*valle* / *chiusa* / *sospir* / *sassi*) with the following sonnet, where they appear almost in inverse order.

Poem 117 again draws attention to the Vaucluse, about which it draws an absurd hypothesis: if the rock face rising above the valley and blocking it from Avignon could turn itself around, placing its back towards Rome, the poet's sighs could enjoy a freer passage down the valley to Laura in Avignon.

Se 'l *sasso*, ond'è piú *chiusa* questa *valle*,
di che 'l suo proprio nome si deriva,
tenesse vòlto per natura schiva
a Roma il viso et a Babel le spalle,
i miei *sospiri* piú benigno calle
avrian per gire ove lor spene è viva:
or vanno sparsi, et pur ciascuno arriva
là dov'io il mando, che sol un non falle. (117, 1–8)

If the steep *rock* that nearly *close*s off
This *vale* – and whence it takes its proper name –
Fastidious in nature, turned its face

Toward Rome and showed its back to Babylon,
My *sighs* would have a more propitious path
To travel where their hope still lives, for now
They wander scattered, yet each one arrives
Where I have sent it; not a one falls short.

Similarly, if this geographical reversal took place, the climb to the peak of the cliff would look towards Italy and distant Rome, the providential city and the rightful home of the Vicar of Christ.

Petrarch bestows on Rome a sense of historical foreboding and prophetic promise.[38] Though he is distant from the city, its symbolic weight remains undiminished: "Roma è per il poeta 'urbs orbis domina' ed il suo nome significa *fortitudo* in greco e *sublimitas* in ebraico" (Rome is for the poet "city mistress of the world" and its name means "fortitude" in Greek and "sublimity" in Hebrew).[39] Avignon (as discussed in chapter 4, section 2) is the anti-Rome or Babylon, while the Vaucluse is the site of the *amor de lonh* and the place of solitude where Petrarch composed his unfinished epic, *Africa*; his dialogues with the great men of the past, *De viris illustribus*; the majority of the *Familiari;* and many of his vernacular poems. When the Vaucluse is ultimately abandoned in 1353 it becomes a kind of shrine to Laura, in memory.

Petrarch's contemplative practice entailed a daily regime of prayer and devotions, an intense study of nature, and unceasing work as a writer and correspondent. Writing to his friend Lelius of a discussion held in early 1355 with Emperor Charles IV, Petrarch extols the solitary life: "Diu enim nil aliud cogitavi plenumque caput rationibus et exemplis habeo" ("There is no subject I have meditated on at greater length, and my head is full of arguments and examples").[40] Many of the examples he cites are related to his empirical study of the living world and his attempt to incorporate natural phenomena into the life of the spirit. If Petrarch refers to nature in a familiar and generic language, that is because of the lexical selectivity of the poetry; but it is also a sign of his vision of nature as something knowable, in contrast to the metaphysical doctrines of his predecessors:

> The spell with which dogmatic medieval ideas had bound nature was first broken by Petrarch's lyric poetry. Nature is now divested of everything strange, everything disquieting and demonic. The lyrical mood does not see in nature the opposite of psychical reality; rather it feels everywhere in nature the traces and the echo of the soul.[41]

For Petrarch, the times of the soul and the shapes of the inner life are found in nature. The landscape observed carries within it the imprint of that human witness. It is imbued with the motivations of the soul. Herein lie the traces of what today is known as the problem of the observer: "Nature is not sought and represented for its own sake; rather, its value lies in its service to modern man as a new *means of expression* for himself, for the liveliness and the infinite polymorphism of his inner life."[42]

In introducing his study *La vita e i tempi di Petrarca*, Karlheinz Stierle writes:

> L'apertura petrarchesca al paesaggio può correlarsi ad una nuova concezione dell'"essere nel mondo." Orizzontalità del mondo e illimitatezza dell'esperienza diventano le condizioni di una prassi di scrittura all'insegna del frammento.
>
> The Petrarchan opening to the landscape can be correlated with a new conception of "being in the world." Horizontality of the world and unlimitedness of experience become the conditions of a praxis of writing under the sign of the fragment.[43]

Stierle develops this thesis in numerous poetical contexts, returning time and again to the idea of the multiplicity, variety, and horizontality of the natural world.[44] Whether the landscape is untouched by humanity or is rich in cultural artefacts and memories, its evocation conveys the strength of perception, not the reliance on metaphysical authority.[45]

Petrarch's writings on landscape show him to be an intense observer of nature and an avid horticulturist who refers to landscapes in their historical and natural specificity.[46] In his orchard, cultivated on an island in the Sorgue opposite his retreat, Petrarch grew figs, apples, grapes, peaches, pears, walnuts, and almonds. From his other, more rustic garden in the Vaucluse, a solitary and primitive belvedere set against the mountainside where the Sorgue cascaded and roared, Petrarch could witness the violent, terrible, awe-inspiring forces of nature.

Before Petrarch's time there were two established ways of interacting with the natural landscape: that of the activist who manipulates nature through cultivation, and that of the rationalist who seeks a contemplative absorption.

> Petrarch was certainly not the first to explore mountain chasms or to cultivate *pomaria* but it is certain he was the first to combine the two experiences,

> whether in practical terms or in his travels and his very system of life [...]. Moreover he is the first to give a literary accounting of those experiences.[47]

These remarks recall Cassirer's comment about Petrarch's discovery in nature of "the traces and the echo of the soul" and his ascription to Petrarch of a functional view of nature, in contrast to the scholastic view that conceived of nature and spirit "substantively" as "two 'parts' of being," a view that resulted in their "reciprocal exclusion."[48] The change to a functional view of nature was accompanied by the development of new theories of art and science, based on empirical observation and inductive reasoning, and by the recognition of nature's role in the individual's moral development. This was in accordance with Petrarch's Neoplatonic vision of a connection between the earthly city and the kingdom of heaven.[49]

According to Eugenio Battisti, the natural landscape is present in the *Fragmenta* in three distinct ways. First, one has the landscape of enamourment in spring, as governed by the Provençal model of *courtoise*: "the idealization of nearly all the attributes of the natural spectacle. [...] The grass is green, the riverbanks are cool, slender and glimmering, the hillside is cool, shady, in bloom, the breeze is gentle, the snow on the mountains is soft, the countryside is gentle." Second, there is "an even more generic process of classical mythologizing of the rural landscape"; here one finds the naturalistic domain of Diana at the fountain and Apollo in the company of the muses. Lastly, one has the rugged moral landscape: "Isolation and solitude, accompanied by discomfort and horror, deserts of stones, roaring streams, caverns and caves, become a kind of spontaneous expansion of what might be called the penitential psychology of the writer."[50] Each of these modalities – of myth, love, and penitence – evolves over the course of the *Fragmenta* as the themes associated with them are developed. Thus many of the earlier poems employ the mythical landscape, while in the poems of the second centenary the idealized natural spectacle assumes prominence together with references to history, after which the rugged, solitary landscape – without and within – establishes itself.

3. The *Secretum* and Canzone 119

In the poems after the *frottola* one notes the persistent thematics of life change, of breaking the chains of habit and desire: "ardomi et struggo anchor com'io solia" ("I am still burning and consumed, as I used to be") (112, 3); "et d'antichi desir' lagrime nove / provan com'io son pur quel ch'i' mi soglio" ("and new tears of old desires / show how I am still that which I am accustomed to being") (118, 12–13). As the iterations of this problem intensify, so does the awareness that desire has a range of permutations from the base to the divine. The subject's severance from intractable behaviour patterns is accomplished over time and is manifested in his cultivation of new relationships. Having sundered with the *frottola* the myth of the complacent victim, Petrarch re-enacts the birth of self-consciousness in the subject by articulating two diegetic positions: that of the narrator, who organizes the time frame of the *fictio* into a moral itinerary, and that of the character, a negative exemplum lodged in the past.[51] Thus memory is put into relief, along with the necessary self-consciousness and detachment of the historian. In the first instance this is the personal historian, but it rapidly becomes an exemplum for the collectivity.

The effect of the divergence of personae is to bring into focus the process of life change in a manner not dissimilar to *Familiare* iv, 1, the Ascent of Mont Ventoux. As Petrarch describes the climb up the highest mountain in Provence with his brother Gherardo, the perils of sin stand in stark relief. The interior and external landscapes are superimposed along with the motif of friendship, a crucial metaphor for the religious life. While there are numerous questions about the letter that go beyond the parameters of this study, certainly the archetype of the spiritual journey it presents is analogous to the journey of the *Fragmenta*. Thus it is important to determine how the letter fits chronologically in Petrarch's life. As Martinelli (who dates the letter in 1343) affirms, by the time Petrarch wrote the Ascent his period of spiritual crisis was behind him:

> L'epistola del Ventoso è stata scritta quando già la tempesta che aveva sconvolto la sua anima era stata da tempo sedata. Il poeta ha infatti la calma e la chiarezza di chi sa disporre ordinatamente dei propri fatti e al tempo stesso li contempla con sereno distacco.

> The letter on Mont Ventoux was written when the storm that had disturbed his soul had long since passed. In fact the poet has the calm and clarity of one who knows how to arrange his life events in an orderly manner and at the same time contemplate them with serene detachment.[52]

In short, to base a reading of the Ascent on the dualism of a subject torn between worldliness and the divine is not supported by the text.[53]

Certainly Petrarch fictionalized aspects of the climb, including the discovery by *sortes* of the passage from *Confessions* that catalyses him to look inward.[54] The fictional date of the climb and the letter – 26 April 1336 – is seemingly intended to match the author's age with that of the Augustine of Book 8 of the *Confessions;* this date also marks ten years since Petrarch's departure from the Studio of Bologna, just as Augustine's dating of his "story" marked twelve years since his reading of Cicero's *Ortensio*.[55] In short, it would be foolish to read the Ascent literally: "l'ascesa del Ventoso non è da intendersi *anche* in chiave anagogica ma *esclusivamente* in tale chiave" (the ascent of Mont Ventoux is not to be understood *also* in an anagogical key, but *exclusively* in such a key).[56] Following Billanovich, who persuasively dates the text in 1353 (thus seventeen years after 1336), the retrospective nature of the letter and its syncretic blending of Christian and non-Christian (Seneca, Livy) sources serves to affirm the primacy of memory in Petrarch's world.[57]

The passage in Augustine's *Confessions* that the narrator opens to at the top of Mont Ventoux concerns the role of memory in the contemplative life.[58] It is through the elevation of memory that one inserts oneself in the history of Christian piety, understood as a process based on humility and compassion.[59] To speak of history in this sense calls to mind the early church as a community of like-minded individuals who sought for practical ways to help people lead an ethical life. As seen above, this tangible history, with its implicit marriage of the immanent and transcendent aspects of religious philosophy, is considered by Petrarch in its progression up to the current day, when Franciscanism presents the most compelling model of the ascetic path, first because of the recognized need among the Franciscans to preserve one's experience of the ineffable in secret, and second because of their commitment not to remain content in pure contemplation but to carry their experience of the sacred back to the world, to the active life.

In his reading of the Ascent, Rodney Lokaj dismisses those critics who have erred by placing the religious model of Gherardo above that of Francesco, who, instead of climbing quickly to the top and then falling asleep (as Gherardo did), surveys the (moral) landscape on the way, understanding each of the low hills as a virtue on the allegorical ascent. The state of saintliness arrived at in the "climb" by Francesco is thus comparable to that of his namesake and model, St Francis. Given the attribution of the letter to the 1350s, it is roughly contemporary with the completion of the *Secretum*, and coincides with a very active period in the composition of the *Fragmenta*. Seen in this light, it is imprudent to insist overly on the emulation of Augustine, since Augustinianism and Western monasticism had exaggerated the importance of reaching the "summit" of one's allegorical-mystical climb, and thus of the obligatory message of transcendence. It was rather in the spirit of St Francis to emphasize what could be learned along the way, at every stage of the journey. And it was in the spirit of Francis to understand the contemplative life and the active life as mutually dependent and interpenetrating, not as existing in the customary hierarchy. Lokaj cites Bonaventure's life of St Francis, *Legenda maior*, as a key model for the Ascent, along with Bonaventure's *Itinerarium mentis in Deum*. In that spirit he cites Francis's use of *sortes* and his experiences on the mountain of La Verna as basic to Petrarch's composition of the letter whose addressee is, in fact, a Franciscan from the area near La Verna, the late Dionigi da Borgo San Sepolcro.

A critical way in which Petrarch differs from Augustine concerns the notion of history. The concept of a finality of history that transcended single human events arose with Augustine, who, by way of the *City of God*, dominated the whole medieval age. But this idea – that religious thought was active in the history of the world – was foreign to Petrarch, as it was to antiquity. If the church carried forward the Thomistic notion of the City of God as the "regno sovrasensibile di Dio che verrà alla fine dei giorni" (supersensory realm of God that will come at the end of days), a concept that became the basis for its temporal dominion and politics, in which it absorbed the world, science, and life within itself, Petrarch offered another understanding of the City of God as the church that prepares the living for the eventual state of perfection by subjugating the sinful life and sanctifying the City of Man.[60]

What this means in practice is that Christian piety and charity have supplanted eschatology as the main focus of the theological poet. Rather than a history that is predestined, one has the intervention of the conscience, which possesses its own history, as in the exemplar of St Francis. As Petrarch recalls the blessed scent of the beloved – "quell'*aura soave* che evoca la cristica soavità nel cui tempo sta fors'anche l'*aura doussa* di Provenza" (that "gentle breeze" that evokes the gentleness of Christ in whose time one might also name the "*aura doussa*" [sweet breeze] of Provence) – he layers his text with biblical sources, charting a path in memory towards the sacred.[61] Thus the adjectives "soave" and "dolce," which modernity has secularized, are theologically informed. As the quality and degree of religious experience waned in society, Petrarch scholarship began to neglect the centrality of sacred texts to the *Fragmenta*.[62]

In short, when an artistic practice based on the sacred, including a daily life of prayer and the practice of the Holy Offices, is torn from its pious contexts, there is a rupture in the reception of that work. It is incumbent on readers, therefore, to restore the question of piety to a central position in consideration of the *Fragmenta*.

Petrarch's capacity to speak on behalf of Christian piety is enabled in the first place by the poetic nature of the Bible. Not coincidentally, it is the poetic use of biblical citation that is most present in the *Fragmenta* (in contrast to the more logical, dialectical use of biblical citation found in the prose). Ultimately the authority to speak of Christian piety is guided by the experience of penitence and grace, which, as Augustine attests, is linked to a "language of tears":

> Le lacrime non sono più un fatto fisico, una reazione corporea a un sentimento, non sono pura sensibilità, ma un modo di comunicare, una loquela, un annuncio, dietro il suggerimento del salmo che invoca "... auribus percipe lachrymas meas" ("... percepisci con le orecchie le mie lacrime")
>
> Tears are no longer a physical fact, a bodily reaction to a feeling, they are not pure sensibility, but a way of communicating, a manner of speech, an announcement, behind the suggestion of the Psalm that invokes "... give ear to my cry".[63]

As I have suggested, the mnestic theme is pervasive in the *Fragmenta* and legible in the iteration of key motifs that tie the sequence together and connect it to other works by the author. One of those is the *Secretum*, a set of three dialogues between "Augustinus" and "Franciscus." Fictionally dated in 1343 when the subject is about to turn forty, the *Secretum* was written in 1347 with subsequent corrections made probably in 1349 and 1353.[64] As the title indicates, this work was ostensibly meant to remain "secret." Among the topics discussed are the morality of love poetry, the nature of the cardinal sins (especially pride and sloth), the role of poetry and eloquence in the life of the spirit, and the pursuit of glory. While the two interlocutors bear the names Augustinus and Franciscus, in many respects it is an internal monologue, with Augustinus being the character who embodies "la coscienza più profonda del poeta" (the deeper conscience of the poet).[65]

Petrarch attributes to Augustinus the accounts of his own turning towards God, his view of death, his attitude towards sloth, and his notion of seeing with the mind, even though these views and notions were not Augustine's.[66] The effect is to strengthen Augustinus's position and adapt it to Petrarch's reality.[67] Clearly the text is to be read allegorically as the characters represent the earlier (Franciscus) and later (Augustinus) stages of either man. Their speeches (witnessed by the silent figure of the Truth) amount to a kind of talking therapy that elevates experience and memory over dialectic or doctrine. Augustinus manifests a high level of psychic and affective maturity; Franciscus, in contrast, is a man oppressed by the power of sin who believes in salvation by grace alone (not unlike Augustine). Augustinus's speeches are consistently longer and more persuasive, while those of Franciscus are brief and conventional, as if to reflect an earlier self. The mode of exhortation that is intrinsic to Petrarch's evangelizing voice (as in the *De otio religioso*, also written in 1347) is embodied by Augustinus.

When Augustinus counsels Franciscus to return to Italy and to avoid the solitary life until his problems of sloth and melancholy are resolved (in Book 3), it is clear the decision has been made and acted on by the mature Petrarch; moreover, Augustinus does not make doctrinal, theoretical references to God, but affirms the value of teaching, learning, and prayer.[68] Given the maieutic content, it is not surprising that the dialogues conclude in a spirit of collaboration, with Franciscus vowing to regather the fragments of his soul (with clear reference to the poetic project of the *Fragmenta*):

> Adero michi ipse quantum potero, et *sparsa anime fragmenta recolligam*, moraborque mecum sedulo. Sane nunc, dum loquimur, multa me magnaque, quamvis adhuc mortalia, negotia expectant.

> I will attend to myself as far as I am able. *I will collect the scattered fragments of my soul*, and I will diligently focus on myself alone. But now, even as we speak, many other obligations, though admittedly mortal ones, still await me.[69]

In short, the *Secretum* is not a work of self-admonishment but rather a lively discussion of questions of poetic theology grounded in the expectation that poetry can speak to questions of the eternal through a discourse of the will: "The central concern of the text is not the religious issue of Franciscus's sinfulness or the psychological dilemma of his divided will but rather the problem of defining the will itself as a faculty of interpretation."[70] Since the *Secretum* was written in parallel to certain poems of the *Fragmenta* and shares with them a fictional time frame, it is natural to look for common elements. Early poems that share a common language with the *Secretum* include *Rvf* 35, 36, 41, 42, 43, and 44. More substantive parallels exist with the dialogued canzoni 119 and 264, both of which involve the poetic pursuit of glory, a prospect that Petrarch understood – philosophically and religiously – as being impossible without virtue.[71]

Canzone 119 is an allegory concerning two women, representing Glory and Virtue, who appear to the subject sequentially and represent two stages of worldly attachment and beauty. The date of composition of the 112-line poem is not known; some place it in 1341 on the occasion of Petrarch's coronation while others put it as late as 1347, the year he wrote most of the *Secretum*. The first woman the subject confronts is the earth-bound figure of pulchritude, a woman whose feet the subject embraces, who creates in him the "flames" and "ice" of desire. As the narrator remembers this woman the repeated use of the verb *vedere* focuses the attention on the image and the imagination as the instrument of self-knowledge.

et io, lasso, credendo
vederne assai, tutta l'età mia nova
passai contento, e 'l rimembrar mi giova,
poi ch'alquanto di lei veggi'or piú inanzi.
I' dico che pur dianzi
qual io non l'avea vista infin allora,
mi si scoverse: onde mi nacque un ghiaccio
nel core, et èvvi anchora,
et sarà sempre fin ch'i' le sia in braccio.
  Ma non me 'l tolse la paura o 'l gielo
che pur tanta baldanza al mio cor diedi
ch'i' le mi strinsi a' piedi
per piú dolcezza trar de gli occhi suoi;
et ella, che remosso avea già il velo
dinanzi a' miei, mi disse: – Amico, or vedi
com'io son bella, et chiedi
quanto par si convenga agli anni tuoi. –
– Madonna – dissi – già gran tempo in voi
posi 'l mio amor, ch'i' sento or sí infiammato,
ond'a me in questo stato
altro voler o disvoler m'è tolto. –
Con voce allor di sí mirabil' tempre
rispose, et con un volto
che temer et sperar mi farà sempre: (119, 22–45)

And I, ah woe, believing
I saw much more of her, passed all my youth
Content, and to recall it pleases me
Since I see more in her now than before.
A short time past, I say,
Since I had never seen her until then,
She showed herself to me: whence in my heart
Ice formed, it still remains
And always shall till I am in her arms.
  But neither fear nor chill could hinder me
From bearing such great boldness in my heart
That I pressed near her feet,
To draw a greater sweetness from her eyes:
And she, who had already taken off
The veil from mine, to me said: "Friend, now see
How fair I am, and ask
As much as to your age seems suitable."
"My lady," said I, "long ago in you
I fixed my love, which I feel kindled so
That in this plight, to wish
For other things – or not – is reft from me."
She, in a voice of wondrous timbre, then
Replied, and with a face
That will forever make me fear and hope:

This woman stands for Glory (the pursuit of Franciscus) and inspires a hope that is mixed with fear. In terms of the Old Testament dichotomy between Leah and Rachel, she is like Leah and represents the active life. In contrast, as the soul moves towards Lady Virtue (in line with Augustinus) and confronts the Rachel figure, the hope in question is the theological virtue.[72]

Canzone 119 is rich in biblical references, notably to the Books of Wisdom and Sirach, and to such poets as Cino da Pistoia, Guittone d'Arezzo, Cavalcanti, and Dante, as regards the divinity of this lady of Virtue, identified as a goddess outside of time. I will limit myself to commenting on the ties to Dante, which include his moral canzoni "Tre donne intorno al cor mi son venute" ("Three women have come round my heart") and "Voi che 'ntendendo il terzo ciel movete" ("O you who move the third heaven by intellection") and a series of passages from *Purgatorio* xxx where Beatrice discusses Dante's progress in the journey of love. In that space of the Earthly Paradise, one is in the presence of the same pastoral mode that Petrarch exploits in poem 119 and his Eclogues.[73] The following lines of Beatrice – "Alcun tempo il sostenni col mio volto: / mostrando li occhi giovanetti a lui, / meco il menava in dritta parte vòlto" ("For a time I sustained him with my / countenance: showing him in my youthful eyes, I led / him with me, turned in the right direction") (*Purg.* xxx, 121–3) – are recalled by these lines of Petrarch – "Questa mia donna mi menò molt'anni / pien di vaghezza giovenile ardendo" ("This lady of mine for many years led me – / All filled with burning, youthful urgency") (119, 16–17) . Similarly, the lines "tutta l'età mia nova / passai contento" ("I passed all my youth / Content") (119, 23–4) recall "questi fu tal ne la sua vita nova" ("he was such in his new life") (*Purg.* xxx, 115); and "onde mi nacque un ghiaccio / nel core" ("whence in my heart / Ice formed") (119, 28–9) recalls "lo gel che m'era intorno al cor ristretto" ("the ice that had tightened around my heart") (*Purg.* xxx, 97). As the subject looks upward to see the second, more brilliant woman of Virtue, the reader notes another calque from the Earthly Paradise, where the pilgrim encounters Beatrice:

> Ratto inchinai *la fronte vergognosa*,
> sentendo novo dentro maggior foco; (119, 65–6)
>
> Abashed, I bowed my head immediately,
> And felt a new and greater fire within;

§

> Li occhi mi cadder giù nel chiaro fonte;
> ma veggendomi in esso, i trassi a l'erba,
> tanta *vergogna* mi gravò *la fronte*. (*Purg.* xxx, 76–8)
>
> My lowered eyes caught sight of the clear stream,
> but when I saw myself reflected there,
> such shame weighed on my brow, my eyes drew back

It is not hyperbole that allows the lady of Virtue, who ignites the poet's spirit, to outshine the lady of Glory of the poem's opening line, "Una donna piú bella assai che 'l sole" ("A lady much more lovely than the sun") (119, 1). There is rather a partnership between the two women, as the lady of Glory states: "– [...] ché questa et me d'un seme, / lei davanti et me poi, produsse un parto. –" ("[…] For one birth has produced / Us both from the same seed – her first, then me") (119, 74–5). The transition between the love of beauty, as symbolized by Glory and existing in time, and the divine love of wisdom associated with the laurel tree and standing outside of time, is, in fact, harmonious. It is also obscure, as stated in the envoi (reminiscent of that of Dante's "Voi che 'ntendendo"), and this obscurity is intrinsic to the nature of Virtue:

Canzon, chi tua ragion chiamasse obscura,
di': – Non ò cura, perché tosto spero
ch'altro messaggio il vero
farà in piú chiara voce manifesto.
I' venni sol per isvegliare altrui,
se chi m'impose questo
non m'inganò, quand'io partí' da lui. – (119, 106–12)

Song, to whoever calls your discourse dark,
Say this: "I do not care, for soon I hope
Another messenger will make the truth
More evident, in a much clearer voice.
Just to awaken people did I come
If he who posed this task
Deceived me not when I set forth from him."

The obscurity of canzone 119 is reminiscent of the biblical parables; in order to penetrate it and arrive at its truth, one must consider the provenance of Glory from the same seed as Virtue, and distinguish it from worldly glory – as exposed by Augustinus in the *Secretum* – which only leads to suffering and error. The envoi can only allude to "another messenger," who is not otherwise identified. This prospect fits with Petrarch's idea of a return to an Age of Gold after the long period of Christianity's adulteration (a corruption dramatized in *Rvf* 136–8 and discussed in chapter 4, section 2).[74] In any case, the figuration of the two women will be revisited in poem 206 and given there its ulterior development, still within the archaic mode reminiscent of the *trobar clus*.[75]

Sonnet 122, "Dicesette anni à già rivolto il cielo" ("Seventeen years by now the heavens have rolled"), was written in Parma in April 1344 and marks seventeen years since the enamourment: the "I" figure is forty years old, the point in life, according to classical texts, when youth is over.

This precedent offers the occasion for an expression of diffidence about the changes that come with age:

> Vero è 'l proverbio, ch'altri cangia il pelo
> anzi che 'l vezzo, et per lentar i sensi
> gli umani affecti non son meno intensi:
> ciò ne fa l'ombra ria del grave velo. (122, 5–8)

> The proverb's true that hair will change before
> One's habits do; with slowing sense, no less
> Intense do human feelings grow. In us
> The dread shade of the heavy veil does that.

The "velo" here is once again the mortal body that covers and conceals the immortal soul. These lines are followed by the interjection "Oïmè" and then by two impassioned questions as to when the subject's desire and suffering will end, so he may see, in calm satisfaction and harmony, the face of Laura. One gathers from the poem a sense of detachment from the emotional turmoil and the pursuit of a path forward that can build on the immanence of the senses and the concrete nature of historical experience.[76]

Chapter Four

In fresca riva: Landscape and History (*Rvf* 125–183)

A die ortus usque ad hanc etatem totam vite mee, fabulam dicam an historiam?

My life from the day I was born until now, shall I speak of it as fable or history?

Familiari xix, 3

1. Canzoni 125 to 129

The great canzoni series, *Rvf* 125 to 129, stands at the centre of all the canzoni in the *Fragmenta* and establishes the mediating role of landscape in the development of the book's major themes.[1] As canzoni of "lontananza" (distance from the beloved), the poems establish the means by which the subject will integrate personal history within the larger collective history of the day and the providential history of Christian piety. Within the macrotext, this series marks the eclipse of a dichotomous view in which the subject and Laura are opposed to one another for the sake of a view of them engaged in a common theological pursuit. For this process to be catalysed the two must be separate.

Poems 125 and 126 have almost identical metric schemes and are the only works in the book in which the majority of lines are not hendecasyllables (in poem 125: 62 of 82 lines are septenaries; in 126: 46 of 68 are septenaries), a fact leading to an intensification of rhyme and lyricism. Both are set in bucolic settings, and their codas reflect one another, though their tones are quite opposite. Canzone 125, "Se 'l pensier che mi strugge" ("If that thought melting me") dramatizes the poet's frustrations at attempting to paint a portrait of Laura with words. It is written in a humble style and includes several borrowings from the *Rime petrose* and other allusions to Dante. Here the poet compares himself to a child bursting to speak, despite his lack of protocol or eloquence:[2]

> Come fanciul ch'a pena
> volge la lingua et snoda,
> che dir non sa, ma 'l piú tacer gli è noia,
> cosí 'l desir mi mena
> a dire, et vo' che m'oda
> la dolce mia nemica anzi ch'io moia. (125, 40–5)

> A child who scarcely can
> His tongue unloose or rule,
> Who cannot speak, but tires of keeping still,
> So I'm led by desire,
> To speak, and my sweet foe
> I want to lend me ear before I die.

The acquisition of speech is a metaphor for the poet's quest for solace. The simile of returning to childhood denotes a return to the language of origins and to a landscape in which the primary desire was the desire to speak. The subject's desire to imagine his "sweet enemy" in her absence is comparable to the urgency felt by the child who wishes to speak. In either case the role of ambiguity and uncertainty is essential:

> Cosí nulla se 'n perde,
> et piú certezza averne fora il peggio. (125, 75–6)

> Thus nothing is lost and having
> greater certainty one would be worse off. (T.P.)

If, on a surface level, the "enemy" is Laura, in a deeper sense it is the subject's former self, with the landscape serving to mediate in his process of purification. As Stierle writes of this situation:

> Ciò che restituisce al poeta la voce è il paesaggio. [...] La "verde riva" funge ora da interlocutrice del poeta in sostituzione della donna. Nasce così una nuova comunicazione immaginaria, da cui potrebbe scaturire anche l'energia per una nuova poesia di "sì largo volo" da venire divulgata presso tutti gli amici della poesia, tanto che anche l'amata potrebbe venirne a conoscenza.

> What restores to the poet his voice is the landscape. [...] The "verde riva" now functions as the poet's interlocutor in substitution of the Lady. In this way a new imaginary communication is born, from which might also spring the energy for a new poetry of "such wide-ranging flight" to be divulgated among all the friends of poetry, so that the beloved herself might come to know of it.[3]

Two poems earlier, when Laura had fallen ill, her colourless face had so impressed the lover's heart that it created a pallor on his face as well. The silent colloquy that ensued between the parties set the tone of distance for the canzone series to follow:

> Quel vago impallidir che 'l dolce riso
> d'un'amorosa nebbia ricoperse,
> con tanta maiestade al cor s'offerse
> che li si fece incontr'a mezzo 'l viso.
> Conobbi allor sí come in paradiso
> Vede l'un l'altro [...]
> [...]
> Chinava a terra il bel guardo gentile,
> et tacendo dicea, come a me parve:
> Chi m'allontana il mio fedele amico? (123, 1–6, 12–14)

> That charming loss of color that concealed
> In amorous mist her sweet smile, to my heart
> Was proffered with such majesty that he
> Came forth to greet it in my countenance.
> I knew then how in paradise one sees
> Another; [...]
> [...]
> Her noble gaze was bent on the earth,
> And, keeping silent, said, or so it seemed to me:
> "Who sends my faithful friend away from me?"

This confrontation of internal forces is apparent in canzone 126, "Chiare, fresche et dolci acque" ("Waters clear and cool and sweet"), a poem situated in the same landscape as canzone 125.[4] The famous incipit speaks to Petrarch's acute powers of observation: "Le 'chiare, fresche e dolci acque' sono infatti caratterizzate da attributi che riguardano le loro proprietà di rifrazione e trasparenza secondo i trattati di ottica ..."

(The "Waters clear and cool and sweet" are in fact characterized by attributes that regard their properties of refraction and transparency according to treatises of optics ...).[5] Petrarch's empirical abilities extend to the music of his language, which seems to spring in many cases from his careful listening to the natural environment.[6] Thematically, canzone 126 concerns the experience of time and memory, and how the memory of Laura leads the subject to contemplate his death (a shared theme with canzone 125).[7] While stanzas 1, 2, 4, and 5 concern the subject's epiphanic memories of Laura, in stanza 3 he projects himself into the future to visualize his own death plot, "già terra in fra le pietre" ("already earth Amidst the stones") (126, 34), as gaining Laura's pity. As in canzone 125, the imagination comes alive in the Vaucluse landscape, a liminal space in which the truths revealed in the past will impact the future.[8] Since the dangers the subject confronts include the excesses of thought and moroseness, the motif of renunciation is linked in both poems to a rustic solitude. This will be taken up again in poem 129: "ch'ogni segnato calle / provo contrario a la tranquilla vita" ("for I find every trodden path to be contrary to a tranquil life") (129, 2–3).

Canzoni 127, 128, and 129 were written during Petrarch's second stay in Parma (December 1343–February 1345). The first and third of these are customarily grouped with poems 125 and 126 as pairs of complementary canzoni "di lontananza" based on the lover's separation from the beloved and his constituting of her phantasm in thought. The distancing coincides with the challenge to escape *acedia* (sloth). It is only by a passionate attention to this weakness of complacency and despair that one can defeat this "enemy" and take action in the sphere of history and actuality. That this battle is underway is signified by the narrator's focus on his self-history in the first stanza of poem 127. Since with this canzone one is not only at the centre of the series 125 to 129 but at the numerical centre of all the canzoni (number fifteen of twenty-nine), the question as to whether this poem has found its proper place – "Quai fien ultime, lasso, et qua' fien prime?" ("Which should be last, ah me! and which come first?") (127, 4) – is not without some irony. From these lines one comprehends the arch value of experience in Petrarch's conception:

> In quella parte dove Amor mi sprona
> conven ch'io volga le dogliose rime,
> che son seguaci de la mente afflicta.
> Quai fien ultime, lasso, et qua' fien prime?

Collui che del mio mal meco ragiona
mi lascia in dubbio, sí confuso ditta.
Ma pur quanto l'istoria trovo scripta
in mezzo 'l cor (che sí spesso rincorro)
co la sua propria man de' miei martiri,
dirò, perché i sospiri
parlando àn triegua, et al dolor soccorro. (127, 1–11)

Wherever I am spurred by Love I must
urge on these doleful rhymes, which are
The rag-tag creatures of my troubled mind.
Which should be last, ah me! and which come first?
He who discourses with me of my pain
Leaves me in doubt with his confused advice.
But since I find inscribed with his own hand
Within my heart the history of all
My martyrdom (which often I consult),
I'll speak, because sighs uttered
Declare an armistice and ease my pain.

In his allusion – "sí confuso ditta" ("his confused advice") – to Dante's declaration in *Purgatorio* xxiv that as love "dictates" in his heart so the poet goes "signifying," the Petrarchan subject has grown sanguine (about Love's advice), redoubling his commitment to transcribe in verse the "history of [his] martyrdom" so as to distinguish himself from the man he once was.[9] This is the process Bakhtin labelled as transgredience. By achieving transgredience, the narrator will order his remembrance of Laura with reference to the ordered cosmos around him. In such a way, as he writes from Italy of the distant Laura, the poet prepares a solid foundation for the great historical poem that follows, *Rvf* 128, "Italia mia, benché 'l parlar sia indarno" ("My Italy, though speech may not avail").

Before approaching this marker poem, some context is required. The era of Petrarch's maturity saw the emergence of the Signorie, oligarchies that suppressed the working-class and middle-class movements that had arisen during the age of the Communes. There was warfare across the Italian peninsula as the loyalties of feudal knights gave way to hired mercenaries in the control of *condottieri*. In his response to this reality, Petrarch acquired a stirring political voice, impugning those of his countrymen who tolerated and benefited from the corrupt baronial system. This is the world in which "Italia mia" is set. It is a canzone of extraordinary range whose material extends from the denunciations of the German invaders of Italy, to exhortations to the Lords of Italy to defend the country, to invocations of a religious nature. This range is enabled by the dialogic and interrogative mode of the 122-line poem, in which Petrarch asserts his love for his homeland and the duty of the *signori* (lords) of northern and central Italy to stop fighting one another and to promote works of value and honest study. As he took on this subject, Petrarch determined that history could not be limited to the naturalistic plane. Since history was a place of moral crisis and error, it needed to be informed by theology if the errors of the past and present were genuinely to be overcome.[10]

One can arrive at an overview of "Italia mia" by a gloss of the six proper nouns that dominate the six stanzas. Stanza 1 opens with an apostrophe to *"Italia,"* elevated through a metonymic listing of her parts, after which the poet invokes God ("Rettor del cielo"), beseeching him to look at the condition of Italy and consider the truth of his speech. Stanza 2 addresses the noble lords of Italy, in whom *"Fortuna"* has placed the responsibility to intervene in order to stem the flow of Italian blood over the land. Stanza 3 invokes "Natura," who provided the Alps to shield Italy from Germany: "Ben provide Natura al nostro stato, / quando de l'Alpi schermo / pose fra noi et la tedesca rabbia" ("Nature made good provision for our state, / To set an Alpine shield / Between us and the Germans' ravening") (128, 33–5). This stanza concludes by returning to the fluvial image of stanza 1, now with rivers of blood. Stanza 4 refers by preterition to *"Cesare,"* continuing the Roman theme begun with the reference to Marius – the ancient Roman victor over the Teutons – and the persistent images of bloodletting of the first three stanzas. As stanza 4 concludes, the poet states his intention to speak the truth (recalling his affirmation in the *Collatio* that he would not indulge in fiction or falsehood):

> Io parlo per ver dire,
> non per odio d'altrui, né per disprezzo (128, 63–4)
>
> I speak to make truth plain,
> And not from hate of others or contempt

Bolstered by this commitment, in stanza 5 the civic theme is related to the *"Latin sangue gentile,"* where the image of blood represents the noble race of Italy to be defended at all costs. In the process of a transition from negative to positive, the poet bestows an ethical dimension on his historical discourse with the help of enigmatic phrases and sententia. In stanza 6 he declares his love of his native land and his yielding to "Dio." Yet though God can ordain, man must act, and the possibility of action currently lies in the hands of the lords of Italy, the addressees of the canzone. Should they not act, the shame and humiliation will be theirs; but if they do, their actions could contribute to a more serene life and a cessation of disputes and agony.

Perdio, questo la mente
talor vi mova, et con pietà guardate
le lagrime del popol doloroso,
che sol da voi riposo
dopo Dio spera; et pur che voi mostriate
segno alcun di pietate … (128, 87–93)

By God, may this sometimes
Arouse your minds, and may you look with ruth
Upon the tears of this grief-stricken folk,
Who, save from God, may hope
For no relief unless from you: but if
You'll show some trace of mercy …

In the envoi, which directs the canzone to go and circulate among the haughty elites, one finds the apothegm derived from Terence's statement that "truth procures hatred":

perché fra gente altera ir ti convene,
et le voglie son piene
già de l'usanza pessima et antica,
del ver sempre nemica. (128, 115–18)

For 'midst smug, haughty people you must go
Whose wills are surely full
Of habit infamous and deep ingrained,
Ever the foe of truth.

The structure of "Italia mia" reinforces the connection between the reality of political struggle and the solace that awaits the virtuous.

This is the sense of the poem's ending, "– I' vo gridando: Pace, pace, pace. –" ("I wander crying, 'Peace, Peace, Peace'") (128, 122). Peace awaits one, though one must cry out for it. Standing opposite the theme of piety – the four instances of *pietà* / *pietate* (lines 8, 19, 88, 92) are the most of any poem – is that of hatred – *odio* (lines 53, 64). According to the theology of history expressed in "Italia mia," only those possessing piety and compassion can steer human events towards unity and virtue. In general, as Stierle has concluded, in canzoni 125 to 129 poetry comes to stand for the power of civilization, with the poet as the agent of peace and the founder of a common language.[11]

Rome is the backdrop for Petrarch's political appeal in "Italia mia," as the locus for the glories and *res gestae* of the past and the potential site for the restoration of the institutions, as well as the return of the papacy from its Babylonian captivity. Yet Rome had fallen into a civil war between rival barons; Florence, too, endured civil strife and in 1339–45 fell into a financial crisis as the Bardi and Peruzzi families supported opposite sides in the English-French war. Against this background of conflict, Petrarch projected the ideal of Rome as the God-given home of the church and the natural home of a unified Italian state. Though Petrarch only visited Rome five times (the last being in 1350), the city enjoyed an archetypal place in his thinking. As the Roman thematic was embedded in the lyric sequence, it underwent variations in its representations. But one constant endured: Rome as the just centre of the Catholic church, the place of the martyrdom of St Peter and St Paul.

2. St Peter and the Avignon Church

Just after the verses in which Christ assigns Peter the role of founding the church, "And I will give unto thee the keys of the kingdom of heaven" (Matthew 16:19), Christ forcefully rejects Peter: "Get thee behind me, Satan: thou art an offence unto me: for thou savourest not the things that be of God, but those that be of men" (Matthew 16:23). When he fails to accept Christ's instruction, Peter, who has been invested with the keys of the church, is a stumbling-block to the faith. This side of Peter is seen at the tomb, where only the women understand that Christ has risen. The figure of Peter tells us much about the logic of scandal that lies at the basis of Christianity's reception and diffusion, and its resolution of the problem of earlier religions, which practised ritual sacrifices and legitimized violence by the invocation of a divine mandate.

Peter's denials of Christ, his falling asleep in Gethsemane, and his slow understanding of the nature of the Crucifixion and Resurrection make him an example to Petrarch, for whom the actual experience of love and weeping had served as a precondition to his own spiritual transformation. With his errors of hubris and sloth, Peter the rock (*Pietro / pietra*) becomes a constitutive part of the linguistic imaginary of Petrarch, be it with respect to the disciple's hesitations or his association with the keys of the church. As Petrarch introduces the figure of Christ the maker of men in poem 4, the figures of John and Peter are singled out:

tolse Giovanni da la rete et Piero,
et nel regno del ciel fece lor parte. (4, 7–8)

And John and Peter from their nets he took
And made them citizens of heaven's realm

Through his engagement of the Gospel story, Petrarch limns his own journey to be a citizen in the kingdom of heaven and a follower of Christ. In poem 27, where he sets forward the idea that the seat of the church would return to Italy and to a religion of love, the keys of Peter are those of a disciple and the human institution he represents:

e 'l vicario de Cristo colla soma
de le chiavi et del manto al nido torna,
sí che s'altro accidente nol distorna,
vedrà Bologna, et poi la nobil Roma. (27, 5–8)

Christ's vicar, laden with his keys and cloak
Returns to his own seat; and so, unless
Some misadventure hinders him, he'll view
Bologna first, and then see noble Rome.

Peter is the embodiment of the role of Christianity in bringing an end to the perceived need for violent sacrifice: the Christian God is the God of the victims, just as the Holy Spirit is the defender of victims.[12]

Petrarch, not unlike Dante, saw the current papacy as abusing the sacrosanct charge given to Peter by Christ, as symbolized by the keys of the church. The papacy in Avignon, "Babylon," was a contemporary equivalent to the judges David urged be cast to the stones in Psalms 140:6. As Petrarch wrote to Gherardo, treating the typological meaning of the

Psalms, the *petram* (crag, stone) onto which the judges or rulers are to be cast is the coming Christ: "'Absorpti sunt iuncti petre iudices eorum', sive, uet translatio vetus habet, 'Absorpti sunt iuxta petram iudices eorum'; petra autem, ut novimus, Cristus est" ("'Their judges were cast down over the crag', or to use an ancient version, 'Their judges were cast down before the crag.' The crag, as we know, is Christ …").[13]

The Avignon papacy represented a failure to learn the lesson of Peter's life. Just as the poet sees his own name as an echo of Peter's, he recognizes the need to break from a Satanic church, as in "I'die' in guarda a san Pietro; or non piú, no" ("Saint Peter I put trust in; no more, now") (105, 16). While the major use of *chiavi* refers to the "keys of the heart," as per an established convention, this overlaps with the evangelical association with the keys of Peter. This is seen in poem 27, just cited, and all the poems where a reference to another Peter, Dante's Pier delle Vigne, is present, such as the cited ballata, "Del mio cor, donna, l'una et l'altra chiave / avete in mano" ("Both this and that key, lady, of my heart") (63, 11–12), or the cited poem 91, "ricovrare ambo le chiavi / del tuo cor" ("take back both the keys / Of your own heart") (91, 5–6), in which "ambo" speaks to the inseparability in Peter of the active life and the Christian life.[14] Insofar as Dante's reference in *Inferno* xiii, lines 58 and 59 – "Io son colui che tenni ambo le chiavi / del cor di Federigo, e che le volsi" ("I am the one who guarded both the keys / of Frederick's heart and turned them") is to Matthew 16:19, the theological implication one arrives at in Petrarch's references – which culminate in sonnet 310 – is that without Laura's guidance towards divine virtue, the lowly ecclesiastic Petrarch would have remained mired in sinful exile:

> tornano i piú gravi
> sospiri, che del cor profondo tragge
> quella ch'al ciel se ne portò le chiavi; (310, 9–11)

> the gravest sighs return,
> From my heart's deepest places drawn by one
> Who's borne away with her the keys to heaven.

Petrarch assumed an ethical mission as an emissary of the true church, as seen in his adoption of the name Petrarca (from his father's "Petracco"). He saw his name as an eponym of the saint buried under the main altar of St Peter's, and perhaps containing the word "arca" ("ark"), so as to signify the Ark of Peter.[15] Therefore it is incumbent on the reader to look for the signs of that polysemy and allegory in the verse.[16]

The echoes of Petrarch's Petrine mission are seen in the uses of "p(i)etra" but also in the verb "impetrare" (to petrify, to beseech). The first usage of the verb, in poem 37, has the first meaning and repeats the sense of the fabulous metamorphosis of poem 23, when the "I" character is turned into stone by the Lady and requests internally that she "unstone" him ("Se costei mi s*petra* ..."). Likewise in canzone 37, where the tone is Cavalcantian, the subject inquires why he is not turned to stone. Two usages of "mi spetro" (I grow tender, I "unstone" myself) occur in poems 89 and 105, as if to prepare the alliterative use of "impetrare" (to beseech) in the celebrated scene of the lover imagining his own tomb: "o *pieta*!, / già terra in fra le *pietre* / vedendo, Amor l'inspiri / in guisa che sospiri / sí dolcemente che mercé m'*impetre*" ("oh how pitiful! – / See me already earth / Amidst the stones. And thus / Love inspire her so / That sweetly sighing, she will win me grace") (126, 33–7). Then when the impetration does not occur, the subject is led to act independently and renounce his past weaknesses and guilt – "da madonna i' non impetro / l'usata aita" ("from my lady I do not / Receive accustomed aid") (207, 4–5). The last, proleptic use of the verb concerns Laura's heavenly prayer on behalf of the subject:

> Sol un conforto a le mie pene aspetto:
> ch'ella, che vede tutt'i miei penseri,
> m'impetre grazia, ch'i' possa esser seco. (348, 12–14)

> One solace only for my woes I wait:
> That she who looks upon my every thought
> Will gain me grace so I can be with her.

Petrarch's considerable derivations from the *Rime petrose* tend to distribute the epithets pertaining to Dante's woman of stone between the Petrarchan subject and Laura. In any case, the "petroso" register of harshness and impenetrability is concentrated in the first third of the *Fragmenta*. In addition, the hardness of stone relates to Peter, who must be chastized by Christ, and to the locus of stone – the Vaucluse – where the subject cultivated the practice of contemplation and renounced profane love, well in advance of the death of Laura. This latter realization should discourage once and for all the notion that Laura's death was the decisive event causing the subject's life to change. To argue as much, writes De Robertis, is to ignore the "sostanziale non-stilnovismo" (essential non-Stilnovism) of Petrarch.[17]

The Petrine theme comes to a head in poems 135 to 138. The first of this tetrad, "Qual piú diversa et nova" ("The strangest, rarest thing"), employs the image of the stone (*petra, scoglio*) to signify the pitiless cruelty of the Lady amidst a catalogue of marvels that denote her superiority to the subject. Archaic and obscure in its style, the canzone recalls the heavily rhymed *frottola* (which also has six fifteen-line stanzas, though *Rvf* 135 has a coda) and has a high frequency of septenaries (40 per cent of the total). Each of the stanzas presents a fabulous or exotic allegorical image for Laura. These are: the phoenix; the magnetic stone (*petra*); the catoblepas that kills with its eyes; a fountain that boils in the night but is cool in the day; a fountain that ignites unlit torches and extinguishes the lit; and two more fountains, one of which is normal and one which causes those who drink from it to die laughing.

In stanza 2, one reads of the legendary power of magnetic stone (*petra*) to pull the iron nails from sailing ships. The idea (of Ptolemy, then Albertus Magnus) that magnetic stones had the power to sink ships is converted into a simile, so that Laura is the magnet – "petra" ("stone"), "scoglio" ("reef"), "calamita" ("lodestone") – that attracts the heart of the lover, leaving him split in two, like the ship deprived of its nails. As Claudia Berra writes,

> I due protagonisti dell'azione si alternano frequentemente nei ruoli sintattici di soggetto e oggetto; la struttura del periodo riproduce così il rapporto fra potere attrattivo e possibilità di essere attratto che caratterizza tanto la coppia "minerale" quanto quella umana.

> The two protagonists of the action frequently alternate in their syntactic roles of subject and object; the structure of the sentence thus reproduces the relation between attractive power and the possibility of being attracted that characterizes the "mineral" as well as the human pairing.[18]

There is, in other words, a reciprocity between the subject and Laura; despite their lack of parity in the current situation, they are joined by a common destiny:

> cosí l'alm'à sfornita
> (furando 'l cor che fu già cosa dura,
> et me tenne un, ch'or son diviso et sparso)
> un sasso a trar piú scarso
> carne che ferro. (135, 24–8)

A stone's thus reft my soul
(Stealing my heart that was a solid thing,
And kept me whole, who now am split and strewn) –
A stone more avid to
Draw flesh than iron.

The coda of this arduous and "polyptychal" canzone leaves behind the paradoxical logic of the stanzas and returns to a concrete, contemplative setting, beneath the "gran sasso" ("great stone") of the Vaucluse. One can conclude that the poem's pursuit of extravagant similes ("diversa et nova cosa") to compare to the subject's state of unhappiness is concluded in the sirma of the final stanza, where he compares the increased flow of the Sorgue River in spring to his increased tears, due to the weight of memory. With the Vaucluse landscape already in place, the coda proceeds in strict detachment from the stanzas, signalling a change in the relationship. If the stanzas reiterated the subject's suffering and Laura's stone-like cruelty, now he can only be seen by Amor and is dedicated to the solitary life. As Berra suggests, *Rvf* 135 is the most suitable marker of the halfway point in Part 1. The archaic text is distinctly non-mimetic and asks the reader to interpret its symbols. Here, I would argue, the stoniness of the woman stands to signify her participation in the winnowing of the heart's desire. This is consistent with the coda in which the subject has returned from the world of legend to the solitary reality of the Vaucluse: "Sotto un gran sasso / in una chiusa valle, ond'esce Sorga, / si sta" ("By a great stone, / Within a closed vale where Sorgue springs, he bides") (135, 92–4).

This locale is the suitable vantage point for the Avignonese sonnets that follow, *Rvf* 136 to 138, a series marked by linguistic violence and an attack on the current papacy. Here Petrarch projects a world view in which politics and prophecy are integrated and linked to the themes of sacred and profane love. Avignon is presented as the anti-Rome, a perversion of the great mission of Peter and Paul, martyred in Rome. As a group these poems concern the theological argument of the two cities, Babylon and Jerusalem, as Petrarch reads of it in Augustine's discussion of Psalm 136.[19] Poem 136 (perhaps the number is not coincidental!) begins by continuing with the flame imagery of canzone 135, where the eating of acorns concerns a bygone age:

Fiamma dal ciel su le tue treccie piova,
malvagia, che dal fiume et da le ghiande

per l'altrui impoverir se' ricca et grande,
poi che di mal oprar tanto ti giova
[...]
Già non fostù nudrita in piume al rezzo,
ma nuda al vento, et scalza fra gli stecchi:
or vivi sì ch'a Dio ne venga il lezzo. (136, 1–4, 12–14)

Let flame from heaven upon your tresses rain,
Malign one; you ate nuts and drank from brooks,
But now from others' ruin grow rich and grand
For doing evil deeds so profits you.
[...]
Indeed, you were not reared in shady ease
But naked to the wind, barefoot 'midst thorns.
Now you live so, the stench must rise to God!

The low mimetic register suits the stench of the Avignon papacy, as the concluding lines recall St Peter's violent invective in *Paradiso* xxvii, one of Dante's most forceful polemics against the corruption of the church, an excoriation that includes the Avignon papacy. As the inverse fortunes of the past and present are dramatized, a key element is the question of virtuous work. The "mal oprar" ("evil deeds") (136, 4) of the current papacy are contrasted with the wise moral leadership of "l'opre antiche" ("deeds of old") (137, 14), as the earlier state of well-being suggests both the Age of Gold and the New Testament, as evident in the allusion to the Beatitudes:

Anime belle et di virtute amiche
terranno il mondo; et poi vedrem lui farsi
aurëo tutto, et pien de l'opre antiche. (137, 12–14)

Then worthy souls and friends of virtue shall
Inherit earth; then shall we see it made
All golden, filled with honest deeds of old.

Then, in contrast to that setting in which the faithful are involved in good works, poem 138 denounces the living hell of the Avignonese papacy, assigning the Curia to "il mondo tristo" ("that living hell") (138, 14) of sin.[20] The poet's anger is not a personal one, but akin to that of St Francis in his struggle to reform the church and return it to its rightful mission:

> Per un'anima cristiana come la sua, il rimedio a tale situazione non poteva venire, certamente, da un ritorno alla realtà storica precristiana, per quanto idealmente questa potesse essere immaginata. I riferimenti all'ira di Dio, a Cristo, alla povertà iniziale della chiesa, alla donazione di Costantino, che abbondano nei sonetti, fanno intravvedere, piuttosto, una soluzione di tipo dantesco e francescano.

> For a Christian soul like his, the remedy for such a situation certainly could not come from a return to the pre-Christian historic reality, however much this could be imagined ideally. The references to the wrath of God, to the initial poverty of the church, to the Donation of Constantine, that abound in the sonnets allow one to see there instead a solution of a Dantesque and Franciscan sort.[21]

Far from being exorbitant poems that depart from the canonical and monolinguistic Petrarch, the series *Rvf* 135 to 138 serves to broaden the canzoniere genre in line with the "vario stile" announced in poem 1. *Rvf* 135, the obscure "canzone of the similes," reinforces the archaic register that was seen in the *frottola* and that will recur in canzone 206, while the Avignon sonnets stress the destiny of the Church of Rome and the need to focus on good works and virtuous actions within the human community. Given the biblical and archaic character of the poems discussed in this section, written under the sign of Peter, it is prudent to recall that the Bible itself is a book of fragments, heterogeneous in style, blending passages of sacred ire, bold prophecy, and intense lyricism.

3. Antithesis and Parallelism

In *Familiari* ii, 9 (probably composed between 1351 and 1353), Petrarch writes to Giovanni Colonna, who had seemingly misunderstood the poet's attachment to fiction and literature, finding it in conflict with his faith and dedication to Augustine:

> Dicis me, non modo vulgus insulsum, sed celum ipsum fictionibus tentare; itaque Augustinum et eius libros simulata quadam benivolentia complexum, re autem vera a poetis et philosophis non avelli. Quid autem inde divellerer, ubi ipsum Augustinum inherentem video? quod

nisi ita esset, nunquam libros *De civitate Dei*, ut reliqua sileam, tanta philosophorum et poetarum calce fundaret, nunquam tantis oratorum ac historicorum coloribus exornaret.

You say that I have been fooling not only the stupid multitude with my fictions but heaven itself. You maintain, then, that I have embraced Augustine and his books with a certain amount of feigned goodwill, but in truth have not torn myself away from the poets and philosophers. Why should I tear asunder what I know Augustine himself clung to? If this were not so, he would never have based his *City of God*, not to mention other books of his, on so large a foundation of philosophers and poets, nor would he have adorned them with so many colours of orators and historians.[22]

Herein lies a fundamental point about the value of letters in the religious life. Whether in the phase of contemplation, worship, or teaching, the religious person is assisted by rhetoric.[23] It is clear that Augustine's example was vital to Petrarch in a literary and spiritual sense; the patterns of narrativity of the *Fragmenta* are often analogous to those of the *Confessions* and, as Iliescu notes, Petrarch's use of antithesis closely resembles that of Augustine: "sia che si tratti di forme nominali, verbali oppure aggettivali, esse si riferiscono sempre a stati d'animo" (whether it's a question of nominal, verbal or adjectival forms, they always refer to states of mind).[24] Petrarchan antithesis thus reveals the subject's ongoing struggle with worldliness and sinfulness, a struggle that proceeds in a positive direction because of the labour of learning and knowledge.[25]

Developed by Petrarch as part of his poetic system, oxymoron and antithesis serve to soften extremes and neutralize polarities, and ultimately point to something beyond themselves, to serenity and quietude.[26] As rhetorical commonplaces or *topoi* they are comparable to the classic enthymeme, as they juxtapose two contrary conditions.[27] They do not serve as emblems of a subject/object dualism or, even worse, an irreconcilable psychic split. Rather, in Petrarch's system, such oppositions are a part of a morphological scheme in which binary terms are not static but productive, usually giving rise to a middle term.[28] If one recalls, for example, Pietro Bembo's canonical division of Petrarch's style into the "piacevole" (pleasant) and the "grave" (grave), more often than not in the *Fragmenta* the two registers are seen to interpenetrate. Beyond the purely "piacevole" or "grave," there is a larger semiotic system. If in the natural language of logic semantic values and attributes tend to be fixed and invariable, in the lyric language of the *Fragmenta* there exists a broad connotative range of semantic variation and ambiguity. Thus in the celebrated incipit below, the middle term that arises is neither "love" nor "not love." By taking the form of a question, the antithesis mediates between the states of mind (or hypotheses) presented, attenuating the apparent crisis in the subject:

> S'amor non non è, che dunque è quel ch'io sento?
> ma s'egli è amor, perdio, che cosa et quale? (132, 1–2)

> If it isn't love, then what is it I feel?
> But dear God, if love it is, what is it and how?

Let us consider the antithetical pairing *dolce / amaro* (sweet / bitter), which occurs fourteen times in the *Fragmenta*. What is the structural and aesthetic import of such a pairing? In ordinary communication in the natural language, the rules of logic and common sense prohibit the identification of semantic opposites: something is either bitter or sweet. But in the language of poetry, the synonymy and antonymy of two terms is possible. In some poems, *dolce* = *amaro*, but when viewed across the span of the work, *dolce* ≠ *dolce* and *amaro* ≠ *amaro* are also possible.[29] The binary terms *dolce* and *amaro* (but also *dolce* and *acerbo* [sour, unripe]) do not possess semantic univocality but attach to median areas of affective meaning. By softening the extremes of an opposition, antithesis and oxymoron become figures of neutralization:

> Cosí sol d'una chiara fonte viva
> move 'l dolce et l'amaro ond'io mi pasco;
> una man sola mi risana et punge; (164, 9–11)

> Thus from one single fountain, living, clear,
> Do sweet and bitter flow on which I'm fed;
> One single hand restores and pierces me.

In a study of Petrarchan parallelism and pluralities, Dámaso Alonso has charted their frequency in the sonnets of each phase of the collection. For Alonso a plurality is a parallel series of beings that have some characteristic in common. The ebb and flow of pluralities contribute to a "biological" order that links the technical progression to psychological factors.[30] The pattern of "pluralities of actions" starts as a "modest and timid" innovation and is then followed by a radical increase of bravura or stylistic extravagance. The heaviest concentration of pluralities and correlations is found in the second centenary, especially in the poems after canzoni 124 to 129: "Il secondo centinaio del *Canzoniere*, in confronto col primo, rappresenta un accrescimento enorme, dalla semplicità alla complessa artificiosità" (the second centenary of the *Canzoniere*, in comparison to the first, represents an enormous increase, from simplicity to complex artificiality); and "Petrarca ha sentito allora con entusiasmo il messaggio estetico di uno stile composito, frequentemente contrastato, dove s'incalzano, in dualità e plurimembrazioni, le immagini o gli esseri reali" (Petrarch then felt with enthusiasm the aesthetic message of a composite, frequently contrastive style, in which images or real beings clashed in dualities and plurimembrations).[31] In the third and fourth centenaries one sees a consolidation of the style with a toning down of the bi- and multi-membral parallelisms, yielding a more mature and serene aesthetics.[32]

In discussing poems 136 to138 I noted how these sonnets were structured around the antithesis between the purity and innocence of the early church and the baseness and corruption of current Christendom. In sonnet 139 this providential theme is engaged again by use of antithesis. Addressing his friends in a moving allusion to Italy, "o dolce schiera amica" ("O my sweet company of friends") (139, 2), Petrarch compares his life to that of Gherardo; he is in exile in a figurative Egypt in contrast to Gherardo's Jerusalem. By way of the allegorical imagery of exile and salvation, a connection is made with the previous sonnets, establishing the need for a personal and religious response to the political and secular crisis.

  I' da man manca, e' tenne il camin dritto;
i' tratto a forza, et e' d'Amore scorto;
egli in Ierusalem, et io in Egipto.
  Ma sofferenza è nel dolor conforto;
ché per lungo uso, già fra noi prescripto,
il nostro esser insieme è raro et corto. (139, 9–14)

  I took the left-hand, he the straight road held,
I, dragged by force, and he led forth by Love;
He to Jerusalem; to Egypt I.
  Endurance, though, brings comfort in my woe,
For by long custom once between us fixed,
Our meetings are infrequent, and are brief.

As was clear in the *De otio*, the direct path taken by Gherardo was not the appropriate choice for Francesco, for whom the experience of error and the eventual return carried valuable lessons: "Ma sofferenza è nel dolor conforto" ("Endurance [...] brings comfort in my woe") (139, 12).

The admission of *acedia* in poem 141, caused by the loss of the love object, coincides with the recognized passivity of the soul; yet in the recognition is the pathway out of despair:

> e chi discerne è vinto da chi vòle.
> E veggio ben quant'elli a schivo m'ànno,
> e so ch'i' ne morrò veracemente,
> ché mia vertú non pò contra l'affanno; (141, 8–11)

> Who judges is o'erthrown by one who wills.
> I see, indeed, how they're avoiding me;
> In truth, I know that I shall die from it,
> Because my strength cannot withstand the pain;

To counter the lassitude and lethargy of the soul, the subject must bolster his powers of discernment and "vertú" ("strength"). Against the image of sloth, one has the germ of a resistance on the part of "chi vòle" ("one who wills"), the will being the essence of the Augustinian interiority that waits to be vindicated.[33]

Sestina 142, "A la dolce ombra de le belle frondi" ("Toward the sweet shadow of those lovely fronds"), concerns the subject's positive pathway towards virtue and faith.[34] This poem, which immediately preceded canzone 264 in the Correggio form, is laden with imagery suggestive of the Passion and Canto I of *Inferno*, and represents a positive resolution to the sylvan predicament discussed in chapter 2, section 1. Given the helical repetition of its six end words, the sestina tends to replicate the cyclicity of natural time; that effect is accentuated here by the presence of "tempo" among the end words (a word that only rhymes with itself in the *Fragmenta*). In the passage of natural time one perceives the inexorable principle of change – "Selve, sassi, campagne, fiumi et poggi, / quanto è creato, vince et cangia il tempo" ("Forests, stones, fields, rivers and hills, / all that is created, time changes and vanquishes") (142, 25–6) – in response to which the subject chooses to embark on "another path," with the six iterations of "altro" confirming that positive change is underway:

Tanto mi piacque prima il dolce lume
ch'i passai con diletto assai gran poggi
per poter appressar gli amati rami:
ora la vita breve e 'l loco e 'l tempo
mostranmi *altro sentier* di gire al cielo
ed di far frutto, non pur fior' et frondi.
*Altr'*amor, *altre* frondi et *altro* lume,
altro salir al ciel per *altri* poggi
cerco, ché n'è ben tempo, et *altri* rami. (142, 31–9)

At first, I was so pleased by that sweet light
That with delight I crossed enormous hills
Just to be nearer those beloved boughs,
but now my brief life, and the place and season
Direct me to another path to heaven,
To bring forth fruit, not merely flowers and fronds.
Another love, *other* leaves, *another* light,
another ascent to heaven do I seek, upon *other*
hills and *other* branches, for the time is nigh.

With the line "ed di far frutto, non pur fior' et frondi" (142, 36), the narrator has entered into a new spiritual terrain distinguished by the potentiality of grace.[35]

The anniversary poem 145 marks fifteen years since the 1327 enamourment; coming after poems 118 (sixteen years) and 122 (seventeen years), it is one of only two anniversary poems out of chronological order (the other is poem 266). Such anomalies make it clear that the time of the narration (*récit*) remains distinct from that of the narrated (*histoire*). In fact, this sonnet seems to recall the intense relation to the landscape (and the move from Avignon to Vaucluse) of the twelve sonnets assigned to 1342 (*Rvf* 107–18), but retrospectively, as the subject lists a series of antitheses concerning his place in the universe, affirming that he will remain the man he has been – "libero spirto" ("a spirit free") – and accept his fate.[36]

ponmi in cielo, od in terra, od in abisso,
in alto poggio, in valle ima et palustre,
libero spirto, od a' suoi membri affisso;
ponmi con fama oscura, o con ilustre:
sarò qual fui, vivrò com'io son visso,
continüando il mio sospir trilustre. (145, 9–14)

Set me in heaven, in earth, or the abyss,
On lofty hills or in low, marshy vales,
A spirit free, or held fast to its limbs;
Give me repute obscure, or great renown,
I shall be what I was, live as I have,
While I continue my trilustral sighs.

In sonnet 148, lines 1 to 6, one has a list of twenty-three rivers and five species of trees that are contrasted to the Sorgue and the laurel: the river whose sound and the tree whose shade offer the necessary solace for contemplation.[37] The "fresca riva" ("cool bank") is a safe dwelling place for the laurel and the one who planted it; it is a place for self-renewal immune from the ravages of time. In the sonnet's conclusion one has a concise affirmation in the form of a prayer

Così cresca il bel lauro in fresca riva,
et chi 'l piantò pensier' leggiadri et alti
ne la dolce ombra al suo de l'acque scriva. (148, 12–14)

May that fair laurel grow on this cool bank,
And in its sweet shade he who planted it
Where waters sound write down high, graceful thoughts.

The prosaic awareness of the world evident in the empirical references, including the lists of rivers and trees, is an example of Petrarch's giving weight to the syntagmatic axis of language, of his using the interaction with the landscape to chart the narrator's progress, internally and with respect to his engagement of reality:[38]

> [T]he point is not – to *be* in the world and to have significance in it, but – to be *with* the world, to observe it and to experience it again and again [...]. Love undergoes [...] an appropriate modification in kind, by associating *not* with the "laurel," but with other values, appropriate to that context.[39]

By stepping forward *qua* writer and penitent the narrator gains outsidedness with respect to the events of the past and is better able to attest to the veracity of experience. This transition is salient in the latter poems of Part 1, in which the laurel imagery has lost its Daphnean and Ovidian associations and acquired an overtly Christic identification.[40]

Rvf 150 to 205 constitute a dazzling and uninterrupted series of sonnets between ballata 149 and canzone 206. In addition to the specular and self-reflective quality present in the earlier sonnet series, *Rvf* 63 to 79, in these fifty-six sonnets one finds a maieutic regard for the reader, who is directed along the same path of growth and learning as the subject. Given the formal and thematic cohesiveness of the series, one is able to cultivate a sensitivity to the prominence given to the act of writing, as seen in the conclusion of poem 151, where the narrator notes how the figure of Amor reveals Laura's beauty uniquely to him:

> Indi mi mostra quel ch'a molti cela,
> ch'a parte entro a' begli occhi leggo
> quant'io parlo d'Amore, et quant'io scrivo. (151, 12–14)

> What he conceals from many, there he shows
> To me, for bit by bit in her fair eyes
> I read all that I say and write of Love.

The motif of Laura's eyes dominates sonnets 154 to 160, with the quartet of poems 155 to 158 centred on weeping and on the eyes as the seat of tears: "occhi sede di pianto."[41] Following logically upon this quartet, poem 159 posits the exemplarity and celestial origins of Laura's beauty, which serves as a point of departure in the construction of a complex Neoplatonic idea:

> In qual parte del ciel, in quale ydea
> era l'exempio, onde Natura tolse
> quel bel viso leggiadro, in ch'ella volse
> mostrar qua giú quanto lassú potea?
> Qual nimpha in fonti, in selve mai qual dea,
> chiome d'oro sì fino a l'aura sciolse? (159, 1–6)

> In which of heaven's parts, in what idea
> Was that original whence Nature took
> The lovely, graceful face, by which she wished
> To show, down here, what could be done above?
> What fountain-nymph or goddess in the woods,
> Lets hair of such pure gold stray in the breeze?

In what "idea" was the exemplar born?[42] What model did nature employ to make the face of Laura? Through this questioning one arrives at the existence of a scale of beings in which the idea of Laura stands above her soul, which in turn stands above her body (as present in the metonymic paranomasia "chiome d'oro sì fino a *l'aura* sciolse"). In response to the questions of the octave, in the sestet Laura's beauty is confirmed as unexcelled such that the power of her figure and gaze enables a transformation in those who see her and come to realize the destructive and restorative powers of Amor:

> non sa come Amor sana, et come ancide,
> chi non sa come dolce ella sospira,
> et come dolce parla, et dolce ride. (159, 12–14)

> Nor knows he how Love cures, nor how he kills,
> If he knows not the way she sweetly sighs,
> The way she sweetly speaks and sweetly laughs.

There is no despair or anguish in the knowledge of this power; there is only the radiant splendour of the Lady's celestial virtues. Part of the archaic charm of this sonnet is carried by its *hapaxes* "idea" and "nimpha," and by the keyword "exempio," which links this poem to the final poem, canzone 366: "Vergine sola al mondo senza exempio" ("O Virgin peerless, in the world unique") (366, 53). The negative assertion "non sa come Amor sana, et come ancide" (159, 12) concerns those who do *not* know the powers of love. The line is a calque of Guittone d'Arezzo's "a lei ch'aucide e sana / lo meo cor sovente" ("to her who often slays and heals my heart"), referring to the sword of Peleus that wounds and heals its victims.[43] The ennobling focus on this knowledge fits with its engagement of the *plazer* form, which provides a list of the wondrous virtues of the Lady.[44]

The next three poems are exclamatory in tone, forming a suite around the theme of earthly and divine beauty, as that same theme was addressed in the *Secretum*. Sonnet 160, "Amor et io sí pien' di meraviglia" ("Full of amazement are both Love and I"), concerns the difficulty of writing the history of a suffering that is ongoing. Sonnet 161, "O passi sparsi, o pensier' vaghi et pronti" ("O scattered steps, O longing thoughts alert"), features thirteen uses of the interjection "O," reinforcing the vocatives that surround the subject's misfortune, as designated in the final line: "deh ristate a veder quale è 'l mio male" ("Ah pause to see what my misfortune is!") (161, 14).[45] And poem 162, "Lieti fiori et felici, et ben nate herbe" ("You joyous, happy flowers, well-favored grass"), concludes the triad of exclamatory poems on a positive note by apostrophizing the Lady, listing her marvellous qualities, and declaring the subject's envy of the water where she bathes and the landscape that surrounds her.

In sonnet 166 Petrarch states his reasons for being a vernacular poet. The counterfactual hypothesis – constructed on the antithesis between the classical languages and Italian – states that if he had persisted in writing Latin poetry, Florence would have its "poeta," as do the home cities of Catullus, Virgil, and Caio Lucilio (an originator of Italian satire). The antithesis is supported by imagery drawn from the worlds of classical and vernacular verse, the "sasso" of Delphi and the "campo" of Petrarch:

S'i' fussi stato fermo a la spelunca
là dove Apollo diventò profeta,
Fiorenza avria forse oggi il suo poeta,
non pur Verona et Mantoa et Arunca;
ma perché 'l mio terren piú non s'ingiunca
de l'humor di quel sasso, altro pianeta
conven ch'i' segua, et del mio campo mieta
lappole et stecchi co la falce adunca.
L'oliva è secca, et è rivolta altrove
l'acqua che di Parnaso si deriva,
per cui in alcun tempo ella fioriva.
Cosí sventura over colpa mi priva
d'ogni buon fructo, se l'etterno Giove
de la sua gratia sopra me non piove. (166, 1–14)

If staunchly I'd remained within that cave –
There where to prophecy Apollo turned –
Its bard, perhaps, would Florence have today,
Not just Verona, Mantua, Arunca;
But as my soil grows no more rushes from
The moisture of that stone, some planet else
Must I pursue, and from my field must mow
The thorns and thistles with my crooked scythe.
The olive tree is sere, and elsewhere turned
That water – from Parnassus once drawn off –
By which it flourished in a time gone by.
Just so will my bad fortune or my guilt

Strip me of every worthy fruit unless
Eternal Jove rain down his grace on me.

The choice to write in the vernacular is viewed in such a way that "the text [...] represents proairesis itself, the author's program of options and the generic differences to be expected from the choice."[46] Since the once universal poetry no longer receives water from its classical sources, a new linguistic terrain must be cleared and cultivated. Following this logic, the dualistic structure of the antithesis (Latin versus vernacular Italian) is mediated by a third element, the adherence to a natural language (and the recognition that Latin was itself once a vernacular).[47] The linguistic complexity of the sonnet is apparent in the toponyms and unusual vocabulary (as in the three *hapaxes* of "*lappole* et stecchi co la *falce adunca*" [166, 8]). In the sestet one sees that the olive, a symbol of peace and poetry, is in need of water; this leads the poet, who naturally identifies with the olive, to pray for the rain of grace.

In poem 172 Laura is impugned for her envy. The seemingly innocent question as to how envy entered into Laura's breast is ironic, as the sonnet recalls other moments that spoke of Laura's negative qualities, in which the virtues and vices are allegorized. This was seen already in the *frottola*: "et in donna amorosa anchor m'aggrada, / che 'n vista vada altera et disdegnosa, / non superba et ritrosa" ("And in a loving lady still I'm pleased / When hauteur and disdain show in her face, / Not pride and bashfulness") (105, 8–10); "Amor et Gelosia m'ànno il cor tolto, / e i segni del bel volto") ("Both Love and Jealousy have seized my heart / As have the lodestars of / Her fair face") (105, 69–70). And it will be again in the discussion below of canzone 206, as it is typically the archaic Petrarch who wields this irony with salutary effects, for in distinguishing the self from the Other the subject establishes his own integrity.

O Invidia nimica di vertute,
ch'a' bei principii volentier contrasti,
per qual sentier cosí tacita intrasti
in quel bel petto, et con qual' arti il mute? (172, 1–4)

O envy, virtue's foe, one who to fair
Beginnings is so eagerly opposed,
Along what ways into that fair breast did
You, silent, steal? Or change it with what arts?

In the conclusion of poem 173 the narrator ("soul") splits from the character ("heart") and repents; having seen the duplicity of Eros, the soul initiates a militant self-distancing from the amorous entrapment:

> ma pochi lieti, et molti penser' tristi,
> e 'l piú si pente de l'ardite imprese:
> tal frutto nasce di cotal radice. (173, 12–14)

> Few are its joyous, many its sad thoughts;
> Its daring deeds it most of all repents;
> From such a root does fruit like this spring forth.

Coming roughly in the middle of the series of fifty-six continuous sonnets, poem 175 is a marker poem in which the chiasmus of the opening and closing lines fixes the date of the enamourment in the remote past with respect to the current time, when Laura's "sun" warms the subject at the hour of vespers (instead of burning him). That change occurs as the figure of Amor outgrows its earlier, imprisoning form, so that in subsequent poems it is elevated to a potential figure of *caritas*.

As the traces of the amorous phantasm are rooted out, the lover ceases being Amor's enemy. Standing at the vertex of the overall parabola of 366 poems, sonnet 183 objectifies the amorous condition and relates the sadness of love to the problem of inconstancy; in so doing, it steps beyond the welter of debilitating emotions:

> Però s'i' tremo, et vo col cor gelato,
> qualor veggio cangiata sua figura,
> questo temer d'antiche prove è nato.
> Femina è cosa mobil per natura
> ond'io so ben ch'un amoroso stato
> in cor di donna picciol tempo dura. (183, 9–14)[48]

> Thus, if I shiver, walk with frozen heart
> At those times when I see her shape transformed,
> That terror has been born from ancient trial.
> By nature, woman is a fickle thing;
> So I know well that any amorous state
> Will not endure long in a woman's heart.

The verses are misogynistic ("femina" is a *hapax*), but their substance lies in the recognition that the enemy is to be found in oneself, not in the love object. Without recognizing one's own inconstancy, one remains trapped in the false happiness of the Epicureans.[49] The gradual expansion of the role of Amor includes a diversification of its roles and implications for the spiritual life. As we have seen, Amor has been a companion to sinfulness, enslaving the character with its arrows; it now facilitates a higher love by enabling the image of the beloved to be planted in the subject's heart where it can evolve from the status of a phantasm into an image of purity and chastity.[50]

In the poems examined in this chapter a contrast was established between the author-narrator's writerly self-awareness and the recollections of his character's entrapment. In the ostensible pursuit of reason and probity, the poet's style grows more decorous and ornate, seemingly more "Petrarchist." Yet, as was shown in the study of antithesis and parallelism, these tropes exceed their conventional usage so as to lend support to the subject's impetus to change and his dynamic approach to the temporality of the lived calendar, as if in the "effort to objectify chronicle time."[51]

Chapter Five

The Penitent Lover (*Rvf* 184–263)

que enim apud vulgus mors est, apud philosophos mortis est finis.

yet what is death for the multitude is the end of death for philosophers

Fam. xvi, 5

1. The Fading Myth of Daphne

In chapter 4 we saw emerge a history of the subject who foregrounded the act of writing by documenting his past and affirming the ethically constructive nature of poetry. In the desire to narrate was discovered a source of the sacred, a spiritual quality intrinsic to the act of self-disclosure. In my analysis of the poet's use of antithesis, I showed how this trope belied the stereotype of psychological inertia and became a source of eurhythmic harmony. So, too, the use of parallelism was seen to bring into focus the problematic of desire and the will, mitigating the presence of binary oppositions in the psyche. In these and other aspects of the poet's operation, there is an intensive focus on the poetic message itself or what Jakobson referred to as the poetic function of language.[1] Giorgio Orelli writes in this regard (citing Baudelaire) of the "deep rhetoric" at work in the *Fragmenta* resulting from the inseparability of signifieds and signifiers, of syntax and semantics, in constituting the Petrarchan style.

There is perhaps no clearer example of Petrarch's engagement of the poetic function than his manipulation of the terms related to Amor, Laura, and the laurel. As the internal life of the spirit assumes a greater role in the second half of the *Fragmenta*, these figures will themselves evolve in parallel with the subject. The transitions in question take place formally and thematically, through the use of narrative and, when necessary, the inenarrable.[2] As one embarks on the second half of the sequence, the figure of Amor is confronted as the cause of much suffering and "vane speranze" ("vain hopes"), echoing that usage in the proemial sonnet – "fra le vane speranze e 'l van dolore" (1, 6) – where the tone was one of stoic resistance. Here, upon the event of a grave illness of Laura's, another hope, a hope that does not concern probabilities, exists in the sacred person of Laura and the allegorized figure of "Pietà" ("Pity"):

> Cosí lo spirto d'or in or vèn meno
> a quelle belle care membra honeste
> che specchio eran di vera leggiadria;
> et s'a Morte Pietà non stringe 'l freno,
> lasso, ben veggio in che stato son queste
> *vane speranze*, ond'io viver solia. (184, 9–14)

> So now from hour to hour the spirit wanes
> Within those lovely, chaste, and precious limbs
> That were the glass of true nobility.
> Indeed, if Pity does not curb Death's course,
> Alas, I see well in what plight stand these
> *Vain hopes* in which I have grown used to live.

The elevation of Laura continues in the following poem, as does the same dialectic of truth versus falsehood: in contrast to the deceit and illusion of the past, Laura is projected as a wondrous phoenix, rising up and flying over the Italian skies, with her "novo habito" ("new gown") symbolic of new life:

> Purpurea vesta d'un ceruleo lembo
> sparso di rose i belli homeri vela:
> novo habito, et bellezza unica et sola. (185, 9–11)

> A crimson dress, with a cerulean hem
> And scattered roses, veils her shoulders fair –
> A new gown and a peerless beauty too.

Poem 186, "Se Virgilio et Omero avessin visto" ("If Virgil and if Homer had but seen"), features the comparison of Petrarch's authorial experience to that of Virgil and Homer. The counterfactual hypothesis is typical of poems (such as 166) that elevate moral choice by foregrounding the writing process. The same contrast between classical myth and current reality is seen again in poem 187, "Giunto Alexandro a la famosa tomba" ("On reaching fierce Achilles' famous tomb"), concerning the self-consciousness of a writer who has suffered: Laura is compared to the hero Scipio, who merited a poet like Homer or Virgil to sing his praises but had to be content with his faithful Ennio at his laurel crowning on the Campidoglio. Likewise, says the narrator, Laura deserves a greater poet than he to sing her praises.

Sonnet 188 blends the myth of Apollo, the sun god who loved Daphne, and the story of the subject's love for Laura. The crafted lines are rich in phonetic and thematic tropes that compare and contrast the pairs Apollo-Daphne and Francesco-Laura. The key to the comparisons is provided by the biblical prefiguration of Christ by Adam, who first saw the nature of sin: "suo male et nostro vide in prima Adamo" ("Adam first saw his lovely woe, and ours") (188, 4). The sonnet presents Laura's Vaucluse as a place where Apollo's rays illuminate the laurel tree in the daytime, bringing joy, then fade in the afternoon, giving rise to shadows. As the sunlight necessary for the illumination of the object fades, the outer vision yields to the inner. As symbolized by the juxtaposition of *"bramo"* in line 8, reordered in the anagram *"ombra"* of line 9, the will to possess has been supplanted by the will to live:[3]

et fuggendo mi toi quel ch'i' piú *bramo*.
L'*ombra* che cade da quel' humil colle, (188, 8–9)

And fleeing, snatch from me my heart's desire.
The shadow falling from that lowly hill –

The object of Apollo's worship early in the day, where "fronde" ("tree") (188, 1) is a metonym for the lady, becomes in the sestet "'l gran lauro" ("this great laurel") (188, 11). This progression from the part to the whole suggests that as shadows lengthen and yield to darkness, the laurel arrives at a greater significance. The outer eye trained to the sunlight yields in the shadows to the greater richness of the inner eye. Thus in the nighttime absence of the sun (Apollo), the subject confronts the tree of darkness (the Cross) and finds his lady abiding in his heart: "ove 'l mio cor co la sua donna alberga" ("Where my Heart with his lady now abides") (188, 14).

Poem 189 was the final poem in Part 1 of the Chigi form. As such it is a marker poem that stands to illustrate the larger moral issues at stake for the subject; to occupy the final position in Part 1 is to anticipate a radical turn in the life of the subject. "Passa la nave mia colma di oblio" ("My vessel, with oblivion awash") is a poem on the recognition of one's ignorance and the need for the Socratic Christian to recognize his potential for self-deception. As the personification of Amor steers the "I" figure's storm-tossed ship to its dubious fortune, the atmosphere is suffused with ignorance and error:[4]

le già stanche sarte,
che son d'error con ignorantia attorto (189, 10–11)

slacken shrouds already strained –
They're formed from error spliced with ignorance

If reason and art are said to have died for the subject, this must be seen as a necessary and positive event.[5] Once the navigational metaphor is established in this way, it can be returned to in subsequent poems where the moral interpretation of the tempest will not be so bleak.[6]

In poem 190, "Una candida cerva sopra l'erba" ("A pure white doe with gold horns appeared") – the final poem of Part 1 in the 1366–7 Malpaghini form – the subject's vision of a white doe with golden horns is interrupted when he falls into a pool of water and is awakened from his reverie:

Et era 'l sol già vòlto al mezzo giorno,
gli occhi miei stanchi di mirar, non sazi,
quand'io caddi ne l'acqua, et ella sparve. (190, 12–14)

The sun had already turned at midday;
My eyes were worn with gazing, though not filled,
When I fell in the water, and she fled.

The awakening at noon (recalling the midday hour in poems 54 and 135) seems to compensate for the remorseful midnight of poem 189 and to "disacerba[r]" ("disembitter") the lover, who is content now that the period of indolence is past.[7] Perhaps the most cogent interpretation of this enigmatic event is that one is at a transition in the conscience of the lover: "il cadere in acqua non è figura del pianto per il presentimento della morte di Laura. L'infortunio simboleggia bensì la *defaillance* dell'amante, è 'la coscienza e il segnale del negativo abdicare della coscienza nel rapimento estatico' cui egli va soggetto" (falling in the water is not a figure of weeping in anticipation of the death of Laura. The accident symbolizes rather the lover's weakness, it is "the conscience and the signal of the negative abdication of conscience in the ecstatic rapture" that he is subjected to).[8]

The allegorical vision of poem 190 concerns a theological question of great moment in Petrarch's day, dealt with more directly in poems 191 to 193. This is the question of the beatific vision of God in the afterlife, which also related to debates over whether the sensory image of things impressed on the eye could convey a state of blessedness among persons still living. Pope John XXII had preached that the souls of the pure do not see the divine essence face to face until the Last Judgment, but only see humanity as glorified by Christ (he also condemned the idea of the absolute poverty of Christ and the Apostles). This pope's doctrine was overturned by his successor, Benedict XII, who upheld the immediate beatific vision of the divine essence by the blessed upon their deaths (before they were reunited with their resurrected bodies). Benedict's solution marginalized the question of the soul's desire to be rejoined with the body and overlooked the view of Augustinians and others "che ammetteva [...] una mediazione *per speciem* (ειδος), mediante la quale una creatura finita accedeva alla conoscenza (*visio*) dell'essenza di Dio: questa possibile ai *viatores* sulla terra, mentre la conoscenza completa (*comprehensio*) potrà avvenire solo *in patria*" (which allowed for [...] mediation by images, through which a finite creature accessed the knowledge [*visio*] of the essence of God: this being possible to those still "in transit" on earth, while complete knowledge [*comprehensio*] can only occur once "home" [in heaven]).[9] By not addressing the doctrine of the *specie* by which images could convey a state of blessedness, the pope essentially rejected that prospect. Petrarch was not concerned about the doctrine per se but sought to translate the ecclesial question about beatific visions into an experiential question about the happiness gained by gazing on the beloved, and the related need to arrive at a higher, more sublimated form of desire for God:

Sí come eterna vita è veder Dio,
né *piú* si *brama*, né *bramar piú* lice,
cosí me, donna, il voi veder, felice
fa in questo breve et fraile viver mio. (191, 1–4)

Just as eternal life is seeing God,
And for no more one yearns, nor may one yearn,
So, lady, looking on you gives me joy,
Here in my all-too-brief and fragile life.

The chiasmus of line 2 suggests a definitive end to physical desire and longing ("bramar") and the enhanced role of Laura as a mediatrix sponsoring the subject's desire for God.[10] The "donna" here possesses subjectivity and is a positive moral presence. Similarly, Amor is seen in its divine provenance, as a mediator that allows one to see the exalted vision of the creation. For Petrarch the ability of mortal creatures to reflect the blessedness of the divinity and the belief that the blessed look down on the living with favour were one and the same idea.[11] He ties this idea of the interpenetration of the transcendent and the immanent to his view of Rome as the divinely mandated seat of the church, a place existing on earth that is comparable with what the blessed souls see after leaving their bodies.[12]

Petrarch's meditation on this and other theological questions leads to a transformation of the Daphnean theme at work in the poems. As I have suggested, the Petrarchan poetic term is semantically overdetermined. This is obvious in the case of *Laura, lauro/alloro* (laurel), *l'auro/ l'oro* (gold), *l'aura* (breeze), *l'aria* (air), the meanings of which accrue through repetition and include an array of associations depending on the changing contexts. Peter Hainsworth provides a list of fifty-one "Daphnean" poems that occur in all sections of the sequence, asserting that the meaning of this myth, as it evolves, unifies the 366 poems.[13] He argues that once the Daphnean myth has passed beyond its direct Ovidian references it becomes an equivalent of the poetic art; thus Laura and the laurel are seen as emblems of poetry. Furthermore, he argues that "within the work as a whole the status of the ethical qualities which are discerned in Laura is uncertain," and that the "most important of the features [...] [is] the elusiveness of Laura."[14] Martinelli takes a different stance better able to deal with the moral presence of Laura, as just seen in poem 191. For Martinelli there are three stages in Petrarch's use of the laurel. In the first stage, the tree stands for the poet in his quest for love and glory; in the second stage, it stands for Daphne/Laura; and in the third stage, the laurel is Christological in nature and Laura a Mary figure. Boyle adopts a view similar to Martinelli's, asserting the "moral dimension of meaning" of the laurel as a figure of the Apolline Christ, the same one suggested by St Francis.[15] If Laura is elusive it is because she can only be known through the relationship. She is a catalyst; her undecidability draws in the reader to participate, to seek out the actual person. In Part 2, this undecidability diminishes, as does the ambivalence of the subject, allowing dialogue to increase, albeit dialogue *in absentia*.

Pozzi has noted that the motifs and attributes of Petrarch's qualifying words for Laura are reduced to a minimum, the effect being to define beauty in the "high lyric genre" in terms of a series of lexical and figurative "reductions" due to a heightened degree of abstraction.[16] One sees the reduction of the number of body parts and the qualities of the beloved that are referred to; one also sees the extreme limitation of the metaphors and other tropes used to refer to her, and the limitation to three colours, all within set patterns. The use of a restricted vocabulary to convey Laura's beauty and virtue ultimately has the effect of intensifying them in the imagination. This is evident in poem 192, in which the subject imagines Laura in terms both immanent and transcendent: she is comparable to nature but also to "cose sopra natura altere et nove" ("things above all nature lofty, rare") (192, 1–2). The dual perspective is enabled by the subject's choice of the path to wisdom and the inner life as the repertory of images used for the Lady of Virtue in poem 119 now accrue to Laura herself:

Stiamo, Amor, a veder la gloria nostra,
cose sopra natura altere et nove:
vedi ben quanta in lei dolcezza piove,
vedi lume che 'l cielo in terra mostra,
vedi quant'arte dora e 'mperla e 'nostra
l'abito electo, et mai non visto altrove,
che dolcemente i piedi et gli occhi move
per questa di bei colli ombrosa chiostra.
L'erbetta verde e i fior' di colour' mille
sparsi sotto quel' elce antiqua et negra
pregan pur che 'l bel pe' li prema o tocchi;
e 'l ciel di vaghe et lucide faville
s'accende intorno, e 'n vista si rallegra
d'esser fatto seren da sí belli occhi. (192, 1–14)

Love, on our glory let us pause to look,
See things above all nature lofty, rare.
Indeed, you see what sweetness rains on her
You see the light revealing heaven to earth.

You see what art empearls, makes crimson, gilds
That chosen flesh, seen nowhere else before;
And with what sweetness feet and eyes she moves
Throughout this shadowed cloister of fair hills.
The new green grass, the thousand-colored blooms
Scattered beneath that holm-oak ancient, black,
Pray her fair feet to touch or treat on them.
All round with vagrant glowing sparks the sky's
Aflame; before our eyes it fills with joy
At being made serene by eyes so fair.

Among the wonders of Laura depicted in the Vaucluse setting is "l'abito electo, et mai non visto altrove" ("That chosen flesh, seen nowhere else before") (192, 6), an apparent calque of Aquinas's use of *"habitus electivus"* (habit issuing in choices) in his commentary on Aristotle's *Ethics*, signifying moral virtue and the proper balance of the will and the intellect.[17] The same term, when used poetically, comes to signify the supernatural, celestial body of Laura in the *hortus conclusus* (enclosed garden). While 192 continues the motifs of divine vision from 191, the former poem dwelt on earthly happiness and the fleetingness of time, while the latter is fully absorbed in the sacred dimension of the vision (referencing the doctrine of the Resurrection) and conveys to that extent a greater unity in the perceiving subject.[18]

It is this unified persona of the author-narrator that is evident in *Rvf* 194 and 196 to 198, the sonnets of "L'aura" (the breeze). While some uncertainty about the dates of composition exists, the consensus places poems 194, 197, and 198 among the very last written by the author, in 1368. The four poems concern the fluctuating and ephemeral nature of Laura's presence and absence, as echoed in the variants on the *senhal* – "l'aura gentil" ("noble breeze"), "l'aura serena" ("tranquil breeze"), "l'aura celeste" ("heavenly breeze"), and "l'aura soave" ("soft breeze") – sounded in the opening lines. As a sublime phenomenon of nature, Laura resists efforts to define her in language.[19] The terms *l'aura, l'auro (l'oro), Laura,* and *lauro* are generally overdetermined and move in a space of poetic neutrality. By virtue of their phonetic similarities and semantic distinctions, one alternates in the reading between denotative and connotative values, as between the real and the imaginary dimensions of language.[20]

In the last of these sonnets, poem 198, "L'aura soave al sole spiega et vibra" ("The soft breeze strews and ruffles in the sun"), the subject oscillates between seeing and not seeing, as in the experience of the writer who cannot describe what he sees in words. The sonnet alternates, in both the octave and the sestet, between its presentation of the Lady and the subject. While the subject is still vulnerable to Amor, finding his heart tied in knots, the true reason behind his bedazzlement is not the appeal of her hair (an emblem of physical desire) but the beacon of her eyes:

> Non ò medolla in osso, o sangue in fibra,
> ch'i' non senta tremar, pur ch'i' m'apresse
> dove è chi morte et vita inseme, spesse
> volte, in frale bilancia appende et libra,
> vedendo ardere i lumi ond'io m'accendo, (198, 5–9)

> In fiber, blood, in bone no pith have I
> That does not shiver if I but come near
> Where she is, who ofttimes suspends and weighs
> In fragile balance death and life at once;
> I see those lights ablaze that kindle me

This illumination pushes the subject to a threshold experience, as he ascertains that Laura (ambiguously referred to as "chi") "suspends and weighs / In fragile balance death and life at once."[21] Thus, the physical debilitation suffered in the nearness of the beloved brings with it a liberating insight.

In her physical presence, Laura-Daphne embodies the figure of the beloved that Petrarch derived from vernacular and classical sources, devising an essential vocabulary to describe her beauty. Certainly by the end of the second centenary the subject's libidinal impulse has faded, and along with it the feminine phantasm of the pneumo-erotic tradition. Laura's beauty grows immaterial and is referred to by reticence and absence, paleness and silence. One has seen that Laura can be ill or pensive, volatile or haughty, and that her vulnerability and her stoniness can serve to prod the subject towards self-understanding and penitence. But finally there is a serene Laura, a moral guide towards atonement, in life and death. Well in advance of the transition to Part 2, when the distance/proximity dichotomy that has defined the relationship is concretized in Laura's death, the composite symbol of the laurel speaks moral truths to the subject. Thus all the later "Daphnean" poems concern the symbology of the laurel: "Est insuper arbor sacra, metuenda et venerabilis" ("a sacred tree, to be held in awe, and to be reverenced").[22]

2. Out of the Labyrinth, Away from the World

As one enters the third centenary, the question of Laura's nearness or distance is framed by the theme of the good neighbour, as in the parable of the Good Samaritan (Luke 10:25–37).[23] The subject's devotion to the Lady is now synonymous with his separation from his former life, as is seen in two contiguous canzoni written in opposite registers: the arduous medieval canzone 206 and the more conventional and retrospective canzone 207, centred on the topic of the Lady's eyes. Canzone 206 is composed of six indivisible strophes linked by *coblas capcandadas* and is an imitation of the Provençal *escondig*, the "excuse" of the poet to the Lady and a protest against the *lauzengiers*. The poem is an emphatic denial by the subject that he has spoken ill of his Lady. The phrase "S'i' 'l dissi mai" ("If I said that") is iterated twelve times in the first four stanzas until the rhythm is broken with "Ma s'io nol dissi" ("But if I said that not"), accompanied by a vow of faithfulness to the truth and to Laura:

> Ma s'io nol dissi, chi sí dolce apria
> meo cor a speme ne l'età novella,
> regg'anchor questa stanca navicella
> col governo di sua pietà natia, (206, 37–40)

> But if I said that not, may one who in
> My youth unsealed my heart so sweetly to
> Its hope still guide this small tired vessel with
> The rudder of her native clemency.

The use of "navicella" ("vessel") to refer to the subject's life recalls Dante's use of that word in the opening of *Purgatorio* to refer to the "ship" of his poetic talent, just as, in the envoi of the canzone, the affirmation that he has served Rachel not Leah – the contemplative life, not the active life – is a reminiscence of Dante's Earthly Paradise (*Purg.* xxvii, 94–108). Intratextually, the alliance with Rachel closes the discourse begun with canzone 119, with the distinction being that here Laura is clearly conflated with Rachel and assumed to possess the same celestial qualities as the Lady of Virtue.

Canzone 207, "Ben mi credea passar mio tempo omai" ("I thought that I could surely spend my time"), recapitulates the "excuse" of poem 206 amid traces of the *trobar clus*: it is comparable in that regard to poem 105, with which it shares a certain obscurity, "Chiusa forma è più ardente ..." ("Flame closed within's more ardent") (207, 66) recalling "Una chiusa bellezza è più soave" ("A beauty that's reserved is gentlest") (105, 52). As in that poem, the poet resolves to initiate a new form of verse, to resist the vanity of the world:

O mondo, o penser' vani;
o mia forte ventura a che m'adduce! (207, 72–3)

O world, O idle thoughts;
O my hard fortune, what you lead me to!

The use of the noun "mondo" (world) calls to mind the sirma of poem 1, where the intention to distance oneself from the evils of mundanity was established: "che quanto piace al *mondo* è breve sogno" ("That worldly joy is but a passing dream") (1, 14). And in the envoi to this canzone, which concludes with an address to the reader as one of Love's faithful, the world is denounced as an unsuitable place to look for the good needed to assuage the wounds of Amor:

Servo d'Amor, che queste rime leggi,
ben non à *'l mondo*, che 'l mio mal pareggi. (207, 97–8)

Love's servant, you who read these lines, this world
Possesses no good that can match my ill.

The need to look beyond the world is a major theme of the poems of the third centenary, where "mondo" tends to signify (as in the *De otio*) the failure of humanity to heed Christ's model and instructions on how to behave in the world. "Mondo" designates the world visited by scandal, as the lexeme was used in each of the Avignonese sonnets. It is increasingly clear in the latter poems of Part 1 that the subject has distanced himself from the world. In lifting up the importance of knowledge and disillusionment, Petrarch takes joy in the creation, as is consistent with his Franciscanism: "Fu forse il primo intellettuale dell'età moderna a teorizzare la vita solitaria come condizione necessaria dello spirito" (He was perhaps the first intellectual of the modern age to theorize the solitary life as the necessary condition of the spirit).[24]

De vita solitaria and *De otio religioso*, written during Lent in 1346 and 1347, respectively, concern asceticism and the solitary life but have distinctly different content and rhetorical characters. *De vita solitaria* presents Petrarch's contemplative philosophy and includes a biographical catalogue of famous solitaries. Here Petrarch amplifies his views on the ancient and Augustinian notions of the soul and the self. Rather than adopting Cicero's elevation of the self to the realm of the divine and eternal, a perspective from which the mind can only scorn human things, Petrarch converts Cicero's two terms for the self – *animus* and *mens* – to mean an autonomous self that lacks access to the eternal but thrives on the elevated human dimension. Petrarch's "noble soul (*generosus animus*) [...] appears as the autonomous self making its own decisions about values and goods" and is distinct from Augustine's conception of the self, which is limited to resting in God.[25] Petrarch's conception of the individual conscience is not detached from the social-quotidian world but affirms the goodness of human life and the possibilities of joy and happiness, and the calm acceptance of death.

De otio religioso augments the doctrine of the free will presented in *De vita solitaria* by advancing a doctrine of grace.[26] It is written as a long allocution to a collective addressee, the Carthusian monks who had recently hosted him at their monastery in Montrieux (where Gherardo had entered in 1343). What is remarkable about the text is its insistence on a few practical and ethical points concerning the spiritual life. By lowering the rhetorical register, the author is able to preserve the communicative sense of a conversation among friends who share the communal interest of a spiritual life together. But there are also aspects of the sermon in what is a predominantly paratactic text. One goal of the *De otio* is to correct a prevailing understanding of *otium* as an idleness that needed to be rectified by prayer and meditation. In contrast, true religious retreat is understood as an activity absorbed in prayer.

Taking as his focus Psalm 45:11 – "*Vacate et videte*" ("Take time and see [that I am God]") – Petrarch explores the nature of prayer, contemplation, and religious community, with frequent reference to the Gospels, Paul's Epistles, the Psalms, and the writings of Augustine: "Postremo dicitur omnibus: 'Nolite diligere *mundum*, neque ea que in *mundo* sunt, quia omne quod in *mundo* est concupiscentia carnis est et concupiscentia oculorum et ambitio seculi'" ("Finally this is said to all people: 'Love neither this world nor those things which are in this world, because every worldly thing involves the desire of the flesh and the desire of the eyes and the striving of this world'").[27] This, in fact, was the focus of Augustine's discussion of the same psalm in *De vera religione*: "Quod si haec intueri palpitat mentis aspectus, quiescite; nolite certare, nisi cum consuetudine corporum: ipsam vincite, et victa erunt omnia. Unum certe quaerimus, quo simplicius nihil est. Ergo in simplicitate cordis quaeramus illum. *Agite otium,* inquit, *et agnoscetis quia ego sum Dominus*" ("Do not strive except against being accustomed to material things. Conquer that habit and you are victorious over all. We seek unity, the simplest thing of all. Therefore let us seek it in simplicity of heart. 'Be still and know that I am God'").[28] In his gloss of the key term "otium" (religious leisure), Petrarch declares his opposition to the work-obsession ("negotium") and urges the Frati to find repose in the spirit. While Aristotle and Virgil urge the virtuous to labour – to work now in order to rest later – Petrarch disagrees, saying that intense work leads to more work, and that only asceticism produces rest.

The *De otio* is structured as a sequential examination of the ways of the "enemies" of humanity: "Occurrite paratibus impiis et vitate tria in primis hostium atque armorum genera, mundi laqueos, carnis illecebras, demonum dolos" ("Oppose their wicked devices, especially three kinds of weapon of the enemy: the traps of this world, the enticements of the flesh, and the guiles of demons").[29] Only by overcoming these enemies can one come to a self-knowledge distinct from the one promulgated by the classical thinkers: "Itaque cum illustres gentium philosophi omnia ad virtutem referant, Cristi philosophus virtutem ipsam ad virtutis auctorem Deum refert utensque virtutibus Deo fruitur, nec usquam citra illum mente consistit" ("Although the illustrious philosophers of all nations relate everything to virtue, the philosopher of Christ relates virtue itself to God, the Creator of virtue. Using virtues, he enjoys God and never lets his mind stop short of that goal").[30] As stated in the *De otio*, the reality of God is not available to man's senses but only once they are quieted, in contemplation and prayer.

One gathers in the *De otio* a sense of Petrarch's awareness of the historicity of the problem of evil. The sacrifice revealed by Christ in history is placed at the centre of the text as the basis for faith; faith is not enlisted as a charismatic or subjective matter or as a matter of dogma. As a layman addressing a monastic community, Petrarch is committed to dispelling certain assumptions that were undermining the religious life. He understood that laicism was enabled by Christ's coming and supplanting of the sacrificial religions in which the sovereignty of the priesthood was not questioned. Petrarch understood with Augustine that there were "wolves" within the church and "sheep" without. Just as Christianity encouraged the development of lay society, those in the religious communities who opposed the developments of humanism by insisting on the apparatus of scholasticism were bogged down in the

City of Man –the strivings and attachments of the world – and failed to aspire to the City of God. As one reads in the Letter to the Hebrews and in Augustine, the City of God must be pursued in history, as the historical crises in the church have made apparent.

In distinguishing Christianity from Christendom Petrarch was diffusing a newly humanistic and syncretic intellectual culture. His view of history might aptly be called "surrational" in that sacred history and eschatology are seen to include secular history.[31] This theological-historical awareness matures in the third centenary of poems as the subject's self-examination as a sinner yields to an intense focus on contemplation and the generative life of the soul; at the same time, the *petroso* (stony) style of many of the earlier poems is eclipsed.[32]

The following three incipits – "Rapido fiume" ("Swift stream," being the Rhone) (208, 1), "I dolci colli" ("Those sweet hills") (209, 1), and "Non da l'hispano Hibero a l'indo Ydaspe" ("from Indic Hydaspes / To Spanish Ebro") (210, 1) – refer to precise geographical locations, in contrast to the dramatic temporal thrust of poem 211, which cites the day and hour when the subject first entered into the "labyrinth," an ambiguous space of entrapment and potential liberation:

Mille trecento ventisette, a punto
su l'ora prima, il dí sesto d'aprile,
nel laberinto intrai; né veggio ond'èsca. (211, 12–14)

In thirteen hundred twenty-seven, just at
The first hour – April sixth the day – into
The labyrinth I stepped; I see no gate.

The date contains a reference to Christ's Passion, as 6 April was used in the Middle Ages as a universal date for the Crucifixion. As is known, the figure of the labyrinth was inscribed on the floors of many cathedrals to guide the faithful in their access to the Christian mystery.[33] In psychical terms, one must consider the labyrinth as a path that has been prepared for one. If in poem 211 that was a path of loss and confusion with no exit, in poem 224 the labyrinth of error is historicized and the reciprocity of the relationship with Laura made tangible:

S'una fede amorosa, un cor non finto,
un languir dolce, un desïar cortese;
s'oneste voglie in gentil foco accese,

un lungo error in cieco laberinto;
[…]
s'arder da lunge et agghiacciar da presso
son le cagion' ch'amando i' mi distempre,
vostro, donna, 'l peccato, et mio fia 'l danno. (224, 1–4, 12–14)

If amorous faith, and if a heart sincere,
A languor sweet, a longing courteous,
If chaste desiring, lit in noble fire,
If roaming long a dark, blind labyrinth;
[…]
If burning from afar and freezing near
Make up the reasons I'm unstrung by love;
Yours, lady, is the fault, and mine the harm.

It is significant that Laura shares intersubjectively in the "peccato" (sin) and "errore" (error), which are qualified by the positive moral terms "fede" ("faith"), "cortese" ("courteous"), "oneste" ("chaste"), and "gentil" ("noble"). In this way, the long and errant wandering in sin suggests its opposite, the correction of error that occurs on the metaphorical road to Jerusalem.

In the poem immediately preceding, sonnet 223, "Quando 'l sol bagna in mar l'aurato carro" ("When in the sea his golden chariot"), the subject tells his painful story to "one who does not hear" (perhaps God, as Bettarini suggests):

Poi, lasso, a tal che non m'ascolta narro
tutte le mie fatiche, ad una ad una, (223, 4–5)

Alas then, to that one who does not hear,
One at a time my hardships I recount

The key verb "narro" (I narrate) foregrounds the narration amidst a flurry of *hapaxes* and rare words that position this sonnet at a psychological nadir, an existential dark night of the soul, of insomnia and anguish, in which the cloaked name of Laura appears at dawn as "l'aura fosca" ("the dark breeze") (223, 12). Then in poem 224 – following a frequent pattern in the sequence whereby contiguous poems having common themes express opposite moral outcomes – one has the sense of moral correction noted above.

As was seen in chapter 4, the figures of antithesis and oxymoron play an important role in the overall moral itinerary and offer a path of mediation between extremes. This is the case in sonnet 226, "Passer mai solitario in alcun tetto" ("There never was a sparrow on some roof"), the first of a chain of six sonnets in which happiness is the result of renunciation: happy is the air that Laura breathes and happy is the prayer of the poet's adoration. In the opening lines the tears of the "passero solitario" (not the noble species of that name, the blue rock thrush, but a "solitary sparrow") allude to Psalms 101:7 and 8; and in the second quatrain, with reference to Job, the subject declaims his solitude and constant sorrow in a series of four antitheses (seen in italics) that denote his helplessness and impotence:[34]

Lagrimar sempre è 'l mio sommo *diletto,*
il *rider doglia,* il cibo assentio et tòsco,
la notte affanno, e 'l ciel *seren* m'è *fosco,*
et *duro campo* di battaglia il *letto.* (226, 5–8)

To *weep* forever is my highest *joy;*
To *laugh* is *woe,* my food is poison, gall;
For me the night is sorrow, *bright* sky *dark;*
And *bed* for me a grievous *battleground.*

The persistence of weeping and the motif of solitude anticipate Part 2 of the *Fragmenta,* as if Laura's death was forecast by this foreboding sonnet.[35] As death is compared to sleep and the "paese almo" ("happy land") – presumably the Vaucluse – is said to possess Laura, as when a body is interred, she is endowed with a figural or typological dimension, being implicitly compared to Mary, singular among women:

Il sonno è veramente, qual uom dice,
parente de la morte, e 'l cor sottragge
a quel dolce penser che 'n vita il tene.
Solo al mondo paese almo, felice,
verdi rive fiorite, ombrose piagge,
voi possedete, et io piango, il mio bene. (226, 9–14)

Ah, truly, sleep is what men say it is,
Death's kinsman, and it takes my heart away
From that sweet worry which sustains my life.

You fertile, happy land; green blooming shores
And shady slopes, in this world only you
Possess, and I bewail, my dearest good.

Laura's absence is no longer cause to plaintively recapitulate the motifs of the *amor de lonh*. Rather, in the duality of Laura, present and absent, near and far, one sees emerge the biblical figure of the good neighbour.

3. A Poetics of Quietude

In his continuing meditation on poetic forms, Petrarch is guided by the stylistic models of the Bible and the Church Fathers. The moral and ethical dimensions of this pursuit are enacted over time and traceable in the final poems of Part 1. A key moment is marked by the rapid composition, sometime in 1347 or 1348, of the *Psalmi penitentiales*, a prayer book that will be instrumental in his later life.[36] Given the precedent of seven penitential Davidic psalms (numbers 6, 31, 37, 50, 101, 139, and 142 in the Vulgate), these Latin poems have been labelled as penitential, though Petrarch – who employed them for many years in his prayers – simply referred to them as his "sette salmi." Claudio Bellinati – whose Italian translation I draw on – argues that the *Psalmi* mark an important religious change in the poet's life: "I *sette salmi* penitenziali di Francesco Petrarca si ergono come una luminosa insegna nel displuvio di due epoche della sua vita" (Francesco Petrarch's seven penitential psalms arise like a bright sign at the watershed between two epochs of his life).[37] This watershed is apparent in all of Petrarch's writings after 1348, in his passionate return to a moral centre. Many of the linguistic markers of his errancy and self-correction are found in the *Psalmi*, including the reference to life as a journey on which one must choose the right path in order to oppose the "enemy" within oneself, a choice that is not without struggle and fatigue as one recognizes the "nets" and "yokes," traps and burdens, placed before one: "Quando comincerò a ritornare a te?" (When will I begin to return to you?).[38]

Previous models of self-recognition and cleansing are provided by the *Confessions* and the *Purgatorio*, works dominated by verbs of turning and ascent in which the process of *mutatio vitae* occurs over time, incrementally. Petrarch followed Augustine from his early years on when the saint's works stood out in a library dominated by classical authors. For the subject, the return towards virtue and the correction of errors is comparable to Augustine's representation of the life of faith as a long transformational journey. Despite the tendency to "read back into the famous 'conversion' narrative in *Confessions* 8" the idea of "a one-time event of conversion," Augustine's illumination in Milan concerned his decision to be baptized, to become part of the Ecclesial body of the Church.[39] It was only with the writing of the *Confessions*, ten years after his decision to be baptized, that Augustine eschewed the doctrinal language that had prevented him from seeing how God was manifest in his life "in Pauline terms, as the incursion of a power (grace) that man cannot summon on his own."[40] So, too, with Petrarch, one detects critical changes in the voice of the subject over the years of his maturity, when many of the poems were written and finalized.

The change in course is given a powerful emblem in the following first lines: "Cantai, or piango" ("I sang once, now I weep") (229, 1) and "I' piansi, or canto" ("I used to weep but now I sing") (230, 1). The progression from weeping to song stands to indicate that the subject, once possessed by a "denatured love," in conflict with the harmony of the natural world, has, through the exercise of the free will, realized the possibility of a serene, "transnatured love."[41] This condition is dramatized in sonnet 231, centred on the representation of the divine Lady, whose immaterial beauty is seen in her reticence, paleness, and silence. As the narrator separates himself from any worldly form of happiness, he speaks in the present, contrasting himself with recollected time of the character:

I' mi vivea di mia sorte contento,
senza lagrime et senza invidia alcuna,
che, s'altro amante à piú destra fortuna,
mille piacer' non vaglion un tormento.
Or quei belli occhi ond'io mai non mi pento
de le mie pene, et men non ne voglio una,
tal nebbia copre, sí gravosa et bruna,
che 'l sol de la mia vita à quasi spento.
O Natura, pietosa et fera madre,
onde tal possa et sí contrarie voglie
di far cose et disfar tanto leggiadre?
D'un vivo fonte ogni poder s'accoglie:
ma Tu come 'l consenti, o sommo Padre,
che del Tuo caro dono altri ne spoglie? (231, 1–14)

I used to live contented with my lot
With neither tears nor any envy, for
Though happier fortune other lovers have,
Their thousand joys aren't worth one pang of mine.
Now those fair eyes on whose account I'll not
Repent my pains nor wish them one whit less
Are hidden by so thick and dark a fog
That my life's sun has almost been put out.
O, Nature, mother fierce, compassionate,
Whence comes such power, and whence such wills opposed,
To fashion, then destroy such graceful things?
All power from one living fount is drawn,
But how, O highest Father, can you let
Another strip your precious gift from us?

Now distant from his former self, the narrator wishes neither to regret nor to relive his earlier actions. Referring to an ailment of Laura, he questions first nature (a mother), then God (a father), as to how the innocent can be harmed. Prosaic and opaque, the poem is a kind of theodicy, asking how God could tolerate the extent of suffering in the world.

Poem 232, "Vincitore Alexandro l'ira vinse" ("Wrath conquered Alexander, conqueror"), interrupts the series of sonnets of Laura's illness to catalogue the befogging effects of anger, where the keyword "ira" is repeated four times, once in each quatrain and tercet.[42] One is reminded of the second dialogue of the *Secretum*, where Franciscus critiques the imperturbability of the Stoics and insists on an *ordo caritatis*, stating that a return to innocence involves struggle, and that, in addition to expelling sorrow, one must sublimate anger.[43] The classical figure who illustrates this necessity is Ajax, an anti-Ulysses figure whose deeds speak louder than his words, who dies by his own hand as a result of excessive anger:

Ira è breve furore, et chi nol frena,
è furor lungo, che 'l suo possessore
spesso a vergogna, et talor mena a morte. (232, 12–14)

Wrath is brief madness, or long madness for
One who restrains it not; it often leads
Its owner to disgrace and sometimes death.

It is worth noting the presence in Petrarch of an Ajax figure, naturally suppressed and controlled, but guided by his personal recognition of the perils of anger. As Petrarch/Ajax chooses a higher order than the natural virtue of the classical warriors, he recapitulates the conflict in the self among Eros, glory, and the spirit.

As the subject evolves in his relationship with the world and with Laura, the passions of Eros and glory are attenuated. The desire to achieve simple-mindedness reflects this choice to recover a restorative pleasure based on self-awareness within a world in fragments. This is evident in sonnet 234, "O cameretta che già fosti un porto" ("O little room, you sometimes were a port"), where the subject recognizes the irony of his decision to plunge into the crowd: "(Chi 'l pensò mai?)" ("Who'd ever credit that?") (234, 13). Though he has insisted on separating himself from the masses, the subject is willing to cast himself as Everyman, to insert his moral parable into history, trusting that God sees into our most private and intimate spaces.[44] The reason for this flight towards the *volgo* is that he does not find the peace he expects from his "cameretta," as in the crying beds of David and Job in Psalms 6:7 and Job 7:3 and 13, and as referenced in the second *Salmo penitenziale*: "La mia camera sia il mio purgatorio, / il letticciolo mio conosca le mie lagrime" (Let my room be my Purgatory, / let my bed know my tears).[45]

Poem 238, "Real natura, angelico intelletto" ("A nature regal, an angelic mind"), is a vignette about the visit of an illustrious regal personage to Avignon, a handsome well-proportioned man of lofty thoughts, magnetic charm, and good judgment who selects the fairest lady present at court. He kisses her eyes and forehead, a gesture that delights the other ladies while it awakens envy in the heart of the subject, for whom this gentleman is a foil. Sonnet 238 stands at the centre of an impressive symmetrical construction in the macrotext; framed by two sestinas, the group of three poems (D) serves as a hinge between two lengthy sequences of sonnets (C, C'), on either side of which, after shorter intervals of mixed canzoni and sonnets (B, B'), there are even longer sequences of sonnets (A, A'). The result is that the two large groups – poems 150 to 205 and 215 to 236; and poems 240 to 263 and 271 to 322 – each includes two canzoni, with eighty-four and seventy-eight sonnets, respectively. As figure 5.1 indicates, the poems are arranged chiastically (ABCDCBA) in a way that reinforces the continuity of the macrotext as it transitions into Part 2.

The sonnet sequence that concludes Part 1 (C') contains a proleptic sorrow, as if in anticipation of the events to come. In 1348 the Black

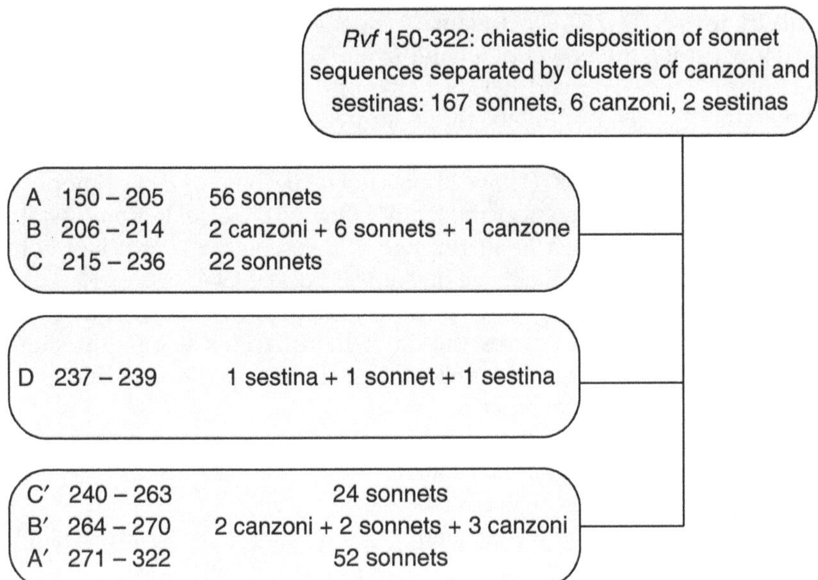

Figure 5.1. Macrotextual patterns in the distribution of poems 150–322

Death swept Europe, with 100,000 dead in Florence alone. Beyond the death of Laura, the numerous deaths of Petrarch's friends and associates give this year a unique status and weight, making it the turning point of the *Fragmenta*. It is in 1348 that Petrarch writes "La mia favola breve è già compita, / et fornito il mio tempo a mezzo gli anni" ("My little fable is already done / And my life ended in my middle years") (254, 13–14). Recalling the only other use of "favola" – "favola fui gran tempo" ("I long have been a fable") (1, 10), the author-narrator declares an end to the character of his past such that in the final poems of Part 1 there is no trace of that persona whose self-pity surpassed his pity for others. The end of the "favola" comports the expectations of the spiritual life.

The use of parenthetical inserts is extensive in these poems. While the digressions are not addressed to the reader per se, their naturalness and suppleness bring the reader closer to the personal sphere of the subject who reflects on his destiny: "(et fe' gran senno, et piú se mai non riede)" ("(and / Great sense showed – more if never he returns)") (243, 6); "(lasso, non so che di me stesso estime)" ("(alas! / I know not how to weigh this by myself)") (252, 7); "(quanto è 'l poder d'una prescritta usanza!)" ("(How great's the power of a habit fixed!)") (258, 10); "(le rive il sanno, et le campagne e i boschi)" ("(The banks of streams, the fields and woods know that)") (259, 2); "(or che mi pò far peggio?)" ("(how can it treat me worse?)") (266, 3); "sa ben Amor qual io divento, et (spero) / vedel colei ch'è or sí presso al vero" ("Love knows what I become, and she (I hope) / Can see it too; she is so near the truth") (268, 55); "se col tempo fossi ito avanzando / (come già in altri) infino a la vecchiezza" ("if it had with time / Kept growing till old age (in some it does)") (304, 10).

Within the darkening view of peril and risk, the subject hates the coming of night and praises the day, when Laura's sun might shine alongside the actual sun: by articulating these opposite conditions he achieves a state of detachment.

> Cosí di me due contrarie hore fanno;
> et chi m'acqueta è ben ragion ch'i' brami,
> et tema et odï chi m'adduce affanno. (255, 12–14)

> Thus two contrary hours have their will of me,
> and it is natural that I desire the one that
> calms me, fear and hate the one that brings me suffering.

By externalizing his desire for serenity, the subject is approaching the double peace attainable by Christians who switch their desire for worldly things to a pure desire for God (*pax inchoata*), which accedes to the divine vision of God (*pax plena*):

> Ma la vista, privata del suo obiecto,
> quasi sognando si facea far via,
> senza la qual è 'l suo bene imperfecto.
> l'alma tra l'una et l'altra gloria mia,
> qual celeste non so novo dilecto
> et qual strania dolcezza si sentia. (257, 9–14)

> Yet sight, denied its object, still contrived
> To find that pathway – as if in a dream –
> Without which its well-being is impaired.
> Between my glories two, this one and that,
> My soul experienced I know not what
> New joy celestial, and what sweetness rare.

With respect to the struggles with Amor, such positive solutions as this often beget negative consequences, suggesting a non-progressive pattern. Yet as the experiences of vision and contemplation increase, the subject realizes outsidedness with respect to that persistent pattern.

As the poems of Part 1 wind to a conclusion – poem 259 marks the last vision of Laura alive in Avignon – the narrative changes its outward focus to an inward focus on charity, peace, renunciation, and the solitary life. Accompanying this transition is the metonymic sign of the "rive" ("banks") of religious consciousness:

Cercato ò sempre solitaria vita
(le rive il sanno, e le campagne e i boschi) (259, 1–2)

I've ever sought the solitary life
(The banks of streams, the fields and woods know that)

Rivers and streams are the sites of spiritual transformation. The profusion of liquid and fluvial images in the *Fragmenta* cannot be understood without reference to the biblically inspired literature of tears and weeping, as the numerous rivers in the text constitute a place of convergence between the natural element and the soul in its experience of life change.[46]

As this sonnet concludes, one has the startling image of a Marian Laura ("madonna") against the backdrop of immoral Avignon and its "fango" ("mire"). The unpredictability of fortune has arranged for this meeting between the couple to be their last, as Laura favours him with a handshake:

Ma mia fortuna, a me sempre nemica,
mi risospigne al loco ov'io mi sdegno
veder nel fango il bel tesoro mio.
A la man ond'io scrivo è fatta amica
a questa volta, et non è forse indegno:
Amor sel vide, et sa 'l madonna et io. (259, 9–14)

My fortune, though, who ever was my foe,
To that place goads me where I grow enraged
To see my lovely treasure in the mire.
But this time, now, my writing hand has she
Befriended, not unworthily, perhaps,
That Love saw, and my lady and I know.

A similar anticipation of quietude occurs in poem 262 in Laura's dialogue with an old woman about the relative merits of "onestà" ("chastity") and "vita" ("life"); in privileging the former over the latter, Laura surpasses the "filosofi" ("philosophers").[47] She has become, in advance of her death, an Apollo figure, in the syncretic sense of a biblical and Christological god of the sun. She is also the laurel tree that foreshadows the cross in poem 263, "Arbor victorïosa trïumphale" ("O you victorious and triumphal tree").[48] The *capoverso* of this final poem of Part 1 is unique in being limited to three words, suggesting the Trinity (as does the first syllable of "*trï*umphale"):

  Arbor victorïosa trïumphale,
onor d'imperadori et di poeti,
quanti m'ài fatto dí dogliosi et lieti
in questa breve mia vita mortale!
  vera donna, et a cui di nulla cale,
se non d'onor, che sovr'ogni altra mieti,
né d'Amor visco temi, o lacci o reti,
né 'ngano altrui contr'al tuo senno vale.
  Gentileza di sangue, et l'altre care
cose tra noi, perle et robini et oro,
quasi vil soma egualmente dispregi.
  L'alta beltà ch'al mondo non à pare
noia t'è, se non quanto il bel thesoro
di castità par ch'ella adorni et fregi. (263, 1–14)

  O you victorious and triumphal tree,
Glory of poets, and of emperors,
How many doleful days, and happy too
You've caused me in my brief and mortal life!
  True lady, only honor do you prize,
And far above the rest you garner it;
Love's birdlime you fear not, no springes, nets;
No ruse against your judgment can avail.
  Nobility of birth, those other things
Precious to us, like rubies, pearls, and gold,
You equally disparage as vile dross.
  Your lofty beauty, peerless in the world,
Proves vexing but as it seems to adorn
And grace your treasure fair of chastity.

The "bel thesoro" of Laura's chaste body is a veil, an *integumentum*, as that term is used by Martianus Capella to represent the material world; it refers in the first instance to one's clothing or dress but also stands for the "veil" at the heart of a figural discourse.[49] Petrarch is attempting in his farewell to the mortal body of Laura to blend secular and religious truths, much as Capella did by conflating the Capitoline trinity, the Christian Trinity, and the classical triad of Wisdom, Virtue, and Eloquence. These aspects of medieval figuration are present in Petrarch's text as he seeks to reconcile, in the spirit of the Platonist Augustine, the classical and contemporary perspectives. The isotopy of the body as one's worldly dress – "abito" (gown), "velo" (veil), "gonna" (dress), "scorza" (bark) – is consistent with Augustine's belief that the soul, not the body, is the origin of sin; thus the body is potentially incorruptible and free to be resurrected.[50] In this way the earthly body comes to signify the celestial body, the risen spirit.

In the anticipated grief of the final poems of Part 1, Laura emerges as a teacher, taking a more active role in the story at the moment when her mortal trajectory is about to end. The laurel tree of poem 263 symbolizes the Tree of Golgotha as it recurs in the life of Laura. Just as Laura has acquired the Marian characteristics of "alta beltà" and has reaped honour (Galatians 6:8), she will be a victim for the faith and be victorious.

Chapter Six

Songs of Grief and Lamentation (*Rvf* 264–318)

Raros veritas testes habet. Inter hec vivimus; in hanc temporum particulam coniecti sumus.

Truth has few witnesses. We live in this situation. We have been cast into this little block of time.

De otio religioso[1]

1. "Quelle pietose braccia" (264, 14)

Five blank pages in Vat. Lat. 3195 separate Part 1 and Part 2; the break comes between poems 263 and 264 and does not coincide with the death of Laura. If the poems of Part 1 immerse us in the story of the Petrarchan subject, whether in the fabulous mode of homodiegetic fiction or that of historical narrative, in Part 2 the voices of character, narrator, and author converge, consolidating the mode of spiritual autobiography.

With the advent of a unitary subject in Part 2, we see the intervention of a contemplative time frame that vitiates the dichotomy between the linear time of history and the circular time of nature, as these two are supplanted by contemplative time/atemporality. As the image of a transcendent Laura serves to mediate between the past and future, the subject comes to realize the finitude of retrospection and grief and gains a circumspect view of time. As death and salvation become an overarching theme, the dyads of order/disorder, harmony/disharmony, and love/chastity diminish in importance. There is greater directness and simplicity in the dialogues, dreams, and encounters, many of which are vignettes set within the encompassing narrative of Laura's death, the subject's grief, and his contemplation of his own death.[2]

If in the troubador tradition the figure of the poet was a servant-liege to the imperious Lady-Domina, an invariant utilizable by poets of diverse temperaments, Petrarch's use of this figure in Part 1 was eclectic and neutral and depended on metonymic substitutions and inversions. The result was that he directed much irony at the tradition of courtly love. By the inception of Part 2 the traces of this tradition are no more than literary simulacra. The debts to the Dolce Stil Nuovo are highly formalized and can be considered a conscious use of anachronism. As the subject confronts the reality of loss and destruction, he is forced to absorb the reality of death into a larger self that seeks its sole consolation in God. Herein lie the sacred nature of the grieving process and the state of quietude that can grow out of it as, through the contemplation of death and the process of self-examination, one regains the capacity for joy and happiness.[3]

Stylistically, the use of tropes is simplified in Part 2 so that a single analogy may suffice to provide the structure for an entire poem; the syntax grows more paratactic and the tone more Davidic, allowing comparisons to the *sermo humilis* of the Bible. At the same time the lexis is more ambiguous, allowing for the double readings and limit-expressions typical of parable. Christ's kenosis or emptying out of his divinity into a human creature forms the basis of the subject's *imitatio Christi* as he grieves for the beloved and consecrates her Christlike nature. In this poetic development, the act of raising one's eyes to the sky – *contemplare* – derives from the act of thinking – *pensare* – the act of weighing (*pesare*) with the intellect: meditating, imagining, judging.

The prevalence of the verb *pensare* in the great canzoni that open Part 2 is an indicator of the turn towards contemplation, as the subject seeks a harmony between the *vita activa*, restored to its full participation in the moral and ethical life, and the *vita contemplativa*. Since most of the poems in Part 2 concern the response to Laura's death and ascent to heaven, sacred themes dominate, including that of revelation, understood as part of universal history. As Paul Ricoeur has written, "Revelation is the transfer from *this* history to *our* history."[4] Seen in this light, the transition to Part 2 is a passage from the personal to the universal; as one proceeds to analyse the poems, therefore, contemplation will serve as a unifying theme along with the figural view provided by religious typology.

The transition to Part 2 comports great gravity. Within the calendrical structure that aligns poem 1 with Good Friday, poem 264, "I' vo pensando, et nel penser m'assale" ("I wander thinking, and within me my thoughts"), corresponds to Christmas Day, the first day in the New Year as it was commonly considered in Petrarch's day. This second-longest poem of the collection takes the form of an interior dialogue between two voices representing the positions of the will and the intellect (or of desire and the pursuit of glory). After the exordium of stanza 1, the "thoughts" of these motivations oppose one another in stanzas 2 to 7. While on a worldly plane the opposing motivations arrive at an impasse, as in the tragic experience of Ovid's Medea, on a sacred plane a ternary element emerges to resolve the conflict. There are suggestions of this opening up to a third alternative earlier in the poem, in the lines "Quelle pietose braccia / in ch'io mi fido, veggio aperte anchora" ("Those arms compassionate, / In which I trust, I see still open wide") (264, 14–15). By heeding such signs, the reader can grasp the author's subjectivity and the alternating states of his soul, divided between the attitude of prayer and the struggle with sinfulness. This condition is manifested in the thoughts themselves, weighed down by frustration and distrust. At the same time, in the following lines one finds the *claritas* in which a transformed figure of Amor states that the love of Laura, whose gaze has penetrated to the lover's soul, was intended to have celestial, not worldly rewards:

et se l'ardor fallace
durò molt'anni in aspectando un giorno,
che per nostra salute unqua non vène,
or ti solleva a piú beata spene,
mirando 'l ciel che ti si volve intorno,
immortal et addorno:
ché dove, del mal suo qua giú sí lieta,
vostra vaghezza acqueta
un mover d'occhi, un ragionar, un canto,
quanto fia quel piacer, se questo è tanto? – (264, 45–54)

["…] and if
Misleading ardor for so many years
Endured in expectation of a day,
One which for our salvation does not come,
Now raise yourself to a more blissful hope
Watching the heavens that, immortal and
Bespangled, round you wheel.
For if, so joyful in its ill down here,
Your longing's quieted

By glancing eyes, or discourse, or a song,
How great will be that joy if this is such?"

Here the subject is informed of the urgent need to discern the worldly limits of love and glory. Thus the figure of the "barchetta" ("small boat") (264, 82) prepared for sea – suggesting the boats of the Apostles in Matthew 8:24 and of Peter in Matthew 14:24 – "è ritenuta anchor da ta' duo nodi" ("[is] still retained by two such knots"), leading the subject to make direct address to the Lord: "Signor mio, ché non togli / omai dal volto mio questa vergogna?" ("why not, my lord, / now rid my countenance / Of this disgrace of mine?") (264, 83, 86–7). The crux of the poem is found in the acknowledgment that the pursuit of "pregio" ("merit") forbids one from loving a mortal being with the love preserved for God. Through the calques of speeches by the dying Medea, the "I" figure anticipates the death of Laura. In the process, "una pietà sí forte di me stesso" ("such fierce self-pity") (264, 2) comes to an end, because of the greater goal of having pity for another. Here too the macrotextual discourse of Glory, begun in canzone 119, finds its final closure, as worldly fame is reduced to a gust of wind:

ma se 'l latino e 'l greco
parlan di me dopo la morte, è un vento: (264, 68–9)

If Latins and if Greeks
Speak of me after death, it's but a wind:

No other poem in the sequence posits the problem of sin with such dialectical force. One is positioned as it were between the warp of the everyday and the weave of the eternal. One has the view of sin as a universal problem, a condition innate to humanity. The past limitations of the subject are revealed to him in the present, when his "barchetta" is no longer impeded by the tragedy of Medea, precisely because it is centred on faith, conceived as a prayerful return to the right path:

et sento ad ora ad or venirmi al core
un leggiadro disegno aspro et severo
ch'ogni occulto pensero
tira in mezzo la fronte, ov'altri 'l vede:
ché mortal cosa amar con tanta fede
quanta a Dio sol per debito convensi,
piú si disdice a chi piú pregio brama. (264, 95–101)

And hour by hour I feel grow in my heart
A worthy scorn, severe and harsh, which sets
Forth all my secret thoughts
Upon my brow for others to observe.
Indeed, to love a mortal thing with faith
As great as that due but to God, is most
Denied him who the most for merit yearns.

The distinction between the love of God's creatures and the love of God is unequivocal. This clarity allows for the twofold principle of the love of God and the love of one's neighbour, as Petrarch cites the same passage (Matthew 22:37–8) cited by Augustine in *De doctrina Christiana*.[5] In the poem's conclusion a third option in the contest between love and glory is established, the way of penitence and life change:

cerco del viver mio novo consiglio
et veggio 'l meglio, et al peggior m'appiglio. (264, 135–6)

At hand, new counsel for my life I seek.
The best I see, yet seize upon the worst.

The essence of the poem's theological message is found in the penultimate line: "cerco del viver mio novo consiglio" (264, 135). This "new counsel" will absorb the pursuit of truth and glory and replace it with a more dynamic and penitential force. The calque in the final line from Ovid's Medea, who "sees the best yet seizes on the worst," also suggests the condition of Paul in Romans 7:14–15: "For we know that the law is spiritual: but I am carnal, sold under sin. For that which I do I allow not: for what I would, that do I not; but what I hate, that do I."[6]

While the internal clock of the subject's lifespan continues to run (even oscillating backwards in poem 266), his thoughts of time are now conducted *sub specie aeternitatis*. The fact that poem 266 celebrates the eighteenth anniversary of the enamourment – while poem 212 already marked the passage of twenty years – clarifies the distinction between the narration (*récit*) and the internal narrative (*histoire*). It is only with poem 267, "Oimè il bel viso, oimè il soave sguardo" ("Alas, that lovely face, alas, that gentle look"), that one arrives at the fatal year 1348. Here the death of Laura is announced in a series of five "Oimè" ("Alas!") in lines 1 to 5 (recalling that usage in Cino da Pistoia's death ode for

Selvaggia). Laura is remembered in her physical presence and stature, her laughter and smile:

> et oimè il dolce riso, onde uscío 'l dardo
> di che morte, altro bene omai non spero:
> […]
> Di speranza m'empieste e di desire,
> quan'io partí' dal sommo piacer vivo;
> ma 'l vento ne portava le parole. (267, 5–6)

> And that sweet laugh, alas, whence flew the dart
> From which I hope for no good else but death.
> […]
> You filled me with desire and hope when I
> Departed from the highest joy alive,
> But the wind blew all those words of it away.

Though it is often viewed as a poem of division, sonnet 267 functions as a bridge and sign of unification: "La scomparsa di Laura è infatti elemento di distacco ma soprattutto di *unificazione* (contrariamente a quanto pensarono antichi commentatori e moderni editori)" (Laura's death is in fact an element of detachment but especially of *unification* (contrary to what ancient commentators and modern editors thought)).[7] Though the winds of change have blown away the words of hope and desire, the hope and desire remain in the subject and will steer him through his grief.

At this most solemn point in the sequence comes canzone 268, the great threnody, underlain with citations from Lamentations, the Gospels, and Paul's Letters to the Corinthians and Hebrews.[8] The first thing that strikes the reader on a formal plane is the presence of four septenaries in the eleven-line strophes, making it the richest canzone in septenaries in Part 2. In the arresting incipit, "Che debb'io far? che mi consigli, Amore?" ("What must I do? What do you counsel, Love?"), one sees the metamorphosis of Amor from a figure of cupidity to a spiritual comrade. The principal answer to the opening query will be supplied by the subject's renunciation of the affairs of the "world":

> Ahi orbo *mondo*, ingrato,
> gran cagion ài di dever pianger meco,
> ché quel bel ch'era in te, perduto ài seco.

Caduta è la tua gloria, et tu nol vedi,
né degno eri, mentr'ella
visse qua giú, d'aver sua conoscenza,
né d'esser tocco da' suoi sancti piedi,
perché cosa sí bella
devea 'l ciel adornar di sua presenza. (268, 20–8)

Ah, ingrate world bereaved,
You have much cause that you should weep with me;
What beauty you possessed, you've lost with her.
Your glory's fallen, and you see it not,
Nor did you merit her
Acquaintance while she lived upon the earth,
Unworthy for her sacred feet to touch,
Because a being so fine
With her fair presence should adorn the Heavens.

The blindness of the world to the innocence and glory of Laura amounts to its ignoring of the City of God. Laura's "sancti piedi" (268, 26) naturally recall those of Christ. The fact that the world was unworthy of her acquaintance during her lifetime is obviously a reference to humanity's not having known the Christ.

In historical terms, the unawareness of Christ's actuality in the world was manifest for Petrarch in the schism of the church, which marked a separation between Christianity and Christendom. As one reads in the *De otio*, the world in Petrarch's day persists in two complementary "heresies": "quarum altera Cristum Deum tantum et non hominem, altera hominem et non Deum decepta contendit" ("One states that Christ was only God and not a human being, the other contends that He was only a human being and not God").[9] Nor were the monks Petrarch addressed in that work immune from these heresies, or from the envy and sloth of a Christendom deprived of its Christianity. Similarly, in the work of mourning undertaken in "Che debb'io far?," the poet summons up a group of elect souls, the blessed "donne" who can join him in his *planh*. These women call to mind Mary and Mary Magdalen, those who remained the longest at the cross and were the first at the tomb. One notes the sanctity of these women – "Donne, voi che miraste sua beltate / et l'angelica vita" ("You ladies who her beauty once admired / And her angelic life") (268, 56) – who are entreated to pity the subject and observe with compassion and charity the soul's internal discourse with virtuous Amor.[10]

The quietude of Petrarch's experience during the years immediately prior to Laura's death prepared him in a sense for the mourning, or what Martinez calls "the conversion of joy into woe, *versatio in luctum*."[11] Eventually, as we progress towards the end of the *Fragmenta*, the motifs of grief will be displaced by those of consecration and happiness mediated by the life of prayer.[12] Reminders of the need, from the standpoint of the faith, to reject the worldly and commonplace form a leitmotif in this process: "Come va 'l mondo!" ("How this world goes!") (290, 1); "Misero mondo, instabile et protervo ..." ("Poor arrogant, unstable world") (319, 5); "Ahi, nulla, altro che pianto, al mondo dura!" ("Woe! Nothing, save for tears, in this world lasts") (323, 72).

As one considers the transition to Part 2, one recalls Guittone d'Arezzo's "Ora parrà s'eo saverò cantare" (We will soon find out if I can sing), an iconic poem of religious and political exile and renunciation. But in contrast to Guittone, who didn't allow for *Amore* to become *virtù* but wrested the one from the other, for Petrarch *Amore* was mutable, committed to its own renunciation and separation from the past. This process of Amor's maturation into virtue, similar in many respects to the one predicated by Dante, can be pointed to in poems 1 and 366 and elsewhere. But it is felt most intensely in the span of poems ending Part 1 and beginning Part 2: 257, 259, 264, 268, 270, and 272.

Canzone 270, "Amor, se vuo' ch'i' torni al giogo anticho" ("If in your ancient yoke you want me back") (270, 1), is a prayer spoken by a unified subject standing before an elevated, celestial figure of Amor who is assisting the subject in his reconciliation with the past:

> (perché qui fra noi
> quel che tu val' et puoi,
> credo che 'l sente ogni gentil persona), (270, 11–13)

> (because here among us
> your great worth and ability, I believe
> is known by every gentle person)

The opening line alludes not to the yoke of desire and physical love but to Christ's invitation to the followers of John the Baptist: "Take my yoke upon you, and learn from me; for I am gentle and humble in heart, and you will find rest for your souls. For my yoke is easy, and my burden is light" (Matthew 11:29–30). Just as the heaviness of slavery becomes a light burden in Christ's speech to the followers of John, in the poem one has a seriously spirited debate between the lover and Amor, who is challenged amid a recapitulation of the devices of his art to bring profane love to life again. The challenge is made by the lover who has reversed the sign of Amor's persona from negative to positive, assuming the position of the mournful victor over the defeated pagan god.[13] The lover addresses Amor with the antithetical verbs *legare* and *sciogliere,* to tie and untie (as in Matthew 18:18: "I tell you the truth, whatever you bind on earth will be bound in heaven, and whatever you loose on earth will be loosed in heaven"), and exists in syntony with the "ardent spirit" of Laura:

spargi co le tue man' le chiome al vento,
ivi mi *lega,* et puo' mi far contento.
  Dal laccio d'òr non sia mai chi me *scioglia,*
negletto ad arte, e 'nnanellato et hirto,
né de l'ardente spirto
de la sua vista *dolcemente acerba,*
la qual dí et notte più che lauro o mirto
tenea in me verde l'amorosa voglia, (270, 62–7)

Her locks with your own hand strew to the wind;
There tie me fast, and you'll make me content.
  No one will ever free me from that snare
Of gold, ruffled and curled, with art unkempt,
Nor from the ardent spirit
Of her face, sweetly cruel, which night and day
Maintained that longing amorous in me,
More green than laurel or than myrtle

In this elevated context, the oxymoron "dolcemente acerba" serves to invalidate the worldly understanding of love and reinforce the way of heaven as Laura is transformed into an angel whose primary gesture is to laugh or smile:

il pensar e 'l tacer, il riso e 'l gioco,
l'abito honesto e 'l ragionar cortese,
le parole che 'ntese
avrian fatto gentil d'alma villana,
l'angelica sembianza, humile et piana,
ch'or quinci or quindi udia tanto lodarsi; (270, 80–5)

Her thoughtfulness and silence, laugh and play,
Her forthright nature, discourse courteous,
Those words that, grasped, would have
Ennobled any soul though lowly bred,
Her countenance, angelic, modest, calm,
Which near and far one heard so greatly praised.

The simulacra of troubadoric motifs accompany a cathartic look backwards to the history of love's slavery and a telescoping forward to the grieving in which the memory of Laura's sense of calm, joy, and felicity will guide the poet:

Morte m'à sciolto, Amor, d'ogni tua legge:
quella che fu mia donna al ciel è gita,
lasciando trista et libera mia vita. (270, 106–8)

Death from your every law has freed me, Love;
That one who was my lady passed to heaven,
And left my life in grief and liberty.

In poem 272, he allows for the fact that his self-pity has saved him from suicide: "se non ch'i' ò di me stesso pietate, / i' sarei già di questi penser' fòra" ("In truth, if piety did not prevent, Beyond these cares I would already be") (272, 7–8). If such self-pity was the point of departure for Part 2 – "Io vo pensando, et nel penser m'assale / una pietà sí forte di me stesso" ("I wander thinking, and within my thoughts / Such fierce self-pity lays me siege …") (264, 1–2) – the point of arrival will be a complete absorption in the pity for the Other.

In the summer of 1351 Petrarch returned to Provence. During the difficult winter that followed, he wrote sonnets 279 to 282, 288, 300 to 303, 305 and 306, 308, 310, 311, 320, and 321. These poems develop a theological theme based on a new sense of being in the world that revives the sense of the transcendental. As regards the rapprochement of the voices of narrator, character, and author, one can stipulate that the fiction is no longer accomplished at a distance, but that a parabolic time has intervened in which the subject's worldly experience is perceived in terms of signs that concern the dispensation of the soul and the existence of grace. As in the New Testament parables, the world is appraised with a cold eye as a place of trial.

Images arise that are reminiscent of the Gospel, like the field that receives the seed or the treasure that is found in the field. Endured faithfully, the experience of the world guides the soul towards reconciliation and moral understanding. Parable includes within it other forms, such as aphorism, proverb, allegory, metaphor, and simile. It often depicts a strange or obscure event occurring in the otherwise natural setting of the rural daily life. These practices give rise to isotopies, or shared structures and sets of imagery, as they pertain to the literal level of planting, harvesting, or labouring, and to the anagogic level of the life of the spirit.[14] The oddness of the parabolic event is a sign of its symbolic character and causes one to distinguish it from the normal course of affairs.

In his essay "The Bible and the Imagination," Paul Ricoeur aims to "to seek *in* reading itself the key to the heuristic functioning of the productive imagination."[15] Ricoeur specifies that the imagination is a "rule-governed form of invention" and can be "considered as the power of giving form to human experience."[16] Armed with this definition, which rejects the view of the imagination as fancy, reverie, or speculation, Ricoeur states that in the biblical context, "the parable is not an exceptional literary genre, rather parabolization is a general procedure of the narrative form of imagination."[17] Drawing on the parables of the wicked husbandmen and the sower (the only ones shared by all the synoptic gospels), Ricoeur shows how structural similarities within and between the parables inform the larger, encompassing discourse of Christ's journey. Each parable possesses a dual function, being a discourse and the metaphorization of a discourse. By tracing the interconnections between the micro patterns of the parables and the macrotext in which they are inserted, one can develop a theory of biblical intertextuality capable of negotiating the presence of "enigma-expressions" (such as "the Kingdom of God") and limit-experiences. Such a theory extends beyond parables to the figural relationship between the Old and New Testaments, passing from "the restricted intertextuality of the parables to the generalized intertextuality of the whole Bible considered as a single book."[18]

Ricoeur's essay is pertinent to a text like the *Fragmenta* in which microtexts are embedded in a larger narrative to which they are linked by interlacing figurative and figural relationships. Petrarch alludes to the Gospels parables at diverse points, as exempla from the life of Christ serve as a catalyst for developing the narrative. The parabolic poems exploit the reciprocity of the microtext and macrotext in order to suggest the englobing of human discourse by the Logos, the Word of God. Given the complexity of such an arrangement, the reading of the texts depends on the identification of isotopies that characterize the events recounted and relate them to their deeper significance, as we have just seen in the case of "giogo" in poem 270.

The sequence of fifty-two uninterrupted sonnets, *Rvf* 271 to 322, features worldly images in narrative vignettes that also function on a deeper, symbolic level. The imaginary milieu of the sequence is liquid, as if to suggest the interpenetration of water and tears. This is seen in poem 275, a dialogue between the subject and his body parts: the eyes, ears, and feet, all incapacitated by grief. He instructs them to praise God and states that there will be an end to mourning and a cause for joy. These are the very themes of humility, praise, and prayer that will lift the subject to the *gaudium et spes* (joy and hope) of the final poems:[19]

Morte biasmate; anzi laudate Lui
che lega et scioglie, e 'n un punto apre et serra.
e dopo 'l pianto sa far lieto altrui. (275, 12–14)

Reproach Death then—or rather, give her praise
Who binds and frees, unseals and shuts at once,
And, after grief, knows how to bring one joy.

If the hope for "novo consiglio" enunciated at the close of canzone 264 is to be satisfied, the subject must be an adequate interlocutor. For that to occur, he must confront the new morality that has surfaced in the interiority of the conscience. When he realizes in sonnet 277, "S'Amor novo consiglio non n'apporta" ("If Love will offer me no new advice"), that Amor has no counsel forthcoming, he must imagine another "guide," and from the sense of disarray there arises a potential for joy:

Imaginata guida la conduce,
ché la vera è sotterra, anzi è nel cielo
onde piu che mai chiara al cor traluce: (277, 9–11)

A pilot that I picture guides my life:
The real one's in the earth – that is, in heaven,
Whence, brighter than before, she lights my heart.

While three years pass in the *histoire* between poems 267 and 278, only seven years pass between poems 278 and 364, meaning that the temporal curve of the fiction flattens out.[20] The timeline of the anniversary poems was progressively loosened by additions made after the Correggio manuscript, supplanting the time of history with that of memory and contemplation ("within-time-ness"), including elements of prayer, vision, and parable. The first of a cycle of three poems written after the return to Vaucluse in 1351, poem 279 is a simple dialogue; as the subject sits contemplating the absent Laura on the "fresca riva" of the Sorgue, her spirit calls out to him:

> Se lamentar augelli, o verdi fronde
> mover soavemente a l'aura estiva,
> o roco mormorar di lucide onde
> s'ode d'una fiorita et fresca riva,
> là 'v'io seggia d'amor pensoso et scriva,
> lei che 'l ciel ne mostrò, terra n'asconde,
> veggio, et odo, et intendo ch'anchor viva
> di sí lontano a' sospir' miei risponde.
> "Deh, perché inanzi 'l tempo ti consume?
> – mi dice con pietate – a che pur versi
> degli occhi tristi un doloroso fiume?
> Di me non pianger tu, ché' miei dí fersi
> morendo eterni, et ne l'interno lume,
> quando mostrai de chiuder, gli occhi apersi." (279, 1–14)

> Where some hear mourning birds, or verdant fronds
> That rustle softly in the summer breeze,
> Or quiet murmuring of lucent waves,
> Beside a cool and flowering bank, there I
> Sit lost in thoughts of love, and write; there I
> See her, and hear, and understand; for she
> Whom heaven showed us, whom the earth conceals,
> Yet lives; my sighs she answers from afar.
> "Alas, before your time, why waste away?"
> She asks me with compassion, "Why still do
> Your mournful eyes spill forth a woeful stream?
> "Weep not for me! Lo, dying makes my day
> Eternal; to that inner light my eyes,
> When I appeared to close them, opened wide."

As the Lady in heaven speaks to the poet, it is through the act of writing ("scriva") that he comes to understand ("intendo") her exemplum, as shown ("mostrò") by heaven. Let weeping come to an end, says Laura, in a familiar form of address that will be reciprocated by the subject. (The *tu* pronoun is used exclusively when addressing Laura in death, but rarely in the poems *in vita*, where *voi* is preferred.)[21]

2. "Come va 'l mondo!" (290, 1)

It was Petrarch's genius to conceive of poetical equivalents for the Christian experience of time and history in which one witnesses the coming to fruition, in a single life, of the changes precipitated by faith. When Laura's image returns as something familiar and intimate that seeks to deliver the subject to unity, that communion carries with it the memory of repentance and of the sinful condition that preceded it. As we have just seen, Laura's spirit is more likely to occur in those solitary places in the world where her presence is still felt:

Cosí comincio a ritrovar presenti
le tue bellezze a' suoi usati soggiorni, (282, 7–8)

Thus I start to find your beauties again
present in the accustomed locales

In poem 290, the subject recapitulates the story of being driven towards moral death before being guided "a miglior riva" by the Lady. The poem begins with the exclamation "Come va 'l mondo!" ("How this world goes!") (290, 1), and is followed by two other exclamations:

Benedetta colei ch'a miglior riva
volse il mio corso, et l'empia voglia ardente
lusingando affrenò perch'io non pèra. (290, 12–14)

Bless her who toward the best shore set my course,
Who curbed with blandishments my ardent will,
So impious, that I might not be lost.

In poem 291, "Quand'io veggio dal ciel scender l'Aurora" ("When I see the dawn descend from heaven above"), the figure of Amor is invoked amidst a reminiscence of the myth of Tithonus and Eos (the Dawn). In contrast to Tithonus, who receives his lover in his arms with every sunset, the subject has only Laura's name to repeat as he points skyward and states, "Ivi è Laura ora" ("There's Laura now") (291, 4).

Unlike in earlier poems in which the hypnotic presence of a name without a body resulted in despair, here the subject, addressing Tithonus, has attained a kind of melancholy detachment:[22]

> I vostri dipartir' non son sí duri,
> ch'almen di notte suol tornar colei
> che non â schifo le tue bianche chiome:
> le mie notti fa triste, e i giorni oscuri,
> quella che n'à portato i penser' miei,
> né di sè m'à lasciato altro che 'l nome. (291, 9–14)

> Your separations aren't so difficult,
> For every night, at least, to you returns
> She whom your hoary locks do not offend.
> My nights she saddens and obscures my days –
> That one who bore away my thoughts, and left
> Me nothing of herself except her name.

In the third poem of the triptych, poem 292, the poet is again grieving over the death of Laura and declares he will write no more poetry:

> Or sia qui fine al mio amoroso canto:
> secca è la vena de l'usato ingegno,
> et la cetera mia rivolta in pianto. (292, 12–14)

> Here let me finish now my amorous song;
> The well-spring of accustomed skill is dry,
> And my lyre is to lamentation turned.

These are the final lines of the last poem in the Correggio form, and designate an ending. So, too, sonnet 293 marks a new beginning and provides a rationale for the continued writing of verse. This "connection of transformation" can be summed up symbolically in the conclusion of poem 297, where the narrator declares his intention to "consecrate" Laura's noble name with his pen.

> et s'al seguir son tardo
> forse averrà che 'l bel nome gentile
> consecrerò con questa stanca penna. (297, 12–14)

if I'm slow to follow, it
May come to pass that her fair noble name
I shall make sacred with this weary pen.

The larger sense of this development is found in the author's realization that attempts at verisimilitude will not persuade the reader as to the truth of the account. Rather, what may do that are overt signs of fictionality that foreground the act of writing, as is consistent with the medieval author's focus on production and the self-representation of production.

Poems 302 to 304 repeat the same sort of recapitulation of the earlier temporalities of fable and history that we saw in poems 290 to 292. The marker poem 302, "Levommi il mio penser in parte ov'era" ("My thought raised me to regions where she dwelt"), conveys a vision of Laura in Heaven, an exemplum modelled on Paul's *raptus* of II Corinthians 3:16: "Whenever anyone turns to the Lord, the veil is taken away":

Per man mi prese e disse: "In questa spera
sarai anchor meco, se 'l desir non erra:
i' so' colei che ti die' tanta guerra,
et compie' mia giornata inanzi sera.
Mio ben non cape in intelletto humano:
te solo aspetto, et quel che tanto amasti
e là giuso è rimaso, il mio bel velo. – (302, 5–11)

She took me by the hand and said, "In this sphere, yet
You'll be with me, if such desire's not wrong;
I'm she who brought such war to you, and who
Completed my day's tasks ere evening fell.
"No human mind can grasp my peace; for you
Alone I wait, and – what you loved so much –
My lovely veil, which there below remained."

Laura's defence of holy desire and her assertion "Mio ben non cape in intelletto humano" (302, 9) makes it clear that there are human limits to the comprehension of the work of the Holy Spirit. As philosophy is redefined by Petrarch, the contemplative view is increased; the mode of argumentation is required to incorporate the affect and the paradoxes of the self; ethics is absorbed into theology. The most synthetic presentation of this philosophy is found in the late text *De sui ipsius et aliorum ignorantia* (*On His Own Ignorance and That of Many Others*).

Poem 303 provides a retrospective view of the landscape of love and the interlocution with Amor, a discourse now complete. The river invoked is no longer the Sorgue but a universal river, just as the "valli chiuse, alti colli et piaggie apriche" ("closed vales, high hills, and sunny slopes") (303, 6) are not just the Vaucluse but stand for the totality of the natural landscape in which sacred love will endure.

o vaghi habitator' de' verdi boschi,
o ninphe, et voi che 'l fresco herboso fondo
del liquido cristallo alberga et pasce:
i dí miei fur sí chiari, or son sí foschi,
come Morte che 'l fa; cosí nel mondo
sua ventura à ciascun dal dí che nasce. (303, 9–14)

O wandering dwellers in the verdant woods,
O nymphs, and you who dwell and feed within
The liquid crystal's cool and grassy deeps,
My days, which were so bright, are now as dark
As Death who makes them so; thus in this world
Each has his fortune from his day of birth.

By juxtaposing the brilliance of days past to the final fact of mortality, the subject converts the sylvan register of the "ninphe" and "vaghi habitor" to the pastoral mode of the Psalms, as in the *Bucolicum Carmen* (where the persona of Silvano espoused the goal of a Franciscan hermitage). Thus the *sententia* of the final lines is not bleak, since what is implicitly forecast after the darkness of death is the clarity and brilliance of the next life. In the realization of one's earthly blindness – in the experience of the ineffable – one attains a guide to right living.[23]

Poem 304, "Mentre che 'l cor dagli amorosi vermi" ("As long as worms of love devoured my heart"), begins with a recollection of youth, when the heart was devoured by worms. The use of a gruesome *memento mori* (reminiscent of Jacopone da Todi's *contrasto* in which the eyes and nose of a dead man are devoured by "vermi") to describe the heart of a vigorous man conveys the gap between the hopeless time of the past and the current time of possibility and hope.[24] In the sestet the poet presents this hypothesis: Laura is dead and her burial site marked by a small headstone ("picciol marmo"); but if she had lived, the poetry of praise I could sing would shatter stones ("romper le pietre"). Positioned at the end of the Chigi manuscript, the sonnet marks with dramatic finality the poet's dismissal of all illusions concerning Amor and the songs of love.

Poem 308 is a marker poem, ambiguous and mysterious, concerning the poet's inability to "paint" in words the image of Laura; as in poems 77 and 78 on the portrait of Laura by Simone Martini, one sees confirmed the artist's inability to reproduce an image of Laura that conveys her divine nature. In the opening lines in which Laura is praised for her "franca povertà" one sees a reference to St Francis and his marriage to Lady Poverty, recalling the pairing of Laura and Francis in poem 4.[25] In addition the virtue of humility pertains to the Sorgue River, which stands metonymically for Laura:

Quella per cui con Sorga ò cangiato Arno,
con franca povertà serve richezze,
volse in *amaro* sue sante *dolceze*,
ond'io già vissi, or me ne struggo et *scarno*.
Da poi piú volte ò riprovato indarno
al secol che verrà l'alte belleze
pinger cantando, a ciò che l'alme et preze:
né col mio stile il suo bel viso *incarno*. (308, 1–8)

That one for whom I changed Arno for Sorgue,
Left servile riches for free poverty,
Has turned to gall her sacred sweetness that
I lived by; by it now I'm melted, flayed.
Since then, in song I've often vainly tried
To sketch her lofty beauties for the age
To come, so it may love and value them,
Yet her fair face my style can't body forth.

With reference to the *dolce / amaro* antithesis discussed in chapter 4, section 3, Petrarch now uses "bitterness" in a manner consistent with Augustine, for whom *amaritudo* designates the condition of the soul before its reception of Christ (and, as the translation suggests, the "gall" given to Christ on the Cross).[26] The Christological reading is evident in the antithetical verbs "incarno" and "scarno," *hapaxes* that suggest the incarnation and flaying of Christ. In the bitterness of the subject at his inability to reproduce the image of the beloved, there is faith in the Resurrection. In the sonnet's conclusion, amid allusions to Dante's portrait of St Francis in *Paradiso* xi, 38: "in terra fue" ("was on earth") and 50: "nacque al mondo un sole" ("a sun was born into the world"), the poet employs the inexpressibility topos:[27]

ma poi ch'i' giungo a la divina parte
ch'un chiaro et breve *sole* al *mondo fue,*
ivi manca l'ardir, l'ingegno et l'arte. (308, 12–14)

But when I come to what's divine in her
Who was a bright, brief sun to all the world,
There courage falters, skill and art as well.

Sonnet 309 continues in the same mode of the inenarrable, foregrounding the finite act of writing in order to persuade the reader of the "silent truth" of Laura's beatitude, despite the inadequacy of the present account:

Chi sa pensare, il ver tacito estime,
ch'ogni stil vince, et poi sospire: – Adunque
beati gli occhi che la vider viva. – (309, 12–14)

May thinking men esteem the silent truth
That conquers every style, and sighing, say:
"Let eyes that saw her living, then, be blest."

Sonnets 310 to 312 constitute a final and definitive reversal of the stilnovistic and Cavalcantian attraction to the world, as seen in the *plazer* genre. This triad reverses the *plazer* by means of a negative enumeration of the beauties and pleasures of the world. Its structures and allusions support a set of sacred references that allow the subject to correct earlier passages. Thus, in poems 310 and 311 the figure of the nightingale may be identified with Christ (as I discuss in chapter 7). The final tercet of poem 312 stands in sharp contrast to the suicide motifs in poems 36 and 273, as one is attracted to death as a means of embracing renunciation, not to ask that it come any sooner:

né altro sarà mai ch'al cor m'aggiunga,
sí seco il seppe quella sepellire
che sola agli occhi miei fu lume et speglio.
Noia m'è 'l viver sí gravosa et lunga
ch'i' chiamo il fine, per lo gran desire
di riveder cui non veder fu 'l meglio. (312, 9–14)

Nor will another ever touch my heart;
How to inter it with her, she knew well,
She, the sole light and mirror for my eyes.
To live so long and sadly vexes me,
So for life's end I call, through great desire
Once more to see her I'd best not have seen.

Such intratextual references to earlier poems recapitulate negative experiences in a corrective light. When the subject relates how the sound of Laura's words educated him in the ways of love, "col suon de le parole / ne le quali io imparai che cosa è amore" ("the music of her words. / Where, as before, I learned / What thing love is") (270, 52–3), one hears the distant sound of how his own words once punished him: "mi struggo al suon de le parole" ("at the cadence of the words I melt") (73, 14). In poems 328 and 330 on the topic of Laura's eyes, one recalls the *canzoni degli occhi* (71, 72, 73). And in sonnet 329, "O giorno, o hora, o ultimo momento" ("O day, O hour, O final instant"), one hears an echo of the telescoping temporality of poem 61, 1-2: "Benedetto sia 'l giorno, et 'l mese, et l'anno, / et la stagione, e 'l tempo, et l'ora, e 'l punto" ("Ah, blessed be the day, the month, the year, / The season, time, the hour, the very stroke"). And when the world without Laura is described as "questo inferno" ("this hell") (345, 10), one recalls the earlier description of Avignon as "di vivi inferno" ("Hell for the quick") (138, 7).

3. Augustinian Time and the Process of Grieving

In te, anime meus, tempora mea metior.

In you, my mind, I measure time.

Augustine, *Confessions*, xi, 27

While almost all the poems in Part 1 were written by 1351, the work of ordering and compiling the poems, of both Parts 1 and 2, continued on parallel tracks for years to come. Working in the area of what he calls "la filologia delle strutture" (the philology of structures) Domenico De Robertis argues that the "strutture intermedie" (intermediate structures) connecting Parts 1 and 2 contribute to the overall unity of the *Fragmenta*. These structures are not inferred or denied on the basis of linearity and consecutive order but are constituted by syntagmatic similarities and correlations between the poems, at times over a great textual distance.[28] De Robertis's idea of "un unico canzoniere 'in morte'" (a single canzoniere "in death") finds its most concrete examples in two interconnected sets that Petrarch was working on in the final years: poems 319, 191, 192, and 193, and poems 194, 196, 197, and 321.[29] In addition to reminding one of the highly constructed nature of the spiritual autobiography, these additions admit to the later poems of Part 1 a more theological understanding of time, as based on contemplation and vision. This is the time of the spirit discussed by Augustine in the conclusion of Book xi of the *Confessions*: "nam et expectat et adtendit et meminit, ut id quod expectat per id quod adtendit transeat in id quod meminerit. [...] sed tamen perdurat attentio, per quam pergat abesse quod aderit" ("The mind expects and attends, and remembers, so that what it expects passes by way of what it attends to into what it remembers. [...] Yet our attention does endure, and through our attention what is still to be makes its way into the state where it is no more").[30] Augustine compares this flow of future events, through the present into memory, to the recitation of a poem:

> quod quanto magis agitur et agitur, tanto breviata expectatione prolongatur memoria, donec tota expectatio consumatur, cum tota illa actio finita transierit in memoriam. et quod in toto cantico, hoc in singulis particulis eius fit atque in singulis syllabis eius, [...] hoc in tota vita hominis, cuius partes sunt omnes actiones hominis, hoc in toto saeculo filiorum hominum, cuius partes sunt omnes vitae hominum.
>
> As the poem goes on and on, expectation is curtailed and memory prolonged, until expectation is entirely used up, when the whole completed action has passed into memory. [...] What is true of the poem as a whole is true equally of its individual stanzas and syllables. [...] The same thing happens in the entirety of a person's life, of which all his actions are part; and the same in the entire sweep of human history, the parts of which are individual human lives.[31]

To know a song or a poem by heart in its syllables and silences, its *sonoritas*, is a means of approaching the mystery of faith, to conceive in the fragility of one's mind, the mind of God, in which past, present, and future are absorbed into eternity. Augustine writes of this process in a passionate language that pertains to the span of poems discussed here, as the Petrarchan subject attempts to recount the contrast between eternal time and worldly time, as the fire of worldly desire is eliminated and replaced by the fire and the desire of God.[32]

Poem 314, "Mente mia, che presaga de' tuoi damni" ("My mind, you had foretold your injuries"), recalls the last encounter between Petrarch and Laura. The recollection stands symbolically for the end of linear time and its replacement by universal time, in which past, present, and future interpenetrate. In the following lines, which echo the Meeting at Emmaus, the situation of "within-time-ness" is reflected by the flames of God's love and is enabled by a series of verbs in the present, past absolute, and imperfect tenses:[33]

Questo è l'ultimo dí de' miei dolci anni.
  Qual dolcezza fu quella, o misera alma!
Come ardavamo in quel punto ch'i' vidi
gli occhi i quai non devea riveder mai, (314, 8–11)

"This is the final day of my sweet years."
  What tenderness was there! O my poor soul;
How, in that instant when I saw those eyes
That I must never see again, we flamed.

The narrative use of the imperfect tense continues in the trio of sonnets 315 to 317, each of which begins with the consonantal sound "t." This cluster stands as a triptych at the midpoint of Part 2 and is inscribed under the sign of the past conditional tense, constituting a unit that recounts what might have occurred had Laura survived. There is a focus on what the "lovers" might have said to one another in their mature years when the flames of passion had dwindled and love and chastity were no longer at odds with one another. De Robertis notes the presence in these poems of a humble, prose-like style having quotidian and proverbial features. The lower register allows for a narrative development at the centre of which is time, presented by the classical construction of the *cum inversum* – first seen in *Rvf* 3, 1: "Era il giorno ch'al sol si scolararo … *quando* i' fui preso …" ("It was the day on which the sun's rays paled") (3, 1) – in which a past context is introduced within which a certain event occurred. The poems function as a single unit interconnected in memory, aided by the force of classical and biblical allusions that recapitulate the pattern (seen above in poems 290 to 292) of a triptych in which the first sonnet proposes a problem that the second and third sonnets resolve, set within a landscape that is morally coherent but physically imprecise. Regarding poem 317, Santagata refers to the "*escamotage* narrativo" (narrative camouflage) of the dialogue between the spirit of Laura and the subject: since the amorous error ("falsa opinione") of the subject has been corrected, the love can mellow into friendship, even after the death of the beloved: "il desiderio cede all'amore, la passione al sentimento, l'amante diviene una amica" (desire yields to love, passion to sentiment, the lover becomes a friend).[34]

If there is a threshold point where the *Fragmenta* crosses over into a purer manifestation of the Augustinian time, it is after poems 315 to 317 and after the provisional conclusion of poem 318, the final poem of the form of Giovanni (1366–7).[35] That sonnet exploits an expressionistic register of verbs of tearing and uprooting ("si svelse," "sterpe") centred on the image of the dead laurel that is yet alive ("Quel vivo lauro") and that leaves its roots ("radici") in the lover's memory where it establishes a nest ("far nido"):[36]

Al cader d'una pianta che si svelse
come quella che ferro o vento sterpe,
spargendo a terra le sue spoglie excelse,
mostrando al sol la sua squalida sterpe,
vidi un'altra ch'Amor obiecto scelse,
subiecto in me Callïope et Euterpe;
che 'l cor m'avinse, et proprio albergo felse,
qual per trunco o per muro hedera serpe.
Quel vivo lauro ove solean far nido
li alti penseri … (318, 1–10)

When one tree fell, ripped out as if it were
By wind uprooted, or dislodged by iron,
Strewing its lofty foliage on the earth,
While showing to the sun its death-white root,
I saw a tree next Love chose as my goal,
And Calliope and Euterpe as my theme,
It won my heart, and there it made its home,
As ivy twines upon a trunk or wall.
That living laurel, where my lofty thoughts
Once nested …

The sonnet proceeds from the violent to the sublime register, encapsulating a pattern seen in the macrotext and reaffirming the subject's faith in a Christian meaning to history, as built on the collective memory of the community. By reaffirming this theme, Petrarch provides the textual bridge between the poems in which memory had a role in the mourning of Laura (274, 280, 305) and those in which it assisted in her consecration (321, 323, 326, 327).

Chapter Seven

Songs of Consecration (*Rvf* 319–366)

1. The In-between Time of Parable

In the final forty-eight poems, many of which are rearranged during the late 1360s, one is abreast of the ultimate dilemma, that of time.[1] The emotional oscillations of the earlier poems of Part 2 recede as the narrative incorporates the events of the personal story into the metaphysical prospects of eternity and timelessness. We saw in chapter 6 the confrontation between the progressive time of history and the circular, repetitive time of nature. Now the neutral (kairotic, rhythmic) time of contemplation has assumed prominence. The appropriate narrative form for this "in-between" time is the parable, a mode that is accompanied by an intensified use of religious symbolism and the figurative language of the mystical tradition.

In a discussion of religious symbolism and poetry, Ricoeur argues that poetry is suited to manifestations of faith but not its proclamations (or *kerygma*). The ability to manifest faith comes to poetry by way of religious symbols, which, when genuine, emerge from reality: "Symbolism is significant only when borne by the sacred valences of the elements themselves."[2] Petrarch's use of religious symbols in the final phase of the *Fragmenta* is reminiscent of the Gospel parables: "tesoro" (treasure), "seme" (seed), "gemma" (gem/jewel), "nido" (nest). In this span of poems, such nouns stand alongside the generic symbols "lauro / alloro" (laurel), "oro" (gold), "albero" (tree), "ale/ali" (wings), "colonna" (column), "riva" (shore).[3] As in those biblical parables in which a rustic setting provides the backdrop for the lessons of death and destiny, the landscape is rendered vertically, suggesting the intimate, hidden connections between this world and the Kingdom of God (as symbolized by the parable of the hidden treasure in Matthew 13). In the parables, concrete physical details refer to the life beyond the world and serve to indicate a return to the world, healed and whole, after trial and suffering. In Petrarch's view, the return to the world is preferable to the anchorite's self-isolation, as it comports a view of how the Kingdom of Heaven is actually at work on the earth.[4]

As seen in the conclusion of chapter 6, the subject's unification under the sign of the will intensified around the midpoint of Part 2, notably in the three sonnets in "t" (315–17), a juncture at which one can speak of the completion of the process of mourning and the readiness of the subject to engage in dialogue in parity with the spirit of Laura. From this point forward, the Pauline focus on the Crucifixion and Resurrection of Christ is palpable, as the exposure of human frailties and sinfulness reinforces the need for the flesh to die for the spirit to be reborn, a purpose for which the knowledge of sin is a necessary gateway to wisdom. The penitent motif of the fleetingness of time is a reminder of the Pauline character of Petrarch's apocalyptics and eschatology:[5] "La vasta tela dei riferimenti biblici [...] è estremamente preziosa per determinare il clima di densa religiosità che alleggia per tutto il *Canzoniere*, ma essa è pur sempre secondaria rispetto alla ben più massiccia presenza della dottrina e delle note peculiari della spiritualità paolina" (The vast network of biblical references [...] is extremely precious for determining the climate of dense religiosity that leavens the entire *Canzoniere*, but it is still always secondary with regard to the more massive presence of the doctrine and peculiarities of Pauline spirituality).[6]

In these final poems one sees two sets of imagery juxtaposed, representing a narrative and a theological level of understanding. On the narrative level the reconciliation with Laura and the alteration of the figure of Amor carry one beyond the subject's experiences of grief and penitence in the final year of the internal history, 1358. On the theological level one is presented with the continuity of past, present, and future, each with its respective "advent": the past advent concerns Christ's life on earth, Crucifixion, and Resurrection; the present advent occurs in the "in-between" time of one's life on earth; the future advent marks the end-time or *parousia*.[7] In the final forty-eight poems, Petrarch's major means of integrating narrative and theology is the use of religious symbolism, with a particular emphasis given to the imagery of the Gospel parables. In this concluding span the spiritual condition of the subject is one of wonder and vigilance.

After Petrarch loses the services of scribe Giovanni Malpaghini in 1368, he continues the copying of the final version of the *Fragmenta* on his own. Poem 319 is the first text he transcribes, both in the working notebook of "scartafacci" (Vat. Lat. 3196) and in Vat. Lat. 3195

I dí miei piú leggier' che nesun cervo,
fuggîr come ombra, et non vider piú bene
ch'un batter d'occhio, et poche hore serene,
ch'amare et dolci ne la mente servo.
Misero *mondo,* instabile et protervo
del tutto è *cieco* chi 'n te pon sua spene:
ché 'n te mi fu 'l cor tolto, et or sel tène
tal ch'è già terra, et non giunge osso a nervo.
Ma la forma miglior, che vive anchora,
et vivrà sempre, su ne l'alto cielo,
di sue bellezze ogni or piú m'innamora;
et vo, sol in pensar, cangiando il pelo,
qual ella è oggi, e 'n qual parte dimora,
qual a vedere il suo leggiadro velo. (319, 1–14)

My days, more swift than any deer that flees
Away like shadow, no more good have seen
Than one blink of an eye, a few bright hours
Which, sweet and bitter, in my mind I store.
Poor arrogant, unstable world, to all
One's blind who rests his hope in you. In you
My heart was seized, and now is held by one
Already earth, with flesh disjoined from bone.
Her better form, though, living even now,
Which will forever live in Heaven above,
Still makes me love her beauties more and more.
I wander, turning gray, and only think
Of what she is today, of where she dwells
And what it's like to see her graceful veil.

As Gianfranco Folena has noted, the expression "un batter d'occhio" ("one blink of an eye") (319, 3) is one of many usages Petrarch coined (including "momento") to indicate a passing instant, and is representative of the development of a more completely measured and scaled system of time than existed previously.[8] This sonnet echoes the rejection of the "mondo" voiced in the *De otio* and shares that work's message of humility before the fact of death and the need for redemption. After the opening use of the Psalmic image of the deer to indicate the fleetingness of time, one has a seeming reference to the speech of Marco Lombardo to Dante pilgrim, "'Frate, / lo *mondo* è *cieco*, e tu vien ben … da lui […]'" ("'Brother, / the world is blind, and you come from … the world […]'" (*Purg*. xvi, 65–6), a monition that echoes the earlier infernal epithets "cieco mondo" (*Inf*. iv, 13) and "mondo cieco" (*Inf*. xxvii, 25). After this denunciation of the blind world, consumed by solipsism and ignorance, the subject gazes skyward to contemplate Laura's "forma miglior" ("better form") (319, 9), or spirit, a "leggiadro velo" ("graceful veil") on which the mind can rest. As time is interiorized in consciousness and memory, the present moment is exposed as fleeting and ungraspable.[9] The subject is now aware that the memorializing of Laura and the reconstitution of the self are two aspects of the same redemptive process. By gathering up the fragments of his experience he arrives at a detachment from error and a fuller understanding of piety and compassion.[10]

This is apparent in sonnet 320, which opens with the veiled *senhal*, "l'aura." The octave is dominated by five verbs in the past absolute tense as the love of old is recalled amidst images of disintegration:

Sento *l'aura* mia anticha, e i dolci colli
veggio apparire, onde 'l bel lume nacque
che tenne gli occhi mei mentr'al ciel piacque
bramosi et lieti, or li tèn tristi et molli.
O caduche speranze, o penser' folli!
Vedove l'erbe et torbide son l'acque,
et vòto et freddo 'l nido in ch'ella giacque,
nel qual io vivo, et morto giacer volli,
sperando alfin da le soavi piante
et da begli occhi suoi, che 'l cor m'ànn'arso,
riposo alcun de le fatiche tante.
O' servito a signor crudele et scarso:
ch'arsi quanto 'l mio foco ebbi davante,
or vo piangendo il suo cenere sparso. (320, 1–14)

That ancient breeze I feel, and those sweet hills
I see appear, where that fair light was born
Which kept my glad eyes yearning, while it so

Pleased Heaven; now it keeps them tearful, sad.
  O fleeting hopes, O thoughtless lunacy!
The grass is widowed, waters have grown dark,
Empty and cold the nest in which she lay,
In which I live, in which I dead would lie,
  Expecting at the last from her soft feet
And hoping from her fair eyes, which so parched
My heart, to have some rest from such great trials.
  O, I have served a cruel and stingy lord,
For while my fire before me blazed, I burned
Now I go weeping for its scattered ash.

The "nido" ("nest") (320, 7) in which Laura once lay and where the subject now lies, is the symbol of rebirth, of infancy in the life of the spirit. The usage recalls the "nido" of poem 318 and anticipates that of poem 321, as an image of incineration and rebirth. In the final tercet one sees that as a fire burned externally – the sun of Laura – the subject burned as well; given the sacred register employed, the ashes are a clear symbol of the Resurrection and the spiritual transformation of the subject.[11]

Poem 321, "È questo 'l nido in che la mia fenice" ("Is this the nest in which my phoenix poised"), repeats the parabolic image of the nest seen in 318 and 320.[12] In lines suggestive of the Psalms (17:8; 36:8; 57:2), the subject has returned to honour the ground of the Vaucluse that Laura had consecrated:

  Et m'ài lasciato qui misero et solo,
talché pien di duol sempre al loco torno
che per te consecrato honora et còlo; (321, 9–11)

  You have left me wretched, lonely here; so I
Return, forever woeful, to that place
You hallowed, which I honor and revere.

Petrarch's use of parable, exemplum and allegory is evident in poems that assume the form of the medieval *visio*. The most celebrated of these, poem 323, "Standomi un giorno solo a la fenestra" ("While one day at my window as I stood"), contains a synthesis of many of the dominant themes of the final poems. Each of the six stanzas presents a vision that connects to the wondrous life of Laura and the cataclysm of her passing; each stanza presents a moment of elevation and wonder interrupted by a material catastrophe; each is a microcosm of the whole.

Stanza 1 concerns the human face of the "fera" ("beast") that is Laura amidst reminiscences of the Daphnean theme. Stanza 2 concerns the majestic ship, standing metonymically for the topos of the sea journey and its archetypal importance in the work. Chiappelli considers the first two stanzas "prefatory" to the distinct epochs of life symbolized by the next four stanzas. His analysis of these stanzas, each of which encompasses a previous stage in the life of Laura and her relationship with the subject, articulates a radical difference between the philosopher, the moralist, and the poet:

The philosopher dwells on the recognition of earthly frailty, and deduces a wisdom that is applicable to future experience; the moralist enters the orbit of contemplation, contrasts the myth of mortal delusions with the unfailing religious values, and seeks spiritual determination and even consolation. The poet's pursuit expands in different areas. To him the moments formed by the past in the self-contained entities are not eliminated by the occurrence of death; on the contrary they acquire a new element of importance.[13]

Since the poet is not restrained by the barriers that restrain the philosopher and moralist, he is able to recapitulate the whole canzone in the final stanza; while retaining in memory the superlative qualities of Laura in life, he uncovers in her death the poem's key theme of renewal:

Alfin vid'io per entro i fiori et l'erba
pensosa ir sí leggiadra et bella donna,
che mai nol penso ch'i' non arda et treme:
humile in sé, ma 'ncontra Amor superba;
et avea indosso sí candida gonna,
sí texta, ch'oro et neve parea inseme;
ma le parti supreme
eran avolte d'una nebbia oscura:
punta poi nel tallon d'un picciol angue,
come fior colto langue,
lieta si dipartio, nonché secura.
Ahi, nulla, altro che pianto, al mondo dura! (323, 61–72)

At last amidst the grass and flowers I saw
A pensive lady go, so graceful, fair,
That just to think of her I burn and quake:

One humble in herself, against Love proud;
And she was wearing such a flawless gown,
Woven to seem of gold and snow at once,
But yet her crowning parts
Were all enfolded in a mist obscure;
Then a small serpent pricked her heel, and as
A gathered flower wilts,
She passed not only certain, but in joy.
Woe! Nothing, save for tears, in this world lasts.

Rvf 323 is a narrative tour de force, containing six brief stories. It possesses an initial "narrative stage" in which the discursive fantasy forms the visions as single episodes, after which each episode is redirected to the "parabola interiore" (internal parable) of the subject in order to arrive at the finished version of the poem.[14] It is here that one sees the power of the exemplum, not drawn passively from a mythical repertoire but saturated with reality: "Nel Petrarca è proprio l'exemplum ad essere permeato di realtà, e ad essere nobilitato da essa" (In Petrarch it is precisely the *exemplum* that is permeated with reality, and dignified by it).[15]

2. Friendship and Dialogue, Memory and Solitude

amicum dici facile est, amicum esse difficile

It is easy to be called a friend, but hard to be a friend.

Senili iii, 3[16]

In order to grasp the depth of Petrarch's meditation on time in the final poems of the *Fragmenta,* one must acknowledge that the subject's relationship to sin is not in question. If through his sinful love he had proposed himself as a negative exemplum, that experience is complete and objectified in memory. In the years after 1358 Petrarch was living out his tenets of religious leisure and sacred friendship: "Hunc ego si a solitudine secludendum arbitrer, durus sim; nec vero michi unquam amici presentia interrumpi solitudo videbitur sed ornari. Ad postremum si alterutro carendum sit, solitudine ipsa privari maluerim quam amico" ("It will never be my view that solitude is disturbed by the presence of a friend, but that it is enriched. If I had the choice of doing without one or the other, I should prefer to be deprived of solitude rather than of my friend").[17] Also in the late work *De ignorantia,* as

Nicholas Mann writes, "perfect friendship entails loving one's friends as oneself."[18] And in the *Senili* one gains a personal acquaintance with the author for whom friendship was coextensive with humility and a commitment to teaching.

In 1363 three of Petrarch's closest friends died; this was two years after the death of his son Giovanni and his friend Zanobi da Strada and one year after the death of Azzo da Correggio:

> Ecce, interea, ut devoti tui fratresque mei optimi ferme omnes simul vento citius abiere: Socrates, Cenobius, Lelius, Simonides et, quod novum audio, Barbatus, nostri omnes et qui te prope ut numen aliquod colerent, me supra hominem amarent.

> And now suddenly nearly all who were devoted to you and the best of brothers to me have passed away at the same time, faster than the wind: Socrates, Zanobi, Lelius, Simonides, and, as I heard lately, Barbato, all our dear ones who considered you like some god and loved me beyond all human bounds.[19]

This passage reflects the high value Petrarch placed on friendship. Yet his relationship with Laura was of another order. What strikes one as remarkable and paradoxical in this regard is how the friendship with Laura bridges the catastrophe of her death and how the conversation with her remains alive in the memory-mind of the subject. The connotative values of friendship that accrued to Laura in earlier portions of the sequence have expanded to make her a figure of extraordinary spiritual importance. The radical differentiation of the faithful friend from the carnal attraction, from her physical beauty, and from the author's use of her to achieve fame is conducted through a common friendship in Christ.

The consecration of Laura in memory is confirmed in the conclusion of sonnet 327, "L'aura et l'odore e 'l refrigerio et l'ombra" ("The breeze, the scent, and the refreshing shade"), a poem, like the sonnet that precedes it, addressed to Death.[20] It begins with the sound, "l'aura" (as poem 320 began "Sento l'aura ..."), and concludes with the commitment to consecrate Laura's name:

> et se mie rime alcuna cosa ponno,
> consecrata fra i nobili intellecti
> fia del tuo nome qui memoria eterna. (327, 12–14)

And, if my rhymes have any influence,
Your name here among noble minds will be
Held sacred in eternal memory.

The key to consecration lies in the reciprocity between the world below and the world above: as Laura blessed this ground during her life, so in death her figure will be consecrated in memory.

The imagery employed in the sacred texts at the poet's side in the 1350s and 1360s often involved the eyes of God. His use of this imagery is seen in sonnet 328 where the eyes of Laura are addressed as "cari amici" (a usage borrowed from Cino):

dicean lor con faville honeste et nove:
– Rimanetevi in pace, o cari amici.
Qui mai piú no, ma rivedrenne altrove. – (328, 12–14)

To them spoke thus, aglow with virtue rare:
"Now stay at peace, dear friends, here never, no,
But elsewhere we shall once more meet again."

Notable too is the adjectival use of *amico,* as in "Fra tanti *amici lumi*" ("Amidst so many friendly lights") (325, 72) and "O *lumi amici* che gran tempo / con tal dolcezza feste di noi specchi, / il ciel n'aspetta: a voi parrà per tempo" ("O you friendly lights that long / Your mirrors sweetly made of us, now Heaven / Awaits us; it will seem too soon to you") (330, 10–12).

The Augustinian sense of friendship is derived from those texts that advise the faithful to study wisdom in order to attain friendship with God (*amicitiam Dei*).[21] This is now the sense of Laura's identity:

et spero ch'al por giú di questa spoglia
venga per me con quella gente nostra,
vera amica di Cristo et d'Onestate. (334, 12–14)

I hope, too, when I've shed this mortal flesh,
She'll come for me with all our company,
True friends of Chastity and friends of Christ.

As we have seen, the humbler ballata and madrigal are weighted towards the first centenary, and the eight single sestinas are found in Part 1. This trend is counterbalanced by the final instances of the ballata, in poem 324 (the last poem to address Amor in its incipit), which recalls the earlier ballatas with a sense of dignity, elevation, and detachment, and the double sestina, poem 332, which possesses a greater sense of gravity than the earlier sestinas. A quick overview of the poem can be obtained by glossing the end words: *lieto, stile, morte, pianto, notti, rime.*[22] The nouns *pianto* and *morte* mark the event of Laura's death and the poet's grief, the situation that has left him desiring death ("bramar morte"); as end words, *pianto* and *morte* announce the crisis that the poem seeks to resolve. *Stile* and *rime* concern the conative thematics of dialogue and the self-reflexive nature of this exercise, as poetry allows for the testimony to the beloved and gives sustenance to the poet in the dark nights (*notti*) of the soul, in which, by looking forward, one can become truly glad (*lieto*). The end words *notti* and *lieto* concern the life of the spirit as it crosses over from darkness into the light of joy.

In the double sestina Petrarch uses a genre made for harmony and musicality to express sorrow and weeping. Doubling the number of stanzas from six to twelve, he increases the already extraordinary iterativity of the sestina by repeating additional words (*vivere / vita, dolore / doloroso, dolce / dolcezza,* the *ri-* prefix) and using the end words in additional contexts (*morte, stile*). The flurry of iterations and "redoubling of style" in the following lines, including a quintupling of *morte / morto* in lines 42 and 43, would deal a death blow to the death itself:

Nesun visse già mai piú di me lieto,
nesun vive piú tristo et giorni et notti;
et doppiando 'l dolor, doppia lo stile
che trae del cor sí lagrimose rime.
Vissi di speme, or *vivo* pur di pianto,
né contra *Morte* spero altro che *Morte.*
Morte m'à morto, et sola pò far *Morte*
ch'i' torni a *ri*veder quel viso lieto (332, 37–44)

Than I, no one has ever lived more glad;
No one more woeful lives by day and night,
And twofold woe reduplicates my style
That from the heart draws forth such weeping rhymes.
I lived in hope, now still I live in tears
To counter Death I hope for naught but Death.
Ah Death has murdered me, and only Death
Can make see again that visage glad

As the poet addresses the nature of his "weary rhymes," he asserts that since Laura's death his style has changed, as she herself will recognize:

Se sí alto pôn gir mie stanche rime,
ch'agiungan lei ch'è fuor d'ira et di pianto,
et fa 'l ciel or di sue bellezze lieto,
ben riconoscerà 'l mutato stile,
che già forse le piacque anzi che Morte
chiaro a lei giorno, a me fesse atre notti. (332, 61–6) [23]

If so high they can soar, my weary rhymes,
That they reach her who's free from wrath and tears,
And now makes Heaven with her beauties glad,
She'll surely recognize my altered style
That gave her joy perhaps, before her death,
Made bright her day and, for me, black the nights.

As the negative impressions of the world subside, the immortal Laura emerges, reflecting the mind of God and God's knowledge, and the prospect that the world which knew her not will come to know her:

sol di lei ragionando viva et morta,
anzi pur viva, et or fatta immortale,
a ciò che 'l *mondo* la conosca et ame. (333, 9–11)

And but of her I speak, alive and dead
(Instead, still living, and immortal now)
So that the *world* will know and cherish her.

§

Non la conobbe il *mondo* mentre l'ebbe:
conobbil'io, ch'a pianger qui rimasi, (338, 12–13)

The *world*, while she was of it, knew her not,
I know her, and am left here to lament;

In poems 340 to 343 one has a series of dream visions in which the subject enjoys the company of a celestial Laura. If the "signor mio" of *Rvf* 342 (1–2) – "Del cibo onde 'l signor mio sempre abonda, / lagrime et doglia, il cor lasso nudrisco" ("On food that my lord ever freely shares – / Sorrow and tears – my weary heart is fed") – refers to Amor, his identity must extend to the Lord of the Psalms, the text from which the image of tears as "food" is drawn.[24] This new Amor is endowed with charity and facilitates Laura's communication that she has not died:

"Che val – dice – a saver, chi si sconforta?
Non pianger piú: non m'ài tu pianto assai?
Ch'or fostú vivo, com'io non son morta!" (342, 12–14)

"What use," she says,
"Is knowing to the comfortless? Shed tears
No more. Have you not wept enough for me?
You should be living now, as I'm not dead!"

Laura's admonishment demonstrates that "la fine degli stimoli della carne equivale alla rinascita dello spirito, così come la morte del corpo non è morte ma conquista della piena vita" (the end of the stimuli of the flesh equals the rebirth of the spirit, just as the death of the body is not death but the conquest of the full life).[25] The motif continues in poem 343, the final piece of this oneiric quartet, in which the presentness of Laura signifies the presentness of salvation and grace:

Ripensando a quel, ch'oggi il cielo honora,
[…]
Poi che 'l dí chiaro par che la percota,
tornasi al ciel, ché sa tutte le vie, (343, 1; 12–13)

Recalling that soft look which Heaven reveres
[…]
Then, when broad daylight seems to touch her, she
Returns to heaven (for she knows every way),

In poem 344, the subject is stricken by Laura's absence and suffers an attack of remorse, remembering a time of sweetness amidst the bitter. But, given the awareness that "bitterness" signifies being separated from Christ,

Fu forse un tempo *dolce* cosa amore,
non perch'i'sappia il quando: or è sí *amara*,
che nulla piú; (344, 1–3)

Perhaps there was a time when love was *sweet*,
Not that I know just when; more *bitter* now
Can nothing be;

The awareness that the *dolce* / *amara* oscillation is not a sign of powerlessness but merely an indication of the brokenness of "[il] secol nostro" ("our world") (344, 5) leads the subject to speak out against the world. This speech act is validated by the bridge-words "duol"/"dolore" and "lingua" connecting poems 344 and 345:

Ma dí et notte il *duol* ne l'alma accolto
per la *lingua* et per li occhi sfogo et verso.

Spinse amor et *dolor* ove ir non debbe
la mia *lingua* avïata a lamentarsi, (344, 13–14; 345, 1–2)

But day and night, the *woe* pent in my soul
I vent upon my *tongue*, pour through my eyes.

Both Love and *Grief* had forced my *tongue* to go
Where it ought not when it set forth, to mourn,

The two sonnets highlight the critical role of speech and language in the practices of mourning and prayer. The final tercet of poem 345, with its motif of the internal eye of the soul and Laura seated at the feet of God, captures the extremely limited extent to which Petrarch attempts to "picture" heaven. Even so, this sonnet can be seen as setting the tone for all those that follow:[26]

con Colui che vivendo in cor sempre ebbe.
[...]
a pie' del suo et mio Signore eterno. (345, 8; 14)

Who in her life, was ever in her heart.
[...]
The feet of her eternal Lord, and mine.

Not surprisingly, diverse poems have been signalled by diverse critics as the point where Petrarch starts to bring his story to a close. Santagata and Caputo, for example, cite the final tercet of sonnet 336, which marks the death date of Laura.[27] Rather than isolating a single poem, I prefer to stress the fugue structure of the poems and the interlacing of common elements, such as the motif of the inner eye. In this way, when one arrives at the final canzone, it is seen to flow out of the final fifty poems.[28] The final canzone to the Virgin is only the culmination and logical conclusion to the set of poems begun after poem 304 and theologically intensified after poem 318.

Petrarch focuses throughout the sequence on the eye of the heart, as in Paul's prayer: "that the God of our Lord Jesus Christ, the Father of glory, may give you a spirit of wisdom and of revelation in the knowledge of him, having the eyes of your hearts enlightened, that you may know what is the hope to which he has called you" (Ephesians 1:17–18).[29] Poems 346 and 347 contain prayers that the poet be able to join Laura in heaven; he asks for her intercession as he aims above her to a state of pure contemplation.[30] Poem 346 stages the welcome to heaven of Laura by the gathered angels, a convention derived from Augustine's *In ascensione Domini*: the poet's desire is to spread the fame of Laura to posterity, knowing that her Glory can only reflect the glory of God. In poem 348 one has an archaic portrait of Laura in possession of her physical features, in the company of God. Each of these sonnets concludes with an act of prayer or beseeching:

mirando s'io la seguo, et par ch'aspecti:
ond'io voglie et pensier' tutti al ciel ergo
perch'i' l'odo pregar pur ch'i' m'affretti. (346, 12–14)

If I am following, and it seems she waits,
So all my longing thoughts I raise to Heaven,
Because I hear her pray that I make haste.

§

dunque per amendar la lunga guerra
per cui dal mondo a te sola mi volsi,
prega ch'i' venga tosto a star con voi. (347, 12–14)

And so, in recompense for that long war
Which turned me from the world to you alone,
Pray that soon I may hasten to your side.

§

Sol un conforto a le mie pene aspetto:
ch'ella, che vede tutt'i miei penseri,
m'impetre grazia, ch'i' possa esser seco. (348, 12–14)

One solace only for my woes I wait:
That she who looks upon my every thought
Will gain me grace so I can be with her.

In poem 349, "E' mi par d'or in hora udire il messo" ("I seem to hear that envoy hourly"), the theme of transformation is articulated in a crescendo where "messo" (celestial messenger) rhymes with "dimesso" (exhausted), suggesting the dramatic nature of the change underway:[31]

cosí dentro et di for *mi vo cangiando,*
et sono in non molt'anni sí dimesso,
ch'a pena riconosco omai me stesso;
tutto 'l viver usato ò messo in bando. (349, 3–6)

So I go, changing both inside and out,
And in a few years have I so declined,
That now I hardly recognize myself;
All my accustomed life I've put aside.

The powerful enjambments in lines 9–10 and 10–11 create, together with the interjection ("O"), the sense of an imminent departure from the short vision and bodily integument of mortal man:

O felice quel dí che, del terreno
carcere uscendo, lasci rotta et sparta
questa mia grave et frale et mortal gonna, (349, 9–11)

O happy day when I fare forth from this
Terrestrial prison, leave my mortal garb –
Enfeebled, heavy-scattered and in rags,

The adjective "rotta" (349, 10) recalls the famous incipit on the deaths of Giovanni Colonna and Laura, "Rotta è l'alta colonna e 'l verde lauro" ("The column high, that laurel green as well") (269, 1); so, too, the rhyme of "gonna" and "donna" (349, 14) with "colonna," recalls the opening of canzone 126 – associated with Laura in memory – where the same three rhyme-words – *donna / colonna / gonna* – appear, and where the poet imagines his own grave.

Poem 350 confirms that Laura's body had been fragile and finite as well. The verb "cangiar" is used – echoing "mi vo cangiando" (349, 3) – referring to the exchanging of one's outer vision for the inner eye of the soul.[32] The realization that Laura's earthly beauty is of base coinage when compared to her celestial beauty leads the subject to abandon his memories of the physical person for the sake of her celestial presence:[33]

Non fu simil bellezza anticha o nova,
né sarà, credo; ma fu sí converta,
ch'a pena se n'accorse il mondo errante.
Tosto disparve: onde *'l cangiar mi giova*
la poca vista a me dal cielo offerta
sol per piacer a le sue luci sante. (350, 9–14)

Such beauty, new or ancient, never lived
Nor will, I think; but it was so concealed
This wayward world but little heeded it.
Because too soon she vanished, I found joy
In changing just to please her holy eyes,
That vision brief which Heaven gave to me.

Poem 351, "Dolci durezze, et placide repulse" ("Those sweet severities and mild reproofs"), is dominated by oxymoronic oppositions between positive adjectives and negative nouns. As the positive side prevails, a corrective action is taken against the conventions and stereotypes of courtly love poetry. The effect is to sum up the history of the lover's errors. With the tension between the moral conscience and the force of the will now diminished, the relationship between Amor, the lover, and the beloved is seen in a completely theological dimension.[34] In the spirit of the poems preceding it, the focus in 351 is on a joyful and chastening virtue: its tension is evident in the powerful end words in *-ulse* (two of them being verbs in the past absolute): "repulse" ("reproofs"), "'nsulse" ("witless"), "refulse" ("shone forth"), "m'avulse" ("choked"). Laura is not the technical "donna beatrice" of the Dolce Stil Nuovo but the lady of Peace promising happiness, in whom the soul is satisfied. Nor is she an eschatological figure like the Beatrice of the *Commedia* but a contemplative one whose presentness in salvation and grace is reinforced by the fact that her beauty was vulnerable to the ruins of time. One can speak of a mediation occurring on the narrative plane as the author recapitulates Laura's behaviour towards the lover – "questo bel varïar fu la radice / di mia salute" ("This sweet variety became the root / Of my soul's health") (351, 13–14). As if to reflect the poem's integration of the past into the present, it comprises a single period with four verbs in the past absolute tense, two in the present, and one in the pluperfect.

The poems discussed in this section present a series of vignettes and visions in which the theme of divine friendship is combined with the motifs of consecration to situate Laura in heaven, in the company of the saints. What has been prefigured over the course of the *Fragmenta* is now fulfilled; that fulfilment is also available to the subject who comprehends that, when viewed within the time of the kairos, "il mondo errante" ("the wayward world") (346, 7; 350, 11) is but the negative sign of salvation.[35] As fault and error arise in human relations, the individual is pressed into decisions concerning the life of the spirit. Conceived in this sense, civilization is a temporal means of projecting a more concrete style of existence in the future, of humanity willing itself towards the Kingdom of God.[36]

3. Seeds of Grace

The final poems of Vat. Lat. 3195 are dominated by the imagery of silence, the ineffable and the inenarrable, providing closure to the macrotext on the phonetic, verbal, and syntagmatic planes. Sonnet 353, "Vago augelletto che cantando vai" ("Ah, charming little bird that singing strays"), involves the continuation of a conversation between the subject and Laura that Death was unable to stop. Until the final reordering of Vat. Lat. 3195, "Vago augelletto" occupied the position immediately before the canzone to the Virgin (*Rvf* 366). This status suggests that *Rvf* 353 cannot be seen in isolation or as a reminiscence of a classical lyric theme. Indeed, "Vago augelletto" completes an avian triad begun with poem 226, "Passer mai solitario in alcun tetto" ("There never was a sparrow on some roof"), and continued with poem 311, "Quel rosignol, che sí soave piagne" ("That nightingale that weeps so gently"), as each of them establishes an analogy between the "I" figure and a bird who, by weeping, sings its laments over love and death. As we have seen in chapter 5, section 2, poem 226 possesses a typological dimension, as Laura prefigures Mary. Seen in the company of its two avian partners, poem 226 anticipates the end of sorrow and worldly cares, in the sense in which Christians interpret the Psalms as prefiguring the arrival of Christ: "I am like a vulture of the wilderness, like an owl of the waste places; I lie awake, I am like a lonely bird on the housetop."[37] Poem 311, "Quel rosignol, che sí soave piagne" ("That nightingale that weeps so gently"), employs a motif – the nightingale's pre-dawn song – that was a medieval symbol for the Resurrection (as in the *Carmen Paschale* of Sedulius Scottus). The subject compares himself to the nightingale who weeps over a departed companion; he had assumed that a goddess such as Laura would be immune from the power of death:

ch'altri che me non ò di ch'i' mi lagne,
ché 'n dee non credev'io regnasse Morte. (311, 7–8)

For no one but myself have I to blame:
I thought that death could not rule goddesses.

And yet, as confirmed in the sestet, all mortal creatures die. In this light, the bird who sings by night and whose song increases in intensity before dawn symbolizes the searching and finding of the Saviour, as well as Christ's victory over death.

This is consistent with my reading of "Vago augelletto," where the subtext of Paul's Letter to the Romans concerns the illumination of the power of death provided by the advent of Christ.[38] More than a plaint based on the dual absence of the avian and human companions, the poem constitutes a map of the subject's memory as he projects himself beyond the "sweet and bitter years" of the past into the future:[39]

I' non so se le parti sarian pari,
ché quella cui tu piangi è forse in vita,
di ch'a me Morte e 'l ciel son tanto avari;
ma la stagione et l'ora men gradita,
col membrar de' *dolci* anni et de li *amari*,
a parlar teco con pietà m'invita. (353, 9–14)

I know not if our shares would be the same,
The one you weep for may be still alive –
That's why, toward me, so grudging are Death and Heaven.
The season, though, and this unwelcome hour,
The memory of sweet and bitter years
With pity urge me to converse with you.

Enabled by memory's accomplishments, "Vago augelletto" marks a liberation from memory's sorrows. The conversation the subject now has with the bird is to be read parabolically as a conversation with the Holy Spirit (nor can one overlook the precedent of St Francis's preaching to the birds). The sonnet is a recapitulation of the earlier avian poems but is distinct from them as its projection into the future is based on the reaffirmed presence of Franciscan humility. In this sense the "pietà" ("pity") of the final line does not belong to the bird (Spirit) or the subject alone but is shared by them in prayer. As a meditation on time the poem involves the subject's penetration to a deeper layer of self-reflection that frees him from the weight of memory. As in poems 226 and 311, the activity of weeping binds the lover and the bird, confirming in the transmutation of tears the poems' common theological focus.

Sonnet 354 responds to and completes the situation of "Vago augelletto," as Amor is seemingly in cooperation with the forces of heaven and the time of universal history:

> Responde: – Quanto 'l ciel et io possiamo,
> e i buon' consigli, e 'l conversar honesto,
> tutto fu in lei, di che noi Morte à privi. (354, 9–11)

> Love answers: "All that heaven and I can do,
> And counsel wise, and conversation chaste,
> All was in her whom Death has seized from us. ["]

Sonnet 355 is Petrarch's recapitulation of Augustine's view of time past, present, and future, as enunciated in Book xi of the *Confessions*. Here the subject pardons Time and declares that while the "yoke" of Love persists, its ills have vanished: "né dal tuo giogo, Amor, l'alma si parte, ma dal suo mal" ("Not from your yoke, Love, is my soul set free, But from its ills") (355, 12–14). As Amor has been transformed, its "yoke" has become liberating; this "giogo" becomes – as its root word *giungere* (to unite) suggests – a union, as in Matthew 11:29–30: "Take my yoke upon you, and learn of me; for I am meek and lowly in heart: and ye shall find rest unto your souls. For my yoke is easy, and my burden is light." Through the lens of a time not conquered but reconciled, one sees the impact of a radically altered approach to one's life in the world, as one is positioned under the sign of the Cross:

> Né minaccie temer debbo di morte,
> che 'l Re sofferse con piú grave pena,
> per farme a seguitar constante et forte; (357, 9–11)

I must not fear the threat of death my King
Endured with such grave suffering, so I
could follow him with constancy and strength.

§

et Quei che del Suo sangue non fu avaro,
che col pe' ruppe le tartaree porte,
col Suo morir par che mi riconforte. (358, 5–7)

And He who was not sparing with His blood,
Who with His foot smashed Tartarean gates,
Assures me by His death I am restored.

Poem 359, "Quando il soave mio fido conforto" ("When that sweet faithful comforter of mine"), is a dialogued canzone that features a lexicon of saying and telling, questioning and answering. As the author states that the truth of Laura's beatitude does not depend on his humble skills as a poet, he recalls Augustine, for whom a commitment to truthfulness grew out of a focus on the will and the positioning of love at the centre of his theology.

Augustine's disputes with Jerome on the subject are well known: Christians cannot and must not lie or deceive however they choose to rationalize a falsehood in support of the faith. Fearing for the condition of his soul, Augustine was reluctant to judge others. His suspension of judgment was based on his reading of the Gospel as mandating a church that included saints and sinners alike. When Petrarch exposes his vulnerability and anguish, it is a sign of commitment to honesty. His combing of conscience reveals the extent to which he embraced Augustine's tenet that the believer must begin by uncovering his own evil. By exposing one's sins to the light – in particular the Adamic sin of pride, but also sloth, ire, and envy – one probes deeper into oneself to find the image of God. As one embarks on the final sequence, there is an emptying out (or kenosis) by means of which the subject is unified as a Christian Everyman who has arrived at the truths of suffering and error and the ultimate friendship offered by God, as mediated by and through the creation. Thus as he closes the circle on his book, Petrarch reinforces poetry's heroic position and its sacred role in the development of human culture.

In the attack of canzone 360, "Quel'antiquo mio dolce empio signore" ("When that sweet wicked ancient lord of mine"), the opening string of adjectives creates a sublime emphasis on the referent "signore," the figure of Amor. The canzone presents a lively debate between the subject and Amor, a *contrasto* mediated by the figure of Reason (as Truth sat by as a witness in the *Secretum*). The rhythm of the dialogue – which represents an internal debate in the mind of the subject – is enlivened by the presence of four septenaries in each fifteen-line stanza. In the first half of the poem (ll 9–75) the subject lists the deceits of Amor and defends himself, charting a path away from love's illusions and towards the "pietà celeste" (360, 58), God's mercy from which he had too long been distant. When the Lover ends his speech and yields to Amor, "Il mio adversario" ("my adversary") (360, 76), an allusion is made to the parable of the widow before the judge (Luke 18:3), the lesson being that the Lord will vindicate those who cry out to him day and night. In the second half (ll 77–147), a different figure of Amor from the one the subject has imagined speaks of God as having favoured the Lover. In his discourse, Love refers to the parable of the good seed (Matthew 13:24, 27, 37): "Di bon seme mal frutto / mieto: et tal merito à chi 'ngrato serve" ("Good seed yields me bad fruit, / And one who aids the thankless merits it") (360, 108–9), the parable Augustine cited to refer to the church, in which saints and sinners commingle until they are separated in the final judgment when the "bad fruit" will be cast into "the furnace of fire; there men will weep and gnash their teeth" (Matthew 13:42). There is some irony in Amor's spiritual contentions. In claiming his great gift to the Lover, Amor espouses the Neoplatonic theory of love concerning a ladder to God, a theory that Petrarch "repudiated," as did Augustine in the *Confessions*:[40]

> Anchor, et questo è quel che tutto avanza,
> da volar sopra 'l ciel li avea dat'ali
> per le cose mortali,
> che son scala al fattor, chi ben l'estima; (360, 136–9)

> "Yet more, and this surpasses all, I gave
> Him wings to soar above the heavens through
> Things mortal, valued right
> A stairway to our Maker; [...]"

When the speech of Amor has ended and the subject has rebutted it, a vainglorious Amor replies that God, in calling Laura home, wanted her for Himself:

ch'i' li die' per colonna
de la sua frale vita. – A questo un strido
lagrimoso alzo et grido:
"Ben me la die', ma tosto la ritolse."
Responde: "Io no, ma Chi per sé la volse." (360, 146–50)

" [...] I gave
Her as a pillar for his feeble life."
At that a tearful shriek
Rings out; I cry: "Yes, gave, but soon stole back."
"Not I, but One who wanted her Himself."

In the envoi, the figure of Reason says she has enjoyed the debate but that more time is needed before a conclusion can be reached. This leads Bettarini to consider the canzone (along with canzone 359) in terms of "un'agostiniana *epoché*," a suspension of judgment.[41] Certainly in the wake of Amor's self-aggrandizement, the reader has sufficient material to decide the argument on the side of the subject.[42] The demurring by Reason has to do with Reason's limitations; as Cherchi writes, in the final seven poems (360–6) the poet enters into a different kind of knowing from what preceded it:

> non più un sapere che gli serve a guidare la propria anima ma un sapere in cui il saputo diventa oggetto di amore così intenso da attrarre a sé la vitalità di chi l'ama, suscitando in lui quell'appetizione così intensa che si chiama volontà.
>
> no longer a knowing that aids him in steering his own soul, but a knowing in which the known becomes the object of a love so intense as to attract to itself the vitality of the one who loves it, stirring up in him that intense appetition that is called the will.[43]

Sonnet 362, containing a dialogue with Laura and God, confirms the radical alteration of the subject's behaviour. The opening quatrain employs the leitmotif of Laura as "t(h)esoro" ("treasure") that has appeared in other poems of Part 2 – "Tolto m'ài, Morte, il mio doppio thesauro" ("My double treasure, Death, you've snatched away") (269, 5); "Il mio amato tesoro in terra trova" ("Find my dear treasure in the earth") (270, 5); "O felice Titon, tu sai ben l'ora / da ricovrare il tuo caro tesoro: / ma io che debbo far del dolce alloro?" ("Happy Tithonus!

O you know full well / What hour brings again your treasure dear, / About sweet laurel, though, what must I do [...] ?") (291, 5–7); "di mie tenere frondi altro lavoro / credea mostrarte; et qual fero pianeta / ne 'nvidiò inseme, o mio nobil tesoro?" ("My noble treasure, I'd show you, I thought, / Another labor of my budding leaves; / What planet fierce grudged our companionship?") (322, 9–11):

Volo con l'ali de' pensieri al cielo
sí spesse volte che quasi un di loro
esser mi par ch'àn ivi il suo thesoro,
lasciando in terra lo squarciato velo. (362, 1–4)

Upon the wings of thought I fly to heaven
So often that I almost seem to be
One of those who have their treasure there,
They who have left their rent veils in the earth.

The violent image of the body abandoned after death – "lo squarciato velo" ("rent veils") (362, 4) – references the Crucifixion (Luke 23:45, Matthew 27:51, Mark 15:38) and the parable of treasures in Heaven (Matthew 6:19–20).[44] When the subject states "mi discoloro" ("I blanch") (362, 6), he means he is ready to abandon the body. Then the spirit of Laura, recognizing his outer and inner changes, utters her final words in the book – "– Amico, or t'am'io et or t'onoro / perch'à i costumi varïati, e 'l pelo –" ("My friend, I love you now and honor you, / For as your hair has changed, so have your ways") (362, 7–8) – after which God himself informs Petrarch that he has twenty or thirty years to live, but the time will pass quickly.

The same spirit of readiness before death is expressed in sonnet 364, whose *capoverso*, "Tennemi Amor anni ventuno ardendo" ("Love held me burning one-and-twenty years"), gives the final date to the *histoire*, 1358, as the subject acknowledges his sin and vows his faithfulness to the sacrament of Holy Confession:

Signor che 'n questo carcer m'ài rinchiuso,
tràmene, salvo da li eterni danni,
ch'i' conosco 'l mio fallo, et non lo scuso. (364, 12–14)

Lord, you've enclosed me in this prisonhouse,
Release me from it saved from endless pain;
I know my fault and offer no excuse.

Poem 366 recapitulates a number of themes that have populated the *Fragmenta*: friendship, specifically an unequivocal friendship with God; the divine feminine principle, including the *via pulchritudinis* and medieval worship of Mary; repentance and contrition, figured in the familiar images of the ship without a pilot or rudder; hope and humility, as communicated in the act of prayer; and the *mutatio vitae*. The addressee and honoree of canzone 366 is the Madonna, from whose entrails the son was born, as is stated in the rosary.[45] To examine this figure in context is to accord the Madonna the reverence and essential role she was accorded in the medieval culture. As I have suggested, the effectiveness of this poem as a conclusion to the collection was guaranteed by certain late changes made in the sequence of poems preceding it.

Poem 366 is a just completion of the whole. This bold canzone of ten thirteen-line stanzas and a seven-line coda knits together a host of references to earlier poems, other poets, and the Bible. The technique of accumulation, with respect to these references and to the active qualities of the Madonna in the life of the Christian, reinforces the poem's accessibility and integrality with the sequence. Its major themes are the theology of grace and the centrality of prayer. The Virgin is praised in the *fronte* of each stanza, while a prayer is contained in every *sirma*. Here is an essential and canonical vocabulary that belongs to Mary alone: she is unique among women. Once again, Petrarch's faith is founded in penitential prayer, for intercession and forgiveness; this has yielded the *mutatio vitae* indexed by occurrences of the verb *cangiare* in poems 332, 346, 350, 360, 361, and now in the final poem where, with "desire transformed," the subject prays to the Madonna to guide him:[46]

Vergine humana, et nemica d'orgoglio,
del comune principio amor t'induca:
miserere d'un cor contrito humile.
Che se poca mortal terra caduca
amar con sí mirabil fede soglio,
che devrò far di te, cosa gentile?
Se dal mio stato assai misero et vile
per le tue man' resurgo,
Vergine, i' sacro et purgo
al tuo nome et penseri e 'ngegno et stile,
la lingua e 'l cor, le lagrime e i sospiri.
Scorgimi al miglior guado,
et prendi in grado i *cangiati* desiri. (366, 118–30)

Virgin human, foe of arrogance,
Be led by love of our shared origin;
Have mercy on a humble, contrite heart,
For if my habit is to love that small
Frail, mortal clay with such a wondrous faith,
What, noble creature, must I do for you?
If from my plight, so mean and vile, to life
By your hands I rise up,
Virgin, I will devote
To you, and in your name, I'll purify
My skill, thoughts, style, my tongue, heart, tears, and sighs.
Guide me to the better ford,
And, with good will, receive desire transformed.

In contrast to views of *Rvf* 366 as an anomaly or as an appendage to the greater sequence (in conformance with the classical practice of closing a longer work with a song in praise of the divinity), and in contrast to the readings of the canzone as a palinode after a book-long dedication to a sinful love, the canzone continues and reinforces sacred themes developed through the sequence: "è solo l'apoteosi di una sostanza diffratta per tutto il Libro, l'acme di natura, qualità e attributi mariani commisti e genericamente legati a fonti scritturali" (it is but the apotheosis of a substance scattered throughout the Book, the acme of nature, qualities and attributes of Mary mixed together and generically tied to scriptural sources).[47] The story of Laura in death effectively merges with that of the female saints, including Mary, in a concretization of the spirit of piety. It is in this spirit of integration that Silvia Chessa writes "Petrarca [...] è inoppugnabilmente il punto dinamico della mariologia fra Medioevo e Umanesimo, e la piena coscienza di questo ruolo è manifestamente espressa dall'ufficio di *Vergine bella* [...]" (Petrarch is irrefutably the dynamic point of Mariology between the Middle Ages and Humanism, and the full awareness of this role is manifestly expressed by the office of *O Virgin fair*).[48]

Some have referred to the *Fragmenta* as an unfinished work, suggesting that there was something provisional about the concluding poems. But as codicologists and textual scholars have demonstrated, the high degree of consistency and the purposeful redundancy of Vat. Lat. 3195 prove otherwise. Savoca dismisses claims that Vat. Lat. 3195 was a working copy, arguing on the basis of paleographic and philological evidence that "il libro del Canzoniere si presenta rigorosamente compiuto e definito, tanto sul piano della scrittura e della lezione dei singoli testi quanto su quello dell'architettura e della organicità narrativa dell'insieme" (the book of the Canzoniere is presented as rigorously complete and definite, both on the plane of the writing and reading of the single texts and that of the architecture and narrative organicity of the whole).[49]

If anything, one could postulate that the book is open-ended by virtue of its adherence to the canzoniere genre itself. Obviously one cannot expect a dramatic conclusion as would befit a romance or an epic, but rather a drawing together – paradigmatically and syntagmatically – of the intersubjective, personal, and universal strands of the Christian story. What is fragmentary in this view is the condition of the soul before death. But even so the impeccable ordering and cohesiveness of the collection leave no doubt about the finality of Vat. Lat. 3195.[50] This was forecast years earlier when Petrarch arrived at the form of the bipartite structure: "La bipartizione dell'opera [...] riflette la tipologia esistenziale di S. Paolo. Con la morte di Cristo è morto l'uomo vecchio nato secondo la carne di Adamo; con la resurrezione l'uomo è risorto a una nuova vita, restaurato dalla grazia" (The bipartition of the work [...] reflects the existential typology of St Paul. With the death of Christ the old man born according to the flesh of Adam died; with the resurrection man is risen to a new life, restored by grace).[51] Order became language and language became order as Petrarch arrived at the final arrangement of his poems, analogous to the *ordo caritatis* proposed by Augustine. The regathering of the fruits of his labours was based on the suggestions of scripture, a fact not in contradiction with his status as the veritable founder of humanism.

Conclusion

1. Historical Reception and the Figure of Petrarch

As new critical perspectives unfold, today's reader can better grasp how the publication and reception of *Rerum vulgarium fragmenta* has varied over the centuries, revealing the literary biases of different eras. Starting with Velutello's *Il Petrarca* (1525), the original structure and sequence of the *Fragmenta* was lost sight of as the work was cut apart and rearranged. Though later editions included all 366 poems in the proper order, the convention of beginning Part 2 at poem 267 and titling the parts "in vita" and "in morte" persisted. Writing in the second half of the sixteenth century, Antonio Minturno perceived the dangers of conflating the Petrarchan narrator and character into a single persona, a practice that has continued until our day, with the predictable result of enervating the theological core of the work, the journey of a Christian *viator*.[1] Though a history of the diffusion and reception of the *Fragmenta* far exceeds the scope of this study (and the abilities of its author), it will be useful to establish some parameters for judging how our thinking about Petrarch has been influenced by the past.

According to Savoca, editors have historically made unjustified interpolations in Petrarch's text, overlooking his system of indicating the musical rhythms, accents, and cadences of the oral reading. This has resulted in errors of orthography and punctuation, and a failure to understand the graphic layout of the poems. Savoca asks: How should the essentially oral components represented in the text experimentally by Petrarch be conveyed in modern editions? In his 2008 critical edition of *Rerum vulgarium fragmenta* Savoca drastically reduces the punctuation that has become canonical through the major diplomatic and critical editions.[2] The effect of this is to allow for a greater range of associations in support of the natural ambiguity of the lyric. Modern codicologists have advanced Petrarch studies as well by rejecting received opinion in order to give the contemporary reader the opportunity to re-view the original manuscript of Vat. Lat. 3195 and understand the novelty of Petrarch's scribal and editorial process and beliefs. As H. Wayne Storey points out, "l'ideale editoriale e culturale probabilmente piú caro a Petrarca [...], [è] fondato sul concetto di indivisibile unità dell'oggetto-libro" (the editorial and cultural ideal probably most dear to Petrarch is founded on the concept of the indivisible unity of the book-object).[3]

Some of the problems in the modern reception of Petrarch may be linked back to a brand of medievalism that arose in the nineteenth century, at once romantic and positivistic, that restricted philology by limiting it to the so-called "facts."[4] As Paul Zumthor has stated, the generation of his mentors "attached themselves to contingent criteria, posed as absolutes: unity, organicity and others."[5] Texts were assumed to possess an original source, a definitive order, intransitivity, and the possible status of "masterpiece."[6] One saw

> the refusal of what was ambiguous, plural, or implied [...], that prejudice according to which "cultural" history, moving either backward or forward in time, was clarified on the basis of a central epistemic moment, identified with "classicism" [...] in relation to which any opposition could be defined.[7]

Failing to heed that "only the slimmest area of overlap exists between the psychic universe of the medieval author and that of the modern medievalist," some modern philologists claimed objectivity and imposed on the medieval author a "personal" or "confessional" voice. In the process they failed to address the empirical, social, and linguistic evidence that alone can offer access to the poet's subjectivity.[8]

There are numerous points of contact between this general situation and the modern reception of Petrarch. Scholars have often failed to enter into the medieval cosmos and codes, its historicity and imaginary. They have taken for granted a personal and confessional voice in the *Fragmenta*, leading to a monolithic conception of Petrarch as an author without moral development, "without history."[9] The "fragment" was reified and held up as being incompatible with unity, a defect compensated for by the presence of a formally perfect style and monological lyric language.[10] One also found projected onto Petrarch a fear of death due to his concern for the fleetingness of time. In reality this theme concerns the need to eliminate attachments to the transitory and to view change from the perspective of the unchanging.[11] In poetry it signifies the unrepeatability of experience and the pre-eminence of the human voice over the written word.[12]

Though most Petrarch scholars have moved away from the romantic historiography of De Sanctis, the culture of "destitution" and anti-classicalism of the Risorgimento and post-Unification periods has persisted in certain quarters and led to a general disregard for classicist literature from the late Renaissance through the Enlightenment. De Sanctis relegated Italy's humanistic past to the lower realms of literary history, reducing Petrarch's poetry to that of a *letterato* cut off from the "real" world of the nation and reduced to courting powerful leaders for favours.[13] Categorizations such as De Sanctis's have led to the dismissal of Petrarch's political persona. This is ironic given the poet's struggle on behalf of Italian unity, including his tireless insistence that the church and the pontificate return to Rome.[14] One might say that De Sanctis's levelling of the classical, and Petrarch along with it, culminates one phase in the Italian construction of a national literary identity and commences another, that of the post-Risorgimento and twentieth century. Both phases have in common the opposition of Dante to Petrarch and the elevation of the former at the expense of the latter. By creating a national canon around the figure of Dante, many Italianists were dismissing three centuries of literary activity, "dall'Umanesimo e dal Rinascimento fino al Barocco e al Neoclassicismo" (from humanism and the Renaissance until the baroque and neoclassicism).[15] Evidence that the Dante-Petrarch dichotomy lives on is seen in a recent comparison of De Sanctis to Contini, alleging that both men harboured polemical reasons to support their "antipetrarchismo" (anti-Petrarchism).[16]

Quondam provides a compelling assessment of how literary historians have underestimated Petrarch. In many cases there were historiographical or nationalistic biases that skewed the vision of critics. Contrasted with Dante in the most stereotypical of ways, Petrarch emerged for much of the tradition as a lesser Italian, a self-absorbed conservative whose vernacular poetry stood at the beginning of a tradition deemed to be aristocratic and even snobbish. In De Sanctis's view, Dante, the national poet and inspiration of the Risorgimento, towers above the cosmopolitan and disinterested Petrarch, the friend of rulers and the cultivator of his own space of retreat and contemplation.

This myth is spurious: "Il Petrarca romanticizzato è figura senza dubbio suggestiva e letterariamente piena di fascino, ma assai poco perspicua e risulta del tutto incongrua rispetto all'idea che il poeta aveva inteso tramandarci di sé" (The romanticized Petrarch is without a doubt a suggestive and literarily fascinating figure, but quite vague and entirely incongruous with respect to the idea of himself that the poet intended to pass down to us).[17] Even Erich Auerbach was susceptible to this myth, writing in 1943: "He was a great poet, delicate, pampered by his contemporaries, often unhappy, because of his easily disturbed soul, and very vain. He wrote a good deal about himself; in fact, it was his only subject."[18] Auerbach later modified his position: "With Petrarch lyrical subjectivism achieved perfection for the first time since antiquity, not impaired but, quite on the contrary, enriched by the motif of Christian anguish that always accompanies it."[19] Perhaps Auerbach had come to understand the importance of the *sermo humilis* and sacred recitation to Petrarch's poetic practice. Certainly, the suppression of contemplation in the West from the seventeenth century onward contributed to anachronistic and superficial understandings of Petrarch.[20]

A bright spot in the reception of Petrarch has been provided by poets. Alfieri, Foscolo, Leopardi, and Carducci stand out for their critical writings on Petrarch. Foscolo considers the poet "come padre dell'Umanesimo, volto a 'dissipare le tenebre, per entro le quali i secoli di mezzo avevano avvolto la letteratura degli antichi'" (as the father of humanism, who aimed at "dissipating the shadows, within which the Middle Ages had enveloped the literature of the ancients").[21] In his "Saggio sopra la poesia del Petrarca" (Essay on Petrarch's Poetry) Foscolo notes that Petrarch is still awaiting the historian he deserves.[22] In parallel with his assertions about the emotional depth of the *Fragmenta*, he cites its unprecedented musicality:

> [L]a dolcezza del Petrarca è animata da varietà e ardore tale, che nessun lirico italiano ha mai conseguito l'uguale. La facoltà di serbare e variare a un tempo il ritmo è tutta sua: – la melodia ne' suoi versi è perpetua, e pur non istanca l'orecchio mai.
>
> The sweetness of Petrarch is animated by such variety and ardour that no Italian lyric poet has ever equalled him. The ability to maintain and vary the rhythm at the same time is all his: – the melody in his verse is perpetual, and never wears on the ear.[23]

Foscolo reaffirms the centrality of Petrarch's derivation from sacred texts:

> Le sue più belle imitazioni sono tratte dalle sacre carte; nè tali imitazioni credo essere state per anche avvertite da verun critico, sebbene deggia essere ovvio ad ognuno quanto profondamente tutti i suoi pensieri fossero inspirati dalla religione.

> His most beautiful imitations are drawn from sacred texts; nor do I believe that such imitations were noticed by critics, though it must be obvious to anyone how deeply his thoughts were inspired by religion.[24]

Giacomo Leopardi is the great nineteenth-century interpreter of Petrarch. Though his 1826 edition and commentary is understated, its paraphrases and glosses are accessible and authoritative. Leopardi's *Canti,* it has been said, amount to a continuous dialogue with Petrarch. As the poet makes clear in the *Zibaldone,* the deeper sense of Petrarch's humanism was ignored by a literary tradition that had lost its philological rigour.[25] Thus while in his canzone *Alla primavera o delle favole antiche* (To Spring, or On Ancient Fables) Leopardi expresses enthusiasm over Angelo Mai's work with ancient documents – "perché con lui sembrano tornare i tempi degli umanisti" (because with him the times of the humanists seem to return) – he profoundly doubted that the Italian reading public could understand the documents of antiquity or the enormous contribution made by the era of humanism.[26] Rather he sensed that with Petrarch and the humanists a window had been briefly opened that was then closed again, irrevocably.[27]

Giosue Carducci attempted to reopen that window with his 1899 edition of the *Canzoniere* (with Severino Ferrari), supported by a rigorous philology though entirely secular in its focus. And let us not forget the trenchant analysis of poet Andrea Zanzotto, whose notion of a Petrarchan "history of return" addresses the cognitive dimension of Petrarch's verse and its humanistic rejection of the reigning historiography of the day.

2. "Altr'uom" (Narrative, Style, Theology)

I have attempted in this study to test the narrator's assertion that he was, in his youth, another man from the one he later became – "in sul mio primo giovenile errore / quand'era in parte altr'uom da quel ch'i' sono" (1, 3–4) – and also to show he became yet another man from the one who made that stoic assertion circa 1348. This latter man was suggested in a 1352 letter to Barbato da Sulmona in which Petrarch reminds his friend of the need to subjugate secular concerns to the religious life: "negotium literarum, [...] nisi tamen ad unum verum finem redigatur, infinitum quiddam et inane est" ("scholarship is limitless and vain unless directed toward a single true purpose").[28] To which he adds, "iam sum quicquid ut essem ex alto permissum erat" ("I have now become whatever was destined for me from above").[29] The conceptualization of an ongoing moral change and purification is of vital importance to the *Fragmenta* as it concerns the subject's ability to discern between the past life and the present, even as that present life is evolving. It is by listening to the critical changes in the voice of the subject that the reader finally comprehends the unity of the book as a synthesis of the author's narrative intent, his variable style, and his theology.

As we have seen, the narrative of the *Fragmenta* is discontinuous and partial, often eclipsed by the non-narrative aspects of the lyric. The "plot" it tells does not concern an outward story but reveals the development of a multifold relationship, before and after the death of the beloved, as well as the subject's involvement with the contemporary world.[30] The narrative involves the construction of a self. If in the Middle Ages this type of construction generally followed the parameters of a "double consciousness," as inherited and adapted from classical and Christian thought, in which reason and faith operated in two distinct areas of human activity, Petrarch alters that scheme.[31] In doing so he redefines what is meant by "reason" and plots a convergence, in humanistic terms, between reason and faith. If for Augustine there was no question as to the proper allocation of human activities or the need for the Christian to subordinate his rational and civic activities (the City of Man) to the life of faith and the theological virtues (the City of God), Petrarch takes a different view. While it is true, as Kenelm Foster writes, that the *Fragmenta* follows a continuous moral and autobiographical time, comparable to the gradual opening up of Augustine in his journey towards God, there are numerous respects in which Petrarch's thinking deviates from that of the Bishop of Hippo (as is consonant with the epigraph of this book).[32]

As a man of the Middle Ages, Petrarch needed to develop his moral vision and his narrative in the sphere of immanence – of temporality, contingency, and history.[33] It is useful to recall in this regard the narrative of the Ascent of Mont Ventoux (*Fam.* iv, 1). The famous letter recounts a climb ostensibly taken with Gherardo, which, if taken at all, occurred many years before the letter was written. A key narrative motif employed in the letter is its use of *sortes* – the practice of selecting a reading by chance that could serve as inspiration. This practice (and literary technique) was seen in Augustine, as when he cited Romans 13:13 and 14 in *Confessions* viii. This latter passage is a model in the Ascent, where it is cited after Petrarch has himself opened by *sortes* to *Confessions* x.[34] As I argued chapter 3, section 3, the Ascent is an allegorical text in which the Petrarchan subject makes a critical decision, after his spiritual illumination, to return to the world, to the suffering City of Man. It is this Franciscan return, in short, that distinguishes Petrarch's theology from Augustine's. The idea of a return to the world is evident in Petrarch's understanding of the solitary life as distinct from monasticism and involving a repeated movement towards and away from society: "si tratta [...] di un ritirarsi dal mondo per rientrare subito in esso e giudicarlo nei suoi valori e disvalori" (it was a matter of [...] withdrawing from the world only to then re-enter it and judge it in its values and its defects).[35] And it is seen in his defence of the role of the passions, and deep emotions, on the path to salvation. All these are aspects of Petrarch's narrative – especially resonant in Part 2 – as the subject who has learned to dwell in crisis is opened up to the existence of grace and the understanding that grace is innate within him. This latter voice is quite distinct from the stoic voice present in the palinode of poem 1.

Petrarch's style depends on its artful manipulation of language; it is woven into the lyrical syntax and demands to be studied on the verbal and phonetic level: "La *forma elocutionis* è caratterizzata dalla reciproca attrazione verbale, dall'impulso isofonico-isosemico" (The elocutionary form is characterized by recriprocal verbal attraction, by the isophonic-isosemic impulse).[36] My attention to style has considered Petrarch's involvement with the poetry of his predecessors, his use of semantic neutrality and lexical variability, and the ways in which the style supports the moral and theological development of the protagonists. In deriving his style from the poets of the Sicilian, Bolognese, and stilnovist schools, Petrarch paid special attention to Dante and Cino da Pistoia, who universalized the lover's melancholy in a religious vision and a reflection on worldly suffering. In Cino's *Poesie* Petrarch found a medium tonality and involvement in the progressive phases of love. He was also deeply indebted to Cavalcanti – whose philosophical verse provided him with a compelling model of the psychological extremes of love. All of these predecessors shared in the medieval period's preoccupation with systems of analogies and hermetic connections between the world of the senses and the world beyond the senses.

The presence of Dante is critical. The *Vita nuova,* even more than Guittone's *Rime,* served as the clearest model for a bipartite canzoniere. The adoption of this schema is first verifiably present in the Chigi form (1359–63), though in all likelihood it was present in the Correggio form (1356–8).[37] The *Rime petrose* exert a strong stylistic influence on the poems of Part 1.[38] And surely in his reading of the *Commedia* – despite claiming that he was unfamiliar with it – Petrarch drew on Dante's depictions of sin. The *Purgatorio,* in particular, with its earthly atmosphere and pervasive theme of spiritual ascent, served as a model of theological poetry engaged in the process of soul-change and reawakening.[39] Like Dante, Petrarch employed classical sources – notably Virgil, Horace, Ovid, Cicero, and Seneca – in a manner that conveyed an inclusive cultural and collective memory and the will to integrate secular and sacred sources. If Dante, in his realistic portrayals of ancient characters confronting their moral destinies, had progressively liquidated the transcendent structures which the church had applied to the pre-Christian world, it is Petrarch who provides a coherent system of thought in which the recovery of the Latin classics can occur.[40] It is Petrarch, the founder of humanism and discoverer of philology, who restores the dignity to the *humane litterae* that Christian dogma had eroded over time.[41]

Dante brought to the fore the role of immanence in the spiritual life; in contrast to Boethius, who argued that art is immanent and amounts to a lie or a seduction, Dante defended the need of the artist to *make,* and to experience earthly suffering. He engaged the world of actions and individual destinies, and the role of the passions in historical events.[42] Petrarch builds on these achievements, according a positive role to the passions in the spiritual life, a position that places him in conflict with those theological doctrines that condemned the passions *tout court.*[43]

Petrarch's theology is coextensive with his humanism and is focused on the care of souls, in dialogue and communication.[44] If his library represents a composite body of the secular and religious knowledge of the past, his use of it assumed that interiority and subjectivity are critical to the philological labour. His work on the letters and orations of Cicero and on Livy's history of Rome has as its fundamental aim the sounding of an inner compass. But it is especially his vernacular poems that resonate with the deeper truths of Petrarch's humanism.[45] As he drew on classical sources, he was exploiting ancient verbal resonances but also investing in something completely new: "Situazione e lettera, svincolati dal soavissimo giogo dell'antico, si rigenerano profondamente in un nuovo linguaggio spirituale" (The situation and the letter, set free from the very gentle yoke of the ancient, are deeply regenerated in a new spiritual language).[46] This new humanistic theology generates a new space in the *Fragmenta* that is at once a space of the word and of the world, that includes textual places – topoi and figures, allegories and symbols – and real places – the mountain, valley, sea, river, forest, or city – codified in Petrarch's poetic language.[47] The places are organized locationally in terms of visual images and verbal registers, and keyed into memory. One can speak of an overall Gestalt in which the intersubjectivity of the self and the Other is articulated and historicized, according to the temporalities of the work.[48]

As I have argued in this study, narrative intent, stylistic variability, and theology are mutually supportive components of the Petrarchan text and its development of the theme of *mutatio vitae*. As one draws together one's own "fragments" in the conclusion of a critical study, it is only natural to consider the closure of the work under study. While there is no need to return to discussions made in the last chapter, it will be of some profit to examine the critical opinions of respected scholars concerning this matter.

In surveying the diverse emphases that characterize the progressive forms of the *Fragmenta*, Marco Santagata writes of Petrarch's "rinuncia alla narratività" (giving up on narrative) in the latter redactions, especially Vat. Lat. 3195.[49] The transition Santagata refers to is purposeful and serves to refine the relation of continuity between Parts 1 and 2. As regards the final sequence of poems, Santagata argues that "il *canzoniere* dell'Io" (the canzoniere of the I), regarding the narrator and his redemption, is transformed into "il *canzoniere* di Laura" (the canzoniere of Laura), leaving the former theme unresolved.[50] Enrico Fenzi disagrees with this position, stating that the "io" and "Laura" are intertwined because of Petrarch's new conception of love, which is consistent with his "radical Augustinianism."[51] Without the "relationship" the "I" doesn't become real to itself or perceivable as a protagonist; thus the "game of contradictions" between the subject's love for Laura and his Augustinianism – seen by Santagata as a negative *impasse* – can be seen "internally" as a sign of "growth" and "come un elemento positivo e [...] come il contenuto vero e proprio della vicenda" (as a positive element and [...] as the true and proper content of the situation):[52]

> [P]er la prima volta nella nostra tradizione lirica, l'amore non è concepito come "stato" dell'"io," più o meno patologico a seconda delle varie teorie in proposito, ma essenzialmente come "rapporto." Un rapporto che la

stessa petrarchesca condensazione dell'"io" rende ineludibile, perché nel momento stesso in cui l'"io" pone se stesso, pone anche il suo movimento rispetto all'altro da sé che lo condiziona, e insomma costruisce i parametri di verità della sua propria storia.

[F]or the first time in our lyric tradition, love is not conceived as a "state" of the "I," more or less pathological according to the various theories in that regard, but essentially as a "relationship." A relationship that the Petrarchan condensation of the "I" itself renders unavoidable, because in the very moment in which the "I" asserts itself it also asserts its motion with respect to the Other that conditions him, and in short constructs the parameters of truth of his own history.[53]

In his study of the closure of the *Fragmenta*, Paolo Cherchi argues for the work's theological unity, stating that all inherited views of it need to be re-examined:

I *fragmenta*, che tradizionalmente hanno guidato l'interpretazione fatta di letture puntuali, ci appaiono ora come un *corpus* unitario, organizzato secondo una storia che presenta una tesi e un protagonista esemplare, secondo quanto preannuncia il sonetto introduttivo.

The *fragmenta*, which have traditionally fostered a criticism centred on individual poems, now appear to us as a unitary *corpus*, organized according to a history that presents a thesis and an exemplary protagonist, according to what is announced in the introductory sonnet.[54]

If poem 1 is largely negative in tone, being dominated by "'la vergogna', la 'vana speranza' e il 'van dolore'" ("shame," "vain hope," and "vain sorrow"), the conclusion of the collection

ci porterà al punto in cui la vergogna non avrà più ragione di esistere poiché verrà rimossa la causa che la genera, la "vana speranza" si trasformerà in "vera speranza," e il "van dolore" diventerà "dolore verace" in quanto sacrificio o amore di carità.

will take us to the point where shame no longer has any reason to exist since the cause that generates it will be removed, the "vain hope" will be transformed into "true hope," and the "vain sorrow" will become "true sorrow" insofar as sacrifice or the love of charity.[55]

For Cherchi, those critics who treat the subject's penitential turn with scepticism have not asked the right questions and failed to perceive the sincerity of Petrarch's working through the problems of the soul he had the temerity to propose. Thus one can speak of the exemplarity of the "I" figure – in whom being and knowing are one – and the ethical value of the sentiments in steering the positive conscience along the right path.

3. An Autopoietic Unity

In adapting the medieval systems of types and registers, Petrarch was extremely innovative. This is seen in such technically archaic poems as *Rvf* 85, 105, 206, and 325, as it is throughout the collection whenever the focus is on poetry itself. The key to the style is not in Petrarch's monolingualism but in the variability and plurivocality with which that code is put into practice, "per attirare [...] l'attenzione sull'accordo profondo di suono e senso, di 'esterno' e 'interno' della parola poetica" (so as to attract attention to the deep agreement of sound and sense, of the "external" and "internal" of the poetic word).[56] As a dynamic textual system, the *Fragmenta* resists external appraisals that fail to assess its autopoietic, or self-generating, nature. One essential criterion that Petrarch employed to construct his system is the variability of genres or types. Particular genres possess inherent qualities and responsibilities within the whole.

The humble forms of the madrigal and ballata occur primarily in Part 1, the only exceptions being ballata 324 and the double sestina, poem 332. The madrigal and the ballata forms pertain to the earliest stage of the *Fragmenta*: poem 121 is the fourth and final madrigal. The unity of the four madrigals stands for the unity of the whole, and of the other lyric genres within it. The final ballata is poem 149; as a "plebeian" form, the ballata presents a structural and musical homology to its designated themes. Symmetrical and chiasmic in structure (or, as Bigi writes, "circular"), the ballata illustrates the property of poetry to replicate its message in its form, metrically, musically, and choreographically. Petrarch's ballata has strong stilnovistic and Dantesque metric affinities, and is one of his least innovative strophic forms.

The sestina form is carried by Petrarch to a new level of complexity and cannot be reduced to the category of the technical or antique; it is an exquisite example of Petrarch's versatility in adapting the canzone form. So, too, is the canzone-frottola, *Rvf* 105, which adopts the popular register of proverbs and aphorisms (in line with the frottola) and combines it with the elevation and intellectual scope of the canzone. As a particularly obscure text, *Rvf* 105 served to introduce critical questions – regarding friendship, personal autonomy, the Gospel, St Francis, St Peter, and the Catholic church – that are dealt with more directly in later poems.

The sonnet, too, is the site of linguistic and stylistic variation. The Petrarchan sonnet includes lines that are, at one time or another, dialectical, violent (suggesting the derivation from Dante), liquid and ineffable, and epigrammatic.[57] Beginning with poems 1 to 10, sonnets are used to knit together the temporal and thematic order, an order based on the juxtaposition of a narrator and character over thirty-one years of narrative time.[58] In the form of the ordered, bipartite canzoniere, the sonnet has the role of reinforcing the author's mnemonic system of recollected images and iterated motifs. As physical and musical images accumulate, they acquire material weight and historical value that are expanded on and developed in the canzoni.

Petrarch's canzoni stand out for their unity among variety. They are the architectural pillars that carry the weight of the story. By virtue of their being thematically and formally diverse the canzoni can address occasional or civic contents as well as the more usual amorous and religious subject matters. When they appear in clusters or in close proximity (125–9; 264, 268, 270; 359, 360, 366) they constitute the grand movements of the Petrarchan symphony. Nor can it be overlooked that, in each of Petrarch's canzoni, the metrical form has a direct and specific bearing on the thematic message.[59]

Petrarch never authorized a single poem of the *Fragmenta* save as a part of the whole. Research into the "forms" of the manuscript-in-progress and the two extant redactions have shown that many poems written at a later date are inserted in "earlier" positions in the sequence, abiding by the overall plan of a work in two parts divided by a partition.[60] Petrarch culled out many poems that did not fit within the unitary plan. In 1358, the chronology established by the anniversary poems is intact and will not be altered further, though subsequent changes condition the narrative, deepening and interiorizing its qualities and relations. After this point (of the non-extant Correggio form) there is a lack of narrative "progettualità" (projectuality), meaning that the new material added in the Chigi and Giovanni forms, and finally in the Vatican redaction, is arranged around the existing narrative and allowed to support its own weight.[61] This suits perfectly the autopoietic nature of the text, which disallows external manipulations aimed at imposing order on the whole.

By inscribing his lyrical text with an ongoing narrative, Petrarch "invented" the genre of the canzoniere as a linear yet multiplicitous and multivocal form.[62] The new genre possesses a temporal and mnemonic dimension put in motion by a dialogic engagement with the reader, a relation cultivated through the work's temporal stratifications and linguistic ambiguities.[63] Just as the chronological time of the narrative is linear and progressive (as seen in the anniversary poems) and the synchronic time of the lyric imitates the circularity and iterativity of nature, there is a third, ascensional, (a)temporality that coincides with the "within-time-ness" of Ricoeur's theorization. As one assesses the self-generating order of the work, the ascensional time is only suggested in the early poems, is emergent in the second centenary, and is salient in Part 2, where the narrative assumes the parabolic shape of a return to God, consistent with the leitmotif of collecting and reunifying.[64] If Martinelli can state that the early portions of the *Fragmenta* constitute a "parabola negativa del peccato" (negative parable of sin), the same mode of parable can be seen to extend in a positive manner over the work as a whole.

Insofar as Petrarch saw the need to devise a poetic theology able to contend with the ineffable and inenarrable aspects of the religious experience, it was incumbent on him to incorporate into his verbal regime the kind of limit-expressions – of parable, proverb, and eschatology – that could refer to the life of the spirit. So, too, the dialogic, responsory, and antiphonic nature of the Petrarchan text allows for its expansion into intersubjective relations, within and between characters, and between them and God. Finally, as one considers the word *fragmenta,* it is critical to retain its connotation as the crumbs of the loaves that were scattered and will be gathered up. That reading assumes the brokenness of the world, the corruptibility of the flesh, and the illusory nature of worldly pleasure. Similarly, the "rime sparse" ("scattered rhymes") connote, with the verb *spargere,* the act of sowing, such that the words of the text are seeds to be cultivated and grown to maturity.

Notes

Epigraph

1 Petrarch, *Le familiari*, 1968, v. 4, 108; *Fam.* [xxii, 2], v. 3, 214. In this 1359 letter to Boccaccio, Petrarch contrasts his commitment to wandering in search of the truth, understood as a process of open inquiry guided by the free will, to the itineraries of Juvenal or Horace or Lucretius or Virgil, none of whom he wishes to emulate. The working analogy of writing (and *imitatio*) to a physical journey is a recurrent feature in Petrarch's moral writings.

Preface

1 R. Bettarini, *Bett*, x–xi.
2 N. Iliescu, *Il Canzoniere petrarchesco e Sant'Agostino*, 15–27. I include in this list Martinelli, Santataga, Bettarini, Dotti, Savoca, Quondam, Pozzi, Orelli, Cherchi, Chessa and others.
3 F. Petrarca, *Inediti*, 317 ; "Petrarch's Coronation Oration," 1243.

Introduction

1 The text cited throughout the book is *Petrarch's Songbook, Rerum Vulgarium Fragmenta*, Italian text by Gianfranco Contini, abbreviated as *Rvf* and referred to as *Fragmenta*. Unless otherwise indicated, the English translations are those of James Wyatt Cook. Cited passages from the *Fragmenta* are referenced by poem number and line number; for example: "Voi che ascolatate in rime sparse il suono" (1, 1). All translations presented without quotation marks are my own. Unless otherwise indicated, English versions of Dante's *The Divine Comedy* are from Allen Mandelbaum's translation. Biblical citations are from

The Holy Bible, Revised Standard Version, though references to the Psalms follow the numbering of the Vulgate.

2 I have relied on the commentary in the critical editions of the *Canzoniere* by Rosanna Bettarini (abbreviated as *Bett*) and Marco Santagata (abbreviated as *Sant*). I am also indebted to the editions of Savoca, Dotti, Contini, Carducci and Ferrari, Zingarelli, Chiorboli, and Leopardi. Among other Petrarch scholars whose work has been indispensable, I would mention Cherchi, Chessa, De Robertis, Fenzi, Iliescu, Martinelli, Orelli, Picone, Pozzi, Stierle, and Wilkins.

3 M. Santagata, *I frammenti dell'anima*, 342.

4 Ibid.

5 R. Bettarini, *Bett*, xv. T. Barolini, "Petrarch at the Crossroads of Hermeneutics and Philology," reaffirms the hypothetical status of Wilkins's nine "forms" of the *Canzoniere*, asserting that the interpretive systems that critics have devised on the basis of those forms are unsupportable. Indeed, Wilkins acknowledged that only two authoritative draft copies of the *Fragmenta* exist – the Chigi edition and Vat. Lat. 3195 – but he also reconstructed Petrarch's ordering and polishing of the collection over the decades with a degree of coherence that scholars continue to recognize while paring back on some of Wilkins's chronological theses in *The Making of the "Canzoniere."*

6 H. Cochin, *La Chronologie du Canzoniere de Pétrarque*, 15.

7 M. Santagata, *Dal sonetto al canzoniere*, 22.

8 See G. Contini, "La lingua del Petrarca"; D. De Robertis, *Memoriale Petrarchesco*; B. Martinelli, *Petrarca e il Ventoso*; G. Orelli, *Il suono dei sospiri*; G. Pozzi, "Petrarca, i Padri e soprattutto la Bibbia"; M. Santagata *Dal sonetto al canzoniere*; M. Santagata, *I frammenti dell'anima*; and Santagata's edition of the *Canzoniere*, 1996, updated 2004.

9 See R. Bettarini, "Perché 'narrando' il duol si disacerba (Motivi esegetici dagli autografi petrarcheschi)," 305: "In altre parole, l'editore d'un testo in quanto puro tecnico che si adopera con disciplinata dottrina a trasferire un codice storico (sia pure d'autore o di copisti) in un altro codice, è un commentatore frustrato, costretto a rimuovere tutte le informazioni che gli sono necessarie per andare avanti, a censurarle nel punto stesso della loro piú vivace efficienza, ed infine a bilanciarle in un sistema di spese e controspese secondo un calendario sincronico che andrà probabilmente perduto" (In other words, the editor of a text, to the extent that he is a pure technician who employs a disciplined doctrine in order to transfer a historic codex (whether of the author or a copyist) into another codex, is a frustrated commentator, forced to repress all the information that he needs to go forward, to censor it exactly at the point when it is most lively and useful, and finally to balance it in a system of receipts and expenditures according to a synchronic calendar that will probably get lost).

10 See Dante Alighieri, *Vita nuova* [III, 10–12], 5. The "fedeli d'amore" (love's faithful) or those in love are the addressees of Dante's first sonnet in the *Vita nuova* and stand more generally for the select group of followers of love poetry in Dante's day.

11 Since the Correggio manuscript is not extant, some scholars consider discussion of it to be hypothetical. Santagata, Bettarini, and Dotti refer to the Correggio manuscript routinely as having been organized "a tesi" (topically) and containing strongly marked narrative components, with attention given to spatial continuity and to the linear progression provided by the anniversary poems.

12 See *Le familiari*, 1968, v. 1, 4: "Et erat pars soluto gressu libera, pars frenis homericis astricta, quoniam ysocraticis habenis raro utimur; pars autem, mulcendis vulgi auribus intenta, suis et ipsa legibus utebatur" (*Fam.* [i, 1], v. 1, 4: "Part of the writing was free of literary niceties, part showed the influence of Homeric control since I rarely made use of the rules of Isocrates; but another part intended for charming the ears of the multitude relied on its own particular rules").

13 I am referring to the narratological distinction (in French) between: *narration* (the act of narrating by an author); *récit* (the recounting of the story by a fictional narrator); and *histoire* (the story itself, as enacted by its characters).

14 M. Santagata, *I frammenti dell'anima*, 252.

15 R. Bettarini, *Bett*, xviii.

16 Ibid., xxii.

17 Ibid., xiv.

18 B. Martinelli, *Petrarca e il Ventoso*, 294.

19 For the opposition of a "closed" and "essentialist" literariness to an "open" and "conditionalist" one, see G. Genette, *Fiction and Diction*, 5–6, 16–29.

20 See G. Leopardi, *Tutte le opere*, v. 2, 716–7: "Così è: la condizione del poeta e del prosatore in quel tempo, quanto ai materiali che si trovano aver nella lingua, è la stessa [...]: il prosatore si trova dunque aver poco meno del suo bisogno, e quasi anche tanto che gli basti a una certa eleganza: il poeta che non si trova aver niente di più, bisogna che si contenti di uno stile e di una maniera che si accosti alla prosa" (*Zibaldone* [2839] 1176: "So it is. As regards the materials available to them in the language, the condition of poet and prose writer in that period is the same. [...] The prose writer finds that he has little less than what he needs, and also nearly as much as he needs for a measure of elegance. The poet, who finds that he does not have any more than that, has to settle for a style and a manner that resemble prose"). In Leopardi's view, Boccaccio the prose writer stood out for his stylistic flourishes and Petrarch the poet stood out for his nonchalance and effortlessness.

21 E. Malato, "Favole parabole istorie," 2000, 21.

22 See P. Ricoeur, *Figuring the Sacred*, 60, who notes that as a mode of discourse, parable employs the logic of "limit-expressions," specifically through its use of "extravagance," or "the extraordinary within the ordinary." It can also be observed that these fictional modes engage narrative time in rhetorically different ways: fable depends on anticipation (prolepsis); history works by reiteration (analepsis); and parable is characterized by suspension (ellipsis).

23 As P. Zumthor writes, *Speaking of the Middle Ages*, 49: "Writing creates an autonomous space, a web of figures in which the author's and receiver's times mingle in a continuous decoding of something that both transcends and engulfs them."

24 As P. Zumthor writes, "From the Universal to the Particular in Medieval Poetry," 820: "the lyrical model, which was worked out by the first troubadours and trovères remained practically unchanged till the end of the Middle Ages. It concentrates on an unnamed and universalized *I*; it excludes narrative elements; it alludes to situations rather than to actions: so it implies no temporal development proper. It is pure play, ritual modulation of a song which is its own purpose."

25 See G. Genette, *Fiction and Diction*, 77–8: "One of the lessons of this state of affairs is that the equals sign, used here in an obviously metaphorical way, does not have precisely the same value on all three sides of the triangle. Between *A* and *C*, it denotes a juridical identity, in the sense of the registry office, which can, for example, hold an author responsible for the acts of his hero [...]. Between *N* and *C* it designates a linguistic identity between the enunciating subject and the subject of the utterance, an identity marked by the use of the first person singular ("I") [...]. Between *A* and *N* it symbolizes the author's serious commitment with regard to her narrative assertions, and for us it suggests quite insistently the dismissal of *N* as a useless agency: when $A = N$, *N* disappears, for it is quite simply the author who is narrating."

26 Ibid., 33.

27 The word "exilio" (exile) only appears in poems 21, 37, 45, 80, and 94.

28 As G. Warkentin writes in introducing James Wyatt Cook's translation, *Petrarch's Songbook*, 1995, 20: "On one hand [Petrarch] presents himself as an *auctor*, a poet of established prestige who, because he speaks in his own person, invites our assent to his account of the situation. Yet at the same time he has suffered a wound which specifically prevents him from narrating its history, its *storia*. In obedience to the pathology of love-malady, submission to such a love results in the impairment of the lover's capacity to discern false semblances from true perceptions."

29 Ricoeur, *Figuring the Sacred*, 50–60, designates the respective logics of such limit-expressions: in parable there is the logic of "extravagance," in the proverb the logic of "hyperbole" and "paradox," and in eschatological sayings "the rupturing of mythic time."

30 See R. Barilli, *Rhetoric*, 53: "To a great extent humanism appears to be a return to the church fathers, and one reason for this is that through their mediation Latin *elocutio*, which as we saw the fathers had inherited, can return in all its splendor. [...] In this light it seems incorrect to ascribe a loss of religiosity to humanism, since in fact the level of religiosity increases. Rather, humanism launches the idea of a direct relationship of the soul with God, following Augustine's model."

31 E. Curtius, *European Literature and the Latin Middle Ages*, 250, comments on the fortuitous provenance of the word "classical," due to an apparent misreading of a passage from Gellius: "There could not well have been any argument over Classicism, if the word *classicus* had been understood." See E. Garin, "Umanesimo e rinascimento," 351–2: "Il moto rinascimentale, insomma, non nacque dagli *studia humanitatis*, affermatisi come demolitori del Medioevo ed instauratori del Rinascimento, ma dal seno stesso della vita e della cultura di un Medioevo in crisi" (The Renaissance revolt, in short, was not born out of humanistic study, claimed as the destroyer of the Middle Ages and the founders of the Renaissance, but actually from the very heart of the life and culture of the Middle Ages, in crisis).

32 M. Santagata, *Sant*, xxxix–xl. See A. Quondam, *Petrarca, l'italiano dimenticato*, 44–5, on the regrettable division between scholars of the Latin Petrarch and the vernacular Petrarch.

33 E. Garin, *Italian Humanism*, 19.

34 See R. Antognini, *Il progetto autobiografico delle Familiares di Petrarca*, for a comprehensive autobiographical catalogue of the 355 letters of the *Familiares*, written over the period 1345–66.

35 Garin, *Italian Humanism*, 19.

36 U. Dotti, *La rivoluzione incompiuta*, 118.

37 See C. Vasoli, *Umanesimo e rinascimento*, 14: "L'elegante scrittore, il poeta squisito, il filologo paziente ricercatore e annotatore di codici concepì la 'rinascita degli studi' non solo come il ritorno ad una 'sapienza' tutta umana, fondata sull'insegnamento degli antichi, bensì come l'integrale restaurazione di una civiltà tradita e corrotta che coincideva con la resurrezione della 'misera Italia' e l'intima 'reformatio' della Chiesa di Cristo" (The elegant writer, the exquisite poet, the patient philologist, researcher and annotator of codexes, conceived of the "rebirth of studies" not only as the return to a completely human form of "knowledge,"

founded on the teachings of the ancients, but as the integral restoration of a betrayed and corrupted civilization that coincided with the resurrection of "poor Italy" and the intimate "reformation" of the Church of Christ). See C. Trinkaus, *The Poet as Philosopher*, 27–51, on the confluence between Petrarch's Stoic and Christian thought. Trinkaus confutes the notion of a Petrarch whose Christianity was diluted by pagan thought (such as one finds argued, for example, by U. Bosco, "Cristianesimo e umanesimo, in *Francesco Petrarca*," 118–27).

38 E. Garin, *History of Italian Philosophy*, 143.

39 See T. Kircher, *The Poet's Wisdom*, 3–41, who explicates the contrast between the thought of P.O. Kristeller and E. Garin regarding philology's contribution to philosophical thinking in this era. While Kristeller discounts it, Garin supports it and "contends that the unsystematic inquiry of the humanists was also philosophical." As Kircher notes, ibid., 15–16, Garin and a like-minded thinker like Charles Trinkaus enable us to see the "conditional, situational way" that Petrarch and other humanists engaged rhetoric to show their philosophical positions. Petrarch differed with orthodox clerics generally, including those of the Augustinian and Franciscan orders, whose theology he found to be more congenial.

40 See P. Tillich, *The Protestant Era*, 72: "Historical realism transcends technological, as well as mystical, realism. Its decisive characteristic is consciousness of the present situation, of the 'here and now'. It sees the power of being, in the depth of 'our historical situation'. It is contemporaneous, and in this it differs from the technological, as well as from the mystical, idea of reality. Neither technological nor mystical realism knows the principle of contemporaneity."

41 As Tillich writes, ibid., 64: "the first slight break in theonomous thinking occurred when Thomas Aquinas interpreted the Augustinian–Franciscan principle that God is truth [...] in Aristotelian terms and said that God is immediately certain for himself but not for us." Regarding Petrarch's rejection of Thomistic rationalism, see B. Martinelli, *Petrarca e il Ventoso*, 214: "Il suo rifiuto per le grandi sintesi razionali e poetiche dell'età precedente, la *Summa* dell'Aquinate e la *Commedia* di Dante, deriva dalla sua reazione al carattere fondamentale di quella cultura, l'enciclopedismo, e alla struttura chiusa di quelle opere" (His refusal of the grand rational and poetic syntheses of the preceding age, the *Summa* of Aquinas and the *Commedia* of Dante, derives from his reaction to the fundamental character of that culture, encyclopedism, and the closed structure of those works).

42 As H. Arendt notes concerning the Platonic and Aristotelian hierarchy of the *bios theoretikos* (vita contemplativa) over the *bios politikos* (vita activa),

The Human Condition, 16: "Traditionally [...] the term *vita activa* receives its meaning from the *vita contemplativa*; its very restricted dignity is bestowed upon it because it serves the needs and wants of contemplation in a living being." As a humanist, Petrarch continuously draws our attention to what Parker Palmer, *The Active Life*, 16, calls "the mistaken notion that contemplation and action are mutually exclusive ways of life."

43 F. Rico, "'Rime sparse,' 'Rerum vulgarium fragmenta,'" 142, notes (citing É. Gilson, *L'esprit de la philosophie médiévale*, Paris, 1943) the convergence in Petrarch's thought of Seneca, Augustine, and the medieval current of "'socratismo cristiano' che percorre il Medio Evo e che indugia, si allarga e si approfondisce nel XII secolo, da San Bernardo o da Guglielmo di Saint-Thierry fino ad Abelardo o alla scuola di Saint–Victor, in una constante esortazione a contemplare Dio nella propria anima" ("Christian socratism" which passes through the Middle Ages and lingers, spreads and deepens in the 12th century, from Saint Bernard or William of Saint-Thierry to Abelard or the school of Saint-Victor, in a constant exhortation to contemplate God in one's own soul).

44 *Le familiari* v. 2, 301; *Fam.* [x, 4], v. 2, 69.

45 See A. Noferi, "Il Canzoniere del Petrarca," 5: "Il fatto è che entrare e dimorare nello spazio del Canzoniere significa appunto entrare e dimorare [...] [nello] spazio dell'abbaglio, dell'ambiguità, dell''artificio' del testo, di quello che Petrarca stesso chiama l'*alieniloquio* (alieniloquium): discorso 'altro' ('procul ab omni plebeio aut publico loquendi stilo' – *Fam.* X 4 – lontano da ogni linguaggio plebeo o pubblico, cioè quello della comunicazione) ..." (The fact is that to enter and dwell in the space of the Canzoniere means precisely to enter and dwell [...] in the space of bedazzlement, ambiguity, the "artifice" of the text, of what Petrarch calls the *alieniloquium*: an "other" discourse ("procul ab omni plebeio aut publico loquendi stilo" – *Fam.* X 4 –, far from any plebeian or public language, that is, from that of communication) ...).

46 Petrarch's poetic theology has not always been appreciated as such. See, for example, E.H. Wilkins, at the end of his *Life of Petrarch*, 1961, 254: "he ever explored the field of theology. [...] His religion was for him less a spiritual experience, less a consciousness of divine love and a response thereto, than a pattern of belief and observance which, if followed faithfully, would greatly increase his prospects of avoiding Hell and winning Paradise."

47 This was in clear contrast to the practice of professional theologians and Aristotelians. See S. Chessa, *Il profumo del sacro nel* Canzoniere *di Petrarca*, 27: "La sua è una teologia [...] di segno monastico, il cui punto nevralgico è l'escatologia amorosa. Rosanna Bettarini la definisce 'una teologia

moderna dell'amore e della conoscenza'" (His theology [...] is of the monastic type, its nerve centre is the eschatology of love. Rosanna Bettarini defines it as "a modern theology of love and knowledge").

48 The medieval practice of the *lectio divina* was compatible with Petrarch's arrival at a threshold of contemplation – of time past, present, and future. The *lectio divina* as practised in the Middle Ages began with the listening by the heart to the Word of God; the listening is followed by the *meditatio* in which the heart ruminates on the Word, the *oratio* of prayer, and the *contemplatio* of communion with God. See E. Bianchi, *Praying the Word.*

49 See P. Cary, *Inner Grace*, 117–19.

50 See C. Bellintani, "Identità e spiritualità di Francesco Petrarca canonico della cattedrale di Padova (1349–1374)," 33: "Nella seconda parte della sua vita sarebbe vissuto sostanzialmente entro questa visione *teologica* dell'esistenza: non è gloria l'ultima e definitiva conquista dello spirito umano, ma la conoscenza delle verità esterne; quelle che guidano, come timone e vele, l'imbarcazione della propria anima, nel periglioso e tempestoso mare dell'esistenza" (In the second part of his life he would live substantially within a *theological* vision of existence: glory is not the final and definitive conquest of the human spirit, but the knowledge of the external truths; those that steer, like rudder and sails, the sea voyage of one's own soul, over the perilous and stormy sea of existence).

51 L. Spitzer, *Classical and Christian Ideas of World Harmony*, provides an acute analysis of this sense of time, at once present in the person, the cosmos, and the poetic language.

52 Petrarch, *On Religious Leisure* [II, 3], 106, 112.

53 F. Petrarca, *Prose*, 454; *The Life of Solitude*, 220.

54 See H. Adams, *Mont-Saint-Michel and Chartres*, 260: "In truth, the immensely popular charm of St. Francis, as of the Virgin, was precisely his heresies. Both were illogical and heretical by essence; – in strict discipline, in the days of the Holy Office, a hundred years later, both would have been burned by the Church."

55 Ibid., 274, 330–1.

56 See R. Antonelli, "'Rerum vulgarium fragmenta' di Francesco Petrarca," 40: "Il trionfo di Maria è iscritto già nel primo sonetto del 'Canzoniere' e nell'arco biografico dell'*exemplum*. costituito dall'«io» dei RVF fino all'ingresso finale nel «porto»" (The triumph of Mary is already inscribed in the first sonnet of the "Canzoniere" and in the biographical arc of the *exemplum* constituted by the "I" of the *Rvf* until the final entry into "port").

57 D. De Robertis, "Contiguità e selezione nella costruzione del Canzoniere petrarchesco," examines manuscript pages from Vat. Lat. 3196 that include

verbal contiguities and clusters among later poems added to both parts of Petrarch's evolving collection. Concerning the relations of "similarity" that arise between poems of Parts 1 and 2, as they appear in Forms prior to Vat. Lat. 3195, De Robertis writes, *Memoriale Petrarchesco*, 73: "Affiora [...] un nuovo tipo di connessione tra le due parti, non lineare o di contiguità, ma correlativa o di similarità, messa *en abîme* nella sistemazione definitiva (di cui importa anzitutto il messaggio globale), ma rivelata dall'atto che la prepara, di natura operativa, e sprofondata nel risultato: spia non solo dell'equiparabilità sostanziale delle due parti del canzoniere, ma della prospettiva bifocale della sua costruzione e del più generale sintagma che costituisce" (There emerges [...] a new type of connection between Part I and Part II, not linear or of contiguity, but correlative and of similarity, placed *en abîme* in the definitive systemization (of which the global message is above all important), but revealed through the act that prepares it, operative in nature, and absorbed in its result: a sign not only of the substantially equal status of the two parts of the *Canzoniere*, but of the bifocal perspective of its construction and of the general syntagm that constitutes it).

58 Thus, a sound critical approach to the work as a whole must combine aspects of verbal criticism, stylistic criticism, and thematic criticism. As P. Zumthor notes, *Toward a Medieval Poetics*, 111–13, verbal criticism is interested in the work's materiality, "its sounds and syntagmatic strings," its "grain"; stylistic criticism is interested in composition, in structural elements, lexical units, and rhetorical figures; while thematic criticism explores the message as communication in terms of dominant motifs and themes.

59 Regarding the "belletristic text" ("a text with heightened features of ordering"), Y. Lotman writes, *Analysis of the Poetic Text*, 37: "The ordered quality of any text can be realized along two lines. In linguistic terms it can be characterized as ordering in terms of *paradigmatics* and *syntagmatics*; in mathematical terms – of equivalency and order. The character and function of these two types of ordering are different. If in narrative genre the second type predominates, then texts with a strongly expressed modeling function (and it is precisely here that poetry, especially lyric poetry, belongs) are constructed with marked predominance of the first."

60 As distinct from R. Jakobson and R. Barthes, who place metaphor on the paradigmatic axis and metonymy on the syntagmatic, Lotman recognizes that metaphor and metonymy both satisfy the Aristotelian definition of metaphor, making the distinctions between them relatively trivial.

61 De Sanctis ignores the knitting together of syntagmatic units into a unified continuum or whole; for him there is no progress in the *Fragmenta* but only the obsessive repetition of the same attitudes and situations. The fact

that Laura is deified on Earth and humanized in heaven, says the critic, means that her death has not led to any spiritual progress in the poet, who therefore has not measured up to his Augustinian model. See R. Jakobson, "Closing Statement: Linguistics and Poetics," 31: "It is no mere chance that metonymic structures are less explored than the field of metaphor. […] [T]he study of poetic tropes has been directed mainly toward metaphor and that so-called realistic literature, intimately tied to the metonymic principle, still defies interpretation …"

62 See Bakhtin, *Art and Answerability*, 150. "Toward the end of the Middle Ages, which knew no biographical values, and in the early Renaissance we can observe the appearance of distinctive and internally contradictory forms that are in transition from confessional self-accounting to autobiography. […] The biographical position in relation to one's own life, i.e., the position governed by biographical value, prevails over the confessional position in Petrarch, even if it does so against some resistance."

63 Petrarch's only mention of the Hercules story is in *De vita solitaria* where he coins the expression *Hercules in bivio* (Hercules at the crossroads). T.E. Mommsen, "Petrarch and the Story of the Choice of Hercules," 190, sees this as reflective of the general "framework of the history of ideas marking the period of transition from medieval to Renaissance thought."

64 See *Le familiari*, 1968, v. 3, 18–19: "Bicornis et exemplaris litera dextro cornu arctior tendit ad sidera, levo latior in terram curvata reflectitur; ea, ut aiunt, ad inferos est via, et illa quidem incessu letior ac dulcior, exitu mestissima, atque amarissima est, et cuius omnino nil possit miserie superaddi; dextrum vero iter ingressis ut labor ingens sic finis optimus" (*Fam.* [xii, 3] v. 2, 142: "This letter, a two-horned symbol, points to the heavens with its narrower right horn, while with its broader left horn it seems to curve toward the earth. The left horn, as they say, represents the path to hell, and while indeed the approach is rather pleasant, the destination is very sad and bitter, so miserable that it could not be more so. For those who enter the path on the right, the rewards are as great as the toil required"). It must also be stipulated that emblematically the "Y" of the *trivium* stood for the unknown, as in the proverb on that letter by Ser Garzo, Petrarch's great-grandfather, as cited by F. Brambilla Ageno, "I 'proverbi' di Ser Garzo," 35: "Y, perché greco, / non si intende meco" (Y, being Greek, is not understood by me).

65 On the importance of rhetoric to theology see G. Mazzotta, "Humanism and Monastic Spirituality in Petrarch," 68: "The *poeta-theologus* […] is the figure empowered to bring together the perspectives of poetry and of theology. Yet Petrarch, unlike the Padua humanists, does not wish to appear as if he simply collapses theology into rhetoric. To this end he sets up an opposition

between style and meaning and seeks to make it valid by evoking St. Jerome's perception of the intractable, untranslatable poetic specificities of the Bible."

66 A. Zanzotto, "Petrarca fra il palazzo e la cameretta," 9.

67 Ibid., 14.

68 Ibid., 15.

69 T.P. Roche, "The Calendrical Structure of Petrarch's *Canzoniere*," concludes that this structure conforms with the ambient fourteenth-century Christian morality, but he does not infer any irony or ambiguity in the calendrical conceits. As L. Del Giudice states, "Il processo narrativo nei componimenti LXI-CV del *Canzoniere* di F. Petrarca,"1985, 156: "Ricordiamo anche quell'ambiguità voluta nel far coincidere il giorno dell'innamoramento con il giorno della Passione di Cristo, un gusto ironico, perfino parodistico, che può sembrarci non di buon gusto!" (Let us also remember the deliberate ambiguity of making the day of the enamourment coincide with the day of the Passion of Christ, an ironic, even parodistic, taste, which might not seem to us to be in good taste!).

70 The anniversary poems are *Rvf* 30, 50, 62, 79, 101, 107, 118, 122, 145, 212, 221, 266, 278, 336, and 360.

71 P. Ricoeur, *Time and Narrative*, 100. Ricoeur, ibid., 103, explores such a relationship in terms of a "hermeneutics of historical consciousness ... [which] aims at directly articulating on the level of common history the three great ecstasies of time: the future under the sign of the horizon of expectation, the past under the sign of tradition, and the present under the sign of the untimely."

72 See A. Hortis, "Della vita religiosa del Petrarca," in Petrarca, *Scritti inediti di Francesco Petrarca*, 277–304.

73 F. Petrarca, *De otio religioso*, 1958, 14: "Hostes itaque vestros scitis neque quid agant aut quid cogitent ignoratis. Occurrite paratibus impiis et vitate tria in primis hostium atque armorum genera, mundi laqueos, carnis illecebras, demonum dolos. Ille vanissima spondet, hec familiariter blanditur, illi autem pessima consilia mortalibus insusurrant" (*On Religious Leisure*, 24: "Therefore, know your enemies, what they are plotting, and what they think. Oppose their wicked devices, especially three kinds of weapons of the enemy: the traps of this world, the enticements of the flesh, and the guiles of demons. The first promises things which are insubstantial; the next lures one as an old friend, but the last whisper their worst counsels to mortals").

74 M. Bakhtin, *Art and Answerability*, 150.

75 M. Bakhtin, *The Dialogic Imagination*, 147. See Bakhtin, ibid., 148: "The essence of this inversion is found in the fact that mythological and artistic thinking locates such categories as purpose, ideal, justice, perfection, the

harmonious condition of man and society and the like in the *past.* [...] A thing that could and in fact must only be realized exclusively in the *future* is here portrayed as something out of the *past,* a thing that is in no sense part of the past's reality, but a thing that is in its essence a purpose, an obligation." Bakhtin goes on to relate eschatology's similar relationship to the future, but states, "here the future is emptied out in a different way. The future is perceived as the end of everything that exists, as the end of all being (in its past and present forms)."

76 Ricoeur, *Time and Narrative,* 18.

77 Ibid.

78 Ibid., 19.

79 Ibid.

80 Ibid., 63.

81 See *Le familiari,* v.1, 4: "Quod genus, apud Siculos, ut fama est, non multis ante seculis renatum, brevi per omnem Italiam ac longius manavit, apud Grecorum olim ac Latinorum vetustissimos celebratum; siquidem et Athicos et Romanos vulgares rithmico tantum carmine uti solitos accepimus" (*Fam.* [i, 1], v. 1, 4: "This last kind of writing, which is said to have been revived among the Sicilians not many centuries ago, had soon spread throughout Italy and beyond, and was once even popular among the most ancient Greeks and the Latins, if it is indeed true that the Attic and Roman people used to employ only the rhythmic type of poetry").

82 F. Kermode, *The Genesis of Secrecy,* 37, citing Augustine, *Homilies on John* (Oxford, 1848), Homily xxiv, I, 375f.

83 See Augustine, *Confessions* 6.5, trans. F.J. Sheed, cited by E. Auerbach, *Literary Language and Its Public in Latin Latin Antiquity and in the Middle Ages,* 49: "The authority of scripture [...] offers itself to all in the plainest words and the simplest expressions, yet demands the closest attention of the most serious minds. Thus it receives all within its welcoming arms, and at the same time brings a few direct to You by narrow ways." This point must not be overstated to justify the claim that the parables can only be understood by priests. As Kermode writes in "Hoti's Business: Why Are Narratives Obscure?," in *The Genesis of Secrecy,* 23–47, such a claim has been used historically with reference to the book of Mark to exclude the commoners from the teachings of the Gospel.

84 The archetypal scene of *Rvf* 34, in which the poet invokes the figure of Apollo-Sun-Amor to protect Laura (the laurel) who shades herself with her hair (branches), is echoed subliminally by *Rvf* 337: "Ancor io il nido di penseri electi / posi in quell'alma pianta" ("Meanwhile the nest of all my chosen thoughts / I built in that life-giving tree") (337, 9–10).

85 Regarding the love of the woman after her death, see C. Giunta, *Due saggi sulla tenzone*, 446: "Ad essere inusuale ed estranea per gli uomini del Medioevo era invece la rappresentazione letteraria di questo sentimento: il che significa che la differenza tra passato e presente è di ordine estetico, non antropologico, e cade quindi nel dominio dell'arte non in quello dell'esistenza" (What was unusual for the men of the Middle Ages was rather the literary representation of this sentiment: which means that the difference between past and present is of an aesthetic, not an anthropological order, and thus falls in the dominion of art and not that of existence).

86 As Zumthor, *Toward a Medieval Poetics*, xxi, writes: "I prefer to distinguish between 'reading' and 'interpretation,' understanding by 'reading' a benevolent reception, an impregnation, almost an initiatory discovery of the text; 'interpretation' implies all that, but goes beyond it as soon as it becomes a sort of conquering aggression, an active and dominating will to appropriate. Reading is immediate; interpretation is mediate, belonging to a different order of reality. Reading puts us in contact with a series of primary facts; interpretation is a means of constituting a secondary fact. In this sense philology appears as a general rule to have more to do with reading than with interpreting ..."

87 M. Carruthers, *The Book of Memory. A Study of Memory in Medieval Culture*, 204–5, has glossed *familiaris* as "a synonym of *domesticus*, that is, to make something familiar by making it a part of your own experience." As Carruthers writes, ibid., 205: "The medieval scholar's relationship to his texts is quite different from modern objectivity. Reading is to be digested, to be ruminated, like a cow chewing her cud, or like a bee making honey from the nectar of flowers. Reading is memorized with the aid of *murmur*, mouthing the words subvocally as one turns the text over in one's memory; both Quintilian and Martianus Capella stress how murmur accompanies meditation. [...] The process familiarizes a text to a medieval scholar, in a way like that by which human beings may be said to familiarize their food."

1. Historical Context and Poetic Form

1 F. Petrarca, *Inediti*, 321; "Petrarch's Coronation Oration," 1246.

2 Giacomo da Lentini, in G. Contini, ed., *Poeti del Duecento*, I, 190.

3 R. Antonelli, "'Rerum vulgarium fragmenta' di Francesco Petrarca," 85, discusses the "presenza importante e non adeguatemente rilevata" (important and not adequately explored presence) of Cavalcanti in Petrarch, starting with the echoes of that poet's sonnet "Voi che per li occhi

mi passaste 'l core" ("You who passed through my eyes to the heart") in the proemial sonnet, "Voi che ascoltate in rime sparse il suono."

4 See F. Suitner, *Petrarca e la tradizione stilnovistica.*

5 See M. Santagata, *Sant*, liv: "Il soggetto che desidera viene con lui ad occupare quello spazio che era riservato alle rappresentazioni della donna, ai rituali del corteggiamento, all'analisi oggettivante di amore. Il palcoscenico sul quale si sceneggiava il rapporto triadico Amore, amata e amante si trasforma nello spazio dell''io'" (With him the desiring subject comes to occupy the space previously reserved for representations of the woman, the rituals of courtship, and the objectifying analysis of love. The stage on which the triadic relation between Love, the beloved, and the lover was acted out is transformed into the space of the "I").

6 According to A. Roncaglia, "Cino tra Dante e Petrarca," 28, Petrarch's borrowings from Cino benefit from that poet's "medianità" (mediumism) with respect to the poets who preceded him: "Insomma, come già nel rapporto con l'eredità siculo-toscana, così all'interno del nuovo stile Cino svolge una funzione eminentemente mediatrice, tanto essenziale al consolidamento della tradizione letteraria ..." (In short, as already in the relationship with the Siculo-Tuscan heritage, thus within the new style Cino carried out an eminently mediating function, quite essential to the consolidation of the literary tradition ...).

7 M. Marti, *Storia dello stil nuovo*, 509.

8 A. Roncaglia, "Cino tra Dante e Petrarca," 29.

9 See Marti, *Storia dello stil nuovo*, 514: "Cino è il poeta più interessante del gruppo, dacché, a differenza del compatto Cavalcanti, e del Dante periodico e coerente, volta a volta, sperimentatore, la sua funzione largamente e ampiamente mediatrice si identifica con una condizione di ricerca permanente [...] all'alba dei tempi moderni" (Cino is the most interesting poet of the group, since, as different from the compact Cavalcanti, and from the periodic and, from time to time, coherent experimenter, Dante, his broadly and thoroughly mediating function is identified with a condition of permanent research [...] at the dawn of the modern age).

10 See E.L. Boggs, "Cino and Petrarch," 46–7, who extends the series of sonnets written with Cino in mind to include the five sonnets after *Rvf* 92 as well. Of particular importance to Petrarch is Cino's concept of memory represented by the painted image of the beloved preserved in one's heart.

11 Santagata, *Sant*, xlii: "Petrarca dà l'impressione di essere un poeta che proviene da un altro mondo, [...] [da] un altrove culturale" (Petrarch gives the impression of being a poet who hails from another world, [...] from a cultural elsewhere).

12 Santagata, *Sant*, xliv.
13 See E. Fenzi, "Petrarca e la scrittura dell'amicizia," 174: "credo che, in qualche modo scavalcando la tradizione italiana e tornando alle origini, Petrarca sia l'unico grande e vero erede della poesia provenzale, quello che l'ha capita meglio [...] perché in essa coglie il nucleo profondo, e profondamente eversivo, che la caratterizza, cio è la pura e inappagata ossessione del desiderio" (I believe that, somehow by skipping over the Italian tradition and returning to the origins, Petrarch is the only great and true heir of Provençal poetry, the one who has best understood [...] why within it is grasped the profound and profoundly subversive nucleus that characterizes it, that is the pure and unsatisfied obsession of desire).
14 See P. Zumthor, *Toward a Medieval Poetics*, 47, regarding the lack of "completeness" of the medieval text, subject as it was to ongoing variations by author and scribe, and even by the reader: "the term *work* cannot, therefore, be understood in its modern sense. [...] [T]he form-meaning nexus thus generated is thereby constantly called in question."
15 See U. Dotti, *Petrarca civile*, 103: "Nella poesia italiana del Petrarca si ha, con grande chiarezza, una concezione del mondo non nuova in sé – l'eterno problema del destino terreno dell'uomo – ma nuova per le forme e il linguaggio che l'esprime; un linguaggio che prima d'ogni altra cosa rappresenta la voce dell'uomo che dialoga con il terreno e con il trascendente, con il mondo e le sue passioni e con Dio e con il cielo" (In Petrarch's Italian poetry one has, with great clarity, a conception of the world not new in itself – the eternal problem of the earthly destiny of man – but new in its forms and the language that expresses it; a language that before anything else represents the voice of man who dialogues with the earthly and the transcendent, with the world and its passions and with God and heaven).
16 On the journey to Rome preceding this event, Petrarch hurt his leg, an injury which left him bedridden in the Imperial-Vatican city.
17 Petrarca, *Inediti*, 317; "Petrarch's Coronation Oration," 1243.
18 Ibid., 1246. Lactantius is cited from the first book of his *Institutes*.
19 Ibid., 1242–3. Regarding the position of poetry among the arts, Petrarch wrote (citing Aristotle's *Metaphysics*), *Le familiari*, v. 1, 52: "Necessariores quidem omnes, dignior vero nulla" (*Fam.* [i, 12], v. 1, 56: "All are indeed more necessary, but none are more worthy").
20 See F. Fido, "Charles Singleton," n.p.
21 P. Zumthor, *Speaking of the Middle Ages*, 57.
22 P. Zumthor, "From the Universal to the Particular in Medieval Poetry," 820.
23 See Zumthor, *Toward a Medieval Poetics*, 50: "Tradition, the world of Ideas in which intertextual relationships are generated, blends so completely

with these models that the production of a text is more or less clearly conceived as a re-production of the model. From a social point of view, tradition lies at the root of the community, linking author and audience through the text, owing much less to an adherence to the text itself than to adherence to a *virtually immutable poetic system.*"

24 Zumthor organizes the types into four general groups, ibid., 61–2: (1) "types that link [the] figurative element to certain lexical choices and to a syntactico-rhythmic mold"; (2) "types linking a figurative element, whose interpretation varies with context, to fairly narrow lexical choices, and also, though less clearly, to certain syntactic preferences"; (3) "types having a major figurative element, weakly lexicalized and with no particular syntactic marker. Most topoi of possible Latin origin can be classified in this group ..."; "a human image, either static [...] or dynamic"; "the image of an object (castle or sword) or even of a situation (the lady in the wood...)"; (4) "types that [...] are weak in figurative content and have a predominantly, or even exclusively, lexicosemantic kernel."

25 Zumthor, "From the Universal to the Particular in Medieval Poetry," 819.

26 Ibid.

27 Ibid., 822.

28 Zumthor, *Speaking of the Middle Ages*, 36.

29 Santagata, *Sant*, xxxiv; see also ibid., xxxii: "le poesie di Petrarca [...] provengono da un altro mondo [...]. Non è il mondo della lirica passata. [...] P. non ha niente a che spartire con quegli epigoni dell'ultima stagione duecentesca che a Firenze, ma non solo, si dedicano alla poesia lirica, e a quella soltanto" (Petrarch's poems [...] originate from another world [...]. It is not the world of the past lyric. [...] Petrarch has nothing to share with those epigones of the late thirteenth century who, in Florence and elsewhere, are dedicated to lyric poetry, and only that).

30 Santagata, *Sant*, liv. As P. Manni notes, *Il Trecento toscano*, 203, Petrarch employs 3,275 separate lemmas in the *Fragmenta*.

31 Santagata, *Sant*, xxxiv.

32 *Le familiari*, v. 3, 203; *Fam.* [xvi, 11], v. 2, 317.

33 E. Garin, *Italian Humanism*, 51.

34 See N. Iliescu, *Il Canzoniere petrarchesco e Sant'Agostino*, 69: "Nell'ambito dell'opera petrarchesca le rime attestano come il dibattito sulla vita, sorto nell'animo dello scrittore fin dalla sua giovinezza, sia stato integrale, e come esso si sia risolto in senso profondamente Cristiano" (In the ambit of Petrarch's work the vernacular poems attest to how the debate on life, which arose in the mind of the writer from his youth on, was integral, and how it was resolved in a profoundly Christian sense).

35 Pietro Bembo writes, *Prose della volgar lingua*, 63, of "due parti" (parts): "La gravità" (gravity) and "la piacevolezza" (pleasantness); the former is characterized by "l'onestà, la dignità, la maestà, la magnificenza, la grandezza" (honesty, dignity, majesty, magnificence, grandeur); the latter by "la grazia, la soavità, la vaghezza, la dolcezza, gli scherzi, i giochi" (grace, softness, beauty, sweetness, amusements, games).

36 Referring to the small number of people who devote themselves to study and leisure in the calm of a remote location, Petrarch writes to Jacopo Fiorentino, *Le familiari* v. 3, 30: "quod quam sit rarum intelliges si vel poetarum vel honestis omnino studiis vacantium animadverteris raritatem" (*Fam.* [xii, 8], v. 2, 153: "You will understand the rarity of such a happening if you consider the scarcity of poets or of men strongly dedicated to honored studies").

37 B. Martinelli, *Petrarca e il Ventoso*, 264.

38 G. Contini, "La lingua del Petrarca," 98–9.

39 See ibid., 101: "nessun esperimento, ove non sia quello di lavorare tutta una vita attorno agli stessi testi fondamentali" (no experiments, other than that of labouring all his life over the same fundamental texts). Contini also names the "experiment" of the *I Triomphi*, which he deems to have been unsuccessful. Giorgio Orelli, *Il suono dei sospiri*, 9, has taken issue with Contini's minimizing of the presence of Dante in the *Fragmenta*: "Dispero insomma di poter definire Petrarca come anti-Dante anzitutto perché non posso aprire il *Canzoniere* senza toccarvi la viva presenza di Dante, il merito del suo linguaggio cosí trasmutabile, il collo d'anatra della sua espressività" (In short, I am disturbed by the ability to define Petrarch as anti-Dante, first of all because I can not open the *Canzoniere* without finding there the living presence of Dante, the merit of his language, so transmutable, its sinuous expressivity).

40 R. Fedi, *Invito alla lettura di Francesco Petrarca*, 125.

41 Contini, "La lingua del Petrarca," 111, 116.

42 Ibid., 104.

43 Ibid., 102.

44 Ibid.

45 Ibid., 117–18, 109, 102: "I sostantivi di Petrarca sono precisamente dei 'neutri', non dei 'maschili'" (Petrarch's nouns are precisely "neuters," not "masculines").

46 R. Bettarini, *Bett*, xix.

47 Y. Tynianov, *The Problem of Verse Language*, 70, 71, 91. See S. Carrai and G. Inglese, "Francesco Petrarca," 239, who write (with reference to the Continian term "unilinguismo") that Petrarch employed multiple registers and orthographic variants in the *Fragmenta*: "Occorre riconoscere […]

quella varietà di registri che Petrarca non intese sistematicamente ridurre ad uno. Non è un caso, per esempio, che forme con dittongamento *ie* e *uo* in sillaba tonica si alternino a forme con riduzione del dittongo (*fiere* e *fere, pie'* e *pe'*, *buon* e *bon, fuoco* e *foco*)" (One must recognize that Petrarch did not intend to systematically reduce that variety of registers to one. It is not coincidental, for example, that dipthonged forms of *ie* and *uo* alternate with the reduction of the dipthong (*fiere* and *fere, pie'* and *pe'*, *buon* and *bon, fuoco* and *foco*)).

48 Bettarini, *Bett*, xxv.

49 As authors such as Petrarch edited their autographic texts, they created textual variants. As is known, Contini is an early and distinguished practitioner of the *critica delle varianti* applied to Petrarch. See Contini, *Saggio d'un commento alle correzioni del* Petrarca *volgare*.

50 A. Petrucci, "La scrittura del testo," 291. Petrucci describes the physical nature of these markings on the manuscripts, 1982–1991, 292: "Molto diversi appaiono, a seconda della natura degli scritti, l'aspetto grafico, l'impaginazione, l'uso degli spazi, della punteggiatura, delle maiuscole. Negli abbozzi e nelle minute la scrittura appare frenetica nella estrema corsività, mentre l'organizzazione testuale nella pagina è fluida per irregolarità e per mancanza di sicure corrispondenze; l'opera di riscrittura, di correzione, di intervento è veloce e imperiosa, scandita da depennature profonde, da sostituzioni continue e multiple, da a volte ambigui segni di richiamo, da sbarrature di annullamento oblique e ripetute" (According to the nature of the writings, the graphic aspect, the pagination, the use of spaces, of punctuation, of capital letters, appear quite different. In the rough copies and drafts the writing appears frenetic in its extreme cursiveness while the textual organization of the page is fluid in its irregularity and lack of sure correspondences; the work of rewriting, of correction, of intervention, is rapid and imperious, marked by deep cancellations, continuous and multiple substitutions, at times by ambiguous reference signs, oblique and repeated cancellation lines).

51 See T. Peterson, Review of Giuseppe Savoca, *Il Canzoniere di Petrarca tra codicologia ed ecdotica*, 1118–19: "Savoca's analysis extends to each of the lyric genres: how they are distinguished and how they cohere into a single architecture. Of great importance are the prosodic signs adopted by Petrarch, as distinct from punctuation; citing over two hundred examples, Savoca rejects the inferences of editors that these 'rhythmic accents' amount to punctuation. [...] Summarizing his conclusions about Petrarch's punctuation practices, Savoca contrasts his own edition with the digital *Canzoniere* published by Nicola Zingarelli (based on Contini),

or the 'contemporary vulgate'. By removing commas, semicolons, colons, and exclamation marks that editors had added over the centuries, Savoca restores to the *Fragmenta* the full weight of the period ('punto')." See G. Savoca, *Il Canzoniere di Petrarca tra codicologia ed ecdotica*, 169: "Ne risulta un testo graficamente più pulito, meglio articolato nella struttura sintattica e pervaso da una 'musica' nuova, più scandita e a volte più nervosa e quasi 'sincopata', mai però frammentata e disorganica. Riportare il punto al ruolo grafico che gli compete significa anche difenderne 'il suo *signficato interno* nella scrittura' (Kandinsky) …" (What results is a graphically cleaner text, better articulated in its syntactic structure and pervaded by a new "music," more articulated and at times more nervous and "syncopated," though never fragmented and disorganic. To return to the period the graphic role it is due also means defending its "*internal meaning* in the writing" (Kandinsky) …). Savoca enumerates errors that have long been accepted as authoritative, noting that in his edition he has followed Petrarch's practice of capitalizing each line of verse; he has added capitals where the "vulgate" has lowercase, usually because of the replacement of a semicolon with a period; and he has eliminated nearly four hundred capital letters that editors had used for emphasis (half of them in *Amor/Amore*).

52 Savoca, *Il Canzoniere di Petrarca tra codicologia ed ecdotica*, 95.

53 The 2003 facsimile edition of the authoritative codex of *Rerum vulgarium fragmenta, Vat. Lat. 3195*, edited by Belloni, Brugnolo, Storey, and Zamponi, was followed in 2004 by a *Commentario* by the same editors.

54 See M. Santagata, "'Io' e 'tu' fra Stilnovo e Petrarca," section 7 [n.p.]: "In linea di massima, Petrarca non cerca testimoni o destinatari privilegiati da iscrivere nei testi (succede perfino che componimenti sicuramente rivolti a un destinatario storico non esibiscano né nomi né pronomi); è vero che si rivolge molto spesso alla donna, però la continuità del libro e, soprattutto, il fatto che quella donna non sia mera destinataria, ma sia a sua volta un personaggio che interagisce, riconfigurano l'allocuzione in dialogo. Ma è una dialogicità strana, più di tipo narrativo che lirico, o meglio, propria di una narrazione integralmente filtrata attraverso lo schermo (lirico) soggettivo" (In general, Petrarch does not seek privileged witnesses or addressees to inscribe in the texts (to the point where compositions surely addressed to a historic addressee show no names or pronouns); it is true that very often he addresses the woman, but the continuity of the book and, especially, the fact that that the woman is not a mere addressee but is an interacting character in her own right reconfigure the allocution into dialogue. But it is a strange type of dialogue, more narrative than lyrical, or better, specific to a narration integrally filtered through the (lyrical) subjective screen).

55 See H. Wayne Storey, in Belloni et al., *Rerum vulgarium fragmenta. Commentario*, 151: "Una delle soluzioni adottate nei *Fragmenta* a salvaguardia dell'armonia dei materiali poetici è la rigorosa diversificazione dei sistemi di trascrizione per ciascun genere lirico. Questa soluzione [...] produce una suddivisione interna dei contenuti in cinque grandi categorie – il sonetto, la sestina, la ballata, il madrigale e la canzone – ognuna delle quali è contraddistina da diversi criteri di trascrizione e da ben riconoscibili peculiarità di *mise en page*" (One of the solutions adopted in the *Fragmenta* in order to preserve the harmony of the poetic materials is the rigorous diversification of the systems of transcription for each lyric genre. This solution [...] produces an internal subdivision of the contents in five large categories – the sonnet, the sestina, the ballata, the madrigal and the canzone – each of which is distinguished by different criteria of transcription and easily recognizable peculiarities in the *mise en page*).

56 See E. Curtius, *European Literature and the Latin Middle Ages*, 79–105.

57 Santagata, *Sant*, xxxix: "È un numero di tutto rispetto, che testimonia come Petrarca non fosse alieno dall'usare il testo poetico come mezzo di comunicazione" (It is a remarkable number, that testifies how Petrarch was accustomed to using the poetic text as a means of communication).

58 As G. Orelli writes, *Il suono dei sospiri*, 4: "Petrarca non inclina certo a far credere che il significante sia autonomo; che ci sia, come si dice, un primato del significante. La sua arguzia luccica come seta quando, nella lettera [*Sen.* II 3], raccomanda: 'Se vuoi piacer sempre, bada al significato'" (Petrarch is certainly not inclined to have one believe the signifier is autonomous; that there is, as is said, a primacy of the signifier. His wit shines like silk when, in a letter he recommends: "If you wish always to please, focus on the meaning").

59 The following poems from the *Fragmenta* are found in the Chigi manuscript: *Rvf* 1–120, 122–56, 159–65, 169–73, 184–5, 178, 176–7, 189, 264–304. The ballata *Donna mi vene* appears after poem 120 but is later removed from the sequence.

60 Martinelli, *Petrarca e il Ventoso*, 408–09. My emphasis.

61 Ibid., 297–9.

62 Ibid., 297.

63 Ibid., 223.

64 See M. Santagata, in Barbarisi and Berra, *Il «Canzoniere» di Francesco Petrarca. La critica contemporanea*, 99: "Mi preme [...] rilevare che questa lettura ideologica, tanto attenta in apparenza all'aspetto macro-strutturale, in realtà elude proprio il problema di fondo, quello del canzoniere. Questa struttura di cui viene riconosciuta la novità, viene assunta come un dato di partenza, senza domandarsi a quali esigenze profonde, letterarie, ideologiche e sociali

essa risponda" (I need [...] to point out that this ideological reading, so apparently attentive to the macrostructural aspect, in reality eludes the deeper problem, that of the canzoniere. This structure whose novelty is recognized, is assumed as a given from the start, without asking oneself what profound literary, ideological and social demands it is responding to).

65 M. Santagata, *Dal sonetto al canzoniere*, 128. U. Dotti writes in a similar vein, *Storia della letteratura italiana*, 89: "Se una vicenda, nelle sue caratteristiche romanzesche, può dissolversi nella profondità della memoria – questa la scoperta di Petrarca – questa stessa vicenda può poi ricomporsi nel miracolo dell'arte" (If a situation, in its novelistic characteristics, can be dissolved in the depth of memory – this is Petrarch's discovery – this same situation can then be recomposed in the miracle of art).

66 Santagata, *Dal sonetto al canzoniere*, 174–6.

67 M. Corti, *An Introduction to Literary Semiotics*, 112. See ibid., 112: "The functionality and information possibility of a collection as such occurs when at least one of the following conditions is present: (1) if there exists a combination of thematic and/or formal elements that runs through all the texts and produces the unity of the collection; (2) if there is a progression to the discourse for which each single text can occupy only one place. Clearly, the second condition presupposes the first, but the reverse is not true. [...] M. Santagata, in an article, 'Intertextual Connections in the *Canzoniere* of Petrarch,' studies the connections of transformation from one text to another and the connections of equivalence (parallel repetition of similar elements, etc.), individuates and distinguishes the superficial structural elements from the 'deep structural elements hypothesized under the form of a thematic paradigm,' and concludes that the *Canzoniere* meets the conditions of both (1) and (2) of our scheme."

68 These well-known lines contain references to Job 30:9; Lam 3:14; Ps 69:12.

69 Ronald L. Martinez, "Mourning Laura in the Canzoniere: Lessons from Lamentations," 1, connects the "voi" interlocutor to Lamentations 1.12 and the general address by a personified Jerusalem, lamenting her captivity and abjection: "O vos omnes qui transitis per viam, adtendite et videte si est dolor sicut dolor meus ..." ("Is it nothing to you, all ye that pass by? behold, and see if there be any sorrow like unto my sorrow ..."). So, too, notes Martinez, ibid., 2, citing G. Pozzi, the lines "Ma ben veggio or sí come al popol tutto / favola fui gran tempo" (1, 9–10) derive from Lam. 3:14 "factus sum in derisum omni populo meo, canticum eorum tota die" ("I am made a derision to all my people, their song all day long").

70 See, for example, *Rvf* 181, 5: "L'ésca fu 'l seme ch'egli sparge et miete" ("[Love's] bait was seed he scatters and he reaps –").

71 Paolo Cherchi has directed attention to the negative values of shame, pain, and vain hope in the proemial sonnet. While the subject enunciates his need for penitence, there is no genuine action taken. See P. Cherchi, *Verso la chiusura: Saggio sul Canzoniere di Petrarca*, 10–11: "[...] il pentimento è il momento della coscienza, ma non è ancora quella della volontà la quale avvia una nuova storia" ([...] the repentance is the moment of conscience, but not yet that of the will that begins a new story).

72 F. Rico, "'Rime sparse', 'Rerum vulgarium fragmenta'. Para el titulo y el primer soneto del 'Canzoniere.'" Rico's is the most exhaustive reading of the proemial sonnet.

73 As P. Vecchi Galli, "Le parole del peccato," notes, in the wake of M. Santagata's commentary, there are parallels between poem 7 and the Babylonese sonnets, notably 136 but also 114. Regarding Petrarch's condemnation of middle-class business practices, U. Dotti, *La rivoluzione incompiuta*, cites the next-to-last *familiare*, *Fam.* xxiv 12 [1360], addressed to Homer, and *Fam.* xviii 9 2, to Nelli, about how he is unknown in his native city of Florence, which is absorbed in its mercantile life and textile production.

74 Here one is in what M. Serres, *Hermes. Literature, Science, Philosophy*, 50–1, describes as "the state of things before the establishment of rational discourse, the time when spaces were poorly joined, when transport and itinerary were only myth."

75 See G. Capovilla, *«Sì vario stile »: Studi sul Canzoniere del Petrarca*, 43

76 See Capovilla, ibid., for whom the multiple strophe ballata would risk "una ipersegmentazione della catena testuale" (a hypersegmentation of the textual chain) and "un gratuito, talora ossessivo effetto cantilenante" (a gratuitous, sometimes obsessive sing-song effect).

77 S. Chessa, *Il profumo del sacro nel* Canzoniere *di Petrarca*, 57. In his study of the poem, Fenzi, *Saggi petrarcheschi*, 26, conveys the sense of the duality that arises from the use of sacred imagery in an erotic context, referring to such allusions to Laura – here and in other early sonnets (*Rvf* 3, 4, 15) – as "eccezionali segni di un destino personale che s'impone con tutta la concentrata evidenza dei suoi simboli e delle loro corrispondenze significative: ma vi è pure in essi un nodo di significati che resta chiuso in sé" (exceptional signs of a personal destiny that imposes itself with all the concentrated evidence of its symbols and their corresponding meanings: but there is also in them a knot of meanings that remains self-enclosed).

78 In a paper on *Rvf* 16 presented to the Yale Petrarch Institute, Thomas Greene, "The Quest for Resemblance in the Poetry of Petrarch," 11,

writes of the character's pursuit of Laura's image as follows: "The poet is condemned to half-resemblances, fragmentary, provisional, deceptive, fleeting likenesses which have no redemptive power and which will always disappoint. This is not a peripheral trait of Petrarchan imagery; it is essential to the psychic structure adumbrated by the poetry and ultimately its implications transcend the psychologistic. They are metaphysical." Greene does not separate the "poet" from his narrator and character when he argues, ibid., 14, that "the profound divisions in Petrarch's own intuitions of himself," lead to a phenomenon of "semiotic disjunction [that] presents itself as inseparable from psychic disjunction."

79 See M.C. Bertolani, *Petrarca e la visione dell'eterno*, 167–81.

80 The physicality of Rome in *Rvf* 16 assumes the position of the creature within the salvific plan guaranteed by the incarnation. See M.G. Blasio, "Il dibattito religioso tra due e trecento," 250: "Petrarca sposta dunque la tensione del discorso sulla dialettica del passaggio terreno, dove la visione della 'dïsiata vostra forma vera' avviene appunto attraverso 'la sembianza', sia essa l'immagine di Roma, di Cristo, della donna" (Petrarch thus displaces the tension of the discourse onto the dialectic of the earthly passage, where the vision of "your true form, yearned-for and desired" occurs precisely through the "resemblance", whether that be the image of Rome, of Christ, or of the woman).

2. Temporality and Desire (*Rvf* 22–100)

1 *Le familiari*, 1968, v. 1, 38; *Fam.* [i, 7], v. 1, 39.

2 In the fable one sees combined two temporalities: the anticipation of the child and the retrospection of the old person. See C. Campo, *Gli imperdonabili*, 21: "Non a caso la lettura delle fiabe, lingua segreta dei vecchi, è così spesso l'evento indelebile dell'infanzia" (Not by chance the reading of fables, the secret language of the old, is so often the indelible event of childhood). The pathway undertaken is often mystifying and illusory, mirroring the psychological experience of the seeker.

3 I. Calvino, *Lezioni americane*, 140.

4 See D. Dutschke, *Francesco Petrarca, Canzone XXIII from First to Final Version*, on the lengthy process of revising *Rvf* 23 over the years.

5 In many respects this recollection of youthful entrapment takes the form of a fable; in so doing it suggests that the fantasy of a child is the perfect analogy for the "prima etade" of the subject's enamourment. See T. Barolini, "The Making of a Lyric Sequence," 13, for whom the "first age" of this canzone amounts to the "only time" that Petrarch allows himself, as he is perpetually

constrained to look backwards: "Petrarch finds ways always to go back, never forward, a fact that highlights the importance of the first verse of the first canzone, poem 23, 'Nel dolce tempo de la *prima* etade': for Petrarch, there are no new beginnings (because there are constant new beginnings), and so the first time – the 'prima etade' – is the only time."

6 In his discussion of canzone 29, which he recommends as "la petrosa del Petrarca" (Petrarch's "stony" poem), R. Spongano, "Francesco Petrarca tentato di morire," notes the troubled history of the interpretations of this obscure poem in which the lyric "I" figure is tempted by suicide. One error – shared by Carducci – is that of designating the praise or laud of Laura in the poem's conclusion as its originating "motive" instead of its "result." The motive instead is the subject's confusion of the phantasm for the woman herself.

7 For S. Agosti the alienation of the Petrarchan subject is mirrored in such deep structures in a way that lends itself to Lacanian analysis. See Agosti, *Gli occhi, le chiome*, 45, regarding the "eternity of desire" in the *Fragmenta*, seen as a function of Petrarch's cult of memory: "il trionfo della memoria, il suo monumento immortale, [...] non è altro che l'affermazione vittoriosa dell'eternità del desiderio" (the triumph of memory, its immortal monument, [...] is nothing other than the victorious affirmation of the eternity of desire). I would add that the ultimate desire in the *Fragmenta* is the desire for God that comes through the subject's Augustinianism.

8 As Michel David wrote in 1967, *Letteratura e psicoanalisi*, 97: "[C]redo non si possa dire che Petrarca sia stato studiato secondo i criteri della psicanalisi, benché la sua enorme produzione, il chiaro autobiografismo delle opere, il problema sessuale [...] offrano una materia di studio straordinariamente propizia ..." (I don't believe one can say that Petrarch has been studied according to the criteria of psychoanalysis, though his enormous production, the clear autobiographism of the works, the sexual problem [...] offer an extraordinarily propitious material for study).

9 See D. De Robertis, "Petrarca petroso," 245.

10 R. Bettarini, *Bett*, 172, citing S. Chessa, *Il profumo del sacro nel* Canzoniere *di Petrarca*.

11 If one accepts the hypothesis that the "tela" refers to the ongoing project of *De viris illustribus*, which Petrarch cannot complete without borrowing a book of Livy assembled by the canon regular and scholar Landolfo, then the reference to "quel mio dilecto padre" ("my cherished father") (40, 11) is probably to Landolfo (who died in 1313) and not Augustine. See G. Billanovich, *La tradizione del testo di Livio e le origini dell'Umanesimo*, 203.

12 Summarizing his *Bucolicum carmen* in a letter to his brother Gherardo, Petrarch writes, *Le familiari*, v. 2, 304: "Pastores colloquentes nos sumus;

ego Silvius, tu Monicus. [...] primi quidem tum quod in silvis res acta est, tum propter insitum ab ineunte etate urbis odium amoremque silvarum, propter quem multi ex nostris in omni sermone sepius me Silvanum quam Franciscum vocant" (*Fam.* [x, 4], v. 2, 72: "We are the conversing shepherds, I Silvius and you Monicus. [...] The first is Silvius because he had spent his life in the woods, and because from an early age there had been planted in him a hatred of the city and a love of the forest. This is why many of our friends generally call me Silvanus rather than Franciscus").

13 See R. Ceserani, "«Petrarca»: Il nome come auto-reinvenzione poetica," 122–4. This sonnet serves as the negative complement or moiety to the positive "Petrine" identification of Petrarch with the phonemes comprising his name in poetry. See below, chapter 3, section 3: "St Peter and the Avignon Church."

14 The same noontime hour is found in *Bucolicum Carmen* III, 85–6: "Forte die medio, dum me meus urget amaror, / Sive amor in silvas ..." ("Hear then: One day around noon I was wandering deep in the forest, / Driven by love and chagrin ...").

15 See C. Segre, "Isotopie di Laura." Segre bases his use of "isotopia" on the research of A.J. Greimas and J. Courtès.

16 G. Capovilla, «*Sì vario stile* »: *Studi sul Canzoniere del Petrarca*, 17.

17 B. Martinelli, *Petrarca e il Ventoso*, 279: "la ballata è stata collocata con notevole anticipo rispetto al posto che le sarebbe spettato se il *Canzoniere* fosse stato allestito secondo un rigido criterio cronologico" (the ballata was positioned quite early with respect to the place one would have expected had the *Canzoniere* been arranged according to strict chronological criteria).

18 See E. Bigi, "Le ballate del Petrarca," 492–6.

19 A. Musumeci's treatment of parentheses notes that they are modest in frequency, brief, and apparently "innocuous"; what the critic finds on deeper investigation is that this syntactic trope involves important key words in important positions. See Musumeci, "Le parentesi nel Canzoniere petrarchesco," 496: "In questo spazio privilegiato, l'incidenza di parole tematiche, cioè di parole che assurgono a funzione di emblemi nella totalità del codice interpretativo petrarchesco, è rilevante" (In this privileged space, the incidence of thematic words, that is of words that rise to the function of emblems in the totality of the Petrarchan interpretive code, is relevant).

20 Parenthesis extends from being a syntactic feature and discursive device (as in digression) to assume the status of a metaphysical category, a means of deferral of the worldly in order to negotiate, however contradictorily, with the ineffable and with God. The position taken here, that Petrarch dialogues with God by opening parentheses in his "normal" interlocution with others and with the reader, runs contrary to Contini's identification of Petrarch's

God as a "psychological theme." See G. Contini, "La lingua del Petrarca," 101: "Il suo non è già il Dio che compone le contraddizioni [...] ma è quel Dio che interviene a sedare il tedio e consolare la stanchezza, s'introduce insomma come tema psicologico ..." (His is not yet a God who composes contradictions [...] but is that God who intervenes to relax tedium and to console fatigue, who is introduced in short like a psychological theme ...). Iliescu strongly disapproves of Contini's remarks about Petrarch's God, seeing them as a continuation of the reductivism of Benedetto Croce's reading of Petrarch. See N. Iliescu, *Il Canzoniere petrarchesco e Sant'Agostino*, 99: "Non è, certamente, nel vero Gianfranco Contini, quando, riassumendo, fa suo, sebbene in forma assai attenuata, il punto di vista della critica che nel nostro secolo fa capo a Croce" (Gianfranco Contini is certainly not in the right when, in summarizing, he makes his own, though in a very attenuated form, the point of view of the critics who in our century descend from Croce).

21 F. Petrarca, *Res seniles*, v. 1, 318; *Sen.* [iv, 5] v. 1, 142.

22 See G. Barthouil, "Petrarca a Avignone," 212: "Petrarca nell'agosto 1342 dà la prima forma ordinata del Canzoniere, redige il *Secretum*, opera d'auto–analisi e di introspezione lucida, appassionante per i lettori" (In August 1342 Petrarch gives the first ordered form of the Canzoniere and he drafts the *Secretum*, a work of self-analysis and lucid introspection, exciting for readers). M. Santagata, *I frammenti dell'anima*, 137, introduces the term "La raccolta del 1342."

23 E.H. Wilkins, *The Making of the "Canzoniere,"* 81–92.

24 Wilkins's research on the nine "forms" of the *Fragmenta* and their dating is widely accepted. Clearly, the earlier forms are not actual sequential editions leading up to the final one.

25 M. Santagata, *I frammenti dell'anima*, 137.

26 R. Antonelli, "'Rerum vulgarium fragmenta' di Francesco Petrarca," 8.

27 The structural idea of a "sonetto al quadrato" (the sonnet squared) is found in Andrea Zanzotto, author of an "ipersonetto" (hypersonnet) of fourteen sonnets, plus a "Premessa" (Premise) and a "Postilla" (Note) in *Il galateo in bosco*. Sonnet xi of the Zanzotto series opens with the incipit of *Rvf* 273: "Che fai? Che pensi?" ("What do you do? What think?"). For an analogous medieval example, one thinks of Folgore da San Gimignano's fourteen "Sonetti dei Mesi" ("Sonnets of the Months"), which include one sonnet for each month plus the "Dedica alla Brigata" ("Dedication to the Group") and the "Commiato" ("Envoi").

28 With reference to this "raccolta," Santagata, *I frammenti dell'anima*, 138, notes "la presenza di ricchi apparati storici e mitologici (41, 42, 43, 44, 45) e il proliferare della tematica dafnea (34, 41, 60, 64)" (the presence of

rich historical and mythological apparatuses (41, 42, 43, 44, 45) and the proliferation of the Daphnean thematic (34, 41, 60, 64)).

29 The religious significance of the scene lies *in potentia*, a feature commented on by M. O'Rourke Boyle, *Petrarch's Genius*, 60: "In the inaugural apostrophe to Apollo, the poet allied himself with that god by whose inspiration 'we shall then see together a marvel.' [...] The laurel was most nobly [...] a 'holy' tree. This religious denotation repeated from the coronation speech his praise of it as 'a sacred tree, to be held in awe, and to be reverenced.'"

30 K. Foster, *Petrarch: Poet and Humanist*, 126. A. Noferi, "Il Canzoniere del Petrarca: scrittura del desiderio e desiderio della scrittura," 9, cites the poem's opening, "Apollo, s'anchor vive il bel desio / che t'infiammava a le thesaliche onde" (34, 1–2) ("Apollo, if that fair desire still lives / Which once inflamed you by Thessalian waves"), as concerning Daphne's transformation "in altro da sé: nel lauro, la pianta sempre verde, sacra ai poeti, la poesia stessa ben visible e tangibile nella sua presenza obbiettiva, materica, letterale, ma che proprio in questa presenza sancisce l'irreparabile assenza del perduto oggetto del desiderio, rappresentante essa stessa dell'oggetto in quanto perduto ed insieme della eternizzazione del desiderio" (into something other than herself: into the laurel, the evergreen plant, sacred to poets, poetry itself quite visible and tangible in its objective, material, literal presence, but which precisely in this presence sanctions the irreparable absence of the lost object of desire, itself representing the object as being lost but also the eternalization of desire). This reading stops short of bestowing on the Apolline and Daphnean imagery a potential to evolve out of the pictorial and "fabulous" discourse into the Christological dimensions of the myth so prevalent later in the sequence.

31 O'Rourke Boyle, *Petrarch's Genius*, 60. As P. Zumthor points out, *Speaking of the Middle Ages*, 63, "every medieval poetic form (on whatever level one may define it) *tends* toward double meaning; and I don't mean the doubling deciphered by an allegoristic reading but, superimposing or complexifying its effects, a perpetual *sic et non*, yes and no, obverse/reverse. Every meaning, in the last analysis, would present itself as enigmatic, the enigma being resolved into simultaneous and contradictory propositions, one of which always parodies the other."

32 E. Taddeo, "Petrarca e il tempo," 87–8, counts twenty-one poems written exclusively in the present tense (all but five in poems 1 to 200). Of these, *Rvf* 35 is identified, as "il più rappresentativo [...]: la monocronia è qui il miglior veicolo della permanenza immutabile della condizione del poeta" (the most representative [...]: monochrony is here the best vehicle for the immutable permanence of the condition of the poet).

33 Wilkins, *The Making of the "Canzoniere,"* 298–9.

34 G. Orelli, *Il suono dei sospiri*, 45. Orelli, ibid., 45, agrees with De Sanctis's assessment of the tone of poem 35 as "cupo e fosco" (dark and sullen) and of its music as "lenta e grave" (slow and grievous).

35 See Campo, *Gli imperdonabili*, 13: "Il vecchio […] sta indicando al fanciullo una meta: non già il proprio passato, ma il suo futuro, il futuro della sua memoria di adulto. Né l'uno né l'altro lo sa, se non per la qualità numinosa delle parole che avvolge l'uno e l'altro nella stessa fascinazione" (The old man […] is indicating a goal to the child: not his own past, but the child's future, the future of his memory as an adult. Neither one of them knows it, save by the numinous quality of the words that enclose them within the same fascination).

36 The epithets in *Rvf* 41, 1, derive from Psalms 85:5 (86:5): "suavis et mitis" ("good and forgiving").

37 See D. De Robertis, *Memoriale Petrarchesco*, 19, for a discussion of these two sonnets' "penetrazione […] capillare" (capillary penetration) and debts to Dante's "canzone petrosa": "Io son venuto al punto de la rota" ("I have come to that point on the wheel"). All translations of citations from Dante's *Rime* are taken from *Dante's Lyric Poetry*, ed. K. Foster and P. Boyde.

38 As M. Santagata writes, *Dal sonetto al canzoniere*, 41: "alle connotazioni disforiche di XLI si oppongono quelle euforiche di XLII" (to the dysphoric connotations of poem 41 are opposed the euphoric ones of poem 42).

39 This example is one of eleven instances of the absolute superlative in the *Fragmenta*. As Diego Valeri writes, the use of the grammatical superlative is consistent with poetry's intrinsic power to elevate reality. See Valeri, "Difficoltà del superlativo assoluto in poesia," 901–2: "La poesia è, per sé, superlativa nel senso che eleva la realtà, posta in noi e disposta attorno a noi, a potenza di sentimento puro, di pura immagine, di pura verità spirituale. La radice di ogni poesia è nella facoltà del poeta di *omnia admirari*; tanto egli è lontano dall'*animus* del filosofo stoico" (Poetry is, in itself, superlative in the sense that it elevates reality, placed within us and arranged around us, with the capacity of pure feeling, pure image, pure spiritual truth. The root of every poem is in the faculty of the poet to marvel in everything, so distant is he from the mind of the stoic philosopher).

40 See G. Pozzi, "Petrarca, i Padri e soprattutto la Bibbia," 144–5: "Non posso però evitare un cenno al mancato ricorso dei commentatori di Petrarca a quella letteratura mariana sbocciata nel secolo XII, che scioglierebbe tanti enigmi; anche una veloce scorsa rivela quanto i detti del poeta risuonino di quelle voci. Già con l'epiteto iniziale di 'bella' egli indirizza alla lunghissima 'via pulchritudinis' che percorsero numerosi scrittori spirituali

attenti alla bellezza, nonché morale, fisica della madonna" (I would be remiss if I did not point to the failure of Petrarchan commentators to draw on that Marian literature that flourished in the 12th century, which would resolve so many enigmas; even a quick look reveals how the poet's sayings echo those voices. Already with the initial epithet of "bella" he points to the very long *"via pulchritudinis"* ["way of pulchritude"] pursued by numerous spiritual writers attentive to the physical as well as the moral beauty of the Madonna). One recalls that Petrarch was part of a wide movement, initiated in France and Italy some 150 years earlier, that included the cult of the Madonna.

41 Pozzi cites these lines as typical of Petrarch's practice of biblical citation. See Pozzi, "Petrarca, i Padri e soprattutto la Bibbia," 149: "Il modo più esplicito si ha quando un evento biblico è assunto come exemplum. Così in 44, 5–8 il pianto di Davide per il figlio Assalonne e per il re Saul è abbinato a quello di Cesare sopra il morto Pompeo per dimostrare, a confronto, la durezza di Laura" (One has the most explicit way when a biblical event is assumed as an exemplum. Thus in *Rvf* 44, 5–8, David's weeping for his son Absalom and for King Saul is paired with that of Caesar over the dead Pompey in order to demonstrate, by contrast, the hardness of Laura).

42 In the passage from Matthew 8:8, a centurion beseeches Christ to heal his paralysed servant: "But the Centurion answered him, 'Lord I am not worthy to have you come under my roof.'" If one ignores the hypothetical quality of the verb and treats it as a simple past tense, one can arrive at the highly speculative conclusion of B. Boysen, "Crucified in the Mirror of Love," 168: "Petrarch is crucified in the reflection (*io v'era con saldi chiovi fisso*) because Laura exiles him from himself, *misero esilio* [sic], mirroring herself in herself (whereby he becomes Echo), and moreover she is placing him in a state of crucifixion […]."

43 Concerning this notion of the Other that surfaces in the fable, see Bakhtin, *Art and Answerability*, 159: "The valued 'fabular' manifoldness of life has the character of an unconscious oxymoron: joy and suffering, truth and falsehood, good and evil – all are indissolubly merged in the unity of the continuous stream of life's manifold *fabulas*, for my acts are determined here not by the context of meaning that urgently confronts my *I–for–myself*, but by the *other* who has possessed me – by the valued being of otherness in me […]."

44 S. Agosti, "Petrarca e la modernità letteraria: una genealogia."

45 See Dante Alighieri, "E' m'increesce di me sí duramente" ("I pity myself so intensely"), *Rime*, 64: "E non le pesa del mal ch'ella vede, / Anzi vie più bella ora / Che mai e vie più lieta par che rida; / E alza *li occhi micidiali*, e grida / Sopra colei che piange il suo partire: / 'Vanne, misera, fuor,

vattene omai.'" ("but she cares nothing for the suffering she sees—indeed, much lovelier than ever now and more full of joy, she seems to laugh; and she lifts her death-dealing eyes and cries out in triumph over her who laments at departing: 'Away with you, wretch, away now!'"). See also the same motif in *Rime*, 167–71, "Così nel mio parlar voglio esser aspro" ("I want to be as harsh in my speech"). It is ironic that J. Freccero, "The Fig Tree and the Laurel: Petrarch's Poetics," 39, fails to note the Dantean source for "i micidiali specchi," since he draws a strong contrast between Beatrice and Laura: "Beatrice is in many senses the opposite of Laura. She was a mediatrix, continually pointing beyond herself to God. Throughout most of the *Paradiso*, for example, the pilgrim looks into her eyes only obliquely so that he sees what lies beyond her. Laura's eyes, by contrast, are 'homicidal mirrors' in which her narcissistic lover finds spiritual death." The *Fragmenta* is rich in examples of Laura's eyes as founts of virtue and blessedness; see my discussion of the *cantilena oculorum* (*Rvf* 71–3) in chapter 4.

46 *Rvf* 46, 12–13 refers to Genesis 1:2 and Isaiah 51:10. It is possible to conjecture here that through Laura's self-reflection one can imagine the self-reflection of Mary, whose cult had become a major component of the Catholic religion, though it was resisted by the schoolmen.

47 G. Cavalcanti, in G. Contini, ed., *Poeti del Duecento*, 511. Trans. Simon West, *The Selected Poetry of Guido Cavalcanti*, 71.

48 M. de Certeau, *The Mystic Fable*, 10.

49 According to Paul Ricoeur, *Figuring the Sacred*, 59, such "antithetical formulas as, 'Whoever would save his life will lose it, and whoever loses his life for my sake will live,'" are typical of proverbs.

50 M. Santagata, *Sant*, 323, cites as biblical references for *Rvf* 64, 9–10: Matthew 7:15–16: "Beware of false prophets, who come to you in sheep's clothing but inwardly are ravenous wolves. You will know them by their fruits. Are grapes gathered from thorns, or figs from thistles?" and Luke 6:44: "for each tree is known by its own fruit. For figs are not gathered from thorns, nor are grapes picked from a bramble bush."

51 See M. Fubini, *Metrica e poesia*, 236 ff, for a discussion of Petrarch's advances, including the unprecedented density of his sonnet and his perfection of the Provençal form of the sestina, to which he adds a melic clarity and rational plausibility that Dante's had lacked.

52 For a discussion of Petrarch's stylistic novelty with respect to Dante and the Dolce Stil Nuovo, see A. Balduino, "Lettura di un sonetto petrarchesco." See L. Del Giudice, "Il processo narrativo nei componimenti LXI–CV del *Canzoniere* di F. Petrarca," 156: "[P.] rinuncia il compromesso stilnovistico che fa della donna scala mobile verso Dio" (Petrarch renounces

the stilnovistic compromise that makes the woman into a moving staircase toward God).

53 Santagata, *Sant*, xx.

54 This stylistic direction will have positive developments in terms of a "Petrarca petroso," starting with *Rvf* 105, the canzone-frottola, and seen in canzone 125 –"parlo in rime aspre, et di dolcezza ignude" ("I speak in rugged rhymes of sweetness bare") (125, 16) – which serves to counterbalance the idyllic sweetness of canzone 126.

55 The cited passages are *Confessions* iv, 3, 4; vii, 5, 7; x, 34, 51.

56 See Bettarini, *Bett*, I, 370–1, for this reference to Cino's "L'alta speranza che mi reca Amore." Cino's phrase "guardo soave" is reversed as "soave sguardo" in *Rvf* 162, 267, 343.

57 A. Gagliardi, *Cino da Pistoia. Le poetiche dell'anima*, 179.

58 Del Giudice's study of poems 61 to 105 indicates in poems 61 to 81 a greater narrative constancy and in poems 82 to 105 a greater attention to formal exercise and bravura. See Del Giudice, "Il processo narrativo nei componimenti LXI-CV del *Canzoniere* di F. Petrarca," 153: "Mentre fino a questo momento (la prima parte) il Petrarca sembra aver privilegiato una struttura logico–narrativa, in questa seconda parte del *Canzoniere* i componimenti tendono invece ad aggregarsi secondo principi formali, e si caratterizza soprattutto per le 'connessioni intertestuali d'equivalenza'" (While up to this moment (the first part) Petrarch seems to have privileged a logical-narrative structure, in this second part of the *Canzoniere* the components tend rather to be grouped according to formal principles, and it is characterized above all by the "intertextual connections of equivalency").

59 The works included by Wilkins as part of the "Liederbuch" that are not part of the Raccolta of 1342 are poems 77, 78, 129, and 179.

60 The theme of Laura's depiction and the historical novelty of painting as an art form is discussed by G. Mazzotta, "Antiquity and the New Arts in Petrarch," 33, who asks: "Is there ever a principle of transcendent order, an objective norm by which the world of history is imaginatively re-formed?" In a discussion of poems 77 and 78, Mazzotta places Martini in the tradition of Duccio and Byzantine miniaturists, who create an iconic and "transfigured space" in contrast to the realistic style of Giotto. What we take from Mazzotta's reading is the importance of seeing the poet as a historian and imitator of the painting style of Simone.

61 E. Fenzi, *Saggi petrarcheschi*, 33–7, considers the historical context of Petrarch's 1336 commissioning of the painting of Laura to Simone and Petrarch's 1337 trip to Rome, as a way to connect the images of Laura's portrait and the Veronica shroud. Fenzi claims that the attachment to the

image in either case (*Rvf* 77–8 and 16) has a "fetish" quality indicative of a general descent by the subject "dal sacro al profano" in these poems.

62 See Dante Alighieri, *Convivio* [4, xxviii], 340: "E qui è da sapere, che […] la naturale morte è quasi a noi *porto* di lunga navigazione e riposo. Ed è così: ché, come lo buono marinaio, come esso appropinqua al *porto*, cala le sue vele, e soavemente, con debile conducimento entra in quello; così noi dovemo calare le vele delle nostre mondane operazioni e tornare a Dio con tutto nostro intendimento e cuore, sì che a quello *porto* si vegna con tutta soavitade e con tutta pace" (Trans. Richard H. Lansing: "Here it should be observed that a natural death [...] is, as it were, a port and site of repose after our long journey. This is quite true, for just as a good sailor lowers his sails as he approaches port and, pressing forward lightly, enters it gently, so we must lower the sails of our worldly preoccupations and return to God with all our mind and heart, so that we may reach that port with perfect gentleness and perfect peace.")

63 The contemporary presence of sacred and amorous themes is an indication of Petrarch's syncretism and opposition to the sharp separation of the spirit and the flesh one finds, for example, in St Paul.

64 Contini, "La lingua del Petrarca," 113–14.

65 *Le familiari*, v. 3, 21; *Fam*. [xii, 3] v. 2, 143.

66 See *Res seniles* v. 1, 158: "[E]xperientia siquidem artem facit, usus autem artem gignit ac perfit verumque … […] Augustinus […] artem rerum expertarum placitarumque memoriam diffinivit" (*Sen*. [ii, 3] v. 1, 63: "If experience really makes art, then practice begets, nourishes, and makes art perfect. […] Augustine […] defined art as the memory of things experienced and enjoyed").

3. The Language of Tears (*Rvf* 92–122)

1 For Petrarch's relations to Cino, see A. Gagliardi, *Cino da Pistoia. Le poetiche dell'anima*, and F. Suitner, *Petrarca e la tradizione stilnovistica*, 99–156.

2 G. Pozzi, "Petrarca, i Padri e soprattutto la Bibbia," 181.

3 See ibid., 173: "Egli si dimostra persuaso che un legame, quale corre fra luce e ombra o voce ed eco, unisca l'aspirazione del poeta secolare e l'ispirazione del profeta biblico. Egli pare convinto che la mozione psichica che spinge e guida al poetare e la grazia che induce nell'anima la fede e la santità possano convivere in nome della anagogia cristiana" (He shows himself persuaded that a connection, such as that between light and shadow or voice and echo, unites the poet's secular aspirations and the inspiration of the biblical prophet. He seems convinced that the psychic

motion that pushes and guides one to write poetry and the grace that induces faith and holiness in the soul can live together in the name of the Christian anagoge).

4 E. Fenzi, *Saggi petrarcheschi*, 59, addresses this situation by referring to the split between the "character" and the "poet" (this latter term referring to both "narrator" and "author"): "Il momento della divaricazione è segnato dall'ambigua posizione del personaggio-poeta: il quale come personaggio vive tra il tempo della fuga e quello della ricaduta, e come poeta lascia (dovrebbe lasciare) *l'altro lavoro* per il poema" (The moment of the split is marked by the ambiguous position of the character-poet: who as a character lives between the time of flight and that of relapse, and as a poet leaves (ought to leave) *the other work* for the poem).

5 See A. Bernardo, "The Importance of the Non-Love Poems of Petrarch's 'Canzoniere.'"

6 "Mai non vo' piú cantar com'io soleva" is probably a late insert in the collection, given the fact that the bulk of its intratextual references are to poems in Part 2. See M. Santagata, *Sant*, 489: "[D]à da pensare, pur costituendo [...] solo un labilissimo indizio, il fatto che la maggior parte dei testi del Canzoniere richiamati nelle note di commento risalga ad anni assai più 'bassi', in molti casi posteriori alla morte di Laura" (The fact that the majority of the texts of the Canzoniere referenced in the notes of the comment are composed in much later years, in many cases after the death of Laura, gives one pause, even if this amounts [...] to a very weak indicator).

7 As Ugo Dotti writes, in U. Dotti, ed., *Canzoniere*, 65, Dante's homage to Brunetto signals his choice of a paternal figure based on his great abilities as a teacher and guide to "una filosofia [...] che s'iscrive sotto il segno dell'etica e della politica e che fa centro, mediante la parola, nell'arte del persuadere e del fondare la convivenza civile. Una concezione del vivere e del sapere, a dirla in breve, di cui si approprieranno Petrarca e gli umanisti ..." (a philosophy inscribed under the sign of ethics and politics and which hits the mark, by means of the word, the art of persuasion and the founding of a civic community. A conception of living and knowing, to put it briefly, that Petrarch and the humanists will appropriate ...).

8 See F. Suitner, *Dante, Petrarca e altra poesia antica*, 170: "Il Petrarca più moderno e più innovatore del resto non era quello della sestina, della frottola, o di certi artificiosi componimenti scritti seguendo techniche provenzaleggianti. Questo è paradossalmente il Petrarca più arcaico, che meno ha avuto fortuna e che si ricollegava a tecniche antiche" (The most modern Petrarch and for that matter the most innovative was not that of the sestina, the frottola, or certain artful compositions written by following

"Provençal-izing" techniques. This is, paradoxically, the most archaic Petrarch who has had less fortune).

9 The genre of the *frottola* is defined by N. Zingarelli, in F. Petrarca, *Rime*, 1963, as "composizione poetica italiana di origine popolare e giullaresca in voga nel XIV e XV sec. di vario metro, spesso di senso oscuro per la presenza d'indovinelli o proverbi" (an Italian poetic composition having a popular and minstrel origin, fashionable during the 14th and 15th centuries, of variable metre, often obscure in its meaning because of the presence of riddles or proverbs).

10 The six fifteen-line stanzas feature a *fronte* of six hendecasyllables, all with *rimalmezzo,* and a double *sirma* of five and four lines made up of two septenaries and seven hendecasyllables, four of which contain *rimalmezzo.* The final lines of stanzas 1 to 5 rhyme with the first hemistych of the following stanza. The metric scheme, excluding the ten *rimalmezzo,* is: ABC. ABC DED, dE.FGgF. With respect to *Rvf* 105, H.W. Storey, in Belloni, et al., *Rerum vulgarium fragmenta. Codice Vat. Lat. 3195,* 162, writes of its anomalous transcription in Vat. Lat. 3195: "non solo è materialmente separata dai componimenti precedenti da uno spazio bianco di ben otto righe [...], ma è anche caratterizzata da una sorta di *tour de force* metrico di rimalmezzo che la distingue graficamente tanto dal suo 'gemello' metrico (la canz. 28 *O aspectata in ciel beata et bella*), quanto da tutte le altre canzoni, facendola quasi assurgere al rango di componimento emblematico di un canto nuovo" (not only is it materially separated from the preceding compositions by a white space fully eight lines long [...], but it is characterized by a sort of metrical *tour de force* with *rimalmezzo* that distinguishes it graphically as much from its metrical "twin" (canzone 28, "O fair and blessed soul whom Heaven awaits"), as from all the other canzoni, making it almost rise to the status of a composition emblematic of a new song).

11 A. Daniele, "La canzone 'Mai non vo' più cantar com'io soleva' (CV)," 163–4.

12 Zingarelli in F. Petrarca, *Rime*, 1963, 656.

13 Daniele, "La canzone 'Mai non vo' più cantar com'io soleva' (CV)," 157–8, states with reference to two Bembian sources, "Bembo [...] sostiene la non consequenzialità logica del componimento" (For Bembo the poem has no logical consequentiality) and "Quello che resta singolare nel Bembo è l'avvaloramento dell'asserto del non senso relativo del genere lirico in questione" (What remains singular in Bembo is the valuing of the assertion of the relative non-sense of the lyric genre in question).

14 G. Leopardi, in F. Petrarca, *Canzoniere* [1828], 1979, 139: "Questa canzone (che che se ne fosse la causa) è scritta a bello studio in maniera che ella non s'intenda. Per tanto a noi basterà d'intenderne questo solo; e io non mi

affannerò a ridurla in chiaro a dispetto del proprio autore" (This canzone (for whatever reason) is written intentionally so as not to be understood. For us it is sufficient to understand this fact; I will not wear myself out to reduce it to clarity as against the author's intent).

15 Zingarelli in F. Petrarca, *Rime*, 1963, 655.

16 G. Carducci in F. Petrarca, *Le rime*, 1899, 149: "È in due parti: nella prima (1–45) sfoga un po' di dispetto nato in lui per le altere ripulse di Laura; nella seconda (46–90) loda ciò che prima aveva biasimato e si consola, perché in tal modo lo sfrenato suo desiderio ha fatto luogo ad un sentimento d'amore onesto e tranquillo che non più gli impedisce la via del cielo" (It is in two parts: in the first (1-45) he vents some irritation born in him due to Laura's haughty rejections; in the second (46-90) he praises what he had earlier blamed and consoles himself, because in such a way his immoderate desire has given rise to a feeling of pure and tranquil love that no longer blocks him from the way of heaven).

17 Daniele, "La canzone 'Mai non vo' più cantar com'io soleva' (CV)," 162, 158, 157.

18 Ibid., 165.

19 F. De Sanctis, *Saggio critico sul Petrarca*, 126, rules out the notion of a Petrarchan sublime: "Manca al poeta il senso del sublime: appena giunge al nobile e al magnifico" (The poet lacks the sense of the sublime: he barely reaches the noble and the magnificent). But if one looks to Petrarch's repudiations in poem 105 of guile and deception of all sorts, one comes to identify a certain positive regression that is conformal with the aesthetic of the sublime.

20 W. Ong has written about this distinction as follows, *Orality and Literacy*, 55: "An oral culture simply does not deal in such items as geometrical figures, abstract categorization, formally logical reasoning processes, definition, or even comprehensive descriptions, or articulated self-analysis, all of which derive not simply from thought itself but from text-formed thought."

21 M. Fubini, *Metrica e poesia*, 296.

22 I share Santagata's reserve with respect to F. Jones's biographical reading of the poem, "An Analysis of Petrarch's Eleventh Canzone," which leans heavily on the hypothesis that "un bel vetro" is a precise woman for whom Petrarch forsook his chaste love for Laura, though no other commentary supports this line of argument.

23 The lines are glossed by Santagata, *Sant*, 500, as follows: "Il diniego opposto da Laura alle mie richieste, che alla fine ha avuto ragione della mia ostinata passione, e che ha dipinto, impresso nel mio animo il vergognoso timore di diventare favola alle genti, cancellando il pensiero da me nutrito sino ad allora (ormai mi sono spinto tanto innanzi che

posso confessare anche questo) di non essere stato sufficientemente ardito nel corteggiamento" (Laura's denial of my requests, which in the end prevailed over my obstinate passion, and which painted, impressed in my mind the shameful fear of becoming the gossip of the people, by cancelling out the thoughts I had nurtured until then (by now I have moved so much further on that I can confess even this) of not having been sufficiently ardent in my courtship).

24 M. O'Rourke Boyle, *Petrarch's Genius*, 154.

25 Ibid., 154–7. According to Boyle, the poet who had "eschewed the elitism of the monastery" was "like Ezekiel the Babylonian captive, the poet of love songs gossiped about at city walls and household doors but spurned for his holy counsel." And here she cites the incipit of 105: "I never used to sing as I used to, for I was not understood, wherefore I was scorned, and one can be miserable in a pleasant place."

26 P. Ricoeur, *Figuring the Sacred*, 149.

27 See M. Santagata, *I frammenti dell'anima*, 137–41.

28 Daniele, "La canzone 'Mai non vo' più cantar com'io soleva' (CV)," 160, notes that the final two stanzas, lacking the use of proverbs of the first four stanzas, "[danno] luogo a un dettato più descrittivo e concludente [...] e infine di anelito di ritorno a Dio (rappresentando così, in piccolo, anche qui la vicenda ideale di tutto il *Canzoniere*)" (give way to a more descriptive and conclusive dictation [...] and finally to the desire of a return to God (thus representing again, on a small scale, the ideal situation of the entire *Canzoniere*)).

29 G. Contini, cited by Santagata, *Sant*, 502, states that poem 106 is "estraneo all'affabulazione generale del *Canzoniere*, come del resto quelli che in esso lo precedono immediatamente [103, 104, 105]; un gruppetto in qualche modo extravagante, che si direbbe preannunciato dal finale del sonetto 102" (foreign to the general storyline of the *Canzoniere*, as are as well those that immediately precede it [103, 104, 105]; a somewhat extravagant little group, seemingly foreshadowed by the end of sonnet 102).

30 See Santagata, *Sant*, 503: "Petrarca rovescia, non senza effetti parodici, la situazione canonica del genere 'pastorella', giocando sull'insolita figura dell'uomo che, solo e indifeso, è catturato dalla donna" (Petrarch overturns, not without parodic effects, the canonical situation of the "pastorella" genre, playing on the unusual figure of the man who, alone and disarmed, is captured by the woman). See also *Sant*, 502: "De Robertis [...] esprime il dubbio che 'in origine' il madrigale sia stato 'laurano'" (De Robertis [...] expresses the doubt that the madrigal was "originally" based on Laura).

31 See C. Segre, "La critica strutturalistica," 59: "i paragrammi violano la linearità del linguaggio, e istituiscono una rete intratestuale che ne

incrocia, magari arricchendoli o contraddicendoli, i significati denotativi" (paragrams violate the linearity of language, and set up an intratextextual network that cuts across its denotative meanings, perhaps by enriching or contradicting them). Segre cites J. Kristeva on the creation by paragrams "al di sopra o al di sotto del piano semantico [di] una sorta di 'testo' non-significativo, volto a realizzare, attraverso modalità sublinguistiche di significazione, la forma o le forme di un comunicare trans-contestuale" (of a sort of non-signifying "text" above and below the semantic plane, dedicated to realizing, by means of sublinguistic modalities of signification, the form or forms of a trans-contextual communication). See O. Ducrot and T. Todorov, *Encyclopedic Dictionary of the Sciences of Language*, 359 (citing J. Kristeva, *Semeiotekè* [Paris, 1969]): "'We call paragrammatic network the *tabular* (not linear) *model* of elaboration' of textual language. 'The term *network* replaces univocity (linearity) by encompassing it, and suggests that each set (sequence) is both end-point and beginning of a multivalent relationship.' The term 'paragram' indicates that each element functions 'as a dynamic mark, *as a moving "gram"* which *makes a meaning* rather than expressing it.'"

32 This variable diction is elucidated by E. Chirilli, "Studio sulle concordanze nel 'Canzoniere' di F. Petrarca," 138: "Il significato originario dei singoli lemmi viene dal poeta piegato e allargato a una graduale espressione di valori affini: e ciò fa in modo che la scarsezza lessicale intravista al primo approccio, venga superata nell'opera e quasi non più avvertita dal lettore, tante e così diverse sono le sfumature semantiche a cui il medesimo vocabolo è chiamato a soddisfare, e tanto agile e duttile è l'abilità dell'artefice" (The original meaning of the single words is broadened and subjected by the poet to a gradual expression of similar values: the result is that the lexical scarsity perceived on the first approach is overcome in the work and almost no longer noticed by the reader, given the many and diverse semantic shadings that the same word is called on to satisfy, and the highly agile and flexible ability of the author).

33 Santagata, *Sant*, 503.

34 I make this point to distinguish between the time of the *narration*, or the narrating itself, and that of the *récit*, which is internal to the story. When in Vaucluse, Petrarch's lone human contact on a daily basis is his faithful *fattore*, Raymond Monet; in the first year there he has only two visits. By 1347 he had written *De vita solitaria* (though the emending process will continue until at least 1361), dedicating it to the local bishop, Philippe de Cabassole (to whom he also addresses *Sine Nomine* 1 and 12), *De otio religioso*, and the *Salmi penitenziali*.

35 While the *Collatio* draws on largely classical sources, gratitude and recognition are expressed to God for the gifts he has bestowed on the poet.

36 See S. Agosti, *Gli occhi, le chiome*, 24: "La sintassi che designa il fantasma come non-reale è sconvolta dall'ordine semantico che lo circoscrive come realissimo: concreto, istante e presente" (The syntax that designates the phantasm as non-real is confused by the semantic order that circumscribes it as most real: concrete, instant and present). Agosti, ibid., 26, notes the numerous references in the poem to Dante's canzone "Così nel mio parlar voglio esser aspro" ("I want to be harsh in my speech"), and the contrast between that poem's "acceso – e magari sadico – erotismo" (burning – and perhaps sadistic – eroticism) and the "castità" (chasteness) of Petrarch's sonnet (though he suggests that purity will again be overtaken by the impulses of libidinous desire).

37 See Fenzi, *Saggi petrarcheschi*, 191–4.

38 See F. Petrarca, *Fam.* [vi, 2], v. 1, 290–5, where the author recalls walking through the Roman ruins years earlier with Giovanni Colonna. At the basis of this itinerary of classic and Christian history, undertaken peripatetically by a tour of the actual sites, is Petrarch's insistence on God as the ultimate "author" of all the wisdom and genius of Rome, before and after the advent of Christ.

39 B. Martinelli, *Petrarca e il Ventoso*, 405.

40 *Le familiari*, 1968, v. 3, 316; *Fam.* [xix, 3], v. 3, 80.

41 E. Cassirer, *The Individual and the Cosmos in Renaissance Philosophy*, 143–4.

42 Ibid.

43 K. Stierle, *La vita e i tempi di Petrarca*, 12. Stierle's appreciation of the Petrarchan landscape contrasts with the view of G. Contini, "La lingua del Petrarca," 106: "Non si sa quanti […] hanno discorso del paesaggio di Petrarca: ma nessuna natura in quanto tale è presente in Petrarca; il paesaggio puro apparterrà ai cosiddetti realisti …" (Many have spoken of the Petrarchan landscape: but no nature as such is present in Petrarch; the pure landscape belongs to the so-called realists …).

44 See ibid., 303: "L'idea del paesaggio come forma di percezione della varietà della terra e del mondo nelle loro relazioni fluttuanti tra soggetto e oggetto, tra il vicino e il lontano, è, tra le innovazioni di Petrarca, quella che si è dimostrata più ricca di conseguenze" (The idea of the landscape as a form of perception of the variety of the earth and the world in their fluctuating relations between subject and object, between the near and the distant, is, among Petrarch's innovations, the one that has been proven to be the richest in consequences).

45 As Stierle writes, ibid., "Lo sguardo del potere viene sostituito dal potere dello sguardo, il quale si costruisce come oggetto uno spettacolo nuovo e originale, che si spinge fino all'estremo della presentazione

visiva, al punto che essa sconfina nell'immaginario" (The gaze of power is substituted by the power of the gaze, which is constructed as a new and original object, which pushes itself to the extreme of the visual presentation, to the point where it crosses the frontier into the imaginary).

46 E. Battisti, "Non chiare acque," draws on the *Familiari*, the *Senili*, the *De remediis*, and other texts, as well as the following poems of the *Fragmenta*: 52, 125, 126, 162, 186, 225, 287.

47 Ibid., 325, 326.

48 Cassirer, *The Individual and the Cosmos in Renaissance Philosophy*, 143.

49 See E. Garin, *Italian Humanism. Philosophy and Civic Life in the Renaissance*, 35: "Nel platonismo, come del resto nella retorica, si cercava un ritorno ai problemi della comunicazione umana, della società umana. Si voleva, in una parola, ritrovare il senso concreto della città terrena, rivalutando quelle virtù politiche alle quali, come Petrarca ricorda sulle orme di Macrobio, e quindi di Plotino, è aperto il regno dei cieli" (In Platonism, as in the rest of rhetoric, one sought a return to the problems of human communication, of human society. One wanted, in a word, to find again the concrete sense of the earthly city, re-evaluating those political virtues to which, as Petrarch recalls in the tracks of Macrobius, and thus of Plotinus, the kingdom of heaven is opened).

50 Battisti, "Non chiare acque," 328, 329, 331.

51 One thinks of the thematic organization of the *Familiari*: the letters are dated by the day but not the year. R. Antognini, *Il progetto autobiografico delle Familiares di Petrarca*, has provided an extraordinary research tool which includes numerous cross-referenced tables cataloguing the 350 letters. As Antognini affirms, too often the *Familiari* have been read piecemeal and not as a continuous, ordered, autobiographical collection.

52 Martinelli, *Petrarca e il Ventoso*, 213.

53 Such a view of *Fam*. iv, 1, arose out of Romantic criticism. See Martinelli, *Petrarca e il Ventoso*, 149–50, who dismisses "il cosidetto tema del dissidio o 'dualismo' dell'anima del poeta, di netta estrazione romantica, per cui il Petrarca appare diviso fino alla fine dei suoi giorni tra due opposte esigenze, il mondo e la donna, da una parte, e il desiderio di purificazione e di ascesi, dall'altra" (the so-called theme of the dispute or "dualism" of the poet's soul, of clear romantic extraction, according to which Petrarch appears split until the end of his days between two opposite demands, the world and the woman, on the one hand, and the desire for purification and ascesis, on the other). R. Durling, "The Ascent of Mt. Ventoux and the Crisis of Allegory," reads *Fam*. iv, 1, as a calque of Augustine's illumination scene in *Confessions* viii, contrasting the two authors' uses of *sortes* in

what are said to be life-changing episodes. Durling is sceptical of the authenticity of Petrarch's account but doesn't address that question in Augustine's story of his conversion.

54 Petrarca, *Prose*, 842, suggests that this passage could not have arisen purely by chance: "Nec opinari poteram id fortuito contigisse, sed quicquid ibi legeram, michi et non alteri dictum rebar" (*Fam.* [iv, 1], v.1, 178: "nor could I believe that it happened by chance but rather thought that whatever I had read there had been directed to me and to no one else").

55 G. Billanovich, *Petrarca e il primo umanesimo*, 173–4.

56 R.J. Lokaj, "Petrarca-alter Franciscus: Un'ascesa francescana al Monte Ventoso," 466.

57 Billanovich, "Petrarca e il ventoso," in 1996, 168–84.

58 The passage turned to is *Confessions* x, 8, 15. See *Sen.* [viii, 6] v.1, 293, where Petrarch states that books i to ix of the *Confessions* concern Augustine's struggles with sin: "in primis novem ab extrema infantia ac materno lacte vite totius errores ac peccata omnia, in decimo etiam adhuc supeerstites peccati reliquias et presentem tunc vite sue statum, in ultimus autem tribus dubitationem suam de Scripturis" ("In the first nine [books], he confesses all the errors and sins of his whole life from his earliest childhood when he was still a suckling, but in the tenth the remnants of sins and the then-present state of his life, and in the last three his doubt concerning the Scriptures and often his ignorance as well").

59 Petrarch uses *pietà* and *pietate* throughout the sequence. The lexical incidences of *pietà / pietate* in the first centenary are: 15; in the second centenary: 15; in the third centenary: 24; and in the final 67 poems: 16. The breadth of definitions of *pietà* include: 1) a feeling of compassion; 2) one of the seven gifts of the Holy Spirit, through which the virtue of justice is developed and perfected; 3) respect and love towards someone; 4) devotion, belief; 5) in the figurative arts, a composition representing the madonna who has the dead Christ in her lap.

60 U. Dotti, *La rivoluzione incompiuta*, 108–9.

61 S. Chessa, *Il profumo del sacro nel* Canzoniere *di Petrarca*, 10.

62 See G. Pozzi, *Sull'orlo del visibile parlare*, 17: "Se l'informazione in materia sacra è declinata nella società, la religione stessa è cambiata. Non solo l'iconografia, ma gran parte della pietà del passato è per noi una lingua morta" (If information about sacred subject matter has declined in society, then religion itself has changed. Not only iconography, but much of the piety of the past is for us a dead language).

63 Pozzi, "Petrarca, i Padri e soprattutto la Bibbia," 183. The cited passage is Psalm 38:12.

64 M. Carruthers assumes a later date of composition, *The Book of Memory. A Study of Memory in Medieval Culture*, 423: "He may have begun *Secretum* at Vaucluse, but the main part was added in Milan, where Petrarch lived from 1353 to 1358; see H. Baron, *Petrarch's Secretum*." T. Kircher, *The Poet's Wisdom: The Humanists, the Church, and the Formation of Philosophy in the Early Renaissance*, 266, assigns the interlocutors of the *Secretum* to the positions of the "absolute" (Augustinus) and the "conditional or transitory" (Franciscus), suggesting that both positions persist through the end of the *Fragmenta*: "What emerges more clearly at the end of the poem cycle is how Laura comes to symbolize both realms for Petrarch, and how his love for Laura itself embraces broad but contrasting emotions that leave him inspired and debilitated."

65 N. Iliescu, *Il Canzoniere petrarchesco e Sant'Agostino*, 64, refers to the *Secretum* as a "monologo."

66 F.E. Cranz, *Reorientations of Western Thought from Antiquity to the Renaissance*, VII, 20, has argued that Petrarch's novelty as a humanist has gone unheeded by those, starting with Leonardo Bruni and arriving at Hans Baron, who see his cultivation of the *studia humanitatis* merely as a restoration of Cicero and others, while the operation undertaken should be seen as a "transformation and transmutation" of the ancient texts.

67 As he did with Augustine, Petrarch attributes to Cicero (in the case of his purported attitude towards melancholy) ideas that are not found in Cicero. See Cranz, *Reorientations of Western Thought from Antiquity to the Renaissance*, VII, 5: "Again one is surprised by the juxtaposition of what Petrarch has to say with an alleged ancient source, which far from being a source, presents us with almost the exact opposite of what Petrarch is saying."

68 See F. Petrarca, *Prose*, 172: "Italiam igitur suadeo, quod moribus incolarum celoque et circumfusi maris ambitu et intersecantis horas Apennini collibus et omni locorum situ, nulla usquam statio curis tuis oportunior futura sit. […] Tam diu cavendam tibi solitudinem scito, donec sentias morbi tui nullas superesse reliquias" (*The Secret*, 148–9: "Italy then would be my choice for you; because the ways of its people, its climate, the sea washing its shores, the Apennine range coming between them, all promise that a sojourn there would be better suited to extirpate your troubles than going anywhere else in the world. […] You must avoid solitude, until you are quite sure that you have not a trace of your old ailment left). See Iliescu, *Il Canzoniere petrarchesco e Sant'Agostino*, 65: "[Augustinus] ripone la sua fiducia nella preghiera e nell'insegnamento, che il poeta trarrà dall'esperienza che desiderava proseguire, anziché in un ennesimo richiamo teorico a Dio" (Augustinus places his trust in prayer and in

teaching, which the poet will draw from the experience that he wished to pursue, instead of in an umpteenth theoretical call to God).

69 Petrarca, *Prose*, 1955, 214; *The Secret*, 2003, 147. My emphasis.

70 V. Kahn, "The Figure of the Reader in Petrarch's *Secretum*," 155. Kahn criticizes the tendency to ideologize the contents of the *Secretum* and has pointed to Petrarch's innovative focus on the reader and the reader's need to interpret the text.

71 This does not justify the epithet for Petrarch given him by T.K. Seung, *Cultural Thematics*, 122: "R.R. Bolgar has rightly called Petrarch the high priest of the Renaissance cult of fame." Bolgar is cited from *The Classical Heritage and Its Beneficiaries* (Cambridge: Cambridge UP, 1954), 147.

72 See P. Cherchi, *Verso la chiusura: Saggio sul Canzoniere di Petrarca*, 69.

73 See R. Poggioli, "Dante 'poco tempo silvano': A Pastoral Oasis in the Commedia," in *The Oaten Flute*, 135–52, for a discussion of the pastoral theme in Dante's Earthly Paradise.

74 See C. Vasoli, *Umanesimo e rinascimento*, 18: "Petrarca [...] considerava il passato come distinto nettamente tra 'l'aetas antiqua', anteriore alla conversione degli imperatori romani, e l''aetas nova' che ancora continuava ed era stata il tempo funesto della decadenza e della corruzione. 'Rinascere', 'restaurare' significava, dunque, *tornare alla vera vita,* chiudere un lungo periodo di tenebre per riemergere finalmente alla purificazione della cultura e della fede cristiana. Per Francesco Petrarca, si schiudeva così nuovamente il mito dell'età d'oro, del tempo in cui 'anime belle e di virtude amiche / terranno il mondo' e l''opre antiche' torneranno alla loro primitiva perfezione [*Rvf* 137, 12–14]" (Petrarch [...] considered the past as clearly distinguished between the "ancient age," prior to the conversion of the Roman emperors, and the "new age" which was still ongoing and had been the grievous time of decadence and corruption. "To be reborn," "to restore" meant, therefore, *to return to the true life,* to end a long period of darkness in order to re-emerge finally to the purification of the Christian culture and faith. For Francesco Petrarca, thus there began a new myth of the age of gold, of the time in which "worthy souls and friends of virtue shall / Inherit earth" and the "honest deeds of old" will return to their primitive perfection). My emphasis.

75 The "two women" theme is also seen in the ballata, "Donna mi vene spesso ne la mente" (A Lady often comes to my mind) removed from the collection and replaced by the last madrigal, poem 121.

76 See Agosti, *Gli occhi, le chiome*, 33: "L'esperienza dei *Fragmenta* è un'esperienza squisitamente interiore, e, per ciò stesso, nella sostanza, estranea a ogni fisicità, di luoghi, di spazi e di date" (The experience of

the *Fragmenta* is an exquisitely interior experience, and, for that reason, in substance, estranged from any physicality, of places, spaces and dates). As the reader of this study will understand, I disagree with Agosti's estimation and find an integral correlation in the *Fragmenta* between the experience of interiority and the author's involvement in "physicality, of places, spaces and dates," albeit one codified in an obscure poetic language.

4. *In fresca riva:* Landscape and History (*Rvf* 125–183)

1 T. Elwert, "La varietà metrica e tematica delle canzoni del Petrarca," 403, discusses the twenty–nine canzoni as metrical expressions of Petrarch's thought, arriving at three groupings: the "Petrarchan," the "Guittonian," and the "Provençal." The dextrous "Provençal-ish canzoni" are balanced by the moralizing "Guittonian canzoni." The fourteen "Petrarchan" canzoni (just under half of the total) thematically regard Laura and share a complex metrical "signature": "canzoni amorose, di omaggio a Laura, di descrizione di Laura, di espressione del sentimento amoroso" (amorous canzoni, of praise for Laura, description of Laura, and expression of amorous sentiment).

2 G. Mazzotta, "The *Canzoniere* and the Language of the Self," 288–9, discusses, in the context of a Petrarchan "polemic" with Dante, the allusions to the *Rime petrose* in canzone 125.

3 K. Stierle, *La vita e i tempi di Petrarca*, 569.

4 One could interpret Laura's status as "enemy" or "friend" in terms of the parable of the Good Samaritan in Luke 10:25–37, where the "neighbour," the one who helps the injured man on the road, is a person traditionally considered an enemy. The antithesis of the Good Samaritan story presupposes two levels of interpretation: the friend on the spiritual level is an enemy in ethno-cultural terms, being unwashed and of different religious beliefs, a heretic. By crossing the cultural divide, the neighbour provides spiritual and material support and sustenance. T. Cahill, *Desire of the Everlasting Hills: The World Before and After Jesus*, states that this parable is a paradigmatic story that institutional Christianity has not heeded.

5 E. Battisti, "Non chiare acque," 315. Battisti is citing the scholarship of Alessandro Parronchi, who drew on Book X of Vitellione's optical treatise, *Perspectiva*.

6 See F. Suitner, *Dante, Petrarca e altra poesia antica*, 152: "mentre gli studiosi si affannano a identificare le fonti massime da cui deriva il celebre suono del più famoso Petrarca volgare, e magari si urtano un po' fra loro per stabilire se più determinanti siano stati i classici o i moderni […], queste 'fonti massime' potrebbero in realtà essere il suono dell'acqua o l'armonioso

rumoreggiare delle fronde degli alberi sospinte dal vento" (while scholars wear themselves out identifying the major sources from which the most famous vernacular Petrarch derives his celebrated sound, and are pained to establish whether the classics or the moderns were more determinative [...], these "major sources" might in reality be the sound of water or the harmonious rumbling of the foliage of trees driven by the wind).

7 E. Fenzi, *Saggi petrarcheschi*, 96, has written of poem 126 as "un lungo complesso ossimoro fondato su un doppio movimento di *memoria* e di *oblio*; sulla *memoria* di un *oblio*, concepita appunto come la riconquista e la riattualizzazione attraverso il tempo e nel tempo di un'estatica fuoriuscita dal tempo" (a long complex oxymoron founded on a double movement of *memory* and *oblivion*; on the *memory* of an *oblivion*, conceived precisely as the reconquest and reactualization through time and in time of an ecstatic exiting from time).

8 For a Lacanian interpretation of the poem see Stefano Agosti, *Gli occhi, le chiome: Per una lettura psicoanalitica del Canzoniere di Petrarca*, 39: "La grande canzone *Chiare, fresche et dolci acque* è, appunto, la canzone dei feticci: e cioè un monumento alla memoria del corpo morcelè, messo in relazione, sull'altro capo della struttura opposizionale, col corpo morto" (The great canzone *Chiare, fresche et dolci acque* is, precisely, the canzone of the fetishes: that is, a monument to the *corps morcelè*, placed into relation, at the other end of the oppositional structure, with the dead body).

9 Dante Alighieri, *Purgatorio* xxiv, 52–4: "E io a lui: «I' mi son un che, quando / Amor mi spira, noto, e a quel modo / ch'e' ditta dentro vo significando»" ("I answered: 'I am one who, when Love breathes / in me, takes note; what he, within, dictates, / I, in that way, without, would speak and shape'").

10 As P. Ricoeur writes, *History and Truth*, 93: "For the Christian, faith in the Lordship of God dominates his entire vision of history."

11 I am paraphrasing the remarks of K. Stierle in a talk given 20 March 2004, at Chapel Hill, NC: "A Manifesto of New Singing: The Group of Canzoni 125–129."

12 The radical novelty of Christianity in resolving and proposing an end to the human appetite for violent sacrifice and the blaming of the victim is the subject of M. Ceruti and G. Fornari's dialogues, *Le due paci. Cristianesimo e morte di Dio nel mondo globalizzato*. As they state in their Premessa, 11–17, the authors' focus in this volume can be summed up with Augustine's expression "Victor quia victima." See *Confessions* [x, 43, 69] 1997, 243: "For our sake he stood to you as both victor and victim, and victor because victim."

13 *Le familiari*, v. 3, 230; *Fam.* [xvii, 1], v. 3, 7. Petrarch supports this typological interpretation with reference to Augustine's *Ennarrationes in Psalmos* (cxl, 19),

a handsome copy of which he received as a gift from Boccaccio on 10 April 1355. See *Fam.* xviii, 3.

14 See T. Zanato, "San Francesco, Pier delle Vigne e Francesca da Rimini," on Petrarch's use of Pier delle Vigne. In *The Life of Solitude*, 1978, 252, Petrarch compares himself to Peter in his willingness to cover great distances. Peter assumed the chair of the church, carrying it from Antioch to Rome.

15 See C. Bologna, "PetrArca petroso," 2003, for an elaboration of this thesis centred on Petrarch's cultivation in the Vaucluse of his own sanctified religious retreat, his own Ark of Peter. See R. Ceserani, "«Petrarca»: Il nome come auto-reinvenzione poetica," who develops the thesis that a comparable network of semantic associations to that developed around the name "Laura" exists in the *Fragmenta* for the name "Petrarca."

16 One can start with the acrostic identified by Orelli, *Il suono dei sospiri*, 29, in *Rvf* 1, 8: "sPEro TRovAR pietà, nonCHE perdono (PE–TR–AR–CHE)" ("If pardon none, compassion then I hope / To find").

17 D. De Robertis, "Petrarca petroso," 247.

18 See C. Berra, "L'arte della similitudine nella canzone CXXXV dei «Rerum Vulgarium Fragmenta»," 181.

19 N. Iliescu, *Il Canzoniere petrarchesco e Sant'Agostino*, 135–9. The gloss in question is from *Enarrationes in Psalmos*, 136, 1, but this is a topic Augustine also discusses in the *City of God*.

20 There is an apparent reference in *Rvf* 137, 12–13, to the Beatitudes.

21 Iliescu, *Il Canzoniere petrarchesco e Sant'Agostino*, 139.

22 *Le familiari*, v. 1, 92; *Fam.* [ii, 9], v. 1, 99. In this letter Petrarch categorically refutes the notion that Laura is a fiction.

23 E. Auerbach writes something similar: *Literary Language and Its Public in Latin Latin Antiquity and in The Middle Ages*, 33: "Augustine himself [...] discussed the use of academic rhetoric in sermons. That it had to be used he took for granted; would it not be absurd, he says in substance, to leave the weapons of eloquence in the exclusive possession of the advocates of the lie and to deny them to the champions of the truth?"

24 Iliescu, *Il Canzoniere petrarchesco e Sant'Agostino*, 75.

25 See E. Bigi, "Alcuni aspetti dello stile del canzoniere petrarchesco," 148: "In verità nell'antitesi, caso particolare del più generale quadro di quella poesia, al movimento di analisi e di opposizione si lega indissolubilmente un secondo e inverso movimento, altrettanto tipicamente petrarchesco, che si potrebbe chiamare di ricomposizione e armonizzazione, che tende cioè a trasformare gli elementi analizzati e opposti in termini perfettamente bilanciati di dolce ed elastica simmetria, di equilibrio euritmico" (In truth,

in the antithesis, a particular case of the more general picture of that poetry, to the movement of analysis and opposition is indissolubly tied a second and inverse movement, just as typically Petrarchan, that could be called recomposition and harmonization, which tends therefore to transform the elements analysed and opposed in perfectly balanced terms of gentle and elastic symmetry, of eurhythmic equilibrium).

26 See A. Badiou, *Handbook of Inaesthetics*, 39: "As Roman Jakobson demonstrated in a fine article, it is in this way that the systematic employment of the oxymoron unsettles all predicative attributions."

27 The general topoi listed by Aristotle include those of opposites, of correlations, and of etymologies. According to J.R. Goetsch (citing Aristotle, *Rhetoric* 1401a6–7 and 1400b27), *Vico's Axioms*, 83: "The antithetic style, which sets two things side by side, is the essence of the enthymeme. Aristotle writes of antithesis that it 'is the "home" of the enthymeme.' He also states that the preferred enthymemes consist in 'the bringing together of opposites in brief form.'"

28 As seen in the above discussion of the landscape, Petrarch's empirical study of nature and his inductive approach to knowledge resulted in his abandonment of the medieval dichotomy of the "I" *versus* nature for the sake of a more integrated understanding of the "I" *in* nature.

29 The fact that the language of art employs the natural language means that tension exists between antithetical terms. As J. Lotman states, *The Structure of the Artistic Text*, 170: "The capacity of transforming different words into synonyms, and of making the same word semantically unequal to itself in different structural positions does not change the fact that the artistic text remains a text in a natural language. This dual existence, the tension between these two semantic systems, accounts for the richness of poetic meanings."

30 D. Alonso, "La poesia del Petrarca e il petrarchismo," 91.

31 Ibid., 90, 93.

32 The relative values depend on context and, thus, ambiguity. But ambiguity in the object often points to ambivalence in the subject. In other words – recalling Petrarch's letter to Colonna – it is vain to study the mechanics of rhetoric without addressing its morality.

33 Following Augustine, Petrarch perceived a gradual movement between the body and soul. As the soul participates in form, order, and beauty, which are divinely ordained, the mystery of the incarnation, of the Advent, and the nature of grace are revealed to it.

34 This kind of sententia is undertaken by the author-narrator, but not the narrator-character.

35 *Bett*, 687, cites as a possible source text the Book of Sirach 24, 22–3: "Ego quasi terebinthus extendi ramos meos, / et rami mei rami honoris et gratiae. / Ego quasi vitis germinavi gratiam, / et flores mei fructus honoris et honestatis" (I spread out my branches like a terebinth, / my branches glorious and graceful / I bud forth delights like a vine; / my blossoms are glorious and rich fruit). Among the passages that have anticipated the "altri poggi" and "altri rami" of the envoi, suggesting the hill of Golgotha and the arms of the Cross, are poem 45: "Ma s'io v'era con saldi chiovi fisso" ("But if I were fixed there with solid nails") (45, 9) and the "altra vita" and "croce" of poem 62.

36 See *Le familiari*, v. 4, 78: "Siquidem a fando fatum dicitur et, ut ait David, «semel locutus est» Dominus et quod Ille locutus est, utique fatum est. [...] Atque ita fatum ac divina providentia unum sunt; quod qui ita intelligit, non fallitur, licet propter eam quam dixi suspitionem nominis, tenendam sententiam, corrigendam linguam admoneat Augustinus" (*Fam.* [xxi, 10], v. 3, 188: "If fate derives from the verb *fari* and if, as David says, the Lord 'spoke once and for all,' then what He said can surely be called fate. [...] Thus fate and divine providence are one; whoever understands this as such is not mistaken, although because of the name's bad connotation, one must, as Augustine warns, retain the meaning but improve the word").

37 For R. Bettarini, *Lacrime e inchiostro nel canzoniere del Petrarca*, 103, the twenty-three rivers named in *Rvf* 148, 1–4, are "fiumi come immagine d'un uomo non mai uguale a se stesso, che si sdoppia e moltiplica specchiandosi e ascoltandosi, sottratto alla solitudine e alla frustrazione dalla somiglianza con l'Altro ..." (rivers as the image of a man never equal to himself, who doubles and multiplies himself by mirroring and listening to himself, withdrawn into soltitude and frustration by his similarity with the Other ...).

38 This is what leads Martinelli to write, *Petrarca e il Ventoso*, 219: "Per dare maggior credibilità ai fatti descritti, il Petrarca ha cercato di ancorare la trama del romanzo (cronologia di finzione) ad una salda base di fatto (cronologia storica), ma la cronologia storica è affatto secondaria rispetto all'idea stessa del romanzo" (In order to give greater believability to the facts described, Petrarch sought to anchor the theme of the romance (fictional chronology) in a solid basis of fact (historic chronology), but the historic chronology is quite secondary with respect to the idea itself of the romance or novel).

39 M. Bakhtin, *Art and Answerability*, 160–1.

40 See U. Dotti, ed., *Canzoniere*, xxxii–xxxvi, for a discussion of the Daphnean myth.

41 R. Bettarini, "Perché 'narrando' il duol si disacerba (Motivi esegetici dagli autografi petrarcheschi)," 313.
42 The use of "l'exempio" recalls Giacomo da Lentini's "exemplo," in "Meravigliosamente," in G. Contini, ed., *Poeti del Duecento*, I, 55.
43 Guittone d'Arezzo, "Gente noiosa e villana," in G. Contini, ed., *Poeti del Duecento*, I, 205. For J. Took, "Petrarch," 94, poem 159 presents "a circular meditation [...] on the irony of love as a principle both of affirmation and destruction," the effect of which is to cast the poet's "mood" into "uncertainty" and a "desperate sense of repetition, of unending sameness." See M. McLaughlin, "Struttura e *sonoritas* in Petrarca (*RVF* 151–60)," 376–8, for a discussion of poem 159's intertextuality with texts of Ovid, Plato, Virgil, and Horace.
44 Here there are references to Cavalcanti's "Chi è questa che ven, ch'ogn'om la mira" ("Who is she that comes, whom every man admires") and Dante's "Tanto gentil e tanto onesto pare" ("So gentle and so full of dignity my lady appears") and "Donne che avete intelletto d'amore" ("Ladies who have understanding of love").
45 The song of a repentant subject is deepening; this echoes *Rvf* 135, 40: "corro sempre al mio male, et so ben quanto / n'ò sofferto, et n'aspetto" ("I / Run ever toward my ill, and well I know / How I have suffered for it, and still yearn").
46 M. Riffaterre, *Fictional Truth*, 32.
47 Here, too, is a stylistic debt to Dante. See G. Orelli, *Il suono dei sospiri*, 152–3, for a discussion of the shared lexis between *Rvf* 166 and *Inferno* xx, 47–52 and *Paradiso* xxi, 112–17.
48 The Virgilian cliché of womanly fickleness is also present in Dante, *Purgatorio* viii, 76–8: "Per lei assai di lieve si comprende / quanto in femmina foco d'amor dura / se l'occhio o 'l tatto non l'accende" ("Through her, one understands so easily / how brief, in woman, is love's fire – when not / rekindled frequently by eye or touch").
49 See *Le familiari*, v. 1, 115: "Nam illa Epycuri, in voluptate consistens, non solum nulla felicitas, sed extrema miseria est; quid enim homini miserius quam humanum bonum bono pecudis, hoc est rationem sensibus, substravisse?" (*Fam.* [iii, 6], v. 1, 128: "The happiness of Epicurus which consists in pleasure is not happiness but extreme misery. For what is more wretched for a man than to surrender the human good, reason, to an animal good, the senses").
50 For Augustine's admonitions against phantasms, see *Of True Religion*, (xxx, 56–xxxv, 65), 52–63.
51 Emile Benveniste, cited in P. Ricoeur, *Time and Narrative*, 106.

5. The Penitent Lover (*Rvf* 184–263)

1 In Jakobson's well-known formulation, the poetic function is that function that refers neither to the addresser or addressee of a message but to the message itself. See R. Jakobson, "Closing Statement: Linguistics and Poetics," 17: "The poetic function projects the principle of equivalence from the axis of selection into the axis of combination."
2 The key role of narrative in this process, including the fact that the act of narrating changes the subject, is signalled by the title of Bettarini's 1985 essay, "Perché 'narrando' il duol si disacerba," whose title refers to *Rvf* 23, 4: "perché cantando il duol si disacerba" ("Because my singing sweetens bitter grief").
3 See C. Segre, "La critica strutturalistica," 328–30, for a reading of poem 188, "Almo sol."
4 The general issue of the poet's ignorance calls to mind the 1370 *De sui ipsius et multorum ignorantia liber* (*On His Own Ignorance and That of Many Others*), in which philosophy is something shared among friends and not the relentless argumentation by syllogisms of Averroist philosophers who claim to explain "scientifically" the rebirth of the phoenix .
5 T.J. Cachey, "From Shipwreck to Port: *Rvf* 189 and the Making of the *Canzoniere*," provides a systematic discussion of the poem's theme of navigation (and shipwreck), as Petrarch inherited it and adapted it to his overall sense of Christian pilgrimage. Cachey draws especially on the *Familiari* and *Fragmenta*, noting Petrarch's fear of the sea after his experience of a terrifying sea journey to Naples, and his positive, humanistic development of the Ulysses theme that he adapted from Dante's (largely negative) model of that sailor in the *Commedia*. Cachey, ibid., 34, suggests that the references to shipwreck are motivated by a need to "repair an imperiled consistency" in one's life.
6 M. Picone spoke at the Yale Petrarch Institute of poems 180 to 189, as a "*mise en abïme*" at the exact centre of the *Fragmenta* of the themes and ideologies on which it is constructed. With respect to the navigation metaphor he indicated three stylistic registers: of the "vita serena," the "vita tempestuosa," and the "vita beata." The first, derived from the *plazer*, the fulfilling journey in the *mare amoroso*, is an illusory reflection of the true felicity, which is only found in Paradise.
7 M. Santagata writes of the mythic and medieval sources of the poem's hunting imagery in *Sant*, 833: "Questo 'idillio venatorio,' peraltro carico di forti intenzioni morali e allegoriche, rivela la sua complessità, anche nella raggiera delle fonti e delle suggestioni culturali a cui attinge ..." (This "venatorial idyll," in addition to being charged with strong moral and allegorical intentions, reveals its complexity, also in the array of sources and cultural suggestions that it draws on ...).

8 S. Carrai, "Il sonetto «Una candida cerva» del Petrarca," 237, citing E. Caldarini, 1975.
9 M.G. Blasio, "Il dibattito religioso tra due e trecento," 247.
10 These lines allude to John 17:3: "And this is eternal life, that they know thee the only true God, and Jesus Christ whom thou has sent." As Contini notes, *Poeti del Duecento*, 671, there is also a probable reference to Cino da Pistoia's ballata "Poi che saziar non posso gli occhi miei" (Since I cannot satisfy my eyes), in which the following analogy is posited: Just as the angel who stands before God becomes blessed in his divine nature, so do I, standing before my Lady, become blessed in my human nature.
11 Petrarch writes in 1337, *Le familiari*, v. 2, 101: "maxime colorem michi videtur habuisse opinio illa, que beatifica visione Dei, in qua consummata felicitas hominis consistit, defunctorum animas tandiu carituras astruebat, donec corpora resumpsissent, quod naturaliter non optare non possunt" (*Fam.* [ii 12], v. 1, 111: "I consider that view especially attractive which held that the souls of the dead were kept from the beatific vision of God (in which the greatest happiness of men consists) until the bodies were finally gathered, something which souls could not refuse").
12 See the second of two metrical epistles to Benedict, *Epistolae Metricae* I, 5.
13 M. Cottino-Jones restricts the topic of Daphne to the early poems and thus forms a briefer list than Hainsworth's. In a manner similar to Bosco, Cottino-Jones asserts that Francesco and Laura are static characters. See M. Cottino-Jones, "The Myth of Apollo and Daphne," 175: "There are in fact two protagonists, the poetic persona and his beloved woman, each of them representing a specific aspect of love, conflictingly related to one another: the former's based on a natural desire, the latter's articulated around a spiritual and virtuous aspiration to heavenly love."
14 P.R.J. Hainsworth, "The Myth of Daphne," 32, 33.
15 A contrasting position with respect to the figures of Laura and the laurel is taken by Umberto Bosco, for whom Petrarch loved the creation as a means to love the creator. Bosco saw Laura as a kind of anti-Beatrice, finding only the latter to be providentially linked to God. Ironically, the same terms that Bosco uses to present Laura as a lifeless abstraction are those that allow one to situate Laura in the Vaucluse as a dynamic presence in the poet's heart and not simply a "figure in the mind" (reducible to a series of images, a phantasm). See U. Bosco, *Francesco Petrarca*, 15–23.
16 See G. Pozzi, *Sull'orlo del visibile parlare*, 148–9: "1. ridusse il numero dei membri nominati ad alcune parti scelte del viso (capelli, occhi, guance, bocca) più una parte anatomica selezionata fra collo, seno, mano; 2. accentuò l'uso di metafore ben definite, preferendole all'impiego del nome proprio designante

i membri elogiati; 3. ridusse il numero delle motivazioni all'alternativa di splendore e colore e per quest'ultimo ai tre dati di giallo, rosso e bianco; con rarissime eccezioni (nero per le ciglia una volta sola); 4. ridusse il numero dei comparanti alla sola rosa per il rosso, ad oro ed ambra per il giallo, lasciando invece un più ampio ventaglio di possibilità per il bianco; 5. sistemazzò i rapporti correnti fra le varie motivazioni di rosso, bianco e giallo e dei loro figuranti secondo due schemi fissi: o la ripetitzione per *x* volte di una coppia o la disposizione dei dati secondo la collocazione asimmetrica di 2:1; 6. sistemazzò le relazioni fra le motivazioni, evitando sul piano delle motivazioni primarie del colore la combinazione omogenea (per esempio fra rose e gigli), ma evitando nello stesso tempo su quello delle motivazioni secondarie l'incontro di una coppia eterogenea (per esempio perle e gigli)" (1. he reduced the number of named body parts to a few select features of the face (hair, eyes, cheeks, mouth) plus a selected anatomical part from among neck, breast, hand; 2. he accentuated the use of well-defined metaphors, preferring them to the specific noun designating the praised body part; 3. he reduced the number of motivations to the alternative between brightness and colour and for the latter to the three cases of yellow, red and white; with very rare exceptions (black for the eyelashes one time only); 4. he reduced the numbers of comparers to the rose alone for red, to gold and amber for yellow, leaving instead a broader range of possibilities for white; 5. he systematized the relations running between the various motivations of red, white and yellow and their figurers according to two schemes: either repetition for *x* times or a pair or the presentation of the pieces in the asymmetrical arrangement of 2:1; 6. he systematized the relations among the motivations, avoiding on the plane of the primary motivations of colour the homogeneous motivation (for example, between roses and lilies), but avoiding at the same time on the plane of secondary motivations the instance of a heterogeneous pair (for example, pearls and lilies)).

17 Aristotle, *Ethica Nichomachea*, 2.6. See M.C. Bertolani, *Petrarca e la visione dell'eterno*, 187–98.

18 See M.C. Bertolani, *Il corpo glorioso*, 88–94.

19 For poem 194, see F. Chiappelli, *Il legame musaico*, 129–38; for poem 198, see A. Noferi, *Frammenti per i Fragmenta di Petrarca*, 155–62. For a discussion of all four poems, see S. Agosti, *Gli occhi, le chiome*.

20 In positing his theory of the Neutral, R. Barthes, *The Neutral*, 130, describes "oscillation" as "one of the linguistic tools of nonarrogance, of nonintolerance."

21 As Bettarini notes, *Bett*, 921, the reference is to Isaiah 40:12: "*quis appendit* tribus diditis molem terrai, et *libravit* in pondere montes et colles *in statera*?"

("Who has [...] enclosed the dust of the earth in a measure, and weighed the mountains in scales and the hills in a balance?").

22 E.H. Wilkins, *Collatio*, 1248. As the symbology of the laurel tree becomes sacred and the pagan myth is eschewed, the tragic fate of Daphne is not forgotten. Writing of poem 198, Agosti, *Gli occhi, le chiome*, 30–1, alludes to the "venir meno" of the subject's libidinous impulse. P. Hainsworth, "The Myth of Daphne," 41, argues that the qualities of the laurel Petrarch identified in the *Collatio* are generally lacking in the *Fragmenta*, stating that Petrarch "fails to achieve a christianization of the laurel until he assigns it a purely spiritual significance in [...] two late poems (313 and 359)."

23 As P. Ricoeur writes, *History and Truth*, 108: "The neighbor fulfills the twofold requirement of nearness and distance. Such was the Samaritan: near because he approached, distant because he remained the non-Judaean who one day picked up an injured stranger along the highway." The figure of the neighbour is not to be confused with the social bond that ties elements of society together. As Ricoeur states, ibid., 108: "[the] social bond [...] is never as comprehensive because the group only asserts itself against another group and shuts itself off from others." For a poetic exemplum of the healing power of friendship at a distance, I recall Guittone d'Arezzo's canzone "Gente noiosa e villana" ("A Noisome and Abject People"), cited in G. Contini, ed., *Poeti del Duecento*, 205: "Va, mia canzone, ad Arezzo in Toscana / a lei ch'auzide e sana / lo meo core sovente, / e dì ch'ora parvente / serà como val ben nostra amistate" (Go, my song, to Arezzo in Tuscany / to her who often slays / and heals my heart, / and tell her that now the / strength of our love will be manifest).

24 U. Dotti, *Vita di Petrarca*, 446.

25 F.E. Cranz, *Reorientations of Western Thought from Antiquity to the Renaissance*, VII, 10.

26 See C. Trinkaus, *The Poet as Philosopher*, 88: "The emphasis on will [...] was powerful throughout Petrarch's works. Grace was brought closer by continuous and earnest striving to become virtuous. Virtue, as he says in the *De otio religioso*, was not enough, nor was it the final goal."

27 F. Petrarca, *Opere latine*, 1975, 590 (citing Augustine, *Of True Religion*, 3–4); *On Religious Leisure*, 15.

28 St Augustine, *De vera religione* [xxxv, 65], 1968, 62 (citing Ps. 46:10).

29 Petrarca, *On Religious Leisure*, 24.

30 Ibid., 130

31 As P. Ricoeur writes, *History and Truth*, 94, "This [sacred] meaning of history [...] remains an object of faith. If progress is the rational part of history, and if ambiguity represents the irrational part, then the meaning of

history for hope is a surrational meaning – as when we say surrealist. The Christian says that this meaning is eschatological, meaning thereby that his life unfolds in the time of progress and ambiguity without his seeing this higher meaning, without his being able to discern the relation between the two histories, the secular and the sacred, or, in the words of St. Augustine, the relation between the 'Two Cities'. He hopes that the *oneness of meaning* will become clear on the 'last day', that he will understand how everything is 'in Christ', how the histories of empires, of wars and revolutions, of inventions, of the arts, of moralities and philosophies – through greatness and guilt – are 'recapitulated in Christ.'"

32 D. De Robertis finds the *petroso* style to be absent from the second half of the *Fragmenta*, including the final sestinas, poems 214 and 332. See D. De Robertis, "Petrarca Petroso," in G. Barbarisi and C. Berra, *Il «Canzoniere» di Francesco Petrarca. La critica contemporanea*, 246: "L'attenuazione e la pratica eclissi della suggestione petrosa è altrettanto impressionante quanto l'intensità di essa nelle celebrazioni in vita" (The attenuation and the practical eclipse of the "'stoniness" is as impressive as its presence was intense in the celebrations in the life of Laura).

33 As J. Villette, "L'énigme du labyrinthe de la cathédrale," 7, writes, the labyrinth on the floor of the Chartres cathedral depicted "le chemin le plus long possible dans la surface la plus ramassie" (the longest road possible upon the most gathered up of surfaces).

34 The allusions in *Rvf* 226, 1 and 2, are to Psalms 101:7–8 and 79:14.

35 Petrarch was no doubt familiar with Augustine's letter to the widow Proba concerning the nature of prayer, *The Works of Saint Augustine* [Letter 130: 10, 20], 193: "For this task [of prayer] is very often carried out more with sighs than words, more with weeping than with speaking. But he places our tears in his sight, and our sighing is not hidden from him who created all things by his Word and does not seek human words."

36 This is the time period given by G. Martellotti, while Claudio Bellinati suggests May 1348, after the news of the deaths of Laura and Franceschino degli Albizzi. E.H. Wilkins, *Life of Petrarch*, 38, dates the writing of the *Psalmi penitentiales* to a single day in 1343.

37 C. Bellintani, in Petrarca, *Salmi penitenziali*, 1997, 14. For the sake of noting analogies with the Italian of the *Fragmenta*, I cite the poems in Bellintani's Italian translation.

38 Petrarca, *Salmi penitenziali*, 1997, 36–7: "Quando incipiam ad te reverti?"

39 Phillip Cary, *Inner Grace. Augustine in the Traditions of Plato and Paul*, n.p. Cary continues, ibid.: "This in fact is not a conversion in the Protestant sense, because Augustine is clear that he already had a personal faith in

Christ as savior at that point (*Conf.* 7:5.7, end, and 7:7.11, beginning). The outcome of this narrative is not faith in Christ, which he already had, but the decision to get baptised, which he had been resisting for many years. And Augustine is abundantly clear that his sins are forgiven and he is born again, not because of the change of heart he narrates in book 8 but because of his baptism, which he narrates in book 9."

40 G. Wills, *Saint Augustine*, 94.

41 See P. Renucci, "L'amore tra natura e storia nella poesia del Petrarca e nella lirica del Rinascimento," 170 (referring to poem 229): "Liberato dall'alternativa fra il gaudio e la sofferenza, il poeta si ritrova qui più al di sopra che al di sotto della natura umana, e anziché snaturato, 'trasnaturato'" (Freed from the oscillation between joy and suffering, the poet here finds himself more above than below human nature, and instead of denatured, "transnatured").

42 See *Fam.* [viii, 1], v. 1, 397–400, written to Stefano Colonna il Vecchio, on the topic of his anger.

43 G. Savoca, "L''ira' di Petrarca fra ermeneutica e concordanze," in *Il Canzoniere di Petrarca tra codicologia ed ecdotica*, 269–82, places in relief an Ajax-like persona (as one of the various personae expressed by Petrarch's "io lirico") by building on the prominence of the theme of anger in sonnet 232 and relating it to the suicide theme in poems 36 and 268.

44 There are references in poem 234 to Ezekiel 8:12: "Son of man, have you seen what the elders of the house of Israel are doing in the dark, every man in his room of pictures? For they say, 'the Lord does not see us, the Lord has forsaken the land'"; and Psalms 54:7: "For thou hast delivered me from every trouble, and my eye has looked in triumph on my enemies."

45 Petrarca, *Salmi penitenziali*, 33: "Fiat michi thalamus meus purgatorium meum, et lectulus meus lacrimarum conscius mearum."

46 In her essay "*Super flumina …*," R. Bettarini, in *Lacrime e inchiostro nel canzoniere del Petrarca*, 87–103, explores the fluvial imagery of the *Fragmenta*, starting with sonnet 148, "Non Tesin, Po, Varo, Arno, Adige et Tebro," connecting the references to actual rivers to the topic of change as a motivating factor in the poet's unceasing dialogue with himself and with the Other, a dialogue in which the shifters and pronouns are constantly changing. A. Bertoni, *La poesia. Come si legge e come si scrive*, 184–8, addresses the fluvial discourse in Petrarch with specific reference to *Rvf* 148, tying that sonnet of the rivers to the Ovidian account of Daphne and her father, the river god Peneus, in such a way as to reinforce the macrotextual narrative.

47 "Filosofi" here is negative, in contrast to Laura, while "filosofia" in poem 7 is the positive solace of study. Both are *hapaxes*. On the presence of dialogue, Edoardo Taddeo writes, "Petrarca e il tempo," 102: "Non pochi sonetti del

Canzoniere portano inseriti in un contesto narrativo o espositivo uno o più tratti in discorso diretto. Ne ho contati quarantasette (compresi tre interamente dialogati), disseminati con sufficiente uniformità per tutta l'estensione dell'opera" (Many of the sonnets of the *Canzoniere* bear one or more of the traits of direct discourse, inserted into a narrative or expository context. I have counted forty-seven of them (including three completely dialogued), disseminated with sufficient uniformity throughout the length of the work).

48 It is worth noting that refutation of the "nobility of blood" seen here is a prominent theme in Book IV of Dante's *Convivio*.

49 Specifically, the *integumentum* is a secular allegory based on a fiction, while sacred allegory is based on biblical history. See Martianus Capella, *The Commentary*, 26: "*Allegoria* is defined as a mode of discourse which covers under an historical narrative a true meaning different from its surface meaning, as in the case of Jacob's wrestling with the angel. This is obviously biblical allegory with its *sensus litteralis* and its *sensus mysticus*. Next, *integumentum* is defined as a mode of discourse which covers a true meaning under a fictitious narrative, as in the case of Orpheus. This is evidently non-biblical allegory. The difference between biblical and secular allegory established here is quite clear. Biblical allegory is conveyed by history, secular allegory by fiction."

50 The following instances of the metaphor of bodily dress – "in vesta negra" (268, 82); "quando si veste et spoglia" (270, 67); "che i vicii spoglia, et vertú veste et honore" (317, 4); "di porpora vestita, e 'l capo d'oro" (323, 50); "Vergin bella, che di sol vestita" (366, 1) ("O Virgin fair, in sunshine all arrayed") – are apparent references to Matt. 6:28, the parable of the lilies of the field ("And why are you worried about clothing? Observe how the lilies of the field grow; they do not toil nor do they spin").

6. Songs of Grief and Lamentation (*Rvf* 264–318)

1 F. Petrarca, *De otio religioso*, 42; *On Religious Leisure*, 64.

2 See P. Ricoeur, *Figuring the Sacred*, 149–50: "Narrative-parables are narratives within a narrative, more precisely narratives recounted by the principal personage of an encompassing narrative. [...] The structure of embedding one narrative in another narrative is the fundamental framework for the metaphorical transfer guided by the enigma-expression 'Kingdom of God.'"

3 See Petrarch's Preface to *Remedies for Fortune Fair and Foul* (*De remediis utriusque fortune*), 1–10.

4 Ricoeur, *Figuring the Sacred*, 148.

5 See Augustine, *On Christian Teaching*, 20: "Scripture says, 'You shall love the Lord your God with all your heart and with all your soul and with all your mind', and, 'you shall love your neighbor as yourself. On these two commandments depend the entire law and the prophets' [Matt. 22:37–40]. The aim of the commandment is love [cf 1 Tim. 1:5], a twofold love of God and of one's neighbour."

6 Castelvetro was the first to identify the Pauline intertext to *Rvf* 136. Bettarini, *Bett*, 2005, 1578, has referred to the state of temporal-attitudinal suspension in the conclusion as an "agostiniana *epoché*."

7 R. Antonelli, in F. Petrarca, *Canzoniere* [1992], xiii. My emphasis.

8 See R. Martinez, "Mourning Laura in the Canzoniere: Lessons from Lamentations," on Petrarch's use of liturgical elements involving the Paschal calendar and the Book of Lamentations, notably in poems 1, 53, 128, and 268. Martinez also draws attention to Petrarch's use of the *Vita nuova* and two of its canzoni, "Donne ch'avete intelletto d'amore" ("Ladies who have understanding of love") and "Li occhi dolenti per pietà del cuore" ("My eyes that grieve because of my heart's anguish"). The Dantean and biblical intertexts are seen to set a pattern for Part 2 under the overall theme of mourning.

9 Petrarca, *De otio religioso*, 41; *On Religious Leisure* [i, 7], 63.

10 Noting the presence of "sintonia fra elementi prosodico-tematici e disposizione materiale" (syntony between prosodic-thematic elements and the material arrangement) of different canzoni, H.W. Storey, in G. Belloni, et al., *Rerum vulgarium fragmenta. Codice Vat. Lat. 3195*, 163, highlights the striking strophic and graphic affinities between canzoni 268 and 206, each of which finds the subject addressing Amor, "ma risalenti a due distinti momenti (entrambi cruciali per il dipanarsi del disegno 'diaristico' del macro testo dei *Fragmenta*)" (but going back to two distinct moments (both crucial for the unwinding of the "diaristic" plan of the macrotext of the *Fragmenta*)).

11 Martinez, "Mourning Laura in the Canzoniere: Lessons from Lamentations," 22. The longer passage regarding *Rvf* 268 reads, ibid., 22: "Although Petrarch clearly backed off making verses closely derived from Scripture for the *cominciamento* of the first canzone *in morte*, the conversion of joy into woe, *versatio in luctum*, was nevertheless destined to function programmatically in the second part of the *Canzoniere*. The force and range of the phrase spring from the wide semantic field comprised by terms like *versare, tornare, rinversare, volgere, voltare, rivolgere, convertire* – in expressions meaning turn to, turn away, turn back, turn over, turn the page, turn fortune's wheel, but also pour forth words and tears ('versai lagrime e'inchiostro', 347.8) – in other words, versify."

12 See *Le familiari*, v. 3, 54–5: "Ora, ne lugeas, atque illam si viventem hic amasti, patere equo animo, gloriosissime pater, ex alto licet terrene conditionis gradu ad summum culmen celestis felicitatis ascendere" (*Fam.* [xiii, 1], v. 2, 174: "Pray, do not mourn; if you loved her alive in this world, allow yourself with a calm heart, O most illustrious father, to ascend from your earthly, though lofty, position to the very highest summit of divine blessedness").

13 The deeper interpretation one could submit to this reversal of identities from worldly to divine is suggested by the verses preceding Matthew 11:29–30, in which John's dignified earthly identity as a prophet and his humble stature in the Kingdom of Heaven are explained: "Truly I tell you, among those born of women there has not risen anyone greater than John the Baptist; yet whoever is least in the kingdom of heaven is greater than he" (Matt. 11:11).

14 See C. Segre, "Isotopie di Laura."

15 Ricoeur, *Figuring the Sacred*, 145.

16 Ibid., 144.

17 Ibid., 148.

18 Ibid.

19 See M. Santagata, "'Io' e 'tu' fra Stilnovo e Petrarca," n.p., who states that Petrarch was the first poet to write love poems after her death to the beloved. Similar is C. Giunta's position, *Versi a un destinatario*, 446–7, that love in old age wasn't represented before Petrarch's carrying of his love of Laura beyond her death.

20 Not coincidentally, there is a marked increase in verbs in the past absolute tense, as the events recounted occur in memory.

21 G. Nencioni, "Antropologia poetica?," 255–6: "Possiamo retrocedere a Petrarca, rilevando che a Laura viva egli si rivolge quasi sempre col *voi* (il famoso 'a cui io dissi: Tu sola mi piaci' di CCV, 8 è la proiezione allocutiva di una determinazione profonda; un caso di metafora sintattica), ma a Laura morta sempre col *tu*, e Laura morta dà del *tu* a lui in sogno. Il *voi* a Laura viva, come il *voi* dei poeti provenzali e siciliani alle loro dame, implica, nell'artificio del dialogo *in absentia*, pur sempre un riferimento sociale ..." (We can go back to Petrarch, pointing out that he almost always addresses the living Laura as *voi* (the famous "To whom I uttered: 'Only you please me'" of 205, 8 is a profoundly determined allocutive projection; a case of syntactic metaphor), but the dead Laura always as *tu*, and the dead Laura addresses him as *tu* in a dream. The *voi* for the living Laura, as the *voi* of the Provençal and Sicilian poets to their ladies, always implies, within the artifice of the dialogue *in absentia*, a still social reference). See

Santagata, "'Io' e 'tu' fra Stilnovo e Petrarca," n.p., for a discussion of the persistent dialogics of the *Fragmenta* and the shift of the poetic "I" in Part 2 to the "tu" pronoun (away from the "voi") for the addressing of Laura.

22 This parabolic side of knowing derives from the kind of self-analysis that Petrarch discussed in his Letter to Posterity (*Sen*. xviii, 1). As A. Scaglione, "The Structure of the *Canzoniere* and Petrarch's Method of Composition," 309, asserts, the key verb in the following passage from the Letter is "*perlegeram*" as it makes clear that the attainment of self-knowledge depends on the "practice of memory": "Adolescentia me fefellit iuventa corripuit, senecta autem correxit, experimentoque perdocuit verum illud quod diu ante perlegeram: quoniam adolescentia et vuluptas vana sunt" ("My youth deluded me, my younger manhood led me astray, but my old age corrected me by teaching me *through the experience of what I read long before*: that youth and pleasure are nothing but vanity"). My emphasis. Poem 291 is one of the three poems (all in Part 2) that mention Laura's name.

23 See G. Savoca, "Letture filologiche del Canzoniere nel Novecento," in *Il Canzoniere di Petrarca tra codicologia ed ecdotica*, 245–68, for a discussion of the theme of the unrepeatability of being and the finite temporal existence of poetry. In commenting on *Rvf* 361, 10–12: "et ch'esser non si pò piú d'una volta; / e 'n mezzo 'l cor mi sona una parola / di lei" ("And that no more than once can we exist; / And then, within my heart, one word resounds / About her"), Savoca argues that the meaning is far from transparent, since, for Petrarch, the true life is another one from that which exists in time.

24 As D. De Robertis notes, "A Farewell to Arms," this imagery of torment derives from a series of biblical passages and is supported by its closed and obsessive structure and intense phonic substrate. It is hard not to think as well of the Franciscan Jacopone da Todi's gruesome *contrasto*, "Quando t'aliegre, omo de altura" (When you rejoice, lofty man), a dialogue between a living man and a corpse that details the body's dissolution, aided by "vermi" that have eaten both the eyes and nose.

25 Castelvetro found the resonance of "Francesco" in the adjective "franca."

26 See S. Morando, "Gli occhi della mente e la preghiera *sine murmure*," 274. Of twenty-three uses of *amaro/i/a/e*, only six are not in the company of *dolce/dolcezza*. None of these pairings, which indicate a stoic equanimity, occur in the poems prior to the canzoni of lontananza (125, 126, 127, 129). Fourteen of the uses occur in Part 2. See N. Iliescu, *Il Canzoniere petrarchesco e Sant'Agostino*, 110–11, 124–5, for an accounting of Petrarch's stylistic debts to Augustine's practice of antithesis.

27 I also detect a reference to *Paradiso*, xiv, 103, "Qui vince la memoria mia lo 'ngegno" ("And here my memory defeats my wit"), where Dante-poet cannot replicate the vision of Christ on the Cross.

28 See D. De Robertis, *Memoriale Petrarchesco*, 72: "Affiora [...] un nuovo tipo di connessione tra le due parti, non lineare o di contiguità, ma correlativa o di similarità, messa *en abîme* nella sistemazione definitiva (di cui importa anzitutto il messaggio globale), ma rivelata dall'atto che la prepara, di natura operativa, e sprofondata nel risultato: spia non solo dell'equiparibilità sostanziale delle due parti del canzoniere, ma della prospettiva bifocale della sua costruzione e del più generale sintagma che costituice" (There emerges a new type of connection between the two Parts, not linear (or of contiguity) but correlative (or of similarity), placed *en abîme* in the definitive systemization (in which the global message is important above all), but revealed by the act that prepares it, of an operational nature, and hidden in the result: an indication not only of the essential equivalency of the two Parts of the *Fragmenta*, but of the bifocal perspective of its construction and of the more general syntagm that constitutes it).

29 Ibid., 83.

30 St Augustine, *Confessionum libri XIII* [xi, 28, 37], 291; *Confessions*, 270.

31 Ibid., 291-2; *Confessions*, 270.

32 See ibid., 292: "at ego in tempora dissilui, quorum ordinem nescio, et tumultuosis varietatibus dilaniantur cogitationes meae, intima viscera animae meae, donec in te confluam purgatus et liquidus igne amoris tui" (*Confessions*, 271: "In the most intimate depths of my soul my thoughts are torn to fragments by tempestuous changes until that time when I flow into you, purged and rendered molten by the fire of your love").

33 D. De Robertis, "Il trittico del T («RVF » 315, 316, 317)," 176. See Luke 24:32: "They said to each other, 'Did not our hearts burn within us while he talked to us on the road, while he opened to us the scriptures?'"

34 M. Santagata, *I frammenti dell'anima*, 267.

35 M. Praloran, "Lo splendore del mondo e la solitudine dell'io (*RVF* 310–20)," 687, cites the verbal phrase "Qual dolcezza fu quella, o misera alma!" (314, 9) ("What tenderness was there! O my poor soul") as an aoristic (or indeterminate) use of the remote past tense.

36 A. Morena, "Autobiografia e struttura nel *mezzo* delle rime sparse," 187, forms a metatextual hypothesis concerning this sonnet. He suggests that by the fallen tree Petrarch refers to the "forma di Giovanni" (the Giovanni form) and "la poesia dell'amante per l'amata" (the poetry of the lover for the beloved), and by the other tree ("un'altra che Amor obiecto scelse"),

Petrarch refers to his own autobiography, a form that will dominate the remainder of the work. As Morena concludes, ibid., 188: "Il trionfo dell'*auctor* sulle spoglie dell'*agens* conferisce unità e misura al libro autobiografico" (The triumph of the *one acting* over the remains of the *one acted upon* confers unity and measure to the autobiographical book).

7. Songs of Consecration (*Rvf* 319–366)

1 See E. Fenzi, "Dalla precarietà del sogno alle sublimazioni dell'intelletto (*RVF* 341–50)"; R. Caputo, "«Et doppiando 'dolor, doppia lo stile » (*RVF* 331–40)"; N. Tonelli, "Vat. Lat. 3195: Un libro concluso? Lettura di *RVF* 360–66"; A. Soldani, "Dialoghi e soliloqui al limitare del tempo (*RVF* 351–59)"; and D. De Robertis, "Il trittico del T («RVF » 315, 316, 317)."

2 P. Ricoeur, *Figuring the Sacred*, 53. See ibid., 53: "Symbols come to language only to the extent that the elements of the world themselves become transparent, that is, when they allow the transcendent to appear through them."

3 Symbols belong to a poetry of experience, not a poetry of rhetoric. According to Ricoeur, religious symbolism possesses a "bound character," meaning that its origins are in nature and not simply invented in the manner of metaphors. In exploring the "distance between manifestation and proclamation," Ricoeur, *Figuring the Sacred*, 52–5, lists four traits of the phenomenology of the sacred that manifest its "antihermeneutical side": (1) "the sacred is experienced as awesome, as powerful, as overwhelming"; (2) "anything by which the sacred shows itself is a hierophany"; this means that the sacred can be preverbal and manifested in an inanimate object or whatever the believer believes, and this conditions the times of the sacred; (3) the sacred is "nonlinguistic"; (4) the "role of nature" functions as a symbolism to manifest how "the sacred, in a word, is dramatic"; these traits are then summarized in a fifth, which asserts that "in the sacred universe the capacity for saying is founded on the capacity of the cosmos to signify something other than itself."

4 As P. Zumthor writes, *Toward a Medieval Poetics*, 94, "Figural interpretation [...] establishes a relationship between two terms, both of which are seen as real, containing no fiction but evincing a firm belief in a plane of higher reality. This difference did not escape the learned in reading and expounding biblical texts and literary practice, which contains only parable and metaphor."

5 B. Martinelli, *Petrarca e il Ventoso*, 1977, 404: "si è visto come il pensiero dell'Apostolo sia da porsi all'origine dei motivi dell'escatologia e dell'apocalittica petrarchesca" (one has seen how the thought of the

Apostle is to be placed at the origins of the eschatological and apocalyptic motifs in Petrarch).

6 Ibid., 403.

7 P. Ricoeur expresses this idea of an in-between time, *History and Truth*, 94: "The meaning of history [...] remains an object of faith. [...] The Christian says that meaning is eschatological, meaning thereby that his life unfolds in the time of progress and ambiguity without his seeing this higher meaning, without his being able to discern the relation between the two histories, the secular and the sacred, or, in the words of St. Augustine, the relation between the 'Two Cities.'"

8 The result of this development is a novel expression, G. Folena, "L'orologio del Petrarca," 280, of "la relatività o circolarità di tempo" (the relativity or circularity of time).

9 Ibid., 277: "Il tempo fisico della natura e il tempo umano della coscienza hanno cioè leggi diverse e sono in conflitto irriducibile come in Agostino. Il tempo è non solo un riferimento continuo, ma anche la struttura portante della cultura e della poesia del Petrarca, e stupisce che questa struttura non sia stata ancora analizzata partitamente" (The physical time of nature and the human time of the conscience thus have different laws and are in irreducible conflict, as in Augustine. Time is not only a continuous reference, but also the supporting structure of Petrarch's culture and poetry, and it is remarkable that this structure has not yet been studied in detail). For E. Taddeo, "Petrarca e il tempo," 76, the "general present tense" in Petrarch (as in similes, periphrases, and gnomic remarks) is "atemporal."

10 Detachment and a return to one's "sources" is the subject of the Eighth Eclogue (*Bucolicum Carmen* viii, 84–6) on the occasion of the poet's departure from Avignon to return to Italy: "(Amiclas:) At, si presagia quicquam / nostra ferunt certi, levis est ad prima recursus / principia" ("(Amiclas:) But still, if my prescient heart within me / Rightly foretells, going back to my sources / Cannot but bring me Happiness"). On the "sweetness of tears" as an integral part of Petrarch's Augustinianism, see N. Iliescu, *Il Canzoniere petrarchesco e Sant'Agostino*, 124–7.

11 See M. Santagata, "'Io' e 'tu' fra Stilnovo e Petrarca," n.p.: "[È] vero che [Petrarca] si rivolge molto spesso alla donna, però la continuità del libro e, soprattutto, il fatto che quella donna non sia mera destinataria, ma sia a sua volta un personaggio che interagisce, riconfigurano l'allocuzione in dialogo. Ma è una dialogicità strana, più di tipo narrativo che lirico, o meglio, propria di una narrazione integralmente filtrata attraverso lo schermo (lirico) soggettivo" (It is true that Petrarch addresses the woman very frequently, however the continuity of the book and, especially, the fact

that the woman is not a mere addressee, but a character in her own right who interacts, reconfigures the allocution into dialogue. But it is a strange type of dialogue, more of a narrative than a lyrical type, or better, precisely that of a narration completely filtered through the (lyrical) subjective screen).

12 The parabolic uses of the "nest" in the Gospel include Matthew 13:31–2: "The Kingdom of heaven is like a mustard seed that someone took and sowed in his field; it is the smallest of all the seeds, but when it has grown it is the greatest of shrubs and becomes a tree, so that the birds of the air come and make nests in its branches"; and Matthew 8:20: "Foxes have holes, and the birds of the air have nests; but the Son of Man has nowhere to lay his head."

13 F. Chiappelli, "An Analysis of Structuration in Petrarch's Poetry," 154.

14 F. Chiappelli, *Studi sul linguaggio del Petrarca. La Canzone delle Visioni*, 29.

15 Ibid., 130. E. Fenzi, *Saggi petrarcheschi*, 92, argues that poem 323 was written after poem 126 since it is doubtful Petrarch could have written "*Chiara* fontana in quel medesmo bosco / sorgea d'un sasso, et *acque fresche et dolci* / spargea, soavemente mormorando" (323, 37–9) ("In that same wood a crystal fountain flowed / Out of a stone, and waters cool and sweet / came gushing, murmuring delightfully") – lines repeatedly corrected on the manuscript – had he not first written "Chiare, fresche et dolci acque" (126, 1). The use of a styleme like "quel medesmo bosco" ("that same wood") reinforces the simultaneity of the two poems written from the standpoint of a contemplative, ascensional time.

16 F. Petrarca, *Res senilis*, 222; *Sen.* [iii, 3], 95.

17 F. Petrarca, *De vita solitaria*, [I, 7, 24], 106; *The Life of Solitude*, 46.

18 N. Mann, *Petrarch*, 99.

19 Petrarca, *Res seniles*, v. 1, 220; *Sen.* [iii, 3], v. 1, 93. This letter is addressed to Niccolò Acciaiuoli.

20 The *capoverso* of poem 327 refers to the four qualities of the laurel listed in the *Collatio*.

21 A reading of *Senili* (for example: *Sen.* iii, 3 and 4; *Sen.* viii, 6; *Sen.* ix, 2; *Sen.* x, 1) shows how the aging Petrarch envisaged friendship as a most elevated relationship that nurtured one's spirit and prepared one for a fuller understanding of the friendship with God.

22 Caputo, "«Et doppiando 'l dolor, doppia lo stile » (*RVF* 331–40)," 726, writes of this work: "E proprio qui si apprezza un risvolto programmatico dell'operazione petrarchesca: la *mutatio vite* passa attraverso l'uso consapevole della poetica che si riconverte in tematica

ovvero viene asservita, per così dire, alla *mutatio operis*" (And precisely here one appreciates a programmatic implication of the Petrarchan operation: the *mutatio vite* passes through the knowing use of a poetics reconverted into a thematics, or rather subjected, so to speak, to the *mutatio operis*).

23 One hears an echo in the antithetical pairing of *stanche* and *lieto* of Dante's address to the reader in *Paradiso* x, 22–4 – "Or ti riman, lettor, sovra 'l tuo banco, / dietro pensando a ciò che si preliba, / s'esser vuoi *lieto* assai prima che *stanco*" ("Now, reader, do not leave your bench, but stay / to think on that of which you have foretaste; / you will have much delight before you tire") – where he warns the reader of the moral difficulty of the paradisical argument.

24 Psalms 80:4–5: "O Lord God of hosts, how long wilt thou be angry with thy people's prayers? Thou has fed them with the bread of tears, and given them tears to drink in full measure."

25 Martinelli, *Petrarca e il Ventoso*, 406.

26 Fenzi, "Dalla precarietà," 747, writes of this poem as the "chiave di volta di tutta l'ultima parte del Canzoniere" (keystone of the entire final part of the Canzoniere).

27 As Caputo, "«Et doppiando 'l dolor, doppia lo stile » (*RVF* 331–40)," notes, the poems of the 330s share mathematical-numerical correspondences around the figures of six and three; the decade marks a turning point in the whole, as the date of Laura's death – 7 April 1348 – is given in poem 336.

28 See R. Barthes, "An Introduction to the Structural Analysis of Narrative," 255: "Functionally the structure of narrative is that of the fugue: narrative 'pulls in' new material even as it 'holds on' to previous material." With respect to the tropic use of "gonna" and "velo" to represent the body, see Romans 7:22; Matthew 26:18; Hebrews 10:19. P. Cherchi, *Verso la chiusura: Saggio sul Canzoniere di Petrarca*, shares this view of the fundamental importance of *Rvf* 366 as a positive and enveloping thematic and moral force, working backward in the sequence.

29 Augustine, *Soliloquies* [I, 6, 12], 41: "For the soul's powers of perception are as it were the eyes of the mind. The most certain truths which are arrived at by the sciences are like those objects which are illuminated by the sun with the result that they can be seen, such as the earth and all the things on the earth." As Fenzi notes, "Dalla precarietà," 748, Augustine's direction to employ the eye of the mind, which impacted Dante as well, was structured in terms of the soul's need of three things: eyes it can use well, the ability to look, and the ability to see.

30 Fenzi, "Dalla precarietà," 740, speaks of the eternal that enters into time and nullifies it. For Fenzi the subject's "lunga guerra" (347, 12), is not, as many have argued, a "war" visited on the subject by Laura but was due to his own vulnerability to love.

31 Martinelli, *Petrarca e il Ventoso*, 407, cites Paul's letters to the Romans and the Galatians as books in which the habits of sinfulness are dramatically juxtaposed to the rebirth of the spirit.

32 As in *Rvf* 338, one sees a reference to John the Evangelist's statement that the world did not know Christ. John 1:10: "He was in the world, and the world was made by him, and the world knew him not."

33 Fenzi glosses this crux as follows, "Dalla precarietà," 756: "'la bellezza incomparabile di Laura presto sparì da questa terra, ragion per cui, pur di piacere a lei fatta santa, è bene ch'io mostri di rinunciare di buon grado a quel poco che mi è stato concesso di vederne' (ove quel *cangiar* fortemente elittico non implica solo rinuncia, naturalmente, ma appunto sostituzione della bellezza fisica con quella spirituale ed eterna)" ("Laura's incomparable beauty quickly disappeared from this earth, and for that reason, though I am pleased she was made a saint, it is good that I show my willingness to renounce that little I was permitted to see of her" (where the strongly elliptical verb *to change* doesn't simply imply renunciation, naturally, but precisely the replacement of physical beauty with spiritual and eternal beauty)).

34 See Augustine, *Confessions* 8, 14: "Love is the act of the lover *and* the love given the loved person. It is a trinity: the lover, the loved person, and love itself."

35 Typically what is registered as *chronos* in the Old Testament is interpreted as *kairos* in the New Testament. See F. Kermode, *The Genesis of Secrecy. On the Interpretation of Narrative*, 89: "Thus the Old Testament becomes the basis for an enormous peripeteia; one finds in its *chronos* prefigurations of the *kairoi* manifested in the New."

36 See Ricoeur, *History and Truth*, 92: "A natural being cannot be guilty; only a historical being can become guilty."

37 See Psalms 102:6–7. Like Augustine, Petrarch read the Psalms figurally as having layers of depth and precise means of interpretation.

38 Romans 5:14: "Yet death reigned from Adam to Moses, even over those whose sins were not like the transgression of Adam, who was a type of the one who was to come"; and Romans 5:17: "If, because of one man's trespass, death reigned through that one man, much more will those who receive the abundance of grace and the free gift of righteousness reign in life through the one man Jesus Christ."

39 See K. Stierle, "Il sonetto CCCLIII," 237: "il dolore dell'io lirico per la perdita dell'amata è assoluto: 'di ch' a me Morte e 'l ciel son tanto avari'. Nessuna speranza in queste parole amare, nessuna luce dell'aldilà" (the sorrow of the lyric I for the loss of the beloved is absolute: "That's why, toward me, so grudging are Death and Heaven." No hope in these bitter words, no light of the hereafter). In his reading of Petrarch by way of Mallarmé and Nerval, Stierle suggests, ibid., 237: "La consolazione è irreale, ma l'irreale forse può essere la sola consolazione: grande tema di tutta la lirica moderna" (The consolation is unreal, but perhaps the only consolation is the unreal: the great theme of all modern lyric poetry). With reference to "Vago augeletto," Stierle, ibid., 242, speaks of "la sua malinconia dolce ma assoluta" (its sweet but absolute melancholy).

40 See Iliescu, *Il Canzoniere petrarchesco e Sant'Agostino*, 112: "rigettando in questa canzone le possibilità elevatrici di Laura, il poeta non soltanto si conforma alla generale lezione derivatagli dall'opera agostiniana, ma ripudia, di fatto, la teoria platonica dell'amore 'scala al Fattor'" (by rejecting in this canzone the uplifting possibilities of Laura, the poet not only conforms to the general reading he had derived from the work of Augustine, but in fact repudiates the Platonic theory of love as the "stairway to the Creator").

41 R. Bettarini, *Bett*, 1578. Bettarini found the same Augustinian *epoché* in canzone 264. As in Augustine's *Soliloquia*, numerous questions are aired that do not receive an answer. N. Tanello's reading of poem 360 faults it for lacking evidence of a "conversione" and suggests that its true religious content is scant or unconvincing. But the critic ignores the basic premise of the poem, which is to recapitulate the discourse of Amor and to distinguish the subject's views from those of Amor despite the changes that have come over Amor in the Christian ambit.

42 B.D. Schildgen, "Overcoming Augustinian Dichotomies in Defense of the Laurel in Canzoni 359 and 360 of the Rime sparse," 158, interprets the unresolved debate before the figure of Reason as a reflection of Petrarch's spiritual inconstancy: "Unlike Augustine, whose *Confessions* are a retrospective unfolding of his conversion which has already occurred, Petrarch's conversion is elusive; he is spiritually still in flux."

43 Cherchi, *Verso la chiusura: Saggio sul Canzoniere di Petrarca*, 157.

44 Matthew 6:19–20: "Do not store up for yourselves treasures on earth, where moth and rust consume and where thieves break in and steal; but store up for yourselves treasures in heaven, where neither moth nor rust consumes and where thieves do not break in and steal." Similar is the parable of the Rich Fool in Luke 12:13–21.

45 See Cherchi, *Verso la chiusura: Saggio sul Canzoniere di Petrarca*, 170: "Le lodi alla Vergine s'incentrano sul suo attributo di madre ricordandone addirittura 'il parto' (v. 28 e v. 43), s'incentrano sul ruolo di mediatrice e di consigliera, oltre ai suoi attributi di purezza e di bellezza" (the praises to the Virgin are centred on her attribute as a mother, even remembering her "delivery" (lines 28 and 43), they are centred on the role of mediatrix and counsellor, as well as her attributes of purity and beauty).

46 With respect to the parable of the virgins, in my reading the lamp oil (or its lack) does not symbolize the virgins' relative knowledge of God; rather it symbolizes their degree of availability and openness to being known *by* God.

47 S. Chessa, *Il profumo del sacro nel* Canzoniere *di Petrarca*, 337.

48 Ibid.

49 G. Savoca, *Il Canzoniere di Petrarca tra codicologia ed ecdotica*, 95.

50 A. Scaglione has written of the text's open-endedness (in contrast to the "closed" system of Dante) as follows, *Francis Petrarch, Six Centuries Later: A Symposium*, 138: "Col *Canzoniere* [...] il testo 'definitivo' è semplicemente l'ultimo scritto. Ma – e questo conta – mentre le varianti sono stadi nel cammino verso una distante, ideale perfezione, esse sono anche, tutte insieme e nella loro successione, il materiale di cui la perfezione è composta" (With the *Canzoniere* [...] the "definitive" text is simply the last one written. But – and this matters – while the variants are stages on the road toward a distant, ideal perfection, they are also, in their totality and their succession, the material of which the perfection is composed).

51 Martinelli, *Petrarca e il Ventoso*, 401–2.

Conclusion

1 See Antonio Minturno, cited in C. Segre, *Intrecci di voci: la polifonia nella letteratura del Novecento*, 143: "quando il poeta parla ad altrui, par che deponga la persona del poeta e ne prenda o tenga un'altra; perciocché nel Petrarca due persone intender possiamo, l'una del poeta quando egli narra, e l'altra dell'amante, quando dirizza a Madonna Laura il suo Parlare" (when the poet talks to others, he seems to set aside the persona of the poet and take on another; for that reason we can detect two personae in Petrarch, that of the poet when he is narrating and that of the lover, when he addresses his Speech to Madonna Laura).

2 Savoca capitalizes each line of poetry, as was Petrarch's practice, and removes the capitalization of nouns such as "amore" that editors have long capitalized, changing the original. This clearly alters one's understanding of the question of allegory and personification. Also with respect to

capital letters and spelling, Savoca enumerates errors that have long been accepted as authoritative. He notes that in his edition he has followed Petrarch's practice of capitalizing each line of verse; he has added capitals where the "vulgate" has lowercase, usually because of the replacement of a semicolon with a period; and he has eliminated nearly four hundred capital letters that editors had used for emphasis, half of them in Amor(e). Savoca compiles a list of 212 differences between the "vulgate" and his edition. The main difference he highlights is syntactic, a fact born out of the radically changed punctuation; this change begets a change in intonation and music, making the text freer and more energetic.

3 H.W. Storey, in G. Belloni et al., *Rerum vulgarium fragmenta. Codice Vat. Lat. 3195*, 133.

4 P. Zumthor, *Speaking of the Middle Ages*, 46.

5 Ibid.

6 Ibid.

7 Ibid., 49–50.

8 P. Zumthor, *Toward a Medieval Poetics*, 40.

9 Umberto Bosco asserted, *Francesco Petrarca*, 7, that Petrarch is "senza storia" (without history), claiming (in error) that we have no writings from the author from before 1338 and that little historical development exists among the writings we do have. Bosco's position is supported by his critical methodology, which avoids any serious discussion of Petrarch's historical poems. Bosco assumed that the narrator and character of the *Fragmenta* were none other than the author himself, thus ignoring the diegesis that confers an internal history to the collection. See U. Bosco, *Francesco Petrarca*, 180–1: "Ma qual è il tono poetico che questi sogni politici trovano nella poesia del Petrarca? Ci dice egli stesso che i suoi versi politici non sono che sospiri, simili a quelli di cui ascoltiamo il suono nel resto del canzoniere" (But what is the poetic tone that these political dreams find in Petrarch's poetry? He himself tells us that his political poems are no more than sighs, similar to those we listen to in the rest of the canzoniere).

10 See, for example, J. Took, "Petrarch," 94: "On the one hand, there is the rapturous transcendentalism of the Dantean *stilnovo*, where the object of the poet's celebration is a *new* (in the sense of a miraculous, even messianic) presence in the historical order. On the other hand, there is the fraught psychologism of the Petrarchan sonnet, where the intuition of an ideal precipitates in one and the same moment a state of spiritual confusion and a sense of imminent demise."

11 See *Le familiari*, v. 4, 220: "nunquam vivimus dum hic sumus, nisi quandiu virtuosum aliquid agentes sternimus iter nobis ad veram vitam, ubi contra

nemo moritur, vivunt omnes et semper vivunt, ubi quod semel placuit semper placet, cuius ineffabilis et inexauste dulcedinis nec modus animo capitur, nec mutatio sentitur, nec timetur finis" (*Fam.*[xxiv, 1], 312–13: "we never live here [on earth] except when doing something virtuous to pave our path to the true life, where in contrast no one dies, everyone lives and will live forever, where what once pleased will ever be pleasing, whose unutterable and infinite charm can scarcely be contained in the spirit, where there are no change and no reason to fear its ending").

12 See G. Savoca, *Il Canzoniere di Petrarca tra codicologia ed ecdotica*, 245–7. It is Savoca's position that philology has historically focused on the "word" of the Petrarchan poem (which aspires in vain to become a "voice") while neglecting the actual – fleeting and finite – voice of the poet.

13 C. Salinari, *La letteratura del Trecento*, 53, provides a picture of the contradictions, and the moral challenges, faced by a humanist like Petrarch: "Cosí l'umanista afferma la dignità dell'uomo nello stesso momento che diventa cortigiano; esalta lo spirito critico mentre si estingue, senza nessuna contropartita, la dinamica politica del Comune; acquista il senso della storia quando egli stesso, e l'Italia intera, non riescono piú a fare storia e vengono tagliati fuori dal grande processo di formazione degli Stati nazionali; prende a modello il mondo classico proprio nel momento in cui il mondo contemporaneo si avvia alla corruzione e allo sfacelo" (Thus the humanist affirms the dignity of man in the same moment that he becomes a courtier; he exalts the critical spirit even as the political dynamic of the Comune dies out, without a worthy replacement; he acquires the sense of history when he himself, and all of Italy, are no longer able to make history and are cut out of the great process of formation of the nation states; he takes the classical world as a model in the very moment that the contemporary world is heading toward corruption and ruin).

14 See Petrarch, *Sen*, vii, 1, letter to Pope Urban. A. Quondam, *Petrarca, l'italiano dimenticato*, 265, writes that in De Sanctis "la liquidazione di Petrarca trascina con sé quella della tradizione che lo scelse come suo *idolo*, anzi [...] è la liquidazione del Classicismo di Antico regime a rendere necessaria quella di Petrarca" (the liquidation of Petrarch drags along with it that of the tradition that chose him as its *idol*, or rather [...] it is the liquidation of *Ancienne regime* Classicism that renders necessary Petrarch's liquidation).

15 Quondam, *Petrarca, l'italiano dimenticato*, 240.

16 See A. Berardinelli, "Il fantasma di Petrarca," 38.

17 B. Martinelli, *Petrarca e il Ventoso*, 272. See also E. Fenzi, "Tra Dante e Petrarca: Il fantasma di Ulisse," in Fenzi, *Saggi petrarcheschi*, 493–517.

18 E. Auerbach, *Introduction to Romance Languages and Literature*, 128. Auerbach, ibid., describes the *Fragmenta* as "a volume of about 350 poems, most of them sonnets," and adds, "Virtually all of them sing the praises of Laura, a woman he had loved in his youth. And within this framework they reveal the movements of a restless soul, at once haughty and prey to anxiety, worshipful of antiquity and yet Christian, enamored of the world and its fame, yet quick to become disenchanted and seek solitude and death."

19 E. Auerbach, *Literary Language and Its Public in Latin Latin Antiquity and in the Middle Ages*, 318.

20 See H. Arendt, *The Human Condition*, 292: "In the modern period, this order is not only reversed, but contemplation is suppressed, replaced by thought. The reversal of the modern age consisted then not in raising doing to the rank of contemplating as the highest state of which human beings are capable, as though henceforth doing was the ultimate meaning for the sake of which contemplation was to be performed, just as, up to that time, all activities of the *vita activa* had been judged and justified to the extent that they made the *vita contemplativa* possible. The reversal concerned only thinking, which from then on was the handmaiden of doing as it had been the *ancilla theologiae*, the handmaiden of contemplating divine truth in medieval philosophy and the handmaiden of contemplating the truth of Being in ancient philosophy. Contemplation itself became altogether meaningless."

21 Quondam, *Petrarca, l'italiano dimenticato*, 216. Even so, Foscolo persisted in the negative comparisons with Dante, as when he cited *Purgatorio* xxv, 47 – "L'un disposto a patire e l'altro a fare" ("one ready to be passive and one active") – as the epigraph to his essay, "Parallelo tra Dante e il Petrarca."

22 U. Foscolo, in F. Petrarca, *Canzoniere*. Commentary by Giacomo Leopardi, 51.

23 Ibid., 45.

24 Ibid., 35.

25 One cause of the oversight is the failure to acknowledge the obscurity of the text. See G. Leopardi, "Scusa dell'interprete" (1826), in 1969, v. 1, 986: "A chi mi dice che il Petrarca non è oscuro, domandando perdono rispondo che il sole non è chiaro, e prometto di provare il mio detto immantinente che egli avrà provato il suo" (To those who say Petrarch is not obscure, I reply, begging their pardon, that the sun is not bright, and I promise to prove my statement as soon as they prove theirs).

26 Quondam, *Petrarca, l'italiano dimenticato*, 124.

27 See ibid., 124–5: "E la consapevolezza della mutazione riguarda anche la stagione del culto di questi scrittori 'vetusti divini', tra la fine del Medioevo e l'inizio dell'Umanesimo, quando la catastrofe dell'Italia non era ancora completa" (And the awareness of change also concerns the season of the

cult of these "divine ancient" authors, between the end of the Middle Ages and the beginning of humanism, when the Italian catastrophe was not yet complete).

28 *Le familiari*, v. 3, 28; *Fam.* [xii, 7], v. 2, 151.

29 *Le familiari*, v. 3, 29; *Fam.* [xii, 7], v. 2, 152.

30 See M. Praloran, "Lo splendore del mondo e la solitudine dell'io (*RVF* 310–20)," 677: "Il significato di un testo [nei *Fragmenta*] si legge [...] alla luce di tantissimi altri testi ma non nel senso di un rivelamento progressivo, del dipanarsi di una trama, a meno che non diamo a questa uno sviluppo soprattutto orizzontale e non diacronico (con queste cautele può essere ripresa la nozione di romanzo, certo non in una accezione classica)" (The meaning of a text in the *Fragmenta* is read in the light of so many other texts but not in the sense of a progressive revealing, of the unfolding of a plot, unless we attribute to this an especially horizontal and non-diachronic development (with these precautions one can take up again the notion of romance, though not in its classical meaning)).

31 See C. Trinkaus, *The Poet as Philosopher*, 27–51.

32 K. Foster, *Petrarch: Poet and Humanist*, 70.

33 See U. Dotti, "Petrarca e la fondazione dell'umanesimo," in *La rivoluzione incompiuta*, 85–125.

34 Augustine, *Confessions* [viii, 29], 1997, 168: "Stung into action, I returned to the place where Alypius was sitting, for on leaving it I had put down there the book of the apostle's letters. I snatched it up, opened it and read in silence the passage on which my eyes first lighted: '*Not in dissipation and drunkenness, nor in debauchery and lewdness, nor in arguing and jealousy; but put on the Lord Jesus Christ, and make no provision for the flesh or the gratification of your desires.*' [Romans 13:13–14]. I had no wish to read further, nor was there need. No sooner had I reached the end of the verse than the light of certainty flooded my heart and all dark shades of doubt fled away."

35 U. Dotti, *Vita di Petrarca*, 446.

36 G. Orelli, *Il suono dei sospiri*, 5. This study of the phonic, metrical, and thematic planes of selected poems of the *Fragmenta* obviously takes its title from the proemial poem "Voi che ascoltate in rime sparse il suono / di quei sospiri."

37 Regarding debts to the *Vita nuova*, see M. Santagata, *L'io e il mondo*, 124–8.

38 See G. Velli, "Il Dante di Francesco Petrarca"; P. Trovato, *Dante in Petrarca*; F. Suitner, *Petrarca e la tradizione stilnovistica*; F. Suitner, *Dante, Petrarca e altra poesia antica*; C. Bologna, "PetrArca petroso"; and Domenico De Robertis, "Petrarca petroso"; as well as the abundant references included in the editions of the *Fragmenta* of Santagata and Bettarini.

39 G. Orelli writes in a positive vein of the "parasitism" of Petrarch's verbal mining of the *Commedia*. See Orelli, *Il suono dei sospiri*, 124: "Forse nessun poeta ha saccheggiato la *Commedia* in lungo e in largo con l'assiduità e, bisogna dire, l'eleganza del Petrarca" (Perhaps no poet has sacked the *Commedia* deep and wide with the assiduousness and, one must say, the elegance of Petrarch). See C. Trinkaus, "Theologia Poetica and Theologia Rhetorica in Petrarch's Invectives," in *The Poet as Philosopher*, 90–113.

40 Referring to Sophocles' *Antigone*, in which the figure of Prometheus struggles between immanence and transcendence, as between the desire to attain clarity or live in obscurity, Dotti notes, *La rivoluzione incompiuta*, 85–7, that already in Virgilian times Prometheus's struggle was judged to be a crime against the gods, which eventually led in the Christian era to the mortification of man faced by the omnipotent transcendence of the triune God; and that Augustine had condemned the human, immanent culture of Latinity in the *City of God*.

41 See *Sen*. xvii, 2, 14.

42 For Dotti, *La rivoluzione incompiuta*, 122–3, Petrarch, like Dante, represents the passions of historical existence: "[S]colpisce gli eventi storici e personali degli uomini, [...] attribuendo all'alta fantasia dell'artista il compito di secolarizzare le concezioni della trascendenza e di ricondurle nell'ambito proprio dell'immanenza dal quale erano state indebitamente strappate" ([Petrarch] shapes the historical and personal events of humanity, [...] assigning to the high imagination of the artist the task of secularizing the concepts of transcendence and bringing them back into the ambit of immanence from which had been unduly extracted).

43 Ibid., 125.

44 See E. Garin, *Italian Humanism*, 19: "There is an insoluble connection between the interior and the exterior, between mind and speech. There is no point in praising the solitary form of speech, or monologue, which man conducts with himself. If we wish to be human, we must communicate with other men."

45 A contrasting view is presented by P. Hainsworth, *Petrarch the Poet*, 7: "Italian poetry, as [Petrarch] conceived and wrote it, was not to be reconciled with humanism in any intellectually coherent fashion."

46 S. Chessa, *Il profumo del sacro nel* Canzoniere *di Petrarca*, 16.

47 As K. Stierle, *La vita e i tempi di Petrarca*, 284–5, writes, Petrarch's view of the landscape dismantles the Dantesque cosmic allegory of the one world ordered by and under the eye of God. In contrast to that hierarchical vision, for Petrarch: "Lo sguardo estetico del soggetto [...] svincola il paesaggio dalla sua referenzialità allegorica e ne fa la scoperta cognitiva di

una nuova accessibilità soggettiva del mondo" (The aesthetic gaze of the subject [...] frees the landscape from its allegorical referentiality and makes the cognitive discovery within it of a new subjective accessibility of the world). While it is true, as Stierle argues, that Petrarch expresses a form of nominalism by introducing a landscape that is open-ended and horizontal – and thus provides a view of the multiplicity that arose in the Trecento – he also retained the vertical and sublime dimension of the landscape.

48 While commentators have largely ignored Petrarch's engagement of artificial memory, earlier scholars such as Agrippa and Diderot singled him out, pointing to *Rerum memorandarum libri*. See Frances A. Yates, *The Art of Memory*, 101–4; Yates ties Petrarch to the arts of memory of St Thomas, as a transitional figure between the Middle Ages and the Renaissance, with specific reference to *Rerum memorandarum libri*.

49 M. Santagata, *I frammenti dell'anima*, 284–8. Since my focus is Vat. Lat. 3195, I do not address the relative presence or absence of narrative tropes in the other forms and redactions.

50 M. Santagata, *Sant*, lxxxvi. Santagata suggests that this transition to "the canzoniere of Laura" undermines the book's closure insofar as the theme of penitence and redemption within the "I" figure is not resolved. See Santagata, *Sant*, 2004, xcii: "E così, con la graduale promozione a personaggio benefico di quella donna a cui il libro avrebbe dovuto riservare il ruolo di antagonista, il canzoniere dell'io', del riscatto del narratore, si trasforma gradualmente nel canzoniere di Laura" (And thus, with the gradual promotion of that woman for whom the book should have reserved the role of antagonist, to a beneficent character, the canzoniere of the I, of the narrator's salvation, is gradually transformed into the canzoniere of Laura).

51 Fenzi, *Saggi petrarcheschi*, 177–82.

52 Ibid., 181.

53 Ibid.

54 P. Cherchi, *Verso la chiusura: Saggio sul Canzoniere di Petrarca*, 8.

55 Ibid., 12–13.

56 Giorgio Orelli, *Il suono dei sospiri*, 3.

57 G. Contini, "La lingua del Petrarca," 117.

58 R. Bettarini, *Lacrime e inchiostro nel canzoniere del Petrarca*, 27, refers in this regard to Petrarch's "presa di distanza dall'*Eneide*, dalle *Metamorfosi*, dalla *Tebaide*, dalla *Commedia*, e da quanto narrativamente più lo toccava, per concentrarsi in quelle infinite operazioni sul linguaggio che fanno dei *Rerum vulgarium fragmenta* una narrazione quasi algebrica di pure forme" (self-distancing from the *Aeneid*, the *Metamorphoses*, the *Thebaid*, the *Comedy*,

and all that narratively touched him the most, in order to concentrate on those infinite operations on the language that make of the *Fragmenta* an almost algebraic narration of pure forms).

59 See T. Elwert, "La varietà metrica e tematica delle canzoni del Petrarca," 392: "la forma metrica non è niente di accessorio o di appiccicato, ma non solo questo, l'esame delle forme metriche porta alla conclusione [...] che essa esprime in se stessa un messaggio che si riferisce al contenuto tematico della canzone" (not only is metrical form not something accessory or tacked on, but the examination of metrical form leads to the conclusion [...] that it expresses in itself a message which refers to the thematic content of the canzone).

60 See Dotti, *Vita di Petrarca*, 422: "Quanto infine alla nona e ultima redazione, essa naturalmente coincide con il Vat. lat 3195. [...] Aggiunse così 20 poesie nella prima parte (i nn. 244–63) e 18 nella seconda (i nn. 343 e 345–61)" (Finally regarding the ninth and last redaction, it naturally coincides with Vat. Lat. 3195. [...] So he added 20 poems to the Part 1 (244–263) and 18 to Part 2 (343 and 345–361)).

61 Santagata, *I frammenti dell'anima*, 288.

62 See S. Carrai, "Petrarca e l'invenzione del «Canzoniere»." See T. Barolini, "The Making of a Lyric Sequence," 7: "From a narratological perspective, the lyric sequence is a peculiarly paradoxical genre, since it insists simultaneously on fragmentation – each lyric is an individual entity endowed with a beginning and ending, with its own *entelecheia* – and on fragmentation's opposite, namely a sequentiality, a linearity brought about by the existence of the larger unit that subsumes the individual parts into a common structure, with a common beginning and ending."

63 See M. Santagata, *Dal sonetto al canzoniere*, 139–40: "È il concetto stesso del libro che è nuovo" (It is the very concept of the book that is new).

64 This was the conclusion foreseen by Franciscus at the end of Book 3 of the *Secretum*.

Bibliography

ABBREVIATIONS

Bett *Canzoniere. Rerum vulgarium fragmenta*. Ed. Rosanna Bettarini. 2 vols. Turin: Einaudi, 2005.

Fam *Letters on Familiar Matters*. Translation of *Rerum familiarium libri* by Aldo S. Bernardo. 3 vols. Baltimore, MD: Johns Hopkins UP, 1978–82.

Rvf *Petrarch's Songbook. Rerum vulgarium fragmenta*. Trans. James Wyatt Cook. Introd. Germain Warkentin. Italian text by Gianfranco Contini. Binghamton, NY: Medieval and Renaissance Texts and Studies, 1995.

Sant *Canzoniere*. Ed. Marco Santagata. Milan: Mondadori, 2004 (incorporating 1996 edition).

Sen *Letters on Old Age*. Translation of *Rerum senilium libri* by Aldo S. Bernardo, Saul Levin, and Reta A. Bernardo. 3 vols. Baltimore, MD: Johns Hopkins UP, 1992.

I. EDITIONS OF PETRARCH'S WRITINGS
(ORDERED BY YEAR OF PUBLICATION)

1. Rerum vulgarium fragmenta

Le rime. Ed. G. Carducci and S. Ferrari. Florence: Sansoni, 1899.

Le "Rime sparse." Ed. Ezio Chiorboli. Milan: Casa editrice Trevisini, 1923.

Il Canzoniere. Ed. Giuseppe Rigutine and Michele Scherillo. Milan: Hoepli, 1925.

Rime. Ed. Nicolò Zingarelli. Bologna: Zanichelli, 1963.

Canzoniere. Critical text and essay by Gianfranco Contini. Annotated by Daniele Ponchiroli. Turin: Einaudi, 1964; reprint: Turin: Einaudi, 1992, with introd. by Roberto Antonelli.

Rime. Ed. Guido Bezzola, with an essay by Andrea Zanzotto. Milan: Rizzoli, 1976.
Canzoniere. Commentary by Giacomo Leopardi, with "Saggio sopra la poesia del Petrarca" by Ugo Foscolo. Ed Ugo Dotti. Milan: Feltrinelli [1828], 1979.
Canzoniere. Ed. Ugo Dotti. Rome: Donzelli, 1996.
Canzoniere. Ed. Marco Santagata. Milan: Mondadori, 2004 (incorporating 1996 edition). Abbreviated as *Sant*.
Canzoniere. Rerum vulgarium fragmenta. Ed. Rosanna Bettarini. 2 vols. Turin: Einaudi, 2005. Abbreviated as *Bett*.
Rerum vulgarium fragmenta. Ed. Giuseppe Savoca. Florence: Olschki, 2008.
Canzoniere. Ed. Sabrina Stroppa. Introd. Paolo Cherchi. Turin: Einaudi, 2011.

2. Translations and Anthologies of *Rerum vulgarium fragmenta*

Selected Sonnets, Odes and Letters. Ed. Thomas G. Bergin. New York: Appleton-Century-Crofts, 1966.
Petrarch: Selected Poems. Ed. T. Gwynfor Griffith and P.R.J. Hainsworth. Manchester: Manchester UP, 1971.
Petrarch's Lyric Poems. The Rime sparse *and Other Lyrics*. Trans. and ed. Robert M. Durling. Cambridge, MA: Harvard UP, 1976.
Petrarch: Selected Poems. Trans. Anthony Mortimer. Tuscaloosa, AL: U of Alabama P, 1977.
Petrarch's Songbook. Rerum Vulgarium Fragmenta. Trans. James Wyatt Cook. Introd. Germaine Warkentin. Italian text by Gianfranco Contini. Binghamton, NY: Medieval and Renaissance Texts and Studies, 1995.

3. Other Works

Lettere senili di Francesco Petrarca. Ed. and trans. Giuseppe Fracassetti. Florence: Le Monnier, 1869.
Scritti inediti di Francesco Petrarca. Includes *Collatio laureationis*. Ed. A. Hortis. Trieste: Tipografia del Lloyd Austro-ungarico, 1874.
On His Own Ignorance and That of Many Others. Trans. of *De sui ipsius et aliorum ignorantia* by Hans Nachod, in Ernst Cassirer, Paul Oskar Kristeller, and John Herman Randall Jr., eds, *The Renaissance Philosophy of Man*, 49–133. Chicago: U of Chicago P, 1948.
Rime, Trionfi e poesie latine. Ed. F. Neri, G. Martellotti, E. Bianchi, and N. Sapegno. Milan: Ricciardi, 1951.
"Petrarch's Coronation Oration." Ed. E.H. Wilkins. *PMLA* 68, 5 (1953): 1241–50.
Prose. Ed. G. Martellotti, P.G. Ricci, R. Carrara, and E. Bianchi. Milan: Ricciardi, 1955.

Il «De otio religioso» di Francesco Petrarca. Ed. Giuseppe Rotondi. Vatican City: Biblioteca apostolica vaticana, 1958.

Le familiari. Ed. Vittorio Rossi and Umberto Bosco. 4 vols. Florence: Sansoni, 1968.

Rime e trionfi. Ed. Raffaello Ramat. Milan: Rizzoli, 1971.

Bucolicum Carmen. Trans. and annotated by Thomas G. Bergin. New Haven, CT: Yale UP, 1974.

Sine nomine. Lettere polemiche e politiche. Ed. U. Dotti. Bari: Laterza, 1974.

Opere latine. Ed. Antonietta Bufano, with the collaboration of Basile Aracri and Clara Kraus Reggiani. Introd. Manlio Pastore Stocchi. 2 vols. Turin: UTET, 1975.

The Life of Solitude. Trans. with introd. and notes by Jacob Zeitlin. Westport, CT: Hyperion Press, 1978.

Letters on Familiar Matters. Trans. of *Rerum familiarium libri* by Aldo S. Bernardo. 3 vols. Baltimore, MD: Johns Hopkins UP, 1978–82.

Il mio segreto. Ed. Ugo Dotti. Milan: Rizzoli, 1981.

Petrarch's Remedies for Fortune Fair and Foul. Trans. with commentary of *De remediis utriusque fortune* by Conrad H. Rawski. 5 vols. Bloomington, IN: Indiana UP, 1991.

Le familiari. Libro primo and Libro secondo. Introd., trans., and notes by Ugo Dotti. 2 vols. Rome: Archivio Guiddo Izzi, 1992.

Letters on Old Age. Trans. of *Rerum senilium libri* by Aldo S. Bernardo, Saul Levin, and Reta A. Bernardo. Baltimore, MD: Johns Hopkins UP, 1992. 3 vols.

Lettere disperse. Varie e miscellanee. Ed. Alessandro Pancheri. Parma: Guanda, 1994.

Salmi penitenziali. Ed. Roberto Gigliucci. Rome: Salerno, 1997.

On Religious Leisure. Ed. and trans. Susan S. Schearer. Introd. Ronald G. Witt. New York: Italica, 2002.

Res seniles. Ed. Silvio Rizzo, with Monica Berté. 3 vols. Florence: Le Lettere, 2006–14.

The Secret. Ed. and introd. Carol E. Quillen. Boston: Bedford/St Martin's, 2003.

Francesco Petrarca. I sette salmi penitenziali. Presentazione e nuova traduzione dal latino. Trans. and introd. Claudio Bellintani. Padua: Il Poligrafo, 2004.

Rerum memorandarum libri. Ed. Marco Petoletti. Florence: Le Lettere, 2014.

Epistolae metricae. http://www.classicitaliani.it/petrarca/poesia/epistole/epistolae_Lexis.htm.

II. SECONDARY BIBLIOGRAPHY

Adams, Henry. *Mont-Saint-Michel and Chartres*. Introd. Ralph Adams Cram. Princeton, NJ: Princeton UP, 1981.

Afribo, Andrea. *Petrarca e petrarchismo. Capitolo di lingua, stile e metrica*. Rome: Carocci, 1979.

Agosti, Stefano. *Gli occhi, le chiome: Per una lettura psicoanalitica del Canzoniere di Petrarca*. Milan: Feltrinelli, 1993.

– "Petrarca e la modernità letteraria: Una geneaolgia." *Il verri* 24 (2004): 5–36.

Alighieri, Dante. *Convivio*. Ed. P. Cudini. Milan: Garzanti, 1980.

– *Dante's* Il Convivio (The Banquet). Trans. Richard H. Lansing. New York: Garland, 1990.

– *Dante's Lyric Poetry*. Ed. K. Foster and P. Boyde. 2 vols. Oxford: Clarendon P, 1967.

– *La divina commedia*. Ed. N. Sapegno. 3 vols. Florence: La Nuova Italia, 1985.

– *The Divine Comedy*. Trans. Allen Mandelbaum. Introd. Eugenio Montale. Notes by Peter Armour. New York: Knopf, 1995.

– *Rime*. Ed. Gianfranco Contini. Turin: Einaudi, 1973.

– *Vita nuova*. Ed. Edoardo Sanguineti. Notes by A. Berardinelli. Milan: Garzanti, 1977.

Alonso, Dámaso. "La poesia del Petrarca e il petrarchismo (Mondo estetico della pluralità)." *Studi petrarcheschi* 7 (1961): 73–120.

Antognini, Roberta. "*Familiarium rerum liber*: Tradizione materiale e autobiografia." In Barolini and Storey, 2007, 205–29.

– *Il progetto autobiografico delle Familiares di Petrarca*. Milan: LED, 2008.

Antonelli, Roberto. "'Rerum vulgarium fragmenta' di Francesco Petrarca." In A. Asor Rosa, ed., *Letteratura Italiana Einaudi. Le Opere*, vol. 1: 1–111. Turin: Einaudi, 1992.

Arendt, Hannah. *The Human Condition*. Chicago: U of Chicago P, 1958.

Asor Rosa, Alberto. *Genus italicum. Saggi sulla identità letteraria italiana*. Turin: Einaudi, 1997.

Atti dei Convegni Lincei: Convegno Internazionale Francesco Petrarca. Rome: Accademia nazionale dei Lincei, 1976.

Auerbach, Erich. *Introduction to Romance Languages and Literature: French, Spanish, Provençal, Italian*. Trans. Guy Daniels. New York: Capricorn Books, 1961.

– *Literary Language and Its Public in Latin Latin Antiquity and in the Middle Ages*. Trans. R. Manheim. Princeton, NJ: Princeton UP, 1993.

Augustine, St, Bishop of Hippo. *City of God*. Trans. Marcus Dods. Introd. Thomas Merton. New York: Modern Library, 1950.

– *Confessions*. Trans. Maria Boulding, OSB. Pref. Patricia Hampl. New York: Vintage, 1997.

– *Confessions*. Trans. with introd. by Garry Wills. New York: Penguin, 2006.

– *Confessionum libri XIII. Editit Martinus Skutella* (1934). Ed. H. Juergens and W. Schaub. Stuttgart: B.G. Teubneri, 1969.

– *Of True Religion*. Trans. J.H.S. Burleigh with introd. by Louis O. Mink. Chicago: Henry Regnery, 1968.

– *On Christian Teaching*. Trans. with introd. and notes by R.P.H. Green. New York: Oxford UP, 1999.
– *On the Trinity. Books 8–15*. Ed. Gareth B. Matthews. Trans. Stephen McKenna. Cambridge: Cambridge UP, 2002.
– *Soliloquies and Immortality of the Soul*. With introd., trans., and commentary by G. Watson. Warminster, Wilts.: Aris and Phillips, 1990.
– *St. Augustine on the Psalms*. Trans. and annotated by Scholastica Hebgin and Felicitas Corrigan. Westminster, MD: Newman Press, 1960.
– *The Works of Saint Augustine. A Translation for the 21st Century. Letters 100–155 (Epistulae)*. Trans. and notes Roland Teske, SJ. Ed. Boniface Ramsey. Hyde Park, NY: New City Press, 2003.
Badiou, Alain. *Handbook of Inaesthetics*. Trans. Alberto Toscano. Stanford, CA: Stanford UP, 2005.
Bakhtin, M. *Art and Answerability. Early Philosophical Essays*. Ed. Michael Holquist and Vadim Liapunov. Trans. and notes V. Liapunov. Austin: U of Texas P, 1990.
– *The Dialogic Imagination*. Ed. Michael Holquist. Trans. Caryl Emerson and Michael Holquist. Austin: U of Texas P, 1981.
Balduino, Armando. "Lettura di un sonetto petrarchesco." In *Boccaccio, Petrarca e altri poeti del Trecento*. Florence: Olschki, 1984. 209–30.
Barański, Zygmunt G., and Theodore J. Cachey Jr, eds. *Petrarch and Dante: Anti-Dantism, Metaphysics, Tradition*. With assistance by Demetrio S. Yocum. Notre Dame, IN: Notre Dame University P, 2009.
Barbarisi, Gennaro, and Claudia Berra, eds. *Il «Canzoniere» di Francesco Petrarca. La critica contemporanea*. Milan: LED, 1992.
Barilli, Renato. *Rhetoric*. Trans. Giuliana Menozzi. Minneapolis: U of Minnesota P, 1987.
Barolini, Teodolinda. "The Making of a Lyric Sequence: Time and Narrative in Petrarch's *Rerum vulgarium fragmenta*." *MLN* 104, 1 (1989): 3–38.
– "Petrarch at the Crossroads of Hermeneutics and Philology: Editorial Lapses, Narrative Impositions, and Wilkins' Doctrine of the Nine Forms of the *Rerum vulgarium fragmenta*." In Barolini and Storey, 2007, 21–44.
Barolini, Teodolinda, and H. Wayne Storey, eds. *Petrarch and the Textual Origins of Interpretation*. Columbia Series in the Classical Tradition, vol. 31. Leiden: Brill, 2007.
Baron, Hans. "The Evolution of Petrarch's Thought: Reflections on the State of Petrarch Studies." In *From Petrarch to Leonardo Bruni. Studies in Humanistic and Political Literature*, 7–50. Chicago: U of Chicago P, 1968.
Barthes, Roland. "An Introduction to the Structural Analysis of Narrative." *New Literary History: A Journal of Theory and Interpretation* 6, 2 (1975): 237–72.

– *The Neutral*. Trans. Rosalind E. Krauss and Denis Hollier. New York: Columbia UP, 2005.

Barthouil, Georges. "Petrarca a Avignone." *Convegno internazionale Francesco Petrarca* . Atti dei Convegni Lincei, vol. 210: 205–31. Rome: Accademia Nazionale dei Lincei, 1976.

Battisti, Eugenio. *L'antirinascimento*. 2 vols. Milan: Feltrinelli, 1962.

– "Non chiare acque." In Scaglione, ed., *Francis Petrarch*, 1975, 305–39.

Bellintani, Claudio. "Identità e spiritualità di Francesco Petrarca canonico della cattedrale di Padova (1349-1374)." In Gilda P. Mantovani, ed., *Petrarca e il suo tempo*, 27–42. Milan: Skira, 2006.

Belloni, Gino, Furio Brugnolo, H. Wayne Storey, and Stefano Zamponi, eds. *Rerum vulgarium fragmenta: Facsimile del codice autografo Vaticano Latino 3195* and *Commentario all'edizione in Fac-simile*. Padua: Antenore, 2003–4.

Bembo, Pietro. *Prose della volgar lingua*. Ed. Mario Marti. Padua: Liviana Editrice, 1967.

Berardinelli, Alfonso. "Il fantasma di Petrarca." *Semestrale di Studi (e Testi) italiani* 14 (2004): 37–42.

Bergin, Thomas G. *Petrarch*. Boston: Twayne, 1970.

Bernardo, Aldo. "Dramatic Dialogue and Monologue in Petrarch's Works." *Symposium* 7 (1953): 92–119.

– "Dramatic Dialogue in the Prose Letters of Petrarch." *Symposium* 5 (1951): 302–16.

– "The Importance of the Non-Love Poems of Petrarch's 'Canzoniere.'" *Italica* 27, 4 (1950): 302–12.

– *Petrarch, Laura and the Triumphs*. Albany, NY: State U of New York P, 1974.

– ed. *Francesco Petrarca. Citizen of the World*. Proceedings of the World Petrarch Congress. Washington, DC, 6–13 April 1974. Padua: Antenore; Albany, NY: State U of New York P, 1980.

Berra, Clauda. "L'arte della similitudine nella canzone CXXXV dei «Rerum Vulgarium Fragmenta»." *Giornale storico della letteratura italiana* 103 (1986): 161–99.

Bertolani, Maria Cecilia. *Il corpo glorioso. Studi sui* Trionfi *del Petrarca*. Rome: Carocci, 2001.

– *Petrarca e la visione dell'eterno*. Bologna: Il Mulino, 2005.

Bertoni, Alberto. *La poesia. Come si legge e come si scrive*. Bologna: Il Mulino, 2006.

Bettarini, Rosanna. "I fiumi di Petrarca." *Studi di filologia italiana* 50 (1992): 5–18.

– "*Fluctuationes* agostiniane nel Canzoniere," *Studi di filologia italiana* 60 (2002): 129–39.

– *Lacrime e inchiostro nel canzoniere del Petrarca*. Bologna: CLUEB, 1998.

– "Perché 'narrando' il duol si disacerba (Motivi esegetici dagli autografi petrarcheschi)." In AA.VV., *La critica del testo. Problemi di metodo ed esperienze di lavoro*, 305–20. Rome: Salerno Editrice, 1985.
– "Verdi panni ..." In *Omaggio a Gianfranco Folena*, 573–80. Padua: Editoriale programma, 1993.
Bianchi, Enzo. *Praying the Word. An Introduction to the Lectio Divina*. Trans. James W. Zona. Kalamazoo, MI: Cistertian Publications, 1998.
Bigi, Emilio. "Alcuni aspetti dello stile del canzoniere petrarchesco." In Barbarisi and Berra, eds, 1992, 145–59.
– "Le ballate del Petrarca." *Giornale storico della letteratura italiana* 152 (1974): 481–93.
– *Dal Petrarca al Leopardi*. Milan: Ricciardi, 1954.
Billanovich, Giuseppe. *Petrarca e il primo umanesimo*. Padua: Antenore, 1996.
– *Petrarca letterato. I. Lo scrittoio del Petrarca*. Rome: Edizioni di Storia e Letteratura, 1947.
– *La tradizione del testo di Livio e le origini dell'Umanesimo*. Vol. 1. *Tradizione e fortuna di Livio tra Medioevo e umanesimo*. Part 1. Padua: Antenore, 1981.
Blasio, Maria Grazia. "Il dibattito religioso tra due e trecento." *Quaderni petrarcheschi* 15–16 (2005–6): 231–59.
Boggs, Edward L., III. "Cino and Petrarch." *MLN* 94 (1979): 146–52.
Bologna, Corrado. "PetrArca petroso." *Critica del testo* 6, 1 (2003): 367–420.
Bonaventure, St. *The Works of Saint Bonaventure*. Ed. Philotheus Boehner and Sr M. Frances Laughlin. St Bonaventure, NY: The Franciscan Institute, 1955.
Bosco, Umberto. *Francesco Petrarca*. Bari: Laterza, 1968.
Boyle, Marjorie O'Rourke. *Petrarch's Genius: Pentimento and Prophecy*. Berkeley: U of California P, 1991.
Boysen, Benjamin. "Crucified in the Mirror of Love: On Petrarch's Ambivalent Conception of Love in *Rerum vulgarium fragmenta*." *Orbis Litterarum* 58 (2003): 163–88.
Braden, Gordon. "Applied Petrarchism." *MLQ* 57, 3 (1996): 397–423.
Brambilla Ageno, Franca. "I 'proverbi' di Ser Garzo." *Studi petrarcheschi*, nuova serie, I (1984): 1–37.
Cachey, Theodore, Jr. "From Shipwreck to Port: *Rvf* 189 and the Making of the *Canzoniere*." *MLN* 120, 1 (2005): 30–49.
Cahill, Thomas. *Desire of the Everlasting Hills: The World Before and After Jesus*. New York: Anchor Books, 2001.
Calcaterra, Carlo. *La selva del Petrarca*. Bologna: Cappelli, 1942.
Calvino, Italo. *Lezioni americane. Sei proposte per il prossimo millennio*. Milan: Mondadori, 1993.
Campo, Cristina. *Gli imperdonabili*. Milan: Adelphi, 1987.

Capovilla, Guido. *«Sì vario stile »: Studi sul Canzoniere del Petrarca*. Modena: Mucchi, 1998.

Caputo, Rino. "«Et doppiando 'l dolor, doppia lo stile » (*RVF* 331–40)." In Picone, ed., *Il Canzoniere*, 2007, 725–31.

Carrai, Stefano. "Petrarca e l'invenzione del «Canzoniere»." In Francesco Bruni, ed., *«Vaghe stelle dell'orsa ...». L'"io" e il "tu" nella lirica italiana*, 119–29. Venice: Marsilio, 2005.

– "Il sonetto «Una candida cerva» del Petrarca. Problemi d'interpretazione e di fonti." *Rivista di letteratura italiana* 3 (1985): 233–51.

Carrai, Stefano, and Giorgio Inglese. "Francesco Petrarca." In *La letteratura del Medioevo*, 207–60. With the collaboration of Luigi Trenti. Rome: Carocci, 2003.

Carrara, Enrico. "Gli 'improvvisi' del Petrarca." *Studi petrarcheschi* 2 (1949): 137–51.

Carruthers, Mary. *The Book of Memory. A Study of Memory in Medieval Culture*. Cambridge: Cambridge UP, 1990.

Cary, Phillip. *Inner Grace. Augustine in the Traditions of Plato and Paul*. Oxford: Oxford UP, 2008.

Cassirer, Ernst. *The Individual and the Cosmos in Renaissance Philosophy*. Trans. with introd. Mario Domandi. New York: Harper and Row, 1963.

Cavalcanti, Guido. *The Selected Poetry of Guido Cavalcanti. A Critical English Edition*. Ed. and trans. Simon West. Leicester: Troubador, 2009.

Ceruti, Mauro, and Giuseppe Fornari. *Le due paci. Cristianesimo e morte di Dio nel mondo globalizzato*. Milan: Raffaello Cortina, 2005.

Cervigni, Dino. "The Petrarchan Lover's Non-Dialogic and Dialogic Discourse: An Augustinian Semiotic Approach to Petrarch's *Rerum vulgarium fragmenta*." In Cervigni, ed., *Petrarch and the European Lyric Tradition. Annali d'Italianistica*, vol. 22: 105–34. Chapel Hill, NC: U of North Carolina P, 2004.

Ceserani, Remo. "«Petrarca»: Il nome come auto-reinvenzione poetica." *Quaderni petrarcheschi* 4 (1987): 121–37.

Cherchi, Paolo. *Verso la chiusura: Saggio sul Canzoniere di Petrarca*. Bologna: Il Mulino, 2008.

Chessa, Silvia. *Il profumo del sacro nel* Canzoniere *di Petrarca*. Florence: Società editrice fiorentina, 2005.

Chiappelli, Fredi. "An Analysis of Structuration in Petrarch's Poetry." In Scaglione, ed., *Francis Petrarch*, 1975, 105–16.

– *Il legame musaico*. Ed. Pier Massimo Forni, with Giorgio Cavallini. Rome: Edizioni di storia e letteratura, 1984.

– *Studi sul linguaggio del Petrarca. La Canzone delle Visioni*. Florence: Olschki, 1971.

Chirilli, Emilia. "Studio sulle concordanze nel 'Canzoniere' di F. Petrarca." *Studi e problemi di critica testuale* 16 (1978): 137–91.

Ciccuto, M. *Figure di Petrarca. Giotto, Simone Martini, Franco bolognese*. Naples: Federico and Ardia, 1991.

Cochin, Henry. *La chronologie du Canzoniere de Pétrarque*. Paris: Bouillon, 1898.

Contini, Gianfranco. "La lingua del Petrarca." In *Il Trecento*, 93–120. Florence: Sanzoni, 1953.

– *Saggio d'un commento alle correzioni del Petrarca volgare*. Florence: Sansoni, 1943.

– ed. *Poeti del Duecento*. Milan and Naples: Ricciardi, 1960.

Cook, James Wyatt, and Germaine Warkentin. "Toward Making a New English Verse *Canzoniere*." *Yale Italian Studies* 1, 2 (1980): 23–43.

Corti, Maria. *An Introduction to Literary Semiotics*. Trans. Margherita Bogat and Allen Mandelbaum. Bloomington: Indiana UP, 1978.

Cottino-Jones, Marga. "The Myth of Apollo and Daphne in Petrarch's *Canzoniere*: The Dynamics and Literary Function of Transformation." In Scaglione, ed., *Francis Petrarch*, 1975, 152–76.

Cranz, F. Edward. *Reorientations of Western Thought from Antiquity to the Renaissance*. Ed. Nancy Streuver. Aldershot, Hants: Ashgate, 2006.

Crossan, John Dominic. *In Parables. The Challenge of the Historical Jesus*. New York: Harper and Row, 1973.

Cudini, Piero, ed. *Poesia italiana del Duecento*. Milan: Garzanti, 1978.

Curtius, Ernst Robert. *European Literature and the Latin Middle Ages*. Trans. Willard R. Trask. Princeton, NJ: Princeton UP, 1973.

Daniele, Antonio. "La canzone 'Mai non vo' più cantar com'io soleva' (CV)." *Lectura Petrarce* 13 (1993): 149–74.

– *La memoria innamorata. Indagini e letture petrarchesche*. Rome: Antenore, 2005.

– ed. *Le lingue del Petrarca*. Udine: Forum, 2005.

David, Michel. *Letteratura e psicoanalisi*. Milano: Mursia, 1967.

de Certeau, Michel. *The Mystic Fable. Vol. 1: The Sixteenth and Seventeenth Centuries*. Trans. Michael B. Smith. Chicago: U of Chicago P, 1992.

Del Giudice, Luisa. "Il processo narrativo nei componimenti LXI-CV del *Canzoniere* di F. Petrarca." *Canadian Journal of Italian Studies* 8, 31 (1985): 145–59.

De Robertis, Domenico. "A Farewell to Arms." In Franca Magnani, ed., *Studi in memoria di Paola Medioli Masotti*, 1–8. Naples: Lofredo, 1995.

– *Memoriale Petrarchesco*. Rome: Bulzoni, 1997.

– "Petrarca petroso." In Barbarisi and Berra, eds, 1992, 203–50.

– "Il trittico del T («RVF » 315, 316, 317)." *Lectura Petrarce* 19 (2001): 167–80.

De Sanctis, Francesco. *Saggio critico sul Petrarca*. Turin: Einaudi, 1952.

– *Storia della letteratura italiana*. Introd. R. Wellek. Notes G.M. Fioravanti. Milan: Rizzoli, 1983.

Desideri, Giovanella, Annalisa Landolfi, and Sabina Marinetti, eds. *L'Io lirico: Francesco Petrarca. Radiografia dei* Rerum vulgarium fragmenta. *Critica del testo* vi, 1. Rome: Viella, 2003.
Dotti, Ugo. *Petrarca a Parma*. Reggio Emilia: Edizioni Diabasis, 2006.
– *Petrarca civile. Alle origini dell'intellettuale moderno*. Rome: Donzelli, 2001.
– *La rivoluzione incompiuta. Società politica e cultura in Italia da Dante a Machiavelli*. Turin: Nino Argano, 2010.
– *Storia della letteratura italiana*. Bari: Laterza, 1991.
– *Vita di Petrarca*. Rome: Laterza, 1987.
Ducrot, Oswald, and Tzvetan Todorov. *Encyclopedic Dictionary of the Sciences of Language*. Trans. Catherine Porter. Baltimore, MD: Johns Hopkins UP, 1979.
Durling, Robert. "The Ascent of Mt. Ventoux and the Crisis of Allegory." *Italian Quarterly* 18, 69 (1974): 7–28.
– "Il Petrarca, il Ventoso e la possibilità dell'allegoria." *Revue des Études Augustiniennes* 23, 3–4 (1977): 304–23.
Dutschke, Dennis. *Francesco Petrarca, Canzone XXIII from First to Final Version*. Ravenna: Longo, 1977.
Eden, Kathy. "Petrarchan Hermeneutics and the Rediscovery of Intimacy." In Barolini and Storey, 2007, 231–44.
Elwert, W.T. "La varietà metrica e tematica delle canzoni del Petrarca in funzione della loro distribuzione nel 'Canzoniere.'" In *Dal medioevo al Petrarca*, 389–409. Florence: Olschki, 1983.
Fedi, Roberto. *Invito alla lettura di Francesco Petrarca*. Milan: Mursia, 2002.
Fenzi, Enrico. "Dalla precarietà del sogno alle sublimazioni dell'intelletto (*RVF* 341–50)." In Picone, ed., *Il Canzoniere*, 2007, 733–57.
– "Petrarca e la scrittura dell'amicizia (con un'ipotesi sul Libro VIII delle *Familiari*)." In Claudia Berra, ed., *Motivi e forme delle* Familiari *di Francesco Petrarca*, 549–89. Milan: Cisalpino, 2003.
– *Saggi petrarcheschi*. Florence: Edizioni Cadmo, 2003.
Fido, Franco. "Charles Singleton." *Lectura dantis* 4 (1989). www.brown.edu/Departments/Italian_Studies/LD/numbers/04/fido.html.
Folena, Gianfranco. "L'orologio del Petrarca." In *Textus Testis. Lingua e cultura poetica delle origini*, 266–89. Turin: Bollati Boringhieri, 2002.
Foresti, Arnaldo. "La canzone dell'amaro riso 'Mai non vo' più cantar com'io soleva.'" *Convivium* 7 (1935): 31–49.
Forni, Giorgio. "Piccoli gesti estremi: I quattro madrigali del *Canzoniere* di Petrarca." *Griseldaonline* 12 (June 2012). Accessed 25 April 2015 at: http://www.griseldaonline.it/temi/estremi/forni-piccoli-gesti-estremi.html.
Foster, Kenelm. *Petrarch: Poet and Humanist*. Edinburgh: Edinburgh UP, 1984.

Freccero, John. "The Fig Tree and the Laurel: Petrarch's Poetics." *Diacritics: A Review of Contemporary Criticism* 5, 1 (1975): 34–40.
Frye, Northrop. *Words with Power: Being a Second Study of "The Bible and Literature."* San Diego, CA: Harcourt Brace Jovanovich, 1990.
Fubini, Mario. *Metrica e poesia*. Milan: Feltrinelli, 1962.
Gagliardi, Antonio. *Cino da Pistoia. Le poetiche dell'anima*. Turin: Edizioni dell'Orso, 2001.
Galimberti, Cesare. "Amate dal sole (*R.V.F.*, XXXIV, CLXXXVIII, CCCLXVI)." In *Dal medioevo al Petrarca*, 427–34. Florence: Olschki, 1983.
Garin, Eugenio. *History of Italian Philosophy*. Trans. and ed. Giorgio Pinton. 2 vols. New York: Rodopi, 2008.
– *Italian Humanism. Philosophy and Civic Life in the Renaissance*. Trans. P. Munz. Oxford: Basil Blackwell, 1965.
– *L'umanesimo italiano*. Bari: Laterza, 1952.
– "Umanesimo e rinascimento." In U. Bosco, ed., *Questioni e correnti di storia letteraria*, 349–404. Milan: Marzorati, 1971.
– ed. *Il pensiero pedagogico dello umanesimo*. Florence: Giuntine and Sansoni, 1958.
Genette, Gerard. *Fiction and Diction*. Trans. C. Porter. Ithaca, NY: Cornell UP, 1993.
– *Narrative Discourse: An Essay in Method*. Trans. Jane E. Lewin. Foreword J. Culler. Ithaca, NY: Cornell UP, 1980.
Giunta, Claudio. *Due saggi sulla tenzone*. Padua: Antenore, 2002.
– *Versi a un destinatario. Saggio sulla poesia italiana del Medioevo*. Bologna: Il Mulino, 2002.
Goetsch, J.R. *Vico's Axioms*. New Haven, CT: Yale UP, 1995.
Goppelt, Leonhard. *Typos. The Typological Interpretation of the Old Testament in the New*. Trans. D.H. Madvig. Foreword E. Earle Ellis. Grand Rapids, MI: Eerdmans, 1982.
Gorni, Guglielmo. "Petrarca Virgini (Lettura della canzone CCCLXVI) 'Vergine bella.'" *Lectura petrarce* 7 (1987): 201–18.
Goux, Jean-Joseph. *Oedipus, Philosopher*. Trans. Catherine Porter. Stanford, CA: Stanford UP, 1993.
Greene, Thomas M. "The Quest for Resemblance in the Poetry of Petrarch." Typescript distributed to Fellows of Yale Petrarch Institute. 20 pp. July 1987.
Hainsworth, Peter. "The Myth of Daphne in the *Rerum vulgarium fragmenta*." *Italian Studies*, XIV (1979): 28–44.
– *Petrarch the Poet. An Introduction to the* Rerum vulgarium fragmenta. London and New York: Routledge, 1988.
Hallock, Ann H. "The Pre-eminent Role of *Babilonia* in Petrarch's Theme of the Two Cities." *Italica* 54, 2 (1977): 290–7.

Harries-Jones, Peter. *A Recursive Vision: Ecological Understanding and Gregory Bateson*. Toronto: U of Toronto P, 1995.

Hawkins, Peter S. "Divide and Conquer: Augustine in the *Divine Comedy*." *PMLA* 106, 3 (1991): 471–82.

Hillman, James. *The Thought of the Heart and the Soul of the World*. Dallas, TX: Spring Publications, 1992.

The Holy Bible. Revised standard version containing the Old and New Testaments. Oxford: Oxford UP, 1962.

Iliescu, Nicolae. *Il Canzoniere petrarchesco e Sant'Agostino*. Rome: Società Accademica Romena, 1962.

Jakobson, Roman. "Closing Statement: Linguistics and Poetics." In Jean Jacques Weber, ed., *The Stylistics Reader: From Roman Jakobson to the Present*, 10–35. New York: St Martin's Press, 1996.

Jones, Frederic Joseph. "An Analysis of Petrarch's Eleventh Canzone: 'Mai non vo' più cantar come io soleva.'" *Italian Studies* 41 (1986): 24–44.

– *The Structure of Petrarch's Canzoniere: A Chronological, Psychological and Stylistic Analysis*. Woodbridge, Suffolk, and Rochester, NY: Boydell and Brewer, 1995.

Kahn, Victoria. "The Figure of the Reader in Petrarch's *Secretum*." *PMLA* 100, 2 (1985): 154–66.

Kennedy, William J. *Authorizing Petrarch*. Ithaca, NY: Cornell UP, 1994.

Kermode, Frank. *The Genesis of Secrecy. On the Interpretation of Narrative*. Cambridge, MA: Harvard UP, 1979.

Kircher, Timothy. *The Poet's Wisdom: The Humanists, the Church, and the Formation of Philosophy in the Early Renaissance*. Leiden: Brill, 2006.

Kirkham, Victoria, and Armando Maggi, eds. *Petrarch. A Critical Guide to the Complete Works*. Chicago: U of Chicago P, 2009.

Kleinhenz, Christopher. "Petrarca, Francesco." In C. Kleinhenz, ed., *Medieval Italy. An Encyclopedia*, vol. 2: 881–8. New York: Routledge, 2004.

Lokaj, Rodney J. "Petrarca-alter Franciscus: Un'ascesa francescana al Monte Ventoso." *Il Veltro* 42 (1998): 465–76.

Leopardi, Giacomo. *Tutte le opere*. Ed. and introd. W. Binni. 2 vols. Florence: Sansoni, 1969.

– *Zibaldone*. Ed. Michael Caesar and Franco D'Intino. Trans. Kathleen Baldwin et al. New York: Farrar, Straus and Giroux, 2013.

Lollini, Massimo. "Return to Philology and Hypertext in and around Petrarch's *Rvf*." *Humanist Studies and the Digital Age* 1, 1 (2011): 66–79.

Lotman, Yury (Jurij). *Analysis of the Poetic Text*. Ed. and trans. D. Barton Johnson. Ann Arbor, MI: Ardis, 1976.

– *The Structure of the Artistic Text*. Trans. Ronald Vroon. Ann Arbor, MI: U of Michigan P, 1977.

Lyotard, Jean-François. "L'interesse del sublime." *Aut aut* 231 (1989): 33–56.

McLaughlin, Martin. "Struttura e *sonoritas* in Petrarca (*RVF* 151–60)." In Picone, ed., *Il Canzoniere*, 2007, 361–81.

Maier, Bruno. "Francesco Petrarca e il 'Canzoniere.'" *Il cristallo* 17, 1 (1975): 15–36.

Malato, Enrico. "Favole parabole istorie. Le forme della scrittura novellistica dal medioevo al rinascimento." In G. Albanese, L. Battaglia Ricci, and R. Bessi, eds, *Favole parabole istorie. Le forme della scrittura novellistica dal medioevo al rinascimento*, 17–29. Rome: Salerno, 2000.

Mann, Nicholas. *Petrarch*. New York: Oxford UP, 1984.

Manni, Paola. *Il Trecento toscano. La lingua di Dante, Petrarca e Boccaccio*. Bologna: Il Mulino, 2003.

Marchese, Angelo. *L'officina della poesia*. Milan: Mondadori, 1985.

Martellotti, Guido. "Storiografia del Petrarca." In *Atti dei Convegni Lincei*, 1976: 179–87.

Marti, Mario. *Storia dello stil nuovo*. Lecce: Edizioni Milella, 1972.

Martianus Capella. *The Commentary on Martianus Capella's* De nuptiis Philologiae et Mercurii *Attributed to Bernardus Silvestris*. Ed. with introd. Haijo Jan Westra. Toronto: Pontifical Institute of Mediaeval Studies, 1986.

Martinelli, Bortolo. *Petrarca e il Ventoso*. Bergamo: Minerva Italica, 1977.

Martinez, Ronald L. "Mourning Laura in the Canzoniere: Lessons from Lamentations." *MLN* 118, 1 (2003): 1–45.

Mazzotta, Giuseppe. "Antiquity and the New Arts in Petrarch." *Romanic Review*, 79 (1988): 22–41.

– "The *Canzoniere* and the Language of the Self." *Studies in Philology* 75 (1978): 271–96.

– "Humanism and Monastic Spirituality in Petrarch." *Stanford Literature Review* 5 (1988): 57–74.

– "Petrarch's Song 126." In M.A. Caws, ed., *Textual Analysis – Some Readers Reading*, 121–31. New York: Modern Language Association, 1986.

– *The Worlds of Petrarch*. Durham, NC: Duke UP, 1993.

Mirollo, James. *Mannerism and Renaissance Poetry. Concept, Mode, Inner Design*. New Haven, CT: Yale UP, 1984.

Mommsen, Theodor E. "Petrarch and the Story of the Choice of Hercules." *Journal of the Warburg and Courtauld Institutes* 16 (1953): 178–92.

Morando, Silvana. "Gli occhi della mente e la preghiera *sine murmure*. Tracce per la 'religione della poesia' in Giovanni Giudici." *Nuova corrente* 44 (1997): 247–82.

Morena, Antonio. "Autobiografia e struttura nel *mezzo* delle rime sparse." *Italica* 82, 2 (2005): 180–93.

Morselli, Guido. *Diario*. Pref. Giuseppe Pontiggia. Ed. Valentina Fortichiari. Milan: Adelphi, 1988.

Mussio, Thomas E. "Fides Amor: Amor as Companion in Petrarch's *Canzoniere*." *Italian Culture* 18, 1 (2000): 1–16.

Musumeci, Antonino. "Le parentesi nel Canzoniere petrarchesco." *Lingua e stile: Trimestrale di Linguistica e Critica Letteraria* 11 (1976): 493–500.

Nencioni, Giovanni. "Antropologia poetica?" *Strumenti critici* 18 (1972): 243–58.

Noferi, Adelia. "Il Canzoniere del Petrarca: Scrittura del desiderio e desiderio della scrittura." *Paragone* 296 (1974): 3–23.

– *Frammenti per i Fragmenta di Petrarca*. Ed. with note by Luigi Tassoni. Rome: Bulzoni, 2001.

Noventa, Giacomo. "A Elio Vittorini." In *Storia di una eresia*, 184–5. Milan: Rusconi, 1971.

Nussbaum, Martha. *Upheavals of Thought: The Intelligence of Emotions*. Cambridge: Cambridge UP, 2001.

Obermeier, Anita. *The History and Anatomy of Auctorial Self-criticism in the European Middle Ages*. Amsterdam: Rodopi, 1999.

Olson, Paul R. "Two Sonnets of Heavenly Vision." *Italica* 35, 3 (1958): 156–61.

Ong, Walter. *Orality and Literacy. The Technologizing of the Word*. New York: Methuen, 1982.

Orelli, Giorgio. *Il suono dei sospiri: Sul Petrarca volgare*. Turin: Einaudi, 1990.

Palmer, Parker. *The Active Life. A Spirituality of Work, Creativity, and Caring*. San Francisco: Jossey-Bass, 1999.

Pancheri, Alessandro. *"Col suon chioccio": Per una frottola "dispersa" attribuibile a Francesco Petrarca*. Padua: Antenore, 1993.

Pascual Argente, Clara. "Visions of Antiquity. Remembering the Classical Past in the Castilian *roman Antique*." PhD diss., Georgetown University, 2010. Available at: cdm15036.contentdm.oclc.org/cgi-bin/showfile.exe?CISOROOT=/p15036coll3&CISOPTR=771&filename=772.pdf.

Pearce, W. Barnett. *Communication and the Human Condition*. Carbondale, IL: Southern Illinois UP, 1989.

Perella, Nicolas J. "Love's Greatest Miracle." *MLN* 86, 1 (1971): 21–30.

Peterson, Thomas E. "The Fabulous Petrarch: *La raccolta del 1342* as Source of the Fabulous in *Rerum vulgarium fragmenta*." *Annali d'Italianistica* 22 (2004): 61–84.

– "Out of Babylon: The *Figura* of Exile in Tasso and Petrarch," *Annali d'Italianistica* 20 (2002): 127–48.

– "Petrarch's 'Canzone-frottola': A Parable of Return." *Symposium* 57, 1 (2003): 15–25.

– Review of Giuseppe Savoca, *Il Canzoniere di Petrarca tra codicologia ed ecdotica* (Florence: Olschki, 2008). *Speculum: A Journal of Medieval Studies* 86, 4 (2011): 1118–20.

Petrucci, Armando. "La scrittura del testo." In A. Asor Rosa, ed., *Letteratura italiana*, vol. 4 (of 9): 285–308. Turin: Einaudi, 1982–91.

Phelps, Ruth Shepard. *The Earlier and Later Forms of Petrarch's Canzoniere.* Chicago: U of Chicago P, 1925.

Picone, Michelangelo. "Petrarca e il libro non finito." *Italianistica* 2 (2004): 83–94.

– "Il sonetto CLXXXIX." *Letture petrarchesche* 9 (1989): 151–77.

– "Tempo e racconto nel 'Canzoniere' di Petrarca." In *Omaggio a Gianfranco Folena*, 581–92. Padua: Editoriale Programma, 1993.

– ed. *Il Canzoniere. Lettura micro e macrotestuale.* Ravenna: Longo, 2007.

Poggioli, Renato. *The Oaten Flute: Essays on Pastoral Poetry and the Pastoral Ideal.* Cambridge, MA: Harvard UP, 1975.

Pozzi, Giovanni. "Petrarca, i Padri e soprattutto la Bibbia." In *Alternatim*, 143–89. Milan: Adelphi, 1996.

– *Sull'orlo del visibile parlare.* Milan: Adelphi, 1993.

Praloran, Marco. "Lo splendore del mondo e la solitudine dell'io (*RVF* 310-20)." In Picone, ed., *Il Canzoniere*, 2007, 677–700.

Prier, Raymond A. "The Ultimate Proscription of Lady Philology and the Self: Canzoniere 366." *Italian Culture* 11 (1993): 45–57.

Propp, Vladimir. *Morphology of the Folktale.* Trans. Laurence Scott. Introd. Svatava Pirkova-Jakobson. Austin, TX: U of Texas P, 1968.

Quondam, Amedeo. *Petrarca, l'italiano dimenticato.* Rome: Rizzoli, 2004.

Raimondi, Ezio. "Una pagina satirica delle *Sine nomine.*" *Studi petrarcheschi* 6 (1956): 55–61.

Regen, Mariann S. "The Evolution of the Poet in Petrarch's *Canzoniere.*" *Philological Quarterly* 57 (1978): 23–45.

Rella, Franco. *Asterischi.* Milan: Feltrinelli, 1989.

Renucci, Paul. "L'amore tra natura e storia nella poesia del Petrarca e nella lirica del Rinascimento." In *Atti dei Convegni Lincei*, 1976, 163–78.

Rico, Francisco. "'Rime sparse,' 'Rerum vulgarium fragmenta.' Para el titulo y el primer soneto del 'Canzoniere.'" *Medioevo Romanzo* 3 (1976): 101–38; partially translated in Barbarisi and Berra, eds, 1992, 117–44.

Ricoeur, Paul. *Figuring the Sacred. Religion, Narrative, and Imagination.* Trans. David Pellauer. Ed. Mark I. Wallace. Minneapolis, MN: Fortress, 1995.

– *History and Truth.* Trans. with introd. Charles A. Kelbley. Evanston, IL: Northwestern UP, 1965.

– *Time and Narrative*, vol. 3. Trans. K. Blamey and D. Pellauer. Chicago: U of Chicago P, 1988.

Riffaterre, Michael. *Fictional Truth*. Introd. Stephen G. Nichols. Baltimore, MD: Johns Hopkins UP, 1990.

Rigolot, F. "Nature and Function of Paronomasia in the *Canzoniere*." *Italian Quarterly* 18 (1974): 29–36.

– "Le poétique et l'analogique." In AA.VV. *Sémantique de la poésie*, 155–77. Paris: Éditions du Seuil, 1979.

Roche, Thomas P., Jr. "The Calendrical Structure of Petrarch's *Canzoniere*." *Studies in Philology*, 71, 2 (1974): 152–72.

Roncaglia, Aurelio. "Cino tra Dante e Petrarca." In *Colloquio Cino Da Pistoia*, 7–31. Rome: Accademia Nazionale dei Lincei, 1976.

Salinari, Carlo. *La letteratura del Trecento*. Rome: Editori Riuniti, 1979.

Santagata, Marco. "Connessioni intertestuali nel Canzoniere del Petrarca." *Strumenti critici* 26 (1975): 80–112.

– *Dal sonetto al canzoniere*. Padua: Liviana, 1979.

– *I frammenti dell'anima. Storia e racconto nel Canzoniere di Petrarca*. Bologna: Il Mulino, 1993.

– *L'io e il mondo. Un'interpretazione di Dante*. Bologna: Il Mulino, 2011.

– "'Io' e 'tu' fra Stilnovo e Petrarca." Text of conference given in Florence in 2004. Available at: santagata.sitonline.it/1/io_e_tu_19178.html. 2010.

– *Per moderne carte. La biblioteca volgare di Petrarca*. Bologna: Il Mulino, 1990.

– "Sul destinatario della canzone petrarchesca 'O aspectata in ciel beata et bella' (R.V.F., 28)." *Rivista di letteratura italiana* 3 (1985): 365–80.

Savoca, Giuseppe. *Il Canzoniere di Petrarca tra codicologia ed ecdotica*. Florence: Olschki, 2008.

Scaglione, Aldo. "The Structure of the *Canzoniere* and Petrarch's Method of Composition." In Bernardo, ed., *Francesco Petrarca*, 1980, 301–13.

– ed., *Francis Petrarch, Six Centuries Later: A Symposium*. Chapel Hill, NC: Department of Romance Languages, University of North Carolina, 1975.

Schildgen, Brenda Deen. "Overcoming Augustinian Dichotomies in Defense of the Laurel in Canzoni 359 and 360 of the Rime sparse." *MLN* 111, 1 (1996): 149–63.

Segre, Cesare. "La critica strutturalistica." In M. Corti and C. Segre, eds, *I metodi attuali della critica in Italia*, 325–41. Turin: ERI, 1970.

– *Intrecci di voci: La polifonia nella letteratura del Novecento*. Turin: Einaudi, 1991.

– *Introduction to the Analysis of the Literary Text*. With the collaboration of Tomaso Kemeny. Trans. John Meddemmen. Bloomington: Indiana UP, 1988.

– "Isotopie di Laura." In *Notizie dalla crisi*, 66–80. Milan: Einaudi, 1993.

Seigel, Jerrold E. *Rhetoric and Philosophy in Renaissance Humanism. The Union of Eloquence and Wisdom, Petrarch to Valla*. Princeton, NJ: Princeton UP, 1968.

Serres, Michel. *Hermes. Literature, Science, Philosophy*. Ed. Josué V. Harari and David F. Bell. Baltimore, MD: Johns Hopkins UP, 1982.

Seung, T.K. *Cultural Thematics. The Formation of the Faustian Ethos*. New Haven, CT: Yale UP, 1976.

Soldani, Arnaldo. "Dialoghi e soliloqui al limitare del tempo (*RVF* 351–59)." In Picone, ed., *Il Canzoniere*, 2007, 759–98.

Spitzer, Leo. *Classical and Christian Ideas of World Harmony. Prolegomena to an Interpretation of the Word "Stimmung."* Ed. Anna Granville Hatcher. Pref. René Wellek. Baltimore, MD: Johns Hopkins UP, 1963.

Spongano, Raffaelle. "Francesco Petrarca tentato di morire." *Studi e problemi di critica testuale* 27 (1983): 55–67.

– *Nozioni ed esempi di metrica italiana*. Bologna: Pàtron, 1966.

Stevens, Wallace. *Collected Poetry and Prose*. New York: Library of America, 1997.

Stierle, Karlheinz. "A Manifesto of New Singing: *Rerum vulgarium fragmenta* 125–29." *Annali d'Italianistica* 22 (2004): 85–103.

– *Petrarcas Landschaften: Zur Geschichte ästhetischer Landschaftserfahrung*. Krefeld: Scherpe Verlag, 1979.

– "Il sonetto CCCLIII." *Lectura petrarce* 16 (1996): 231–47.

– *La vita e i tempi di Petrarca. Alle origini della moderna coscienza europea*. Trans. Gabriella Pelloni. Venice: Marsilio, 2007.

Storey, H. Wayne. *Transcription and Visual Poetics in the Early Italian Lyric*. New York: Garland, 1993.

Suitner, Franco. *Dante, Petrarca e altra poesia antica*. Fiesole (Florence): Cadmo, 2005.

– *Petrarca e la tradizione stilnovistica*. Florence: Olschki, 1977.

Taddeo, Edoardo. "Petrarca e il tempo." *Studi e problemi di critica testuale* 27 (1983): 68–108.

Tillich, Paul. *The Protestant Era*. Trans. James Luther Adams. Chicago: U of Chicago P, 1948.

Tonelli, Natascia. *Varietà sintattica e costanti retoriche nei sonetti dei Rerum vulgarium fragmenta*. Florence: Olschki, 1999.

– "Vat. Lat. 3195: Un libro concluso? Lettura di *RVF* 360–66." In Picone, ed., *Il Canzoniere*, 2007, 799–822.

Took, John. "Petrarch." In Peter Brand and Lino Pertile, eds, *The Cambridge History of Italian Literature*, 89–107. Cambridge: Cambridge UP, 1996.

Trinkaus, Charles. *In Our Image and Likeness; Humanity and Divinity in Italian Humanist Thought*. 2 vols. Chicago: U of Chicago P, 1970.

– *The Poet as Philosopher: Petrarch and the Formation of Renaissance Consciousness*. New Haven, CT: Yale UP, 1979.

Trovato, Paolo. *Dante in Petrarca: Per un inventario dei dantismi nei "Rerum vulgarium fragmenta."* Florence: Olschki, 1979.

Tynianov, Yuri. *The Problem of Verse Language*. Ed. and trans. Michael Sosa and Brent Harvey. Ann Arbor, MI: Ardis, 1981.

Valeri, Diego. "Difficoltà del superlativo assoluto in poesia." In *Studi di varia umanità in onore di Francesco Flora*, 901–2. Milan: Mondadori, 1963.

Valéry, Paul. *An Anthology*. Selected with introd. James R. Lawler. Princeton, NJ: Princeton UP, 1977.

Vasoli, Cesare. *Umanesimo e rinascimento*. Palermo: Palumbo, 1976.

Vecchi Galli, Paola. "Le parole del peccato." *Quaderni petrarcheschi* 15–16 (2005–6): 127–41.

Velli, Giuseppe. "Il Dante di Francesco Petrarca." *Studi petrarcheschi* 2 (1985): 185–99.

Vickers, Nancy J. "Diana Described: Scattered Woman and Scattered Rhyme." *Critical Inquiry* 8, 2 (1981): 265–79.

– "Vital Signs: Petrarch and Popular Culture." *Romanic Review* 79, 1 (1988): 184–95.

Villette, J. "L'énigme du labyrinthe de la cathédrale." *Notre-Dame de Chartres*, 58 (1984): 4–12.

Voci, Anna Maria. *Petrarca e la vita religiosa: Il mito umanista della vita eremitica*. Rome: Istituto Storico Italiano per l'Età Moderna e Contemporanea, 1983.

Waller, Marguerite R. *Petrarch's Poetics and Literary History*. Amherst: U of Massachusetts P, 1980.

Warkentin, Germaine. "*Infaticabile maestro*: Ernest Hatch Wilkins and the Manuscripts of Petrarch's *Canzoniere*." In Barolini and Storey, eds, 2007, 45–65.

Wilkins, Ernest Hatch. "The Evolution of the Canzoniere of Petrarch." *PMLA* 63, 2 (1948): 412–55.

– *Life of Petrarch*. Chicago: U of Chicago P, 1961.

– *The Making of the "Canzoniere" and Other Petrarchan Studies*. Rome: Edizioni di storia e letteratura, 1951.

– "Petrarch's *Exul Ab Italia*." *Speculum: A Journal of Medieval Studies* 38, 3 (1963): 453–60.

– *Studies in the Life and Works of Petrarch*. Cambridge, MA: Mediaeval Academy of America, 1955.

Williams, Raymond. *Keywords. A Vocabulary of Culture and Society*. New York: Oxford UP, 1976.

Wills, Garry. *Saint Augustine*. New York: Viking Penguin, 1999.

Yates, Frances A. *The Art of Memory*. London: Routledge and Kegan Paul, 1966.

Zak, Gur. *Petrarch's Humanism and the Care of the Self*. Cambridge : Cambridge UP, 2010.

Zanato, Tiziano. "San Francesco, Pier delle Vigne e Francesca da Rimini nei 'Rerum vulgarium fragmenta.'" *Filologia e critica* 2 (1977): 177–216.

– "Il sonetto CCCXLIV." *Lectura petrarce* 18 (1998): 425–45.

Zanzotto, Andrea. *Fantasie di avvicinamento*. Milan: Mondadori, 1991.

– *Il galateo in bosco*. Milan: Mondadori, 1979.

– "Petrarca fra il palazzo e la cameretta." In F. Petrarca, *Rime*, ed. G. Bezzola, 1976, 5–16.

Zumthor, Paul. "From the Universal to the Particular in Medieval Poetry." *MLN* 85, 6 (1970): 815–23.

– *Langue Texte Énigme*. Paris: Seuil, 1975.

– *Speaking of the Middle Ages*. Trans. Sarah White. Foreword Eugene Vance. Lincoln: U of Nebraska P, 1986.

– *Toward a Medieval Poetics*. Trans. Philip Bennet. Minneapolis: U of Minnesota P, 1992.

Index

www.ingramcontent.com/pod-product-compliance
Lightning Source LLC
LaVergne TN
LVHW090150080826
844660LV00013B/741/J

* 9 7 8 1 4 8 7 5 0 0 0 2 3 *